GRAVE NEW WORLD

GRAVE NEW WORLD

Security Challenges in
the 21st Century

MICHAEL E. BROWN

EDITOR

GEORGETOWN UNIVERSITY PRESS
In cooperation with the
CENTER FOR PEACE AND SECURITY STUDIES
EDMUND A. WALSH SCHOOL OF FOREIGN SERVICE
   GEORGETOWN UNIVERSITY
WASHINGTON, D.C.

Georgetown University Press, Washington, D.C.
© 2003 by Georgetown University Press. All rights reserved.
Printed in the United States of America

10 9 8 7 6 5 4   2003

This book is printed on acid-free recycled paper meeting
the requirements of the American National Standard
for Permanence in Paper for Printed Library Materials.

Library of Congress Cataloging-in Publication Data

Grave new world : security/challenges in the twenty-first century /
Michael E. Brown, editor.

"In cooperation with the Center for Peace and Security Studies, Edmund
A. Walsh School of Foreign Service, Georgetown University."
Includes bibliographical references and index.
    ISBN 0-87840-142-3   (pbk. :   alk. paper)
  1.   Security, International.   2.   Security, International—Forecasting.
I.   Brown, Michael E. (Michael Edward), 1954–   II.   Georgetown University.
Center for Peace and Security Studies.
    JZ5588.G73 2003
    327.1'7—dc21
                                                        2003006464

Contents

Figures and Tables

Figures

Tables

Preface

When I launched this project in June 2001, one of my main objectives was to raise the level of awareness about national and international security problems. At the time, many people believed that security problems had waned because the cold war had ended. Others claimed that the advent of globalization and the development of a stronger international civil society would minimize the security problems that remained. Many Americans thought that deadly conflicts were tragedies that happened only to other people.

The September 11, 2001, terrorist attacks on New York and Washington suddenly and horribly changed these sanguine patterns of thinking—not just in the United States but around the world. The attacks made it searingly clear that national and international security problems had not gone away, that globalization was not a panacea—indeed, it was a big part of the problem—and that the deadly security challenges of the twenty-first century would require sustained, sophisticated policy responses.

My concern now is that many people—Americans, in particular—might be inclined to focus their attention exclusively on the terrorist threat. Although terrorism poses a clear and present danger to American, Western, and international security in general, it is not the only threat on the security agenda. Losing sight of the rest of the agenda would be foolhardy, and ignoring the desperate problems faced by other people around the world would be unworthy of great nations. Similarly, one hopes that the 2003 war in Iraq, and the aftermath of that war, will not completely preoccupy American, Western, and international attention. Although conflict and postconflict problems in Iraq are immediate and important, grave security problems abound throughout the world.

This project has three main objectives: to advance our understanding of current threats to national and international security, to assess the prospects for the next decade or two, and to derive some policy lessons that will foster national and international security in the future.

This book examines a wide array of military and nonmilitary factors that will shape the security landscape in the twenty-first century, including the proliferation of nuclear, biological, chemical, and conventional weapons; the development of military and nonmilitary technologies, including information technology and genetic engineering; the impact of demographic and environmental factors on stability and security; the changing nature of the energy market and defense economics; and the unique security problems faced by the developing world. Special attention is given to the increasingly important role played by transnational actors—transnational mass media organizations, transnational criminal organizations, and transnational terrorist organizations—in contemporary security affairs. Developing a better understanding of this complex, dynamic security landscape is a prerequisite to the development of effective policies that will foster national, regional, and international security.

A study that examines such a wide range of issues could not be written by any one person in a practical time frame. This book exists because fourteen distinguished scholars—Audrey Kurth Cronin, Dorothy Denning, Bernard Finel, Brian Finlay, Roy Godson, Martha Harris, Timothy Hoyt, Jo Husbands, Charles Keely, John McNeill, Theodore Moran, Janne Nolan, Diana Owen, and Loren Thompson—drew on their wealth of substantive expertise and wrote detailed studies focused specifically on the issues this study seeks to illuminate. Their willingness to commit precious time and energy to the project's agenda was critical to the success of this venture. I am very grateful to my colleagues for their participation in this project.

Several members of the Georgetown University community participated in a one-day workshop that launched our investigation of these issues. On behalf of the entire group, I would like to thank Anthony Arend, Andrew Bennett, Chester Crocker, John Ikenberry, Dana Johnson, and Angela Stent for their insights and contributions to this undertaking.

This project was sponsored by and conducted under the aegis of the Center for Peace and Security Studies (CPASS) of the Edmund A. Walsh School of Foreign Service, Georgetown University. I would like to thank the many people at CPASS who contributed to this effort. Bernard Finel and Elizabeth Stanley-Mitchell provided institutional leadership and organizational support. Erin Roussin managed the project's finances. Jim Ludes and Sandi Nagy handled the logistics for the project workshop. Abha Shankar contributed valuable research assistance on several key issues. Christina Zechman Brown provided extensive administrative and technical support in the project's final stages. I am grateful to one and all.

I would like to express my appreciation to Richard Brown, the director of Georgetown University Press, for his support of this book project. The staff and associates of Georgetown University Press made important contributions to the quality of the final product. Deborah Weiner, Fred Thompson, and Suzanne Wolk deserve special mention.

Finally, I would like to thank Robert Gallucci, dean of the Edmund A. Walsh School of Foreign Service, for his energetic support of CPASS and its programmatic initiatives in the security studies field. It is a pleasure to work with such a thoughtful professional.

Multiperson projects are arduous undertakings, but they can bring exceptional intellectual resources to bear on critical problems. I hope that this project sheds some light on the security challenges of our grave new world.

—MICHAEL E. BROWN
WASHINGTON, D.C.

Introduction # Security Challenges in the Twenty-first Century

Michael E. Brown

National and international security problems are important for one reason above all others: their human consequences are staggering. In the twentieth century, armed conflicts killed tens of millions of people, wounded tens of millions more, and drove tens of millions of people from their homes. In addition, the economic costs of security problems—the costs of defense preparations, the costs of wartime military operations, and the costs of postconflict reconstruction—have been enormous. Many security problems of the twentieth century will persist in the twenty-first, some will evolve and become deadlier than ever, and new problems will be added to the security agenda. National and international security will be momentous policy problems for the foreseeable future.

A brief review of security problems in the twentieth century brings this picture into sharper focus. During World War I more than 8 million soldiers were killed, more than 6.6 million civilians were killed, and more than 21 million soldiers were wounded.[1] Over the course of World War II in Asia and Europe, an estimated 15 million soldiers were killed, at least 26 million and perhaps as many as 34 million civilians were killed, and at least 25 million soldiers were wounded.[2]

The decades after 1945 have been referred to as "the long peace" because the great powers of that era—the United States and the Soviet Union—did not engage in all-out military hostilities even though they had an alarming number of opportunities to do so.[3] One of the most dangerous aspects of the cold war was the nuclear arms race between the United States and the Soviet Union. Between 1945 and 1990 the two superpowers built and deployed tens of thousands of nuclear weapons. At the peak of the arms race in the 1980s, their nuclear arsenals contained approximately 24,000 strategic nuclear weapons deployed on an array of intercontinental-range delivery systems and at least 23,000 tactical nuclear weapons deployed on land, sea, and air around the world.[4] Most of these weapons were many times more powerful than the atomic bombs that were used in the U.S. attacks on Hiroshima and Nagasaki in 1945; some strategic weapons had explosive yields one to two thousand times greater than the bombs dropped on Japan.

There were two main schools of thought about the likely consequences of an all-out nuclear war between the United States and the Soviet Union. Some believed that a war involving tens of thousands of nuclear weapons would kill billions of people, obliterate all of the world's leading powers, and end civilization as we knew it. These were the optimists. The pessimists believed that tens of thousands of nuclear explosions would send vast amounts of dirt and dust into the atmosphere, creating a nuclear shroud that would block sunlight from reaching the earth's surface. The resulting ice age—a "nuclear winter"—would kill every human on the planet, and perhaps all animal and plant life as well. The nuclear arms race brought the self-immolation of the human race into the realm of the possible.

Although no great-power war took place during the cold war, dozens of other conflicts did. According to one noted scholar, the incidence of interstate conflict "plummeted" in the decades after 1945, but intrastate war became increasingly prevalent. Only 30 of the 164 wars fought in the decades after 1945—18 percent of the total—were interstate conflicts. The vast majority—126, or 77 percent of the total—were intrastate conflicts.[5] Approximately 20 million people were killed in the many conflicts of the cold war era.

When the cold war ended, it is no exaggeration to say that hopes and expectations soared in many parts of the world. One of the most moving statements about the possibilities of the post–cold war era came from U.S. President George H. W. Bush. Addressing a joint session of the U.S. Congress on September 11, 1990, he outlined his vision of a "new world order." He foresaw the advent of "a new era—freer from the threat of terror, stronger in the pursuit of justice, and more secure in the quest for peace, an era in which the nations of the worlds, East and West, North and South, can prosper and live in harmony." Bush maintained that a "new partnership of nations has begun, and we stand today at a unique and extraordinary moment." He observed:

> A hundred generations have searched for this elusive path to peace, while a thousand wars raged across the span of human endeavor. And today that new world is struggling to be born, a world quite different from the one we've known, a world where the rule of law supplants the rule of the jungle, a world in which nations recognize the shared responsibility for freedom and justice, a world where the strong respect the rights of the weak.[6]

The end of the cold war had tremendously important positive effects on international security. With the collapse of the Soviet empire in Eastern Europe in 1989 and the disintegration of the Soviet Union in 1991, the Soviet military threat that had loomed over Western Europe for decades vanished. At the same time, the threat of an all-out nuclear war between the United States and the Soviet Union faded. Many of the regional conflicts that had been fueled by superpower patronage—in Cambodia, El Salvador, Mozambique, Namibia, and Nicaragua, for example—wound down and began to move toward settlements.

At the same time, hopes for a new and predominantly peaceful world—so widespread at the beginning of the 1990s—were dashed by the deadly conflicts that followed. The leading powers did not form a new partnership of nations and create "a new world order." International responses to war, slaughter, and starvation in Bosnia, Somalia, and other lethal trouble spots were appallingly inadequate. Nowhere was this more tragic than in Rwanda, where an estimated 800,000 people were killed in a genocidal slaughter that went on for one hundred days in the spring and summer of 1994. The world watched on CNN.

In the first twelve years of the post–cold war era (from 1990 to 2001), fifty-seven major armed conflicts took place in forty-five different countries. In the first half of this period, the number of conflicts in any given year ranged from twenty-eight to thirty-three; since 1998, the number of conflicts has held steady at around twenty-five conflicts per year. As of 2003, conflicts seethed and raged in places as diverse as Afghanistan, Algeria, Burma, Burundi, Colombia, the Democratic Republic of the Congo, India, Indonesia, Iraq, Israel, Ivory Coast, Pakistan, the Philippines, Russia, Somalia, Sri Lanka, and Sudan.[7] The American-led war against Al Qaeda and transnational terrorism continued to unfold on a number of fronts.

Almost all of the deadly conflicts of the post–cold war era have been either intrastate conflicts or intrastate conflicts with regional complications. Only four—the 1991 Gulf War, the 1998–2000 border war between Ethiopia and Eritrea, the 1999 Kargil conflict between India and Pakistan, and the 2003 war in Iraq—could be called conventional interstate conflicts. The prevalence of intrastate conflicts in the post–cold war era is significant. In many intrastate conflicts, the stakes are high—survival, power, wealth, territory. These conflicts frequently escalate into military campaigns designed to drive out or kill civilians from rival groups. Civilians are consequently subjected to direct, deliberate, systematic attacks. Intimidation, expulsion, rape, assassination, and slaughter are commonly employed instruments. The numbers of people killed or displaced in such conflicts are often counted in tens and hundreds of thousands. It is estimated that 6 million people were killed in armed conflicts in the 1990s.[8] At the beginning of the twenty-first century, the number of "internally displaced persons" who had fled their homes but stayed within the borders of their own countries stood at 5.3 million. The number of people who had crossed international borders and acquired refugee status stood at 12 million.[9]

To get a complete picture of the consequences of conflicts in the twentieth century, economic costs should also be taken into account. One can start with the costs of armed conflicts. It is estimated that the economic and financial costs of World War I came to $4.5 trillion, and that those of World War II came to $13 trillion. The Iran-Iraq war of 1980–88 cost an estimated $150 billion, and the Gulf War of 1990–91 cost $102 billion. Recent and current intrastate conflicts in Algeria, Burma, Colombia, Indonesia, Mexico (Chiapas), Russia (Chechnya), and Turkey have cost more than $1 billion each. The complicated conflict in Kashmir has cost an estimated $31 billion since 1989, and the even more complex conflict in the Democratic Republic of the Congo has cost $4 billion since 1998.[10] The economic costs of the 2003 Gulf War will be tens of billions of dollars.

The costs of postconflict peacekeeping and reconstruction are also part of the cost equation. United Nations peacekeeping costs do not reveal the full magnitude of these costs because other international organizations, regional organizations, individual states, and nongovernmental organizations also contribute to postconflict reconstruction efforts, but UN costs are nonetheless revealing. The United

Nations launched fifty-five peacekeeping operations between 1945 and 2002, with forty-two—the vast majority—undertaken between 1988 and 2002; thirteen operations were under way in 2003. The end of the cold war enabled the members of the UN to work together in ways that had theretofore been impossible. Not only did the number of peacekeeping operations soar, but the scope of many operations expanded. In addition to traditional peacekeeping operations that monitored cease-fires, multifunctional operations tried to tackle a wider range of conflict-resolution tasks: disarmament and demobilization of combatants; rebuilding economies; re-creating (or creating) viable, stable political institutions; and reestablishing (or establishing) vibrant societies. The annual costs of UN peacekeeping operations correspondingly increased from $0.4 billion in 1991 to a peak of $3.6 billion in 1993; expenditures in the early 2000s averaged approximately $2.6 billion per year. Total UN peacekeeping costs for 1948–2002 came to $26.1 billion, with $21.5 billion —again, the vast majority—incurred between 1991 and 2002.[11] In addition, the World Bank estimates that it lent $6.2 billion to eighteen countries for postconflict reconstruction in the 1980s and 1990s.[12]

Finally, the costs of defense preparations are massive. The United States spent almost $6 trillion on nuclear weapons and its nuclear establishment between 1940 and the mid-1990s.[13] Total U.S. national defense spending is projected to increase from $397 billion in fiscal year 2003 to $470 billion in FY 2007. Worldwide defense expenditures came to $835 billion in 2001 (with U.S. spending making up 38.6 percent of the total and NATO as a whole contributing 58.5 percent of the total).[14] Worldwide defense spending comes to $137 per capita.[15] This is not to say that these expenditures are unnecessary or frivolous—only that they are substantial and that they inevitably entail opportunity costs.

Three things are clear about the prospects for national and international security in the twenty-first century. First, security problems will continue to be widespread and deadly. It would be naive and irresponsible to assume that current problems will simply go away or that new problems will be neutralized by the positive benefits of globalization. Second, the security agenda will be far more complex than it has been in the past. It will include continuing security problems, such as great-power rivalry, interstate confrontations, and intrastate conflicts. It will also include problems that are changing as a result of the end of the cold war and the advent of globalization. These problems include the changing dynamics of weapon proliferation, the changing character of the defense industry and energy markets, the intensification of demographic and environmental pressures on many countries and regions, and the growing capabilities of transnational actors—criminal and terrorist organizations—that operate outside the parameters of the state system. The security agenda of the twenty-first century will also include genuinely new security challenges, such as those posed by advances in information and genetic engineering technologies. All of this will take place in the context of an intense globalization process that no one controls.

Finally, those who have policy responsibilities in the security arena will have to think ahead, develop true strategies, adapt to changing circumstances, and work together multilaterally. Those who simply react to events will be overtaken by events, and those who try to tackle global problems on their own will simply be overwhelmed. In the complex, increasingly interconnected world of the twenty-first century, multilateralism will not be an option—it will be a necessity.[16]

Purpose of the Book

This book has three main objectives: to advance understanding of current threats to national and international security, to assess the prospects for the next decade or two, and to derive policy lessons that will foster national and international security in the future.

Our starting point in analyzing these issues is a recognition that, although the use of military force and the causes and consequences of wars are central issues in security affairs, security is not *just* a military issue. The origins of most security problems are not limited to military developments, and the solutions to security problems are rarely limited to military actions. This is not to say that the military aspects of national and international security should be set aside altogether. Rather, if we want to develop a thorough understanding of the dynamics of security problems in the contemporary world, we must examine the full range of military *and* non-military factors that influence these problems around the world. Security problems are multidimensional, and they have to be studied in broad, inclusive terms.

We also recognize that, although states and the intergovernmental bodies they create are still the most important actors in international security affairs, transnational actors are increasingly influential. The latter include transnational mass media organizations, transnational criminal organizations, and transnational terrorist organizations. Coming to a determination about the likely impact of these actors is an important challenge for scholars and policymakers alike.

This book analyzes security problems from a functional rather than a regional perspective. The rationale for adopting this approach is straightforward: in an increasingly interconnected world where information, ideas, people, and problems can quickly cross national and regional boundaries, a global perspective on security problems is needed. Even if one's concerns are parochial, understanding the broad scope of contemporary security problems is essential. Focusing on functional issues will facilitate our effort to identify the key factors and driving forces that shape security issues across regions and around the world.

With these objectives and considerations in mind, the contributors to this volume were asked to address three specific sets of questions about their respective issue areas:

- What are the most important recent developments in the area under examination? What are the key factors or driving forces behind these developments?
- What are the prospects for the future? What are the implications of these developments for national, regional, and international security?

• What broad policy lessons and recommendations should national, regional, and international policymakers derive from the foregoing analysis?

By focusing on a common set of questions, the volume's functional studies provide a strong, structured foundation for the development of some general conclusions about the prospects for national and international security as well as some broad lessons for those who have policy responsibilities in these areas.

Overview of the Book

This book examines a wide array of military and nonmilitary factors that are affecting and will continue to affect national and international security in the twenty-first century. The dividing line between "military" and "nonmilitary" factors is not always sharp, however. Many technological developments, for example, are not driven by military considerations and do not initially have military applications, but they nonetheless end up having important military implications. It is therefore impossible to devise a tidy organizational scheme that puts every "military" factor in one box and every "nonmilitary" factor in another. With this caveat in mind, this book is organized along the following lines.

Part I analyzes the impact of weapons and technology on national and international security. It examines both military technologies, such as nuclear weapon technology, and technologies that do not have direct military applications, such as some information technologies. Part II looks at a wide range of predominantly nonmilitary factors—including economic, environmental, and demographic factors—that have important security implications. It concludes with an analysis of the special nature of security problems in the developing world. Part III focuses on the growing roles played by several transnational actors—transnational mass media organizations, transnational criminal organizations, transnational terrorist organizations—in national and international security affairs. A concluding chapter draws on these analyses, looks at national and international security problems from a broad perspective, and develops some policy lessons.

Weapons, Technology, and Security

The first part of the book examines the impact of weapons and technology on national and international security. It focuses on the enduring and evolving security problems posed by the proliferation of nuclear, biological, chemical, and conventional weapons, and on the emerging challenges posed by developments in the areas of information technology and genetic engineering.

In chapter 1 Timothy Hoyt analyzes the complex relationship between technology and security. He begins by observing that, over the centuries, technology has had profound effects on military affairs and the nature of warfare. The gunpowder revolution was followed by the advent of rifled guns and artillery, railroads, steam engines, the telegraph, the telephone, the internal combustion engine, radio, radar and sonar, nuclear weapons, and long-range, high-speed delivery systems such as the airplane, the cruise missile, and the ballistic missile. Many analysts believe that recent developments in sensors, information technology, precision-guided weaponry, and air power are combining to bring about yet another revolution in military affairs. Hoyt contends that, although technological developments will have tremendous implications for military operations in the decades ahead, one should not lose sight of the fact that technology is also having profound effects on nonmilitary aspects of security.

In chapter 2 Bernard Finel, Brian Finlay, and Janne Nolan examine the problems associated with the control of nuclear, biological, and chemical weapons. First, Russia's nuclear establishment continues to deteriorate. This has implications for the stability of the U.S.–Russia nuclear balance as well as for efforts to control nuclear proliferation. Second, several other states have been pushing forward with nuclear programs, and this could have destabilizing consequences for regional and international security. Third, efforts to control the proliferation of biological and chemical weapons have been hobbled by the fact that many biological and chemical facilities can be used to produce either civilian products or weapons. This makes arms control in this area exceedingly difficult. Fourth, the possibility that terrorist organizations might acquire nuclear, biological, or chemical weapons is a growing concern. Unfortunately, international efforts to address proliferation problems have been stymied by a policy split between the United States and most of the rest of the world. Coordinated international efforts to address proliferation problems are therefore stalled at a critical juncture.

In chapter 3 Jo Husbands argues that fundamental changes have taken place in the trade and transfer of conventional weapons since the end of the cold war. The good news is that the overall volume of conventional arms transfers has dropped significantly—perhaps to about half of the cold war peak. The bad news is that the conventional arms trade is still enormous, and conventional weapons are used to kill tens of thousands of people in intrastate and regional conflicts every year. Even more discouraging is the fact that the changing character of the conventional arms market impedes arms control efforts. According to Husbands, the driving forces behind conventional arms transfers have shifted from the geopolitical concerns of the cold war to economic motivations. In addition, the black market is a growing part of the equation. Unfortunately, it is highly unlikely that arms-exporting states and corporations will be able to resist the economic pressures that will continue to drive them to participate energetically in the international arms market.

In chapter 4 Dorothy Denning analyzes the impact of recent developments in information technology on national and international security. She notes that although advanced information technology can enhance the capabilities of well-meaning actors to promote stability and security, they can also strengthen the hands of less benign actors. She reports that cyberspace attacks are increasing in number and severity. Long-term trends are disquieting because information technology is becoming faster, more powerful, more mobile, and more ubiquitous around the world. In addition, computer networks are becoming increasingly integrated with critical infrastructures such as telecommunications and power systems; deadly attacks on increasingly vulnerable systems could be launched in the future. The prognosis, therefore, is not encouraging. Although the United States and other governments have taken some steps to address these dangers, Denning contends that more should be done to generate better data on cyberspace security incidents, to enhance expertise on these issues, and to strengthen international cooperation in this increasingly important area.

In chapter 5 Loren Thompson examines the potential effects that two clusters of emerging technologies—digital networking and genetic engineering—might have on national and international security in the twenty-first century. He argues that both technologies "are sure to have tremendous effects on security and stability, digital networking being the most important for the immediate future and genetic engineering having potentially epochal effects in the long run." Thompson observes that digital networking is already transforming commerce, culture, and politics, but not always in benign ways. Genetic engineering could have truly cataclysmic implications. In the near term, it could be used to fashion extremely potent biological weapons, or weapons targeted at specific groups of people. In the long term, genetic engineering "may change the course of evolution, in the process redefining human nature." Thompson predicts that many of these technological advances will be nearly impossible to control. He concludes, "Major consequences for world order would appear to be inevitable."

Nonmilitary Aspects of Security

The second part of the book examines the impact of several nonmilitary factors on national and international security. It begins by examining changing patterns of defense economics, energy issues, environmental factors, and demographic developments. It concludes with an analysis of the distinctive features of security problems in the developing world.

In chapter 6 Theodore Moran examines the dynamic linkages between defense economics and security. The important military advantages currently enjoyed by the United States and its allies depend to a large degree on advanced technologies in areas such as microelectronics, data processing, and telecommunications. More and more of these technologies are being developed, not by traditional defense industries but by commercial companies seeking to improve their position in commercial markets. The future of these firms is therefore a critical security question. Many countries face formidable challenges. Europe and Japan are hampered by rigidities in labor and capital markets that impede innovation, and most of their defense firms are dwarfed by their American counterparts. Russia and China need to institute economic and management reforms that will enable their high-tech firms to compete internationally. The United States faces challenges of a fundamentally different nature. Foreign ownership of U.S. high-technology firms is likely to increase substantially in the years ahead because of low U.S. savings rates and high U.S. balance-of-payments deficits. This growing economic interpenetration will constrain American economic and political autonomy. The security implications of these developments will be substantial.

In chapter 7 Martha Harris analyzes the increasingly complex linkages between energy and security issues. For most of the twentieth century, states sought to promote energy security by expanding national control over energy resources; cooperation on energy issues was intermittent. However, the global energy market became increasingly integrated in the final decades of the twentieth century. This trend has continued since the end of the cold war and is likely to continue in the future. Harris argues that the increasingly integrated character of the global energy market and rising energy demand call for a fundamental departure from the parochial, national approach that dominated energy policy in the twentieth century. A broader conception of energy security and a multilateral approach to these problems are needed in the twenty-first century. The reality, she says, is that "no country can achieve energy security independently today." She concludes that the United States must take the lead in adopting a global perspective and a multilateral approach to energy security problems.

In chapter 8 J. R. McNeill argues that the relationship between environmental factors and security problems is important but often oversimplified. The contention that environmental change produces political instability and violent conflict, for example, does not receive strong support from the historical record. He finds that the linkage between resource competitions and conflict is stronger. Indeed, if one expands the definition of "resources" to include labor, land, and oil, "then most wars have been over resources." Adding precision to this general proposition, he argues that wars are most likely when valued resources are seen as scarce or when power differentials make resource seizure easy and inexpensive. Perceived resource scarcities can be triggered either by population growth or by technological developments that transform unvalued goods into strategic necessities. This does not bode well for the future. Important ecological buffers—forests, fisheries, fresh water—are shrinking, and this will generate more environmental migration. This, in turn, will generate economic, social, and political tensions, and perhaps violence. Water and oil will continue to be sources of contention and perhaps contributing factors in armed conflicts. McNeill concludes that environmental factors and resource scarcities are becoming increasingly important issues in security affairs.

In chapter 9 Charles Keely observes that in decades gone by the only demographic issue that received sustained attention from security specialists was the population size of key states. In recent years, however, the stability and security implications of a wider range of demographic factors have begun to receive the attention they deserve. Population growth, he observes, "can lead to internal and external security threats." Population movements—economic migrations, refugee flows, and internally displaced persons—can generate social and economic tensions, political instability, and armed violence. Keely cautions that although demographic developments are important factors in the security equation, they are not the only factors. They rarely bring about armed conflict entirely on their own. Rather, they interact with other problems, such as access to land or jobs, to exacerbate social, economic, and political tensions and thereby make conflict more likely. He warns that most of these demographic problems are not amenable to military solutions. Indeed, in many of these areas, appropriate policy responses will fall under the heading of social policy: family planning, female education, and improved health care initiatives to better address child mortality and the HIV-AIDS epidemic.

In chapter 10 Timothy Hoyt focuses on the special security problems faced by people and states in the developing world. During the cold war, conflicts in the developing world were often driven by the politics—as well as the weapons—of the superpowers. This led to the escalation and prolongation of many conflicts, but it also had a moderating effect in some cases because neither superpower wished to see a regional conflict escalate into a nuclear confrontation between the superpowers. Hoyt contends that although the end of the cold war helped to take the steam out of some conflicts in the developing world, others have intensified. Today, conflicts in the developing world are driven primarily by local and regional issues, including environmental and demographic pressures, fierce competitions for power, and crises over the political stability and legitimacy of states. Intrastate conflicts, often with complicated regional entanglements, have become prevalent. Rogue states and failed states have become more of a concern. The future, moreover, is not bright. Hoyt argues that these problems pose increasing threats to international security, but international responses to these problems have nonetheless been woefully inadequate.

Transnational Actors and Security

The third part of the book examines the increasingly important roles played by three sets of transnational actors—transnational mass media organizations, transnational criminal organizations, and transnational terrorist organizations—in national and international security affairs.

In chapter 11 Diana Owen examines the growth of transnational mass media organizations, arguing that developments since the early 1980s have had "vast implications" for the conduct of diplomacy, peacekeeping, military operations, and national and international security in general. The media have long played important roles in security affairs, of course. American media coverage had an enormous impact on U.S. participation in the war in Vietnam, for example. Even so, the arrival of around-the-clock television news operations in the early 1980s represented a watershed development. CNN and its counterparts are far-flung transnational operations with global coverage and immediate, vivid reportage. The attention policymakers pay them has led some to speculate about the existence of a "CNN effect" on U.S. and Western policy. Owen contends that a measured approach to this issue is needed. Although mass media organizations can help to set policy agendas and accelerate or impede policy deliberations, these organizations do not make policy themselves. One must therefore be careful to avoid exaggerating their immediate policy effects.

In chapter 12 Roy Godson analyzes the destructive effects that transnational criminal organizations and corruption are having on governance and security. He argues that collaboration between political establishments and criminal organizations—the political criminal nexus (PCN)—is a large and growing problem. He estimates that 120 of the more than 190 states in the international system are weak, failing, or failed; as a result, "they have medium to strong PCNs." Although PCNs have existed since time immemorial, the magnitude of the problem today is "unprecedented." Godson considers PCNs to be "one of the most dangerous threats to the quality of life in the contemporary world." They are increasingly dominating the political, economic, and social life in many countries, which in turn increasingly undermines governability, the rule of law, human rights, and economic development. Problems that "threaten the political, economic, and social infrastructure of a country cannot be considered ordinary crime problems," he says; they must be deemed security problems. Moreover, they are not just localized security problems. Many PCNs operate across entire regions, undermining governance and stability throughout these regions. Others operate across many regions, while some have global reach.

In chapter 13 Audrey Kurth Cronin examines the dangers posed by transnational terrorism. She argues that although there might be a temptation to treat the September 11, 2001, attacks on the United States as unprecedented and unique, it is more accurate—and wiser, from a policy standpoint—to understand the historical, political, and economic contexts that shape terrorism in the contemporary world. Cronin explains that terrorism—defined as the threat or use of seemingly random violence by nonstate actors against innocents for political ends—has deep historical roots. Terrorism has gone through several distinct phases over the centuries—against authoritarian regimes, against colonial powers, and, more recently, against American leadership of the globalizing international system—but a common thread runs through these phases: in each case, terrorism has been an instrument used by the weak against preponderant powers. The current terrorist assaults conducted by Al Qaeda, she says, must be understood in this context. Although there is a religious component to Al Qaeda's motivations, its actions are primarily the manifestation of a power struggle with the United States and, more generally, the dynamics of globalization.

Policy Lessons

In the book's concluding chapter, I draw on these functional analyses, look at national and international security problems from a broad perspective, and outline some policy lessons and recommendations.

Notes

1. R. Ernest Dupuy and Trevor N. Dupuy, *The Encyclopedia of Military History from 3500 B.C. to the Present*, 2d rev. ed. (New York: Harper and Row, 1986), 990.

2. Ibid., 1198.

3. See John Lewis Gaddis, "The Long Peace: Elements of Stability in the Postwar International System," *International Security* 10 (spring 1986): 99–142. For more analysis of this issue, see John Mueller, *Retreat from Doomsday: The Obsolescence of Major War* (New York: Basic Books, 1989).

4. Estimates of the size of the Soviet Union's tactical nuclear arsenal vary. For more details, see Michael E. Brown, "Recent and Prospective Developments in Nuclear Arsenals," in *Nuclear Deterrence: Problems and Perspectives in the 1990s*, ed. Serge Sur (New York: United Nations, 1993), 17–44.

5. See Kalevi J. Holsti, *The State, War, and the State of War* (Cambridge: Cambridge University Press, 1996), 21–25. Note that Holsti's data are for 1945–95. This corresponds closely—but not precisely—with the beginning and end of the cold war era.

6. George Bush, "Presidential Address: Gulf Crisis an Opportunity for a 'New World Order,'" (transcript), *Congressional Quarterly Weekly Report* 48 (Sept. 15, 1990), 2953–55. Many have wondered if the terrorist attacks that took place on September 11, 2001, were timed to coincide with the anniversary of a previous political event. At this juncture, no one outside of Al Qaeda appears to know for sure. That said, there are two reasons for speculating that President Bush's 1990 speech might have figured in Al Qaeda's calculations. First, Bush was calling for the creation of a "new world order" that would inevitably be dominated by the West and based on Western values; this would not sit well with those who believed that Islam was already under siege from the West. Second, Bush's speech was one of the milestones in his effort to rally U.S. and international support for a campaign to overturn Iraq's August 1990 invasion of Kuwait. This ultimately led to a massive American and Western military buildup in Saudi Arabia. Al Qaeda claims to see this military presence—which remained after the Gulf War of 1991 ended—as an assault on Islam's holiest lands.

7. See Mikael Eriksson, Margareta Sollenberg, and Peter Wallensteen, "Patterns of Major Armed Conflicts, 1990–2001," in Stockholm International Peace Research Institute (SIPRI), *SIPRI Yearbook 2002: Armaments, Disarmament, and International Security* (Oxford: Oxford University Press, 2002), 63–76. A "major armed conflict" is one in which at least a thousand people have been killed. For more discussion of conflict trends in the 1990s, see Ted Robert Gurr, *Peoples Versus States: Minorities at Risk in the New Century* (Washington, D.C.: U.S. Institute of Peace Press, 2000), chap. 2.

8. IISS, Conflict Database Project, Nov. 2002.

9. See UN High Commissioner for Refugees (UNHCR), *Refugees by Numbers, 2002 Edition*; available at www.unhcr.ch. For higher estimates (including an estimate of 20–24 million for internally displaced persons), see U.S. Committee for Refugees, *Refugee Reports*; available at www.refugee.org.

10. Estimated costs include military expenditures, economic losses, refugee costs, and reconstruction costs; costs are adjusted to 1995 dollars. See IISS, "2002 Chart of Armed Conflict."

11. This does not include the costs of UN political and peace-building operations. See UN Department of Peacekeeping Operations, "Statistical Data and Charts" and "Background Note," Sept. 1, 2002; available at www.un.org/depts/dpko.

12. See World Bank Operations Evaluation Department, "Post-Conflict Reconstruction," in *Précis*, no. 169 (summer 1998): 1–5; available at www.worldbank.org.

13. In constant 1996 dollars. See Stephen Schwartz, *Atomic Audit: The Costs and Consequences of U.S. Nuclear Weapons since 1940* (Washington, D.C.: Brookings Institution, 1998).

14. IISS, *Military Balance, 2002–2003*, 241–42, 332–37.

15. SIPRI, *SIPRI Yearbook 2002*, 232.

16. See Chantal de Jonge Oudraat and P. J. Simmons, "From Accord to Action," in *Managing Global Issues: Lessons Learned*, ed. Chantal de Jonge Oudraat and P. J. Simmons (Washington, D.C.: Carnegie Endowment for International Peace, 2001), 690–727, at 722–23.

Part I   Weapons, Technology, and Security

Chapter 1   # Technology and Security

Timothy D. Hoyt

Technology revolutionized warfare in the twentieth century. New inventions—including the airplane, the submarine, the tank, the ballistic missile, and nuclear weapons—fundamentally changed the manner in which states waged wars, the organizations they created to wage wars, and the burdens and costs of military preparedness. These weapons helped redistribute the balance of power in the international system and contributed to an extended hiatus in great-power war through the unpleasant reality of nuclear deterrence.

Today, many analysts argue that the international system lies on the brink of a new revolution in military affairs based on information technologies, precision-guided weapons, and stealth technology. Analysts have identified three visions of this revolution—the Soviet "military-technical revolution," which focused on the narrow impact of technology on land battle; the belief that air power has become a revolutionary force unto itself; and the belief that information technology will provide better knowledge of the battlefield, eliminating friction and the fog of war from future armed conflicts.[1] The Western capabilities that the Soviet Union feared were demonstrated by the remarkably efficient Western destruction of a Soviet-armed and trained Iraqi military in the Gulf War of 1990-91. The importance of air power was demonstrated by the Western coalition's military operations in Desert Storm and other U.S. and allied operations later in the 1990s. The information revolution continues to unfold.[2] All of these trends were on display in the U.S.-led war on Iraq in 2003.

The argument that technology contributes to revolutionary military changes appears to be incontrovertible, but the precise role technology plays in these changes remains an issue of great debate. The limitations of technology, the challenges created by the introduction of new technologies into military environments, and the importance of nontechnological factors in military affairs all play a role in determining the nature and pace of change.

This chapter will assess the role of technology in international security since the end of the cold war. It will first examine military revolutions in history, stressing several analytical difficulties that must be considered as we examine current events. It will then analyze several recent military conflicts—in particular, the spectacular defeat of Iraq in 1991 and the air campaigns against Serbia and Afghanistan—which suggest to some that a new revolution in military affairs is taking place. It will then assess the effectiveness and limitations inherent in the new military capabilities associated with those victories. It will conclude with an assessment of the ramifications of technological change for the international system.

Military Revolutions

Technology is profoundly affected by human choices and social factors. These elements affect technological development at the individual level (where scientists decide what to research and entrepreneurs decide what technologies to develop), at the organizational and political level (where some capabilities will be dismissed or selected on the basis of corporate preference), and at the societal level (where comfort with "science" or particular areas of exploration impedes or enables research). Broader changes in society contribute to significant military change as well.

The idea that social changes are fundamental to revolutionary changes in military effectiveness is not new. Williamson Murray and MacGregor Knox argue, for instance, that revolutions in military affairs are the aftereffects of broader shifts that they refer to as "military revolutions."[3] According to Murray and Knox, military revolutions "have normally resulted from massive social and political changes that have restructured societies and states, and fundamentally altered the manner in which military organizations prepared for and conducted war."[4] They contend that military revolutions transform all aspects of war, from policy and strategy to tactics. This macrolevel approach to military affairs neatly complements the view of Alvin and Heidi Toffler, who argue that "the way we make war reflects the way we make wealth—and the way we make anti-war must reflect the way we make war."[5]

The examples these macrolevel approaches use to demonstrate truly revolutionary change in war differ significantly from the more operationally or technically focused studies examined in the next section of this chapter. The Tofflers examine three great waves of socioeconomic change—the agricultural age, the industrial age, and now the emerging information age—each of which has brought with it fundamental changes in war.[6] Murray and Knox identify five revolutionary shifts in military affairs since the sixteenth century: the creation of the modern state in the seventeenth century, which provided an organizational entity to extract resources and fund permanent, disciplined military forces; the French Revolution, which merged mass politics and warfare; the Industrial Revolution, which made it possible to equip, supply, and maintain forces in far greater numbers and at far greater distances than ever before; World War I, which combined the previous two upheavals and set the pattern for twentieth-century war; and the nuclear revolution, which kept the cold war from developing into an all-out war between the United States and the Soviet Union.[7] This formulation sees revolutions in military affairs in narrower terms: as a means of increasing military effectiveness, often using new technology as a force multiplier.

Finally, some studies attempt to combine both technological and social elements.[8] These studies identify four major periods of significant military change, associated primarily with the rise of European military dominance. The first revolution is the gunpowder era, with the resulting introduction of cannon, fortifications, firearms, and wooden sailing ships. This era is also associated with nontechnological change, including the development of new military organizations and administration. The result is that by the early eighteenth century European armies possessed marked advantages over even the most powerful non-European states, and European navies allowed the projection of power to distant lands.[9]

A second period of significant change occurred during the nineteenth century, when the social dynamics of the French and American Revolutions combined with the economic dynamics of the Industrial Revolution. Technologies associated with this revolution include rifled guns and artillery, steel, railroads, steam engines, and the telegraph. This revolution required considerable investments in heavy industry and infrastructure, which were facilitated by the growth and solidification of state power in Europe and North America. Ability to produce modern weapons—possession of the means of production—is also closely associated with the ability to use them effectively in both this and later periods. Militaries using these new technologies dominated adversaries using more primitive methods, facilitating a new wave of late-nineteenth-century colonization.[10]

The third period of dynamic military change was the interwar period and World War II, as weapons and technologies initially introduced during World War I were improved and mastered. Critical technologies included the internal combustion engine, the radio, telephone, and new electronics systems (particularly sonar and radar), as well as the weapons systems that carried these new capabilities, such as the airplane, submarine, and tank. The maturation of these new technologies provided opportunities for significant changes in warfare, which could only be achieved through the integration of appropriate doctrine, tactics, and organization.[11] The fourth and final revolution to date is the nuclear revolution—the combination of weapons of unparalleled destructive capacity with long-range delivery systems.

This view of revolutions corresponds roughly with studies of patterns in the arms trade and in international technology transfer.[12] According to this view, military-industrial change moves in waves of innovation, adaptation, imitation, and acquisition. Innovating states create and produce new types of weapons. As these new weapons emerge, other states with sufficient industrial capabilities adapt their industries and armed forces to produce the new weapons. States with lesser industrial capabilities or economic endowments attempt to imitate the forces and capabilities of the most successful states, producing what they can and purchasing what they cannot. Some states are simply unable to produce the weapons, but must purchase them for their own security. The diffusion of military industries and military capabilities are, in fact, closely linked, at least in systemic terms.[13] Through this pattern, changes in military technology flow through the international system, affecting the military balance of power.

These broader views of military change put technology in perspective, and help identify key trends that may be emerging in the international system. First, they emphasize that some elements of military change are uncontrollable, but that those elements that *are* controllable tend to be directed toward specific problems. In the absence of an enemy, truly significant military change is difficult to achieve. Military innovation requires an incentive, and the critical innovations of the twentieth and twenty-first centuries occurred in response to a perceived need to solve a problem, whether those innovations were the development of blitzkrieg by a numerically constrained Reichswehr, the development of amphibious warfare tactics by the U.S. Marine Corps, or the use of passenger aircraft as weapons of mass destruction by a small group of terrorists.[14]

A second issue is that technology is not simply a matter of weapons or other hardware. Focusing solely on weaponry risks losing sight of the forest for the trees; some of the most important technologies in military affairs have not been weapons per se.[15] The importance of weapons depends on, and may influence, the duration of conflict—the shorter the war, the greater the importance of superior hardware.[16] But a broader look at war and technology reinforces the importance of nonweapons technology and, in fact, of nonhardware aspects of technology. In the words of one of the leading works on technology and war, "technology is perhaps best understood as an abstract system of knowledge, an attitude towards life, and a method for solving its problems."[17]

The reason for this lies, in part, in the close relationship between technology and science. Science is the study of the way things are, and technology is the application of science to fulfill specific human needs.[18] Science flourishes only in environments where it is supported, either by government or society. Technological development is shaped by these same forces but occurs more rapidly where technological progress is valued for economic purposes.[19] Since the late nineteenth century, science has become closely tied to application, and the market now rewards rapid innovation in high-technology products. The role of the state in scientific research and development expanded dramatically after World War II and continues (albeit at reduced levels) in the twenty-first century—but commercial development of technology now outpaces military-sponsored development, encouraging even the most modern military organizations to buy commercial "off-the-shelf" technology.[20]

The contemporary visions of the revolution in military affairs examined in the next part of this chapter, therefore, show only a part of a greater whole, suggesting broad changes in the international system that will be discussed in the conclusion. These changes are occurring in the scientific and economic arenas, are profoundly affected by social and cultural forces, and are far more "revolutionary" than anything happening in the narrow sphere of military technology.

The "Revolution in Military Affairs"

The decade of the 1990s offered ample proof that the U.S. military had achieved overwhelming dominance in military affairs. After the collapse of the Soviet Union, no state spent even one-fifth as much on defense as the United States, no state maintained military production capacities even remotely comparable to those available to the United States, and no state could match the ability of the U.S. military to project force globally. As soon became clear, the military imbalance between the United States and even powerful regional states had become extraordinarily lopsided, and was based at least in part on technological innovation.

The Gulf War and After

In August 1990 the forces of Iraq's Republican Guard rolled into Kuwait, quickly crushing all conventional military resistance and occupying the country. The Iraqi military, equipped and trained with a wide range of Soviet and Western equipment, had defeated Iran in a vicious war of attrition from 1980 to 1988, ending with a series of dramatic Iraqi victories. Iraq's vaunted "million-man army" (a figure that included large numbers of substandard troops), modern air force, and combat experience made it, in theory, a formidable military force. Respected military analysts anticipated heavy coalition casualties in a ground counteroffensive.[21]

The Gulf War is now widely accepted as one of the single most crushing military defeats in the history of warfare. Coalition aircraft flew tens of thousands of sorties, but coalition losses were improbably low. New high-tech weapons developed to fight the Soviet Union in the 1980s were used by coalition forces with devastating effectiveness against a far less capable Iraqi force. These weapons included "stealth" aircraft capable of evading radar detection; precision-guided weapons, including aerial bombs and cruise missiles; tactical antiballistic missiles; and new sensors and command-and-control networks on satellites and aircraft.

The result was a remarkable military victory in a short campaign. During the first three days of the conflict, air strikes on Baghdad and other Iraqi cities severely degraded the ability of Iraq's leadership to command its troops in the field. Iraq's air force was forced into hiding or exile, its small navy was sunk, and key sectors of its economic infrastructure were severely damaged, all with remarkably low numbers of civilian casualties, particularly when compared to previous strategic bombing campaigns.

The U.S. Navy operated freely in the highly constricted waters of the Persian Gulf, despite the presence of sophisticated Iraqi antiship cruise missiles, suffering damage only from primitive mines. Iraq's ground forces in or near Kuwait were subjected to a month-long bombing campaign with both precision-guided weapons and massive payloads of "dumb bombs," which degraded both Iraqi morale and military capability. When the coalition ground forces began their attack, they were assisted by a near-complete blackout of Iraqi intelligence and reconnaissance that left Iraq's forces blind and vulnerable. The four-day ground operation included a classic armored envelopment, assisted by massive use of helicopters for both assault and supply missions. The United States lost fewer than half a dozen tanks to Iraqi defenses, captured tens of thousands of prisoners, and suffered fewer than two hundred fatalities in battle. Iraq's forces were routed and driven from Kuwait.

Given the remarkable efficiency of this victory, it is hardly surprising that analysts began referring to the emerging military imbalance in the international system as a revolution in military affairs. The United States fought this war with enormous strategic and military advantages, however, including a passive enemy, favorable terrain for operational maneuver and long-range engagement, and an arsenal designed to defeat a much larger and more formidable opponent in a much larger and more intense conflict. Western technology and advanced weapons clearly contributed to the coalition's victory, and particularly to the low coalition and civilian casualties, but an objective observer might well argue that the Gulf War victory was overdetermined.

The next two Western military successes occurred in a different region, against another substantial regional power, and appeared to confirm the contention that air power could independently win wars. Operation Deliberate Force, the Western military intervention in Bosnia in 1995, appears to have been very deliberate indeed, at least in this respect. Carried out with small numbers of aircraft and munitions, Operation Deliberate Force played a crucial role in forcing an end to the slaughter in Bosnia, and in temporarily stopping the bloodshed in the former Yugoslavia.

Operation Allied Force—the NATO military campaign against Serbia in 1999—was another example of the use of modern air power in isolation. The West's public repudiation of a ground-force option severely limited the capacity of NATO forces to achieve one of the important objectives of the conflict—ending the "ethnic cleansing" of the Albanian minority in Kosovo. In fact, the immediate impact of the early bombing campaign was to accelerate and indeed assure the successful ethnic cleansing of Kosovo. A mid-campaign reassessment of this strategy increased the number of NATO air assets devoted to the campaign, changed the targeting priorities, and improved cooperation between NATO air units and the Kosovo Liberation Army. The latter acted both as intelligence assets and as a surrogate for missing NATO ground forces, forcing the Serbs to mass their forces in response to potential offensives and providing more attractive military targets for NATO air strikes.

The combination of air power, special operations forces, and local insurgents also achieved significant results in Afghanistan starting in October 2001. Most U.S. air sorties early in the conflict were staged by bombers originally designed for intercontinental nuclear strikes or from the decks of aircraft carriers far from landlocked Afghanistan. Despite these daunting geographic difficulties, the combination of Western air power with Northern Alliance forces on the ground reversed the effects of the previous five years of Afghan warfare. In November 2001 Taliban military forces dissolved and retreated into strongholds in remote regions of the country, from which they were later dislodged by a combination of military and diplomatic pressure. The establishment of a U.S. air base in the mountains near the Taliban stronghold was one of the keys in this military campaign.

This string of impressive military victories by U.S. forces and its allies provides substantial evidence that the technology-intensive militaries of the West can dominate most potential adversaries in conventional battle. The improved accuracy and destructiveness of basic weaponry, the ability to identify targets and transmit their coordinates to a wide range of potential delivery systems, the coordination of military operations across space and time through new communications capabilities, and the domination of the electronic spectrum provide the United States with unparalleled conventional warfare capabilities. The United States now possesses the ability to carry out military operations with high lethality and effectiveness anywhere on the planet, a capability unique in the history of warfare.

Shortly after the Gulf War, analysts in the United States and elsewhere began speculating about the emergence of a revolution in military affairs.[22] The concept actually evolves from earlier Soviet writings about the introduction of nuclear weapons into the armed forces. However, early Soviet writings also refer to dramatic changes in conventional military capability, brought on by scientific and technical progress, improved industrial capacity, and the selective application of key technologies to the military arena.[23] Soviet authorities identified three basic elements in their studies of technological impact on military affairs: the means of destruction, the means of delivery, and the means of control.[24] These categories were easily applicable to the Gulf War. Precision-guided weapons provided vast increases in destructive power and effectiveness, decreasing the numbers of sorties and, therefore, potential losses necessary to destroy key targets. Delivery systems, including stealth aircraft and cruise missiles, were less detectable and therefore more survivable in addition to being able to deliver more lethal payloads. Dominance of the electromagnetic spectrum and space allowed command, control, and coordination of land, sea, and air forces scattered throughout the Persian Gulf region and, later, the Balkans.

The post–Gulf War discussion of the emerging impact of military technology focused on several different visions.[25] The first, related to the Soviet discussion, saw the emergence of new *weapons* as the dominant feature that permitted revolutionary change. A second saw emerging *technologies*, rather than weapons per se, as bringing about fundamental changes in the ways battles could be fought, through near real-time coordination of intelligence, analysis, targeting, and destruction.[26] A third, which gained support over the 1990s, argued that *air power* was finally "coming into its own" as a capability that could achieve decisive results independently of other elements of military power.[27] One final perception of revolutionary military change is found in the suggestion that information technologies enable new forms of strategic attack against the economies and infrastructure of warring states.[28]

A Revolution in Weaponry

The argument that changes in weaponry define revolutions in warfare is an old one. Some analysts have concluded that an advantage in technology naturally leads to superior military capability: "Tools or weapons, if only the right ones can be discovered, form 99 percent of victory.... Strategy, command, leadership, courage, discipline, supply, organization and all the moral and physical paraphernalia of war are nothing to a high superiority of weapons—at most they go to form the one percent, which makes the whole possible."[29]

A number of studies focus on the evolution of weapons, each correctly noting that changes in armaments play a substantial role in the development of new military capabilities that have helped rearrange regional or global balances of power.[30] Some studies are futuristic at best, if not deeply misguided.[31] Clearly, the idea that the development of certain types of weapons has fundamentally changed warfare is correct. One need only examine the literature on the impact of nuclear weapons on warfare to see that, at times, new weapons have had revolutionary effects.[32] Even nonnuclear weapons have increased enormously in capability. According to one source, the relative capability of a World War II–era 155 millimeter howitzer with unguided shells is 100,000 times greater than a sixteenth-century arquebus.[33]

Weapons alone, however, are insufficient to ensure victory. In World War II, for example, France, which had larger numbers of relatively superior tanks, fell in six weeks to the German blitzkrieg. The Italian Navy was defeated in the Mediterranean by an outnumbered and less modern British naval force. During the course of the war, Germany developed an array of weapons that should sound quite familiar to the modern analyst or military officer, including jet fighter and strike aircraft, submarines that sailed as fast underwater as on the surface, sophisticated airborne and ground-based radar systems, ballistic missiles (the V-2), cruise missiles, precision-guided munitions (radio-controlled glider bombs), and highly sophisticated chemical agents. Germany also fielded tanks that were superior to those in Western arsenals. Germany nevertheless lost the war. The experience of the United States in Vietnam also demonstrated the limits of superior weapons.

Other analysts of military effectiveness have pointed out the limitations of concentrating solely on weapons. One key element of military capability is having military organizations that are able to maximize the effectiveness of available weapons.[34] A second is having military doctrines that embrace innovative ideas.[35] A third factor is military education and training.[36] A focus solely on weapons is misguided. It is a fallacy that is common in the study of technology—the "sin" of technological determinism.[37]

A Revolution in Sensors and Information Processing

This fascination with technology as a determining factor in human affairs is also apparent in the argument of Admiral William Owens on the revolution in sensors and communications technology. Owens argues that new technologies will allow the United States to overcome the obstacles to accurate intelligence in warfare, obstacles outlined by Carl von Clausewitz in his description of friction.[38] The development of military electronics has led to a vast and rapid proliferation of communications devices and sensors. These increase the ability of commanders to have access to information about enemy forces, either by observing them directly or by intercepting their signals, and to coordinate their own forces in response.[39] The ability to coordinate military operations in time and space may be more important than superior weaponry. As Martin van Creveld points out, the radio sets inside German tanks may have contributed more to the effectiveness of blitzkrieg operations in 1939–40 than the combat capability of the tanks themselves.[40]

The experience of the 1990s, however, suggests that the more optimistic assumptions regarding information and communications technologies will not be realized soon. Friction was a constant in the Gulf War, despite the near absence of Iraqi interference and the generally exceptional geography for waging airborne surveillance and warfare.[41] Operation Allied Force was marred by highly publicized targeting errors, including the attack on a Serbian passenger train and the disastrous attack on the Chinese embassy in Belgrade. Under more difficult conditions, the limits of air- and space-based surveillance and intelligence gathering have been demonstrated by the inability to find key leaders of the Taliban and Al Qaeda since September 11, 2001.[42] The U.S. military has recognized some of these limitations, emphasizing both the opportunities and constraints offered by new information technologies in recent strategy statements.[43]

A Revolution through Air Power

A third perspective on the revolution in military affairs is the belief that air power can now be decisive in warfare even when operating independently of other armed forces. This belief, unsurprisingly, is strongly supported by the U.S. Air Force, which has an ideological connection with the concept of independent air power dating back to the 1920s.[44] Early theories of independent air power represented an effort to apply technology to resolve the appalling military dilemmas of 1914–1918. The combination of new forms of destruction and delivery (bombs and long-range aircraft, respectively) would target enemy civilian populations and economic targets in their homelands.[45] This would bypass the bloody, stalemated trench warfare of World War I, breaking either the will or the economy of the adversary and leading to swift victory.[46] World War II saw vast resources poured into strategic bombing campaigns by both Britain and the United States, in part because Britain had few options for harming Germany after the collapse of France in 1940.[47]

Contemporary air power advocates focus less on the destruction of civil society or economic infrastructure and more on the rapid degradation of enemy command and control. In effect, air power now focuses on achieving operational effects that will lower enemy morale and fighting capabilities.[48] Air power can also, of course, inflict tremendous damage on enemy combat units themselves, as demonstrated in Desert Storm, more recent operations in Afghanistan, and in Iraq in 2003. But does this constitute a true military "revolution?"

It is important to note that this "revolution" took eighty years to accomplish, due to the slow maturation not only of doctrine but also of crucial supporting technologies, including bombsights, precision guidance, and long-range delivery systems. In addition, it appears clear that air power, however formidable, still does not constitute a decisive war-winning capability in isolation. There is no evidence that Iraq planned to withdraw its forces from Kuwait prior to the coalition's ground invasion, despite severe battering of both Iraqi military forces and Iraqi infrastructure in the air campaign. Both Operation Deliberate Force and Operation Allied Force benefited from the availability of proxy forces—a significant Croat and Bosnian offensive in 1995, and the skillful use of the Kosovo Liberation Army in 1999. Operations in Afghanistan were decisive because of the skillful use of special forces on the ground and the availability of the Northern Alliance units to fix Taliban forces in place at the front line.

The record of air power in Kosovo was mixed. Operation Allied Force was initiated on the assumption that Serbian leader Slobodan Milosevic would cave in within forty-eight hours—a grossly unrealistic expectation.[49] The Allied commander, General Wesley Clark, concerned about ensuring the destruction of Serbian ground forces, made great exertions to provide either artillery or helicopter support for NATO operations, efforts that were eventually futile.[50] The ultimate impact of air strikes on Serb forces in Kosovo remains hotly debated, but it appears that initial U.S. claims were inflated and that substantial Serb forces retreated in good order after the cease-fire with much of their equipment.[51]

The "primacy-of-air-power" argument rests on technology: improvements in precision guidance for various munitions make these munitions more lethal. For example, in Operation Allied Force, allied forces were able to program eight Tomahawk land attack missiles to destroy the primary sprinkler system in Serbian Socialist Party headquarters. This ensured that the building burned down.[52] Increased accuracy raises expectations as well as lethality. As the 1990s demonstrated, increasing use of precision weapons led to a popular presumption that war would become increasingly antiseptic.[53] As a result, U.S. military force was used more frequently than during the cold war, and primarily in support of nonvital interests.[54]

This demonstrates an interesting and very important phenomenon about technology. Many analysts of technology, and specifically of military technology, see it as an independent variable in international affairs. According to this line of thinking, technologies emerge and are irrevocably put to military use in an orderly, almost predictable fashion.[55] The most extreme variants of this approach are found in Soviet thinking on the "military-technical revolution," which assumed that because the United States was capable of creating certain kinds of weaponry, it would automatically do so.[56]

In fact, technology and innovation have strong social components. In many respects they are dependent variables that are influenced by human factors.[57] In the case of the military-technical revolution feared by the Soviet Union, many of the weapons that Soviet thinkers saw as irrevocably emerging in U.S. arsenals could or would have been delayed or perhaps canceled as the result of U.S. domestic politics and budgetary disputes. Funding for research and development both enables and constrains technological experimentation and innovation. Deprived of funds, some options may never be pursued.[58]

One social aspect of the air-power revolution is the impact of antiseptic precision capabilities on political choices and popular support for military intervention. Desert Storm, thanks in large part to the extensive air campaign, demonstrated that revolutions in military affairs can lead to low casualties. Operation Allied Force was waged without a single allied combat fatality. Assumptions of low casualties, however, also extend to the enemy. Concern over the possible impact of media reports on the so-called "Highway of Death" affected the Bush administration's war-termination efforts in 1991. The tragic bombing of the Chinese embassy in Belgrade during Operation Allied Force embarrassed the U.S. government and significantly increased Chinese suspicions of and hostility to the United States.[59] The combination of increased precision and of improved international media coverage in warfare, both enabled by improvements in sensors and communications technologies, has profoundly influenced the way the United States wages war today.[60] Social pressures have shaped the direction in which technology is applied for military purposes, and the result has not necessarily been the decisive victories generally associated with a new revolution in military affairs, as Operation Allied Force and Operation Desert Fox demonstrate.

New Dimensions of Warfare

A final framework for examining possible emerging revolutions in military affairs focuses on the creation of a new environment in which military operations can be conducted. This is the emerging information sphere associated with new communications and information technologies. Information warfare, information operations, and other concepts crept into the lexicon of military affairs in the 1990s.[61] The creation of a new dimension of war—the information or cyber dimension—is an important facet of technological change. Some analysts see it as enabling vastly increased coordination of conventional military forces.[62] Others see it as a potentially crucial strategic dimension on its own, where warfare can be waged through other means with potentially devastating strategic results.[63]

The creation of a new dimension of warfare may represent a reasonable definition for a revolution in military affairs. Previous examples could easily include the creation of littoral naval power by Athens in the fifth century B.C., which crushed Persia and changed the face of Greek warfare; the discovery of ocean-going sea power by various European states in the fifteenth through seventeenth centuries; the expansion of warfare to three dimensions by the development of aircraft and submarines; and the development of the electronic dimension of warfare during the twentieth century. Each of these developments has fundamentally affected the means through which war is waged and the opportunities available to those powers that mastered the new dimension.

Information technology and improved communications in general play a crucial role in international affairs.[64] It is probably premature to argue that the information sphere has become an arena for decisive operations, for two reasons. First, the adversary must be vulnerable to attack from or in the new dimension. Only those countries that rely heavily on information technology can suffer significantly from information operations. In fact, the countries most vulnerable to these attacks are the very countries innovating and moving toward an information warfare capability—the United States and a number of other states in the developed world.

Second, the evidence of successful information operations, even in a rudimentary manner, is rather limited. It has been reported that information operations were carried out in Kosovo but were deliberately limited in scope.[65] More recently, the Falun Gong spiritual movement jammed the Chinese government's Sinosat-1 satellite for a week in June 2002, affecting as many as 70 million people.[66] Political groups, including opposition parties, separatist movements, and terrorist organizations, use the Internet for fundraising and information dissemination, including the now famous Zapatistas of Mexico. Information technology has proven critical in a supporting role to more traditional dimensions of warfare; information sharing, for example, is an important force multiplier for U.S. forces today. Nevertheless, claims for a decisive role in the near future appear premature.[67]

The Changing Technological Context

New technologies now being exploited for commercial purposes include information technology, new research in biology and genetics, and eventually nano-technology, among others. Computers and the Internet have contributed to the creation of an information sector with significant international economic ramifications. These new areas of research are not necessarily dominated by the West—certainly not to the extent that the United States once dominated global economic and technological competition. In the near future the majority of technological breakthroughs may well occur outside the United States, with the newly industrialized states of Asia providing considerable competition.[68]

These technological changes have profound ramifications for military capability, and more broadly for international security. First, they suggest that states or societies that do not place a high value on science or technology will have increasing difficulty competing in the international economy.[69] This can lead to increased popular disaffection with global order, a trend already noted in observers of the globalization phenomenon.[70] It can also exacerbate tensions between cultures, which may lead to interstate or regional conflict or, as we have seen, international terrorism and other "low-intensity" political violence.[71]

Second, states will be faced with a series of difficult choices in emerging research areas. The opening up of biological and genetic research raises serious moral and ethical dilemmas. The United States already debates the use of fetal tissue for research and the ethics of cloning. As DNA manipulation becomes technologically and commercially viable, it has significant implications for both commercial and military uses that may not be pursued with equal fervor by all societies.

A third issue is the diffusion of technological innovations, particularly those that may have military applications.[72] The rapid and systematic progress in scientific research and technological innovation, particularly in fields such as genetics and the biological sciences, raises troubling questions about the ability of the international system to control their distribution or use. Proliferation of nuclear weapons has been a concern for decades, constitutes a relatively easy monitoring and export control problem, and has still been circumvented by determined states. The chemical weapons convention instituted strict controls on industrial facilities and precursor chemicals. However, controlling biological and genetic research—a high-profit research area with disturbing dual-use aspects—will be much more difficult, as leading economic powers (including the United States) oppose surprise on-site inspections for fear of jeopardizing potential commercial advantage or research.

Warfare in the twentieth century revolved around industrial capabilities, or access to reliable foreign suppliers of arms. Developing these industries required enormous capital outlays, which led in turn to proliferation of both finished weapons and industrial capability ranging from assembly to codevelopment. Warfare since the nineteenth century has been *product*-dominant and *capital*-intensive. Machines were required for modern warfare, and these could only be produced by large, expensive heavy industries. States that opted not to produce these military technologies had to get them elsewhere, which led to an international arms market. States that chose not to use these technologies had to be prepared to accept very heavy losses in manpower when engaged with technologically superior foes. This usually led to defeat.[73]

Reliance on these technologies led to an increasingly centralized and shrinking international defense industry. No state currently provides for all of its defense needs through domestic research, development, and production. Only a handful of states can manufacture modern combat aircraft, main battle tanks, high-performance jet engines. Defense producers in Europe have been forced to seek partners or pursue joint ventures due to heavy capital costs and limited production runs.[74]

The emergence of the information and electronic dimensions of warfare, however, change the potential competition in emerging defense-related areas. These new areas are *process*-dominated and *knowledge*-intensive, very different requirements for competition. Small states such as Israel and Singapore already compete effectively in defense upgrades, using sophisticated local electronics industries to improve the capabilities and extend the service life of existing weapons.

The introduction of new technologies and new dimensions of military capability simultaneously creates new vulnerabilities. States that compete effectively in these new technological "niches" can not only acquire important military capabilities but may also gain significant parts of the international market, possibly even outcompeting the enormous, but relatively inflexible, U.S. defense industry. Israel has gained just such a niche in the production of unmanned aerial and unmanned combat aerial vehicles (UAV/UCAV) and military electronics. Technologically backward North Korea is one of the leading international exporters of ballistic missiles and their associated technologies. Emerging or existing computer software industries in India, Israel, and the Pacific Rim may soon exploit the potential of expansion into the defense sector.

Because commercial technologies are now being created at a rate far beyond the ability of any military, even the U.S. military, to deploy them, new opportunities also exist for military innovation. While the United States retains an almost unsurpassable advantage in traditional arms, states in conflicted regions will continue to experiment with emerging capabilities to resolve specific security dilemmas, including perhaps the deterrence of U.S. intervention. States seeking to deter the United States currently focus on missiles and weapons of mass destruction. It is possible that in the future the threat of information warfare attacks or outbreaks of hoof-and-mouth disease will join this array of tools.

Conclusion

In the short term, American military predominance remains assured. No other state or coalition will be able to create the kinds of capabilities currently available or evolving in the U.S. military. Emerging technologies will enhance the American ability to project power internationally, permitting the United States to intervene with potentially decisive results in regional conventional conflicts.[75] States seeking to compete with the United States will have to focus on deterring U.S. intervention, attacking U.S. bases and ports of entry into various regions, and exploiting other capabilities as a form of asymmetric warfare.[76]

States engaging in warfare with the United States will need to seek to limit the formidable capabilities of American air power in particular. Deception and camouflage will be crucial tools. Resistance through unconventional warfare, including special forces operations and state-sponsored terrorism, will allow states without high-tech force-projection capabilities to retaliate against U.S. bases and facilities and the U.S. homeland in event of a war. As the September 11, 2001, attacks demonstrate, commercial technologies can be used in innovative ways to cause great destruction.

It will be tempting for some regional powers to believe they can imitate the success of the U.S. Air Force in local wars. This would be a mistake, as no regional air force, with the possible exception of Israel, has the reconnaissance, surveillance, and support capabilities necessary for dominance of local air space, and most do not maintain adequate stocks of precision-guided munitions. Both Pakistan (in 1971) and Iraq (in 1980) attempted to emulate the successful Israeli air attacks of 1967. Both failed for entirely predictable reasons and found themselves in trouble in the resulting conflicts. In regional conflicts, with the exception of Israel, technological change may increase existing imbalances but is unlikely to lead to decisive advantage in the near future.[77]

The longer-term aspects of technological change raise interesting questions about the future shape of the international system. The proliferation of technological capabilities and the lowered financial barriers to participation in the emerging technology fields suggest two significant international trends in the coming decades. The first is the gradual breakdown and realignment of the international arms production hierarchy. New producers will be able to compete on more level ground in emerging technological areas, and older established producers may lack the incentive or the capability to compete. The second trend evolves from the first. Most states will lack the financial resources to aspire to "superpower" status—the acquisition of substantial capability in all technological and military niches.[78] Some states will seek to attain some capability in many niches, and others will seek to specialize in existing or emerging niches, as they feel appropriate. Some, of course, will not be able or willing to compete.

The emerging global military order will resemble Renaissance Europe far more than post-Westphalian Europe. There will be wide disparities in military capability based on different concepts and technologies, with many states capable of mobilizing significant local resistance if attacked. Those desiring or capable of significant force-projection capabilities will face high financial costs and difficulties in achieving decisive military success.

This is not a vision where the current U.S. technological advantage will necessarily lead to an extended period of military dominance. The technologies that have made up the American revolution in military affairs to date have only begun to mature, and new capabilities are emerging with enormous speed. The United States leads in information technologies, for instance, because it relies on them so heavily, and therefore is more vulnerable than other states to outside attack. In some technological areas the United States will probably constrain itself, while in others more flexible and adaptable countries responding to immediate or specific threats will innovate first.

The lowered cost of entry and altered costs of competition in emerging defense technologies will also accelerate one of the principal effects of globalization. Education will become a major security asset, and both state and non-state actors will have access to increasingly formidable military-related technologies. Relatively small numbers of scientists, supported by large numbers of technicians and funding, created nuclear weapons capabilities in Pakistan and nuclear and biological weapons capabilities in Iraq in the late twentieth century. The world has already seen nonstate actors with substantial financial capital—such as Al Qaeda, Aum Shinrikyo, and Falun Gong—use technologies for mass destruction or mass political effect. This trend is likely to continue, and technical expertise combined with targeted capital will allow relatively weak groups and states to create significant capabilities, given proper incentives.

The proliferation of technologies will also force military organizations to continue to professionalize, and to seek ways to integrate technicians into current military structures. This will be an uncomfortable change in many militaries, where "geeks" and soldiers are viewed as very different entities.[79] New technologies will also raise troubling questions about the continued validity and applicability of the lessons derived from the last 500 years of European warfare. The distinction between civilian and combatant, while increasingly sharp due to the professionalization of military forces and the erosion of conscription, may well blur in the actual conduct of warfare with new technologies.[80] The emergence of new dimensions of warfare in space and cyberspace may force reconsideration, or at least reinterpretation, of the principles of war used by many militaries.[81]

The American-led victories in the Gulf War in 1991 and in Iraq in 2003 were spectacular successes at the operational level. They represented the culmination of a century of technological exploration and military innovation. In the future, combat—enabled by emerging technologies and waged between adversaries that may range from computer hackers to multinational coalitions of states or consenting elites—may be much murkier, less decisive, and less controlled.[82]

Acknowledgment

The author would like to thank his students at Georgetown University's Security Studies Program for their stimulating discussion of many of the ideas raised in this chapter. The author is particularly grateful for the assistance and comments of Chris Connell, Benoit Durieux, Aaron Frank, and William Philbin. The views reflected in this chapter are those of the author, and do not represent the policy or official position of the U.S. Navy, the Department of Defense, or any other organization of the U.S. government.

Notes

1. See Eliot A. Cohen, "A Revolution in Warfare?" *Foreign Affairs* 75 (March/April 1996): 37–54.

2. Admiral Bill Owens (with Ed Offley), *Lifting the Fog of War* (New York: Farrar, Straus and Giroux, 2000).

3. Williamson Murray and MacGregor Knox, "The Future Behind Us," in *The Dynamics of Military Revolution, 1300-2050*, ed. MacGregor Knox and Williamson Murray (Cambridge: Cambridge University Press, 2001), 175-94; and Williamson Murray, "Thinking about Revolutions in Military Affairs," *Joint Forces Quarterly* 16 (summer 1997): 69-76.

4. Murray and Knox, "The Future Behind Us," 176. This definition is important in that it does not even mention technology.

5. Alvin and Heidi Toffler, *War and Anti-War: Survival at the Dawn of the 21ˢᵗ Century* (Boston: Little, Brown, 1993), 3.

6. Ibid.

7. Williamson Murray and MacGregor Knox, "Thinking about Revolutions in Warfare," in Knox and Murray, *The Dynamics of Military Revolution*, 6. Only the last upheaval is specifically linked with a weapon or weapons.

8. Report of the Future Security Environment Working Group submitted to the Commission on Integrated Long-Term Strategy, *The Future Security Environment* (Washington, D.C.: The Pentagon, 1988); and Notra Trulock III, "Appendix B: Emerging Technologies and Future War: A Soviet View," in *The Future Security Environment*.

9. See Clifford Rogers, ed., *The Military Revolution Debate* (Boulder: Westview, 1995); Jeremy Black, *European Warfare 1660–1815* (New Haven: Yale University Press, 1994); Geoffrey

Parker, *The Military Revolution 1500–1800* (Cambridge: Cambridge University Press, 1988); and Carlos Cipolla, *Guns, Sails, and Empires: Technological Innovation and the Early Phases of European Expansion, 1400–1700* (New York: Minerva Press, 1965).

10. Daniel Headrick, *The Tools of Empire: Technology and European Imperialism in the Nineteenth Century* (Oxford: Oxford University Press, 1981); David B. Ralston, *Importing the European Army* (Chicago: University of Chicago Press, 1990); Michael Howard, *War in European History* (Oxford: Oxford University Press, 1976); Bruce D. Porter, *War and the Rise of the State: The Military Foundations of Modern Politics* (New York: Free Press, 1994).

11. Andrew Krepinevich, "Cavalry to Computer: The Pattern of Military Revolutions," *The National Interest,* no. 37 (fall 1994): 30–42; Cohen, "A Revolution in Warfare?"; Marshal V. D. Sokolovsky, *Soviet Military Strategy,* ed. Harriet Fast Scott, 3rd ed. (1968; New York: Crane, Russak & Co., 1975); John A. English, *Marching through Chaos: The Descent of Armies in Theory and Practice* (Westport, Conn.: Praeger, 1998); Richard E. Simpkin, *Race to the Swift* (London: Brassey's, 1985).

12. See Keith Krause, *Arms and the State: Patterns of Military Production and Trade* (Cambridge: Cambridge University Press, 1992).

13. This linkage has been explored by the author in relation to security in the developing world. See Timothy D. Hoyt, *Military Industry and Regional Power* (London: Frank Cass, forthcoming).

14. For a study of military innovation in the twentieth century, see Stephen Peter Rosen, *Winning the Next War: Innovation and the Modern Military* (Ithaca: Cornell University Press, 1991).

15. Canned food and plasma represent two examples. Information technologies, including maps, have also been crucial in the evolution of warfare. Roads and the development of civilian transport fundamentally changed war in the nineteenth century, enabling Napoleon's armies to move rapidly across Germany and, later in the century, using railroads to provide the logistical support for the massed armies of the American Civil War and the wars of German unification.

16. This explains the strong element of technological determinism in many studies of technology and war. Superior hardware is viewed as the explanation for the short duration of some decisive wars, although human factors such as politics and popular support may be the deciding factors in these conflicts.

17. Martin Van Creveld, *Technology and War,* 2d ed. (New York: Free Press, 1991), 312. This is another way of discussing the distinction between technological *product*—the artifacts or objects that are manufactured, or the artifacts necessary for the manufacture of these objects—and technological *process*—the knowledge of how to create objects and the intellectual and organizational know-how necessary to systematically replicate results and perhaps further innovate.

18. Eugene B. Skolnikoff, *The Elusive Transformation: Science, Technology, and the Evolution of International Politics* (Princeton: Princeton University Press, 1993), 12–15.

19. See William H. McNeill, *The Pursuit of Power: Technology, Armed Force, and Society since 1000 A.D.* (Chicago: University of Chicago Press, 1982) for a discussion of technological progress in command and market economies. McNeill concludes that markets have encouraged innovation much more successfully.

20. Skolnikoff, *The Elusive Transformation,* 30–31.

21. Worst-case estimates of up to 16,465 coalition casualties can be found in Trevor N. Dupuy et al., *If War Comes . . . How to Defeat Saddam Hussein* (McLean, Va.: HERO Books, 1991), 104.

22. Andrew Krepinevich, "Cavalry to Computer: The Pattern of Military Revolutions,"

National Interest, no. 37 (fall 1994): 30–42; James R. FitzSimonds and Jan M. van Tol, "Revolutions in Military Affairs," *Joint Force Quarterly,* no. 4 (spring 1994): 24–31; Brig. V. K. Nair, *War in the Gulf: Lessons for the Third World,* Lancer Paper No. 3 (New Delhi: Lancer, 1991).

23. Sokolovsky, *Soviet Military Strategy,* xx, 113, 260.

24. N. A. Lomov, ed., *Scientific-Technical Progress and the Revolution in Military Affairs (A Soviet View)* (Moscow: Military Publishing House of the Ministry of Defense, 1973), 35–36.

25. See Cohen, "A Revolution in Warfare," 39–40.

26. This argument is found in Joseph S. Nye Jr. and William A. Owens, "America's Information Edge," *Foreign Affairs* 75 (March/April 1996): 20–36. It is developed further in Owens, *Lifting the Fog of War.*

27. Philip S. Meilinger, *Paths of Heaven: The Evolution of Air Power Theory* (Maxwell Air Force Base, Ala.: Air University Press, July 1997). The core of the air-power argument was already emerging before the Gulf War, which served to support the arguments of its leading proponent. See John A. Warden III, *The Air Campaign: Planning for Combat* (Washington, D.C.: U.S. Government Printing Office, 1988).

28. See John Arquilla and David Ronfeldt, *In Athena's Camp: Preparing for Conflict in the Information Age* (Santa Monica, Calif.: RAND, 1997).

29. J. F. C. Fuller, *Armament and History* (New York: Da Capo Press, 1998), 31.

30. Among these are T. N. Dupuy, *The Evolution of Weapons and Warfare* (Indianapolis: Bobbs-Merrill, 1980); Bernard and Fawn M. Brodie, *From Crossbow to H-Bomb,* rev. and enl. ed. (Bloomington: University of Indiana Press, 1973); and Robert L. O'Connell, *Of Arms and Men: A History of War, Weapons, and Aggression* (Oxford: Oxford University Press, 1989).

31. See, for example, Frank Barnaby, *The Automated Battlefield* (New York: Free Press, 1986). An interesting study is I. F. Clarke, *Voices Prophesying War, 1763–1984* (London: Oxford University Press, 1966).

32. See Scott D. Sagan and Kenneth N. Waltz, *The Spread of Nuclear Weapons: A Debate* (New York: Norton, 1995); and Robert Jervis, *The Meaning of the Nuclear Revolution: Statecraft and the Prospect of Armageddon* (Ithaca: Cornell University Press, 1989).

33. T. N. Dupuy, *Numbers, Predictions, and War,* rev. ed. (Fairfax, Va.: HERO Books, 1985), 7.

34. See Andrew Krepinevich, "Cavalry to Computer"; FitzSimonds and van Tol, "Revolutions in Military Affairs"; and Jeremy Black, "Military Organisations and Military Change in Historical Perspective," *Journal of Military History* 62 (Oct. 1998): 871–93.

35. Eliot Cohen, "A Tale of Two Secretaries," *Foreign Affairs* 81 (May/June 2002): 33–46.

36. Stephen Biddle, "Victory Misunderstood: What the Gulf War Tells Us about the Future of Conflict," *International Security* 21 (fall 1996): 139–79; Williamson Murray, "Innovation: Past and Future," *Joint Forces Quarterly* (summer 1996): 51–60.

37. The belief that technology drives human affairs, and therefore represents an independent variable in international affairs, is particularly associated with Marxist-Leninism. See Merritt Roe Smith, ed., *Military Enterprise and Technological Change: Perspectives on the American Experience* (Cambridge: MIT Press, 1985); and Merritt Roe Smith and Leo Marx, eds., *Does Technology Drive History? The Dilemma of Technological Determinism* (Cambridge: MIT Press, 1994). For a classic study, see Lynn White Jr., *Medieval Technology and Social Change* (Oxford: Oxford University Press, 1962).

38. See Owens, *Lifting the Fog of War;* and Carl von Clausewitz, *On War,* ed. and trans. Michael Howard and Peter Paret (Princeton: Princeton University Press, 1976), 117–21.

39. Guy Hartcup, *The Silent Revolution: Development of Conventional Weapons, 1945–1985* (London: Brassey's, 1993), 19–108.

40. Martin Van Creveld, *Technology and War,* rev. and enl. ed. (New York: Free Press, 1991), 180.

41. Barry D. Watts, *Clausewitzian Friction and Future War,* McNair Paper 52 (Oct. 1996).

42. Michael E. O'Hanlon, "A Flawed Masterpiece," *Foreign Affairs* 81 (2): 47–63.

43. *Joint Vision 2020* (Washington, D.C.: U.S. Government Printing Office, June 2000), 6–10.

44. William Mitchell, *Winged Defense: The Development and Possibilities of Modern Air Power—Economic and Military* (New York: G. P. Putnam's Sons, 1925); William Mitchell, *Our Air Force: The Key to National Defense* (New York: Dutton, 1921).

45. See Giulio Douhet, *The Command of the Air,* trans. Dino Ferrari (New York: Coward-McCann, Inc., 1942); Alexander Seversky, *Victory through Air Power* (New York: Simon & Schuster, 1942). Hugh Trenchard, the British Chief of Air Staff from 1919 to 1929, developed theories that called for air power to provide "police" support for colonial authorities. See David MacIsaac, "Theorists of Air Power," in *Makers of Modern Strategy*, ed. Peter Paret (Princeton: Princeton University Press, 1986), 633.

46. In the European campaign, the United States attacked industrial "centers of gravity" through daylight bombing, while Britain attacked population centers (and later dams and other infrastructure targets) at night. These choices were predicated on secondary technologies—bombsights and escort fighters—as well as doctrine and combat experience. In the Pacific theater, geography, weather conditions, patterns of industrial infrastructure, and the materials used in Japanese building construction eventually pushed the United States into a campaign of night-bombing with incendiaries.

47. An excellent study of the U.S. Strategic Bombing Survey is David MacIsaac, *Strategic Bombing in World War II: The Story of the U.S. Strategic Bombing Survey* (New York: Garland, 1976). This book includes a brief section on the British Bombing Survey Unit. For a defense of British air strategy in the war, see Arthur Harris, *Bomber Offensive* (London: Greenhill Press, 1998). A critique can be found in Bernard Brodie, *Strategy in the Missile Age* (Princeton: Princeton University Press, 1959), 107–44.

48. An earlier version of this argument can be found in Timothy D. Hoyt, "Iraq's Military Industry: A Critical Strategic Target," *National Security Studies Quarterly* 4 (spring 1998): 42.

49. William Arkin, "Operation Allied Force: 'The Most Precise Application of Air Power in History,'" in *War over Kosovo: Politics and Strategy in a Global Age,* ed. Andrew J. Bacevich and Eliot A. Cohen (New York: Columbia University Press, 2001), 5.

50. See Wesley K. Clark, *Waging Modern War* (New York: Public Affairs, 2001).

51. Arkin, "Operation Allied Force," 25.

52. Michael G. Vickers, "Revolution Deferred: Kosovo and the Transformation of War," in *War over Kosovo*, 194.

53. Michael O'Hanlon notes that the percentage of precision munitions used increased from less than 10 percent of all bombs in Operation Desert Storm to more than 50 percent in Operation Enduring Freedom. See O'Hanlon, "A Flawed Masterpiece," 52.

54. A very interesting piece on this topic is Andrew J. Bacevich, "Neglected Trinity: Kosovo and the Crisis in U.S. Civil-Military Relations," in *War over Kosovo*, 155–88.

55. An extreme version of this approach can be seen in computer games such as Sid Meier's *Civilization* series. These games have "technology trees," in which new developments are dependent on previous technologies, and military improvements are directly associated with technological change.

56. Soviet military thinking, like much Marxist analysis, had a strong element of technological determinism.

57. Skolnikoff, *The Elusive Transformation,* 10–12.

58. The importance of state funding for both commercial and military technologies during the cold war is discussed in Daniel S. Greenberg, *The Politics of Pure Science* (Chicago: University of Chicago Press, 1999); and David C. Mowery and Nathan Rosenberg, *Paths of Innovation: Technological Change in Twentieth-Century America* (Cambridge: Cambridge University Press, 1998). The cold war alliance of science and state was first explored in Vannevar Bush, *Modern Arms and Free Men: A Discussion of the Role of Science in Preserving Democracy* (New York: Simon & Schuster, 1949).

59. Many actors assume that U.S. technological capabilities are so advanced that mistakes cannot be made. According to this line of thinking, if U.S. forces struck the Chinese embassy, it must have been a deliberate attack.

60. See Bacevich, "Neglected Trinity"; and Eliot A. Cohen, "Kosovo and the New American Way of War," in *War over Kosovo,* 38–62.

61. An excellent introduction can be found in Martin C. Libicki, *What Is Information Warfare?* (Washington, D.C.: National Defense University, Aug. 1995).

62. See Owens, *Lifting the Fog of War.*

63. Russia, for example, has noted in its nuclear doctrine that information operations against it will be considered a "strategic" attack, therefore possibly warranting "strategic" (i.e., nuclear) retaliation. An early consideration of this new type of warfare can be found in Roger C. Molander, Andrew S. Riddile, and Peter A Wilson, *Strategic Information Warfare: A New Face of War* (Santa Monica, Calif.: RAND, 1998).

64. Excellent studies of the historical impact of information technologies include Daniel R. Headrick, *When Information Came of Age: Technologies of Knowledge in the Age of Reason and Revolution, 1700–1850* (Oxford: Oxford University Press, 2000); and Daniel R. Headrick, *The Invisible Weapons: Telecommunications and International Politics, 1851–1945* (Oxford: Oxford University Press, 1991).

65. Vickers, "Revolution Deferred," 196.

66. "Banned Falun Gong Movement Jammed Chinese Satellite Signal," *Washington Post,* July 9, 2002. The operation forced the Chinese government to cancel a live broadcast of a speech by President Jiang Zemin, and transmitted Falun Gong video feed for brief periods of time.

67. Colin Gray, examining air and space power, has argued that the evolution of military capability goes through four stages: experimental/marginal adjunct to terrestrial forces; useful and important adjunct to terrestrial forces; indispensable adjunct; and independent war winner. It could be argued that information power is currently in the first or second stage. See Colin S. Gray, *Explorations in Strategy* (Westport, Conn.: Praeger, 1996), 102.

68. Thomas J. Welch, "Technology Change and Security," *Washington Quarterly* 13 (1990): 111–20. The technological threat of Asia to the West is also addressed in Paul Bracken, *Fire in the East: The Rise of Asian Military Power and the Second Nuclear Age* (New York: HarperCollins, 1999).

69. In this vein, a disturbing study is Pervez Hoodbhoy, *Islam and Science: Religious Orthodoxy and the Battle for Rationality* (London: Zed Books, 1991).

70. The leading anecdotal chronicler of this trend is Thomas L. Friedman, *The Lexus and the Olive Tree* (New York: Anchor Books, 2000). Another example is Benjamin R. Barber, *Jihad vs. McWorld: Terrorism's Challenge to Democracy* (New York: Ballantine Books, 1995). A more academic survey of the globalization phenomenon is Victor D. Cha, "Globalization and the Study of International Security," *Journal of Peace Research* 37 (3) (2000): 391–403.

71. This is a theme in Samuel P. Huntington, *The Clash of Civilizations and the Remaking of World Order* (New York: Touchstone Books, 1996).

72. An introduction to this phenomenon can be found in Everett M. Rogers, *Diffusion of Innovations,* 4th ed. (New York: Free Press, 1995).

73. The exceptions to this rule include the Chinese effort in Korea, 1950–1953, and the independence struggle of the Vietnamese.

74. See, for example, David Mussington, *Arms Unbound: The Globalization of Defense Production* (London: Brassey's, 1994).

75. An examination of these capabilities can be found in Michael O'Hanlon, *Technological Change and the Future of Warfare* (Washington, D.C.: Brookings Institution, 2000); Bevin Alexander, *The Future of Warfare* (New York: Norton, 1995); George and Meredith Friedman, *The Future of War: Power, Technology, and American World Dominance in the Twenty-first Century* (New York: Crown Publishers, 1996); and Barry R. Schneider and Lawrence E. Grinter, eds., *Battlefield of the Future: Twenty-first-Century Warfare Issues,* Air War College Studies in National Security, No. 3 (Maxwell Air Force Base, Ala.: Air University Press, 1998).

76. Robert Kagan and William Kristol, eds., *Present Dangers: Crisis and Opportunity in American Foreign and Defense Policy* (San Francisco: Encounter Books, 2000); Bracken, *Fire in the East.*

77. In the Israeli case, the current Palestinian threat is not easily engaged by the technologies and capabilities of the revolution in military affairs.

78. The United States remains the obvious exception. In addition to existing capital stocks of defense equipment, high U.S. defense expenditures will allow it to compete in most if not all capability niches for the foreseeable future.

79. U.S. Navy ships, particularly aircraft carriers, already have difficulty operating without civilian contractors on board to provide critical technical services.

80. For an interesting discussion of these emerging ethical issues, see Alberto Coll, "Kosovo and the Moral Burdens of Power," in *War over Kosovo,* 124–54.

81. See Robert R. Leonhard, *The Principles of War in the Information Age* (Novato, Calif.: Presidio Press, 1998).

82. Two interesting but controversial studies are James Adams, *The Next World War: Computers Are the Weapons and the Front Line Is Everywhere* (New York: Simon & Schuster, 1998), and Martin Van Creveld, *The Transformation of War: The Most Radical Reinterpretation of Armed Conflict since Clausewitz* (New York: Free Press, 1991).

Chapter 2

The Perils of Nuclear, Biological, and Chemical Weapons

BERNARD I. FINEL, BRIAN D. FINLAY, AND JANNE E. NOLAN

Despite dire predictions to the contrary, the proliferation of weapons of mass destruction (WMD) has actually diminished by most quantitative measures since the end of the cold war. In the nuclear sphere, India and Pakistan publicly tested nuclear devices in 1998, but the number of "threshold" nuclear states with active nuclear programs is at a historic low.[1] Similarly, commerce in biological and chemical weapons capabilities is still constrained and mostly concentrated in a few problem states.

Quantitative measures, however, do not begin to capture the significance of the proliferation problem. The security implications of proliferation have as much to do with the states or substate actors involved in technology acquisition or weapon-development programs as with the volume of trade or the numbers of emerging WMD regimes.[2] Even limited proliferation among so-called "rogue" states and "super terrorists" in a context of a globalizing technology market poses profoundly destabilizing implications for international security.[3]

This chapter examines the problem of the proliferation of weapons of mass destruction in the contemporary environment, focusing in particular on nuclear, biological, and chemical weapons. We will first discuss global trends and then examine specific proliferation problems in a regional and state-specific context. On this basis, the chapter analyzes some of the policy implications associated with different potential proliferation threats.

Proliferation in a Globalized World

Since the advent of the Westphalian system in 1648, the nation-state has been the dominant actor in international politics. From security relations to trade to law and religion, the interaction among states has been organized around sovereign governments operating from defined state boundaries. Today, however, states have increasingly less control over their own territory and borders. Powerful secular trends have recast the foundations of international relations, and sovereignty is increasingly less of a determinant of countries' destinies.[4]

Economic globalization is perhaps the most significant transformational trend undermining traditional state supremacy. Governments, challenged by the intensifying pressures of competitiveness, are acquiescing to the demands of international market forces that have superceded national and even regional demarcations. The

rise of an increasingly influential globalized class of elites, the continued importance of multinational corporations whose far-flung operations transcend sovereign control, and the emergence of genuinely transnational security risks, such as
terrorism, all pose challenges that elude resolution by any single government.[5] The
complexities of economic globalization are beyond the scope of this chapter, but
the phenomenon is relevant to the ascendance of nonproliferation as a genuinely
multinational policy dilemma.

First, globalization is increasing trade and decreasing trade barriers. With the
growing importance of commercially available technologies for weapons development, state-based controls on trade have become ever more ineffectual. Second, globalization has led to increased travel and communication, which inevitably leads to
the wider dissemination of intellectual property. At a more profound level, states
are losing their role as the locus of identity formation in the modern world. Economic globalization, combined with changes in international norms, has eroded
the traditional loyalty of citizens to their nation-states, elevating the importance
of parochial, regional, or supranational affiliations.[6] This helps to explain both the
tendency of states to fragment—which can be seen in the collapse of several states
in the former Soviet bloc and across Eastern and southeastern Europe—and the
move toward economic and political integration, a phenomenon most obvious in
Western Europe.[7]

The effects of these transformations are difficult to understand with precision, but
ultimately, absent the ability to command loyalty, states are increasingly constrained
in their ability to impose sacrifices on citizens for the good of the "state."[8] Efforts to
control proliferation impose real costs on economic and social freedoms for corporations and the individual. In an era of diminishing state authority, the ability of states
to control internal, much less foreign, affairs, is diminished. This has put serious
constraints on the design of effective nonproliferation policies.

Technological Transformation and Nonproliferation

In addition to these broad structural and economic shifts, we can also point to a
number of more concrete developments that can have an impact on trade regulations and other forms of nonproliferation policy. The most important of these are
technological changes that have modified both what needs to be controlled and the
pace and character of technological diffusion.

Over the past decade we have seen an extraordinary convergence between civilian and military technology.[9] Certainly, this is not a completely new phenomenon.
Throughout the nuclear era, the nonproliferation-treaty regime has been based
on the premise of a technological quid pro quo—offering potential proliferators
access to peaceful nuclear technology in return for restraint in developing nuclear
weapons.[10] The challenge of dual-use technologies was recognized early on, and
the regime benefited from relatively clear distinctions between peaceful and military applications of critical technologies. At the same time, the inducement toward
nuclear restraint was limited by the fact that the value of peaceful uses of nuclear

power diminished as the result of cheaper alternatives for energy, as well as political and social concerns about the safety of nuclear plants. For most of the cold war era, the challenge of dual-use technologies focused on the definition of commodities diffusing from the West to nations of the Warsaw Pact, aimed at tightly restricting items of "strategic value," including a range of commercial and all but a handful of military-related goods.[11]

Today the dual-use problem is far more intractable because the problem exists at the broad level of industry rather than being confined to individual items controlled by a small number of advanced states. In the past it was more plausible to segregate trade in military or civilian data or technology, in part because there were limited commercial uses for a majority of advanced products in technically underdeveloped states. Today it is an extreme technical challenge to isolate critical enabling technologies, which could transform a space-launch vehicle into a ballistic missile or augment the ability to use a commercial nuclear plant as the basis for a weapons facility.

In the 1990s chemical manufacturers were forced to accede to oversight procedures in the conduct of trade because of the inherently dual-use nature of their products, particularly precursor materials that can contribute to chemical weapons development. With the development of biotechnologies, in turn, trade in the global pharmaceutical industry was recognized as a potential way to spread sensitive expertise and dual-use items that could result in furthering advances in biological weapons.[12] Biotechnological advances and genetic engineering techniques require skills and equipment similar to those needed at a biological weapons complex.

In the same vein, information technology and increased reliance on the global information networks that underpin the modern economy can leave societies open to potentially debilitating information warfare. The information revolution has radically altered the proliferation threat. The spread of tools such as the Internet and the global positioning system promote the forces of globalization by making national boundaries more porous. The information revolution does not lend itself to effective or long-lasting political controls. A country may attempt to insulate itself from problems associated with globalization—consider North Korea or Iraq—but these efforts are bound to be imperfect and short-lived. Faxes, the World Wide Web, and cheap cellular phones have made border control close to impossible.[13]

Many in the West see the information revolution as a positive development—as weakening the power of government in autocratic societies, for example. The same forces that may enhance democratization, however, can also pose challenges for the security of democracies. Freely available and widely diffused information can include information about manufacturing weapons of mass destruction. Furthermore, access to modern communications, encryption countermeasures, and the Internet can enable transnational actors, including terrorist and criminal factions, to organize across national borders. In short, the information revolution has transformed and exacerbated the proliferation problem.

"Rogue States" and "Undeterrables"

Much of the concern about the diffusion of weapons during the cold war was focused on so-called vertical proliferation—a reference to the progressive buildup of new weapons and weapons designs among the major powers. To the degree that attention was paid to horizontal proliferation—the acquisition of lethal technologies by less developed states—the focus was on the larger regional powers such as Brazil, Argentina, India, and Pakistan. Since the mid-1980s, and particularly since the early 1990s, the locus of concern has shifted to smaller, less-stable states such as Libya, Iraq, and North Korea.

The implications are significant. These new proliferators tend to be less well established in the regional or global order. Some analysts argue that such "rogue" states have a smaller stake in global stability and, lacking traditional instruments of state power, seek unconventional weapons to compensate. Experts have cautioned that weapons of mass destruction have gone from being symbols of great-power status to a "poor man's" source of influence.[14] In short, small states may pose tougher proliferation problems, according to this logic, precisely because their weakness makes them less susceptible to traditional modes of deterrence and adds to their motivation to develop offensive postures by relying on the perceived power of unconventional arsenals.

An increased interest among terrorist groups in acquiring weapons of mass destruction has become a major preoccupation in the United States in the wake of the terrorist attacks on the World Trade Center and the Pentagon. A growing number of groups are increasingly independent of state sponsorship and control. Many analysts believe that some of these are becoming increasingly willing to participate in "mass-casualty" events as a form of warfare, moving away from more contained provocations designed to gain attention and international leverage.[15] The hijackings of the 1970s have reemerged in the use of airliners as guided missiles. As indicated by the testimony from the trials of the Japanese doomsday cult Aum Shinrikyo, the acquisition and use of chemical and biological weapons was done less to achieve political objectives than with the express intent of mass destruction.[16]

Terrorist groups are not only largely immune to most existing nonproliferation strictures; the threat of terrorism tests existing distinctions between different areas of policymaking.[17] Until recently terrorism was conceived of as a law-enforcement problem, whereas proliferation was largely a diplomatic challenge. Policymakers and analysts have yet to fully come to terms with the implications of the existence of terrorist groups capable of disrupting or disabling a modern society. At the micro level, the problem is one of bureaucratic jurisdiction and leadership. Both sets of problems are real and significant. The outcome of the reordering of priorities and institutional alignments following the events of September 11 remains unknown and cannot yet be fully appreciated. Indeed, nearly two years after the fact, the American government is still struggling to determine some of the basic organizational principles behind a new Department of Homeland Security. The attacks also opened up a wide-ranging international debate on such issues as the legitimacy of preemption of potential threatening actors.

Key Trends: Nuclear Weapons

In the early 1960s, President John Kennedy famously predicted that there might be as many as twenty nuclear-armed states in the world by the 1970s.[18] Forty years later, the number is eight: the United States, Russia, Britain, France, China, Pakistan, India, and Israel. Beyond those eight, only three additional states are suspected to have focused research and development programs on nuclear weapons: Iraq, North Korea, and Iran. Altogether, these eleven states can be divided into three groups: the big five, whose nuclear status is confirmed by the nonproliferation treaty; the independent three, whose nuclear programs are longstanding and well established; and the three "rogues," whose programs may violate their international commitments. The following sections discuss trends and recent developments in each category.

The Big Five

The United States. President George W. Bush arrived in Washington having announced publicly his commitment to a fundamental rethinking of U.S. nuclear strategy. Citing a radically changed international security environment, the new administration vowed to rebuild the nuclear posture from the ground up. With the cold war more than a decade past, the Bush administration inherited a nuclear arsenal containing more than 10,000 warheads, almost 8,000 of them in active deployment.[19] Many of these weapons supported an operational plan containing more than 2,200 targets.[20] More than 2,000 of these weapons were on immediate launch-ready status, capable of being fired within fifteen minutes.[21] The Single Integrated Operational Plan (SIOP)—the set of plans for employing U.S. nuclear weapons on a massive scale in the event that deterrence failed—had been reviewed by the first Bush administration and later by President Clinton. Except for reductions in the overall number of nuclear warheads said to be required, neither president achieved significant reforms of the nuclear posture. Preparations for a massive, prompt nuclear attack against Russian military targets using a triad of land-, sea-, and air-based weapons remained the centerpiece of U.S. strategy.

After "looking into President Putin's soul," as President Bush put it after meeting with the Russian president at a G-8 summit in Italy, the administration began working to define a new cooperative relationship with Russia. Denouncing the traditional doctrine known as Mutually Assured Destruction (MAD) and belittling the utility of arms-control agreements, the administration sought to replace the pillars of U.S.–Russian nuclear stability that had been in place since the dawn of the cold war. Secretary of Defense Donald Rumsfeld, in turn, charged the Pentagon with transforming the military to meet the demands of the new post–cold war security environment.

In the nuclear sphere, the centerpiece of a revised policy for guiding the U.S. nuclear posture was the pledge to shift from a "threat-based approach" for planning nuclear contingencies, which focused on a centralized plan to execute the launch of thousands of weapons against hundreds of targets in Russia and China, to a so-called "capabilities-based approach," relying on a reduced arsenal of nuclear weapons to be used flexibly in a wide array of conflicts. These latter forces, in turn, are to be supplemented by other capabilities, such as conventional precision-strike weapons, enhanced and space-based communications, command and control, and defenses against missiles.[22]

During the 2000 presidential campaign, Bush had criticized the existing nuclear posture, describing the thinking that gave rise to such large numbers of weapons as "outdated." In a sweeping declaration in May 2000, he proposed unilateral U.S. reductions and asserted that "it should be possible to reduce the number of American nuclear weapons significantly [below the START II level of 3,000–3,500 strategic warheads each] without compromising our security in any way."[23] In November 2001, when President Bush first met with Russian president Vladimir Putin in Washington and in Crawford, Texas, Bush made good on his campaign pledge by announcing a two-thirds reduction in the U.S. nuclear arsenal, stating, "The current levels of our nuclear forces do not reflect today's strategic realities. . . . The United States will reduce our operationally deployed strategic nuclear warheads to a level between 1,700 and 2,200 over the next decade, a level fully consistent with American security."[24]

The following month, despite opposition in the House of Representatives, the Congress responded to the president's request by repealing section 1302 of the National Defense Authorization Act for Fiscal Year 1998, which prohibited the president from reducing the strategic nuclear arsenal below the 6,000-warhead level set by the START I treaty. This force level was a political imposition on the Clinton administration's latitude to work with the Russians and artificially high for the post–cold war era.

Accordingly, the administration announced that the U.S. reductions would be implemented over a ten-year period, with no verification provisions other than those that already exist for START I and START II. The administration will begin by moving forward with the retirement of eight hundred warheads fixed to the ninety-six missiles carried aboard four Trident submarines that are slated for decommissioning, the transfer of the B-1B to conventional missions, and the elimination of fifty land-based Peacekeeper ICBMs.[25]

The Bush administration has emphasized that the level of U.S. nuclear requirements is no longer based only on the size and character of the Russian or Chinese target base. A new emphasis of American nuclear deterrence strategy is to be prepared to redress immediate threats to the United States from "rogue states" and proliferants, as well as unforeseen future contingencies.[26] That said, the preservation of the sanctity of the triad, the continued emphasis on strategic counterforce, and the correlation between the approximately 2,200 Russian targets in the most recent SIOP and the 2,200-warhead limit proposed by the Bush administration have led many to suggest that nuclear plans are still based on the stated need to hold a large Russian (and growing Chinese) set of targets at risk.[27]

In addition to reaffirming the centrality of nuclear forces for U.S. security, the administration also has taken actions that suggest a more pronounced role for nuclear missions in combating global proliferation. Since the 1970s the United States has pledged that it would not use nuclear weapons against nonnuclear-weapon adversaries; however, Undersecretary of State for Arms Control and Nonproliferation John Bolton aroused attention when he implied that the United States might consider the use of U.S. nuclear weapons against nonnuclear-weapon states. State Department spokesman Richard Boucher moved quickly to state that Secretary Bolton's comments did not indicate a change in policy. The new rhetoric was consistent with the views of those outside the administration who have been urging the adoption of an explicit link between U.S. nuclear deterrence and the threats of chemical or biological attacks.

Following revelations about the size and scope of Saddam Hussein's nuclear, chemical, and biological weapons facilities after the Gulf War, discussions about developing a new class of more usable lower-yield nuclear weapons for managing proliferation challenges have become much more prominent. The first Bush administration, under the direction of then-Secretary of Defense Dick Cheney, had considered this option. Just prior to leaving office, Secretary Cheney issued a revised Nuclear Weapons Employment Policy (NUWEP) instructing the head of STRATCOM to develop a new planning process for the global application of nuclear weapons, including a call for "adaptive targeting" to allow for rapid and flexible retargeting of forces against unplanned threats.[28]

Against this backdrop, President Clinton lobbied the Democrat-controlled Congress three years later to enact legislation prohibiting the research and development of a new low-yield nuclear weapon. In 1994 the Pentagon moved to modify the existing B-61 design, thereby turning it into a de facto mini-nuke with a yield of less than five kilotons. Recalibrating these weapons to lower yields circumvented the congressional restriction.[29]

Congressional support of so-called "miniaturized" nuclear weapons has grown in recent years. By 2000, the Republican-controlled Congress sought to repeal the restriction on the development of miniaturized warheads. At the time, Senator John Warner (R-Va.), among others, successfully pushed to include a mandate to study the utility of low-yield nuclear weapons to destroy hardened and deeply buried targets as part of the FY 2001 Defense Authorization Act. The report was submitted to the Congress in July 2001. It concluded that "We must prepare for those unique and emerging strategic threats that are critical and well protected, both physically and through focused camouflage, concealment, and deception programs. This will require additional investment in intelligence, special weapons, and counter-WMD capabilities, including nuclear weapons."[30]

The report found that while there was no current requirement for a miniaturized nuclear weapon capable of defeating a hardened or deeply buried target, there was a definite need to define a new mission.[31] The Bush administration has not pressed for the development of new systems since then, but neither has it ruled out future research, development, and production of new weapons. Although research, development, construction, and testing of a new nuclear weapon could take years, the Bush administration's nuclear posture review provides an early indication of the administration's decision to leave the door open to the development of new weapons. In June 1998 the Defense Science Board Task Force on Underground Facilities stated that there are more than 10,000 underground military facilities spread throughout more than seventy countries. Approximately 1,400 of these are known or suspected sites for weapons of mass destruction, according to the Defense Intelligence Agency.[32]

At present it is unclear whether the administration will seek modifications to the existing nuclear inventory or move to develop an entirely new weapon. In either case, critics worry that the result will be a more usable nuclear weapon, adding to the potential for the nuclear threshold to be crossed in a crisis.[33] Significantly, the decision could also presage a resumption of nuclear testing.

On September 23, 1992, the United States conducted its last nuclear weapon test, and just over a week later, on October 2, the U.S. nuclear testing moratorium was signed into law. As a result of a 1993 presidential directive, the National Nuclear Security Administration (NNSA) maintains a capability to conduct an explosive underground nuclear test within twenty-four to thirty-six months of a presidential decision to do so.[34]

The administration has opened the door to possible resumption of underground testing, justified as necessary to ensure the safety and reliability of the strategic arsenal and, possibly, to develop an expanded range of nuclear options to satisfy a more adaptive targeting strategy and manage a revised target set. In its final reports, the Bush nuclear review endorsed a proposal by the NNSA to reduce the lead time to prepare for and conduct an underground nuclear test. Moreover, pending completion of a Nevada test-site study, the president's budget request for FY 2003 has allocated $15 million to begin the transition to an enhanced readiness posture. While the review proposes that the United States be able to return to testing, it does not establish guidelines on when testing would resume. Rather, the review calls for enhanced appropriations that would dramatically decrease the two-year time frame necessary for the Department of Energy to return to testing.[35]

Russia. In contrast to U.S. nuclear modernization, Moscow continues to battle a depressed economy and an inadequately funded nuclear infrastructure. The end of the cold war and the collapse of the Soviet Union presaged the end of the threat of deliberate U.S.–Russian nuclear conflict. New concerns over the control of nuclear warheads and fissile material throughout the former Soviet Union have emerged as the more immediate and urgent challenge. With Russia's increasing inability to fund the personnel and hardware necessary to maintain and protect its nuclear infrastructure, concerns have intensified that nuclear weapons could be inadvertently launched at the United States, its friends, or its allies. The U.S. and Russian military have procedures to prevent accidental or unauthorized launch and have gone to extraordinary lengths to ensure strict control over nuclear weapons. But this system is not foolproof, especially when Russia's early-warning and nuclear command systems are deteriorating badly. The CIA has reported that the Russian nuclear weapons command system frequently malfunctions, and that critical electronic devices and computers sometimes switch to combat mode for no apparent reason. Many of the radars and satellites intended to detect a ballistic-missile attack no longer operate.[36]

The implications are dramatic. Within a few minutes of receiving instructions to fire, U.S. and Russian land-based rockets with more than 3,000 warheads could begin their twenty-five-minute flights to their targets. Less than fifteen minutes after receiving the attack order, U.S. and Russian ballistic-missile submarines could dispatch more than a thousand warheads.[37] None of these missiles can be recalled or made to self-destruct.

Although they are no longer enemies, the U.S. and Russia maintain their respective nuclear postures to deter the other from launching a surprise attack. Relying on a "launch-on-warning" strategy, both sides are poised to launch massive retaliatory strikes after early-warning satellites and radars have detected an incoming enemy missile attack. The very few minutes allowed to evaluate whether an attack is genuine increases the risk of a mistaken or unauthorized launch as a result of a technical or human error.

Even when nuclear forces were well funded and personnel highly trained, this practice raised the possibility of catastrophe, as evidenced by the history of U.S. and Russian false alerts. For example, on January 25, 1995, Russian radar operators thought a U.S. scientific rocket launched from Norway might be a missile headed for Russia. (Allied ballistic-missile submarines, carrying multiple-warhead missiles, routinely patrol near the Norwegian coast.) President Yeltsin, holding the "nuclear briefcase" that could order the firing of nuclear missiles in response, was quickly notified and hurriedly conferred with his top advisers. The trajectory of the rocket remained unclear for a few minutes. Radar crews continued to track the missile, and after about eight minutes (just a few minutes short of the procedural deadline for responding to an impending nuclear attack), senior military officers determined that the rocket was headed out to sea. Weeks earlier Norway had informed Russia of the planned launch, but word had not reached the right destination.[38] Since 1995 Russian early-warning and nuclear command-and-control systems have deteriorated significantly.

The collapse of the Soviet Union has raised another concern, one highlighted by the events of September 11, that fissile materials and warheads could be stolen from Russia and turn up in the hands of would-be proliferators or terrorist organizations. In 1991, under the leadership of Senators Sam Nunn and Richard Lugar, the United States embarked on an initiative for cooperative threat reduction to help Russia build down the enormous nuclear arsenal and expertise amassed during the cold war. Ten years later the original program, and those that followed, have achieved impressive results. However, they have only addressed a small percentage of the weapons and materials still held—and often inadequately secured—by Moscow.

Britain and France. In contrast to the United States and Russia, the rest of the "big five" nuclear countries have been engaging in nuclear modernization far more modestly and without publicity. In both Britain and France nuclear modernization is aimed at maintaining a minimal nuclear force, as much for political as for military reasons. The British in particular have debated the necessity of retaining even this minimal force posture. The costs appear to be disproportionate to the benefits, especially in light of growing British commitments arising from its role as the lead partner with the United States in the war on terrorism and the quest for regime change in Iraq.

Britain and France have also stayed aloof from the United States in terms of counterproliferation. Although the prime minister of Britain has signed on to support the United States in demanding regime change in Iraq, this seems to be a specific rather than a general posture. The mid-1990s European rejection of military preemption apparently remains operative in the rest of the world.

China. In contrast to France and Britain, China has provoked significant debate over its nuclear developments and intentions. The Chinese are developing their nuclear arsenal in three ways: increasing numbers, increasing accuracy of weapons systems, and testing mobile missile systems.[39] The Chinese are replacing their obsolescent DF-5 ICBMs with solid-fueled, road-mobile DF-41s, which represents a major change in the sophistication and survivability of their land-based nuclear force. These missiles are also significantly more accurate and may give China some "counterforce" capabilities even against hardened targets. Furthermore, the size of the force is also expected to increase significantly, from fewer than twenty ICBMs to more than one hundred within a decade.[40] The Chinese government is also working to deploy a new generation of nuclear-mission submarines, although these deployments have been hampered by technical difficulties.

China may prove to be a proliferation problem case less for its current plans and export behavior than its potential to be a major supplier of illicit military materiel. China has a very elaborate nuclear complex, and possesses literally tons of unallocated fissile material.[41] China's nuclear ambitions could in principle shift very rapidly in response to international or domestic pressures.

The Chinese continue to rely on minimum deterrence as the foundation of their nuclear doctrine. The net effects of its modernization, however, could be construed as giving China an added capability to threaten American assets in the event of a confrontation—over Taiwan, for example. For some analysts, the growth of a robust, survivable Chinese nuclear force may presage a greater willingness to risk war over Taiwan. This prognosis has to assume that a situation involving Chinese nuclear threats would leave the United States in a state of "self-deterrence" because of its unwillingness to engage in nuclear escalation.

In short, because of the context of Sino-American relations, stable "mutual assured destruction" might be a prerequisite for war in the region, whereas, paradoxically, the one-sided vulnerability that has existed previously may have helped the United States maintain an extended deterrence relationship over Taiwan. But this assessment is hardly a consensus view.

China has had the ability to target West Coast cities with its existing force for many years. Given that, current changes in the Chinese nuclear arsenal may not represent a dramatic departure from the past. The Chinese may still fear and plan against a disarming nuclear first strike from the United States, underscored by the decision to reintegrate Chinese targets in the U.S. SIOP. It is still difficult to imagine any credible scenario under which the United States would embark on such a course of action, especially given American conventional superiority.

Conclusions on the Big Five. Over the past decade, the United States and Russia have drawn down their operational nuclear forces dramatically, while the British and French have largely treaded water. Only the Chinese seem inclined to invest significantly in their nuclear capabilities. But while the United States now deploys fewer nuclear weapons, new missions for nuclear weapons are being actively considered as instruments of deterrence and retaliation against biological or chemical attacks, or as part of a preemptive counterproliferation strategy that would rely on limited nuclear strikes to destroy another country's weapons facilities.

The movement of the People's Republic of China toward a more survivable force would traditionally be seen as a positive development toward more stable deterrence. The particulars of the Chinese case, however, give one pause. To the extent that asymmetrical U.S. advantage has been crucial to maintaining an extended deterrence relationship over Taiwan, the erosion at the margins of American superiority may, in fact, pave the way for conventional conflict between the United States and China. This particular case suggests that for an assessment to be meaningful, the implications of weapons proliferation must take account of the conditions in a specific regional context.

Three Independents

Israel. Israel has a longstanding operational nuclear force, with between 100 and 400 nuclear devices.[42] Though Israel neither confirms nor denies the existence of its nuclear arsenal, there is broad consensus among experts and policymakers about its existence and relative capabilities. The implications of this arsenal for Israeli and international security, however, are widely debated. There are essentially two schools of thought on this matter.

The first school sees Israeli nuclear weapons as a stabilizing factor that has helped prevent full-scale war between Israel and its Arab neighbors since the early 1970s. The second school of thought suggests that the Israeli nuclear force contributes to instability in two ways. First is the argument that nuclear weapons may encourage intransigence on the part of Israeli leaders vis-à-vis the Arab world generally and the Palestinians specifically. The second argument is that Israeli nuclear weapons abet a desire among Arab and the gulf states to develop unconventional countermeasures, including biological and chemical as well as nuclear weapons.

If one believes that the key security problem for Israel currently rests in the Israeli-Palestinian dispute rather than the broader Israeli-Arab conflict, the role of nuclear weapons is minimal. Simply put, no nuclear arsenal is capable of defeating suicide bombers, nor is such a capability relevant in countering the demographic pressures that may ultimately force Israel to choose between being a Jewish state and a multinational democratic state.

India and Pakistan. In 1998 India publicly tested a nuclear device. Pakistan followed suit with a series of tests of its own, most of which were successful. Both states declared the intention to deploy operational nuclear weapons, declaring themselves nuclear-weapons states. Since then relatively little has happened in the South Asia arms race, despite quite significant security tensions between the two countries.

An understanding of the specific regional context is important in understanding the issues of timing, strategy, and intentions that are driving Indian and Pakistani nuclear policy. Both India and Pakistan have had the capacity to deploy nuclear weapons for some time. India has been a de facto nuclear state since at least 1974, when it tested a primitive nuclear device. The key question that has arisen since 1998 is why the two states chose that year to publicize their nuclear capabilities. There is little agreement on this issue. Perhaps the most compelling interpretation of India's timing has to do with the nature of its views about the international regime regulating the development and possession of nuclear weapons. The 1972 nuclear nonproliferation treaty was reviewed for the fifth and final time by all of its members in 1995, culminating in a majority vote to extend the treaty indefinitely. The implementation of the long-awaited comprehensive test ban treaty in 1998, moreover, seemed imminent.

Indian leaders, not surprisingly, may have begun to believe that the window of opportunity for joining the "nuclear club" was closing rapidly and that the political costs of a later declaration would be prohibitive in light of the momentum of international agreements. In addition to domestic political calculations, concerns over China's nuclear modernization, and frustration about the failure of the nuclear powers to live up to their nonproliferation treaty commitments to move toward nuclear elimination, may have convinced the Indian government that the time was right to test.[43]

The Pakistani response was nearly a foregone conclusion despite strong pressure from the West.[44] Given the very tense security competition between the two states, Pakistan felt that it had to respond both for domestic political and for international strategic reasons. The states of the West apparently agreed; despite ritual condemnations, the imposition of sanctions was limited and half-hearted.

Both countries have struggled to develop an appropriate strategy to guide plans for how they would deploy or use nuclear weapons. In many ways both are going through a process of analysis and debate about desirable doctrines and operational plans that the West experienced decades earlier. Indian and Pakistani strategists are actively debating issues of nuclear deterrence and crisis bargaining, revisiting early cold war authors such as Herman Kahn and Bernard Brodie and trying to make their arguments relevant to the subcontinent in the twenty-first century. The debate is far from resolved, although most analysts see the Indians moving toward a doctrine focused on minimal deterrence and a survivable second-strike force.[45]

As a practical matter, cost issues may ultimately limit the Indians to this sort of posture regardless of the outcome of doctrinal debates. An effort to build a classical nuclear "triad" of submarines, bombers, and ICBMs is both redundant and costly. At present most analysts believe that the Indians have "dozens" of weapons, and predictions about future developments are quite varied.

There is less information about Pakistani debates of this sort, and the few hints we do have are less than reassuring. Given Indian conventional superiority, some analysts in Pakistan seem to be leaning toward a war-fighting concept for nuclear weapons, including plans to use nuclear weapons early in a conventional war to destroy massed Indian formations, and the forward deployment of nuclear weapons to make such a doctrine plausible.[46] Pakistan, however, has only limited supplies of fissile material and, combined with the relatively low-tech and inefficient design of their weapons, this constrains future deployments.

Finally, in terms of intentions, India's and Pakistan's plans for the future of their nuclear forces are unclear. While both countries were adamant about their intention to deploy significant nuclear arsenals after 1998, neither has moved particularly quickly to actually deploy a significant force. In part, budget and fissile-material constraints have played a role, but there are also some political dynamics that may result in South Asian nuclear forces remaining largely rhetorical rather than actual. For the Indians, the symbolism of the act was perhaps more important than the military or strategic utility of a large arsenal.

For the Pakistanis, the concern may be political instability. Perceived parity with India, especially in the nuclear sphere, is critical to regime survival in Pakistan. That said, Pakistani leaders might have little interest in taking actions that are seen as outright provocations of their allies. While the United States has been willing to limit itself to token denunciations of Pakistani nuclear ambitions—especially given Pakistan's help in the "war on terrorism"—this would probably not be the case if the United States had reason to fear Pakistan's nuclear weapons' falling into the hands of anti-American extremists.

Three "Rogues"

There are three countries whose nuclear programs and international behavior place them outside the mainstream of international affairs: Iraq, Iran, and North Korea. All three are suspected of pursuing nuclear programs despite strong international responses, although the level of the effort varies in each case.

North Korea. In 1994, following International Atomic Energy Agency (IAEA) concerns over accounting of North Korean nuclear fuel, North Korea threatened to withdraw from the nonproliferation treaty to escape IAEA oversight. This quickly led to a diplomatic crisis, with the United States determined to keep North Korea within the regime. The Clinton administration was committed to preventing North Korea from developing nuclear weapons and was apparently willing to go to war over the issue, even though North Korea had a sovereign right to withdraw from the treaty with appropriate notice.

Happily, the crisis did not lead to war, thanks to a last-minute deal whereby North Korea agreed to freeze its nuclear program in return for oil shipments and a commitment to build two "proliferation-resistant" reactors to provide electricity.[47] This "agreed framework" has been under siege ever since, buffeted by the Asian financial crisis of 1998, which curtailed the ability of the South Koreans to contribute to building the new reactors, and by persistent suspicions that North Korea had simply moved its program underground rather than freezing it altogether. Indeed, in October 2002 North Korea admitted to building a nuclear warhead, although both the nature of that admission and the implications for future North Korean policy are ambiguous.

Though concerns about North Korea are significant, in the final analysis there seems to be a general consensus that whatever limited North Korean program exists is better ignored than confronted. Most analysts see political trend lines on the Korean peninsula as generally positive. Relations between North and South Korea are slowly improving, the North Korean economy is too weak to permit a massive arms-building effort, and more generally there is the sense that North Korea will someday, relatively soon, simply go out of business and be absorbed by the South. Given that strategic context, the costs of confrontation may outweigh the costs of procrastination. As a result, despite North Korean provocations, most analysts believe that some sort of deal will emerge whereby the West will essentially pay off the North Koreans in order to buy time.

A major concern with North Korea, however, is the reluctance of the Bush administration to negotiate publicly with "rogue" states. The North Korean regime has clearly signaled its interest in a new deal to replace the 1994 "agreed framework," but the Bush administration is concerned that agreeing to or even discussing a new deal is tantamount to giving in to blackmail. The result is that even as the United States was launching its preventive war on Iraq in March 2003, the situation on the Korean peninsula was becoming increasingly tense, with the

North Koreans overtly restarting their nuclear weapons program and the United States claiming that a diplomatic solution was likely, while refusing to engage in direct negotiations.

Iran. Iran is similarly suspected of maintaining a covert nuclear-weapons program, although at present suspicion centers on Iranian research into nuclear weapons rather than on the imminent production of a usable device. Concerns about Iranian intentions, however, have been heightened by increasing evidence that the Iranians do indeed plan to move toward a weapons program sooner rather than later. The outlook on the Iranian nuclear program is continually shifting between optimism and pessimism as new developments force people in the nonproliferation community to reassess their views. Still, because Iran has been closely tied to terrorism and the funding of extremist causes, its nuclear problem is a cause of concern.

Mitigating concerns over Iran's nuclear program is the general view that there are a number of positive trends in the Iranian case, most notably a gradual move toward democratization and the rise of a modernizing middle class—one of the few in southwest Asia.

Iraq. Iraq was the hard case in the area of proliferation of weapons of mass destruction. After the Persian Gulf War (1990–91), UN weapons inspectors discovered WMD programs on an order of magnitude few had suspected before the war. These programs violated Iraq's preexisting international commitments, commitments that turned into obligations as a result of the UN resolutions that ended the conflict. From 1991 to 1998 UN inspectors sought to document and dismantle the Iraqi WMD complex in the face of constant resistance and harassment. UN inspectors were finally expelled from the country by Saddam Hussein in 1998, and some evidence suggested that Iraq reconstituted its WMD programs.

Iraq was also a difficult case because of its political context. Saddam Hussein's regime had attacked four regional neighbors—Iran and Kuwait with ground forces and Saudi Arabia and Israel with missiles. Iraq used chemical weapons against Iran. Hussein's regime was brutally authoritarian and systematically used military force, including chemical weapons, against domestic opponents of the regime. Hussein's pursuit of weapons of mass destruction was obsessive and pathological, earning him the enmity of much of the world and costing his country billions of dollars due to sanctions. Hussein was, by all evidence, not suicidal, but he was isolated, prone to misjudgment, and extremely aggressive in his international relations. As a result, Iraq became a test case for nonproliferation. The combination of uncertainty over the nature and extent of Iraq's WMD program and the relative certainty that the regime would pose a threat to regional and international security if its programs came to fruition generated a unique sense of urgency that galvanized the Bush administration's efforts to disarm Iraq.

Following the terror attacks of September 11, 2001, the Bush administration enunciated a doctrine of preemption, focused primarily on terrorists but also on Iraq. During the summer of 2002 the administration engaged in a well-publicized internal debate about how to respond to Iraqi violations of its international obligations vis-à-vis weapons of mass destruction. Many of the "hawks" relied on a simple syllogism to justify extending the war on terror to Iraq, namely, that Hussein could be expected to develop weapons of mass destruction unless countered and that the U.S. could not trust Hussein not to transfer such weapons covertly to groups like Al Qaeda. The "doves" countered that threatening Hussein with regime change was likely to encourage the transfer of these weapons rather than prevent it. By late summer, the administration seemed to have accepted the hawkish position and was working on securing approval for an attack on Iraq from the U.S. Congress and United Nations while making clear that UN approval was preferred but not required.

After initially denouncing this new U.S. policy as illegitimate, Iraq gradually began exploring the possibility of inviting UN inspectors into the country for the first time since they were expelled in 1998. The Bush administration, however, decided not to pursue the inspection process extensively. Although UN inspectors were at work in early 2003, the Bush administration made clear its doubts about the process and insisted on setting an early deadline for full Iraqi compliance. When the Iraqis refused to embrace the inspection regime wholeheartedly, the United States opted for war rather than work through the UN to strengthen the inspection process. The United States, along with Britain and Australia, subsequently launched a large-scale campaign to overthrow Saddam Hussein's regime and to finally dismantle Iraq's WMD programs. This largely unilateral U.S. decision has severely divided the international community. It remains to be seen whether the Iraq case will be an exception or a precedent in future cases of proliferation concern.

Conclusions: Nuclear Weapons

Though there is much good news in terms of nuclear weapons proliferation—namely, the relative paucity of serious nuclear programs among nonnuclear states—nuclear policy has been an area of significant change over the past several years. These changes have occurred in four main areas.

First, the United States and Russia have been engaged in a complex process leading to significant reductions of deployed nuclear weapons. Though the Bush administration has been reticent about accepting formal obligations, it has remained committed to continued reductions. Similarly, the Russian nuclear arsenal is shrinking, although budget constraints have made if difficult for the Russians to dispose of their excess weapons in a safe manner.

Second, the United States has increasingly begun to consider scenarios under which it would use nuclear weapons. During the Clinton years, these discussions led to declarations that the United States ought to consider using nuclear weapons in response to any use of weapons of mass destruction against American assets.[48]

This first-use option was clearly conceived of as a way to bolster American deterrence vis-à-vis unconventional threats. The Bush administration has built on this position by becoming more open to the possibility of using nuclear weapons in specific missions, bunker busting and counterproliferation in particular. The paradox of making nuclear weapons more usable while declaring their possession by states like Iraq anathema seems lost on most of the supporters of this more visible role for nuclear weapons.

Third, India and Pakistan have become nuclear-weapons states in the context of a heated rivalry and an actual, ongoing military conflict in Kashmir. Though this development hinted at an immediate and destabilizing arms race, neither state has moved quickly to deploy a large and usable nuclear force. Indeed, Indian strategists are still debating the nature of the future Indian arsenal, and Pakistan seems largely willing to await the results of these deliberations before matching Indian deployments.

Finally, the war with Iraq has fundamentally transformed the issue of nonproliferation vis-à-vis "rogue" regimes. Both Iran and North Korea have used the distraction provided by the Iraq crisis to accelerate their nuclear programs. The range of possible outcomes makes predictions about the future a daunting task. In the best-case scenario, the Bush administration, having eliminated the threat from Saddam Hussein, will return to a nonconfrontational posture in its dealings with Iran and North Korea, possibly leading to negotiated solutions to both countries' nuclear programs. In the worst-case scenario, American unilateralism and use of force may heighten security concerns in both Iran and North Korea and make them consider the development of a usable nuclear arsenal an absolute imperative. It is easy to imagine how these developments could lead to conflicts with the United States.

Key Trends: Chemical and Biological Weapons

While the threat of nuclear proliferation and the catastrophic consequences that could result continue to dominate the international nonproliferation playing field, the emerging threat of catastrophic terrorism, combined with the awareness of the relatively accessible precursors and ease of production of chemical, and to some extent biological, weapons, has opened previously unrealized opportunities to construct a "poor man's atomic bomb." Both biological and chemical weapons are prohibited by widely accepted international treaties. Inherent inadequacies, born of the practical impossibilities of ensuring seamless proliferation prevention, have impelled efforts to control precursor elements through tightened export controls and inspections, all the way up to unprecedented coercive disarmament measures, as with UNSCOM, and the implementation of a preemptive attack on Iraq by the Bush administration.

The Chemical Weapons Convention (CWC) entered into force in 1997. The CWC includes comprehensive verification measures and allows for on-site inspections. The treaty also provides for the creation of the Organization for the Prohibition of Chemical Weapons (OPCW), whose functions are analogous to those of the IAEA under the nonproliferation treaty. The OPCW has found itself under fire from the Bush administration on charges of mismanagement, lack of responsiveness, and personal misconduct of senior OPCW officials. Not surprisingly, these charges have divided the international community, with many states seeing the American actions as more reflective of a general bias against international treaties than of the specific shortcomings of the OPCW. In any case, Iraq, North Korea, Libya, Syria, and Egypt are not members of the CWC, and even member states are still in the process of slowly destroying their chemical weapons stocks.

The Biological Weapons Convention (BWC) entered into force in 1975 and bans the production and possession of biological weapons. The BWC has no verification mechanisms, however, and adherence to its terms has been spotty even among signatories. At least a dozen countries are suspected of maintaining biological weapons programs, including "Iraq, Iran, Israel, North Korea, Syria, Libya, Russia, and possibly India, Pakistan, China, Egypt, and Sudan."[49] The realization that the BWC was ineffectual—a realization prompted in large measure by the startling discoveries by UNSCOM following the Persian Gulf War—led to a series of negotiations starting in 1994 to provide the convention with verification and enforcement mechanisms. But this effort largely collapsed in the face of the Bush administration's withdrawal from the negotiations in the summer of 2001 over the issue of protecting American intellectual property. The playing field changed somewhat when the United States suffered a series of mail-borne anthrax attacks in October 2001. However, while the attacks reinforced American fears of biological terrorism, they also encouraged even greater unilateralism on the part of the United States. Many in the Bush administration simply do not trust international treaties. It is an article of faith among many in the administration that the United States can count only on its own capabilities to prevent future attacks. In November 2001, Undersecretary of State John Bolton gave a comprehensive statement on the U.S. view of the BWC. He referred to the summer 2001 draft verification protocols as "flawed" and instead called on states to act individually to criminalize possession and production of biological weapons and to implement stronger security measures to guard pathogenic microorganisms.[50] Given American intransigence, it is unlikely that effective revisions to the BWC will occur in the near term.

From a medical standpoint, it may be argued that the scourge of deadly pathogens and the insidious dangers they present are at once the most perilous and the least understood threat to civil society today. According to the World Health Organization, infectious disease remains the leading cause of death worldwide, with one-quarter of all deaths each year attributable to infectious diseases or complications arising from them. Over the course of the next hour, 1,500 people will die of an infectious disease. The emergence of new pathogens—disease-causing microorganisms such as viruses or bacteria—combined with the reemergence of those previously thought conquered, and a growing resistance to antibiotics, pose a fundamental threat to our collective health and security. Increasingly, the perils of disease epidemics are not, as is commonly understood, threats restricted solely to the developing world. The thousands of pathogens that prey upon humanity are unfettered by political, ethnic, and cultural borders, particularly in today's increasingly global economy. Increased international trade and the ease of travel across national boundaries suggests that disease moves more easily and rapidly today than at any time throughout history.

While these observations alone are sobering, to say the least, it should be recalled that each death resulting from infectious disease in modern times has been attributable to ostensibly "natural" causes. Recent revelations from Russia and the Middle East and events in Japan have shown that the dangers posed by dangerous pathogens have implications far beyond that of domestic public health.[51]

The core issue with chemical and biological weapons is that the basic production facilities are dual-use. Unlike a nuclear program, which requires costly and specialized facilities to produce weapons-grade fissile material, chemical and biological programs are relatively easy to reconstitute even if existing stockpiles are destroyed. The Australia Group (an association of thirty-three countries opposed to biological and chemical weapons proliferation) has tried to address this problem by placing a number of precursor chemicals on a warning list. Australia Group members seek to restrict access to their chemicals and to report trade in them to one another. But the long-term effectiveness of the CWC remains in question despite these informal measures.

Perhaps the most significant development over the past decade is that normative constraints against chemical and biological weapons are becoming increasingly entrenched among states.[52] Unfortunately, the existence of a norm against the possession and use of biological and chemical weapons may tempt nonstate actors to violate that norm precisely because its general acceptance will ensure widespread "terror" at its violation. If terrorist groups seek to inflict psychological wounds on their targets, norm-breaking actions may be increasingly favored.

Conclusion

As suggested above, there has been an increasing bifurcation between the United States and the rest of the world on how to control proliferation. While the rest of the world remains focused on traditional, multilateral nonproliferation—that is, on efforts to prevent the spread of weapons of mass destruction and reduce existing stockpiles through multilateral accords—the United States has been increasingly focused on "counterproliferation" and "preemption"—that is, on actions taken to minimize the effects of weapons of mass destruction and to develop the capabilities to forcibly destroy another country's stockpiles.

The U.S. Department of Defense is increasingly concerned about the potential use of weapons of mass destruction on the American homeland and against its forces abroad, and is increasingly engaged in strategies of denial. As a result, Defense has begun working on means to "counter" and respond to such developments. Though the phrase "counterproliferation" has an "inside-the-beltway" bureaucratic definition, it also has a more substantive meaning to scholars and analysts. What has most strikingly differentiated the Pentagon's efforts from earlier initiatives at the Arms Control and Disarmament Agency is that the Defense Department has been only indirectly concerned with *preventing* proliferation. Rather, the department has focused on ways of limiting the damage caused by the use of weapons of mass destruction by an adversary in wartime as well as on managing the consequences of weapons' use. The Pentagon has considered both active and passive damage limitation, with the former receiving the most attention because of the possibility of military counterproliferation, that is, actually attacking WMD production facilities and/or deployed systems in potential adversaries. The Pentagon believes that these efforts have an indirect effect on preventing proliferation because if the U.S. military is capable of fighting and winning any war despite the use of weapons of mass destruction by opponents, then enemies will be less likely to seek such weapons if their main adversary is the United States.

Clearly, however, there are costs to this approach. Unlike the United States' "go-it-alone" approach vis-à-vis biological weapons, which hinders international cooperation but does not necessarily work against it, "counterproliferation" works directly against other nonproliferation effects. Though some analysts refer to nonproliferation and counterproliferation as complementary policies on a broad antiproliferation continuum, the reality is that both the substance and rhetoric of counterproliferation have significant effects on a nonproliferation agenda. First, counterproliferation is inherently unilateralist and its adoption is likely to reduce cooperation between the United States and the rest of the world. Second, because the United States justifies its own continued possession of and experimentation with nuclear weapons in the interests of counterproliferation, it undermines norms against nuclear weapons. Indeed, it was this particular issue the need to test low-yield nuclear devices useful in a counterproliferation role—that prompted U.S. opponents to vote against the comprehensive nuclear test ban treaty. Third, this U.S. policy relies on deterrence and coercion, where traditional nonproliferation relies on reassurance and positive incentives. Though analysts often speak of using carrots *and* sticks, in practice people do not like to accept carrots from people wielding sticks.

In addition to the divide between the United States and much of the rest of world in terms of proliferation policy, there is also a divide between the attention placed on states and on nonstate actors. In particular, after the terrorist attacks of September 11, 2001, the notion that terrorist groups would refrain from mass casualty attacks for fear of generating an overwhelming response went by the wayside. Some terrorist groups clearly cannot be deterred: they operate without normative limits on the number of casualties they cause or the targets they attack. The implications of this insight, however, are unclear. In the short run, the realization that "super terrorists" are out there has encouraged American unilateralism; it is not clear what the longer-term implications will be. Proliferation policy, in short, is at a crossroads. Its future cannot be determined until policymakers in the United States and abroad reach a consensus on core issues—in particular, on the importance of multilateralism and unilateralism in the quest to combat proliferation.

Notes

1. Since the 1980s India and Pakistan have joined the de facto nuclear club, while South Africa has dismantled its nuclear weapons. In addition, Argentina and Brazil have ended their nuclear programs and Ukraine, Belarus, and Kazakhstan gave up the nuclear weapons they inherited from the Soviet Union. Iran, Iraq, and North Korea remain "problem" states, but no other countries have initiated new nuclear programs. For a good summary of global trends, see Joseph Cirincione (with Jon B. Wolfsthal and Miriam Rajkumar), *Deadly Arsenals: Tracking Weapons of Mass Destruction* (Washington, D.C.: Carnegie Endowment for International Peace, 2002), 3–23.

2. See the perspective in Peter R. Lavoy, Scott D. Sagan, and James J. Wirtz, *Planning the Unthinkable: How New Powers Will Use Nuclear, Biological, and Chemical Weapons* (Ithaca: Cornell University Press, 2000).

3. Raymond Tanter, *Rogue Regimes: Terrorism and Proliferation,* rev. ed. (New York: St. Martin's Press, 1999).

4. See, for instance, the interesting collection of essays in Stephen D. Krasner, ed., *Problematic Sovereignty* (New York: Columbia University Press, 2001).

5. Thomas Friedman, *The Lexus and the Olive Tree: Understanding Globalization* (New York: Anchor Books, 2000), esp. 101–11 and 194–211; and Margaret E. Keck and Kathryn Sikkink, *Activists beyond Borders* (Ithaca: Cornell University Press, 1998).

6. See the essays in James N. Rosenau and J. P. Singh, eds., *Information Technologies and Global Politics: The Changing Scope of Power and Governance* (Albany: SUNY Press, 2002).

7. James M. Rosenau, "New Dimensions of Security: The Interaction of Globalizing and Localizing Dynamics," *Security Dialogue* 25 (Sept. 1994): 255–82; Ian Clark, *Globalization and Fragmentation: International Relations in the Twentieth Century* (New York: Oxford University Press, 1997).

8. Consider, for instance, the vocal criticism of various measures of the U.S. government undertaken in response to terrorism such as the detention of material witnesses and the decision to treat some members of Al Qaeda as "unlawful combatants" rather than as common criminals or prisoners of war.

9. A sense of the problem can be gleaned by reading over the list of dual-use items covered under the Wassenaar Arrangement, available at www.wassenaar.org/list/tableofcontents-01web.html#Dulist.

10. Joseph Cirincione, "Historical Overview and Introduction," in Joseph Cirincione, ed., *Repairing the Regime: Preventing the Spread of Weapons of Mass Destruction* (New York: Routledge, 2000), 1–14.

11. Although, even then, the definition of strategic items could often be quite contentious. Michael Mastanduno, *Economic Containment: CoCom and the Politics of East-West Trade* (Ithaca: Cornell University Press, 1992).

12. Indeed, resistance from the pharmaceutical industry was crucial in causing the Bush administration to withdraw support for talks aimed at strengthening the Biological Weapons Convention.

13. See the essays in Bernard I. Finel and Kristin M. Lord, eds., *Power and Conflict in the Age of Transparency* (New York: Palgrave, 2000).

14. Keith Payne, *Deterrence in the Second Nuclear Age* (Lexington: University of Kentucky Press, 1996); cf. Robert S. Litwak, *Rogue States and U.S. Foreign Policy: Containment after the Cold War* (Baltimore: Johns Hopkins University Press, 2000).

15. Richard Betts, "Universal Deterrence or Conceptual Collapse?" in *The Coming Crisis: Nuclear Proliferation, U.S. Interests, and World Order,* Victor Utgoff, ed. (Cambridge: MIT Press, 2000), 76–78.

16. Kyle Olson, testimony, "Global Proliferation of Weapons of Mass Destruction: Case Study on Aum Shinrikyo," Permanent Subcommittee on Investigations, Committee on Government Affairs, U.S. Senate hearing (Oct. 31, 1995).

17. For a fuller discussion of this theme, see Bernard I. Finel, Brian D. Finlay, and Janne E. Nolan, eds., *Opportunity Costs: The Transformation of U.S. Non-Proliferation Policy from the Post–Cold War to Post–September 11* (Washington, D.C.: Brookings Institution, forthcoming).

18. *New York Times*, March 23, 1963, A1.

19. Press release, Natural Resources Defense Council, "Faking Restraint: The Bush Administration's Secret Plan For Strengthening U.S. Nuclear Forces—Table 1. Nuclear Forces," Feb. 13, 2002, accessed at www.nrdc.org/media/pressreleases/020213a.asp.

20. Bruce G. Blair, "Background Paper on the Strategic War Plan and START Reduction," paper presented to the Democratic Thursday Luncheon of the U.S. Senate, May 18, 2000, accessed at www.cdi.org/issues/proliferation/blairbckReduc.html; and Bruce G. Blair, "Trapped in the Nuclear Math," *New York Times,* June 12, 2000, A29.

21. Bruce G. Blair, Harold A. Feiveson, and Frank N. von Hippel, "Taking Nuclear Weapons off Hair-Trigger Alert," *Scientific American,* Nov. 1997, 74–81, accessed at www.sciam.com/1197issue/1197vonhippel.html.

22. At present, there are an estimated 30,000 nuclear warheads in the worldwide inventory. It is estimated that the United States has slightly more than 10,500 and Russia approximately 20,000. Of these totals, the United States and Russia maintain approximately 6,000 operational strategic warheads each. The remaining warheads are nonstrategic—that is, "tactical" forces, retired warheads awaiting dismantlement, or warheads in reserve. *Nuclear Posture Review* (31 Dec. 2001) (Washington, D.C.: U.S. Government Printing Office, 2002).

23. George W. Bush, "U.S. Nuclear Weapon and Security Policies," *Federal News Service,* May 23, 2000.

24. "President Announces Reduction in Nuclear Arsenal," Nov. 13, 2001, accessed at www.whitehouse.gov/news/releases/2001/11/20011113-3.html.

25. Elimination of these systems will account for a 1,300-warhead reduction in the existing force of 6,000 operationally deployed warheads. The plan also calls for further reductions to the level of 3,800 operationally deployed strategic warheads by FY 2007. At that time, the administration will reassess and announce a revised timetable to continue the draw-down to 1,700–2,200 deployed warheads. The enduring force will be based on 14 Trident SSBNs, 500 Minuteman III ICBMs, 76 nuclear-capable B-52H bombers, and 21 B-2 bombers—capable of delivering at least 5,000 nuclear weapons, depending on configuration of the launch platform. Admiral James O. Ellis Jr., "Basic Terminology of the Nuclear Posture Review," submitted in support of formal testimony before House Armed Services Committee on Feb. 14, 2002, accessed at www.senate.gov/~armed_services/e_witnesslist.cfm?id=165.

26. Department of Defense, news transcript, "Special Briefing on the Nuclear Posture Review," presenter, J. D. Crouch, Assistant Secretary of Defense, International Security Policy, Jan. 9, 2002, accessed at www.defenselink.mil/news/Jan2002/t01092002_t0109npr.html.

27. "The Nuclear Posture," editorial, *Washington Post*, March 13, 2002.

28. See Nolan, *An Elusive Consensus,* 31.

29. The B61 modification II entered service in 1997. Other off-the-shelf designs, such as the W54, that can have explosive yields as low as 0.01 kilotons also have the potential to be reengineered and used as deep-penetration munitions. James Gordon Prather, "Micro-Nukes," *American Spectator,* Nov.-Dec. 2001: 24.

30. Department of Energy, "Report to Congress on the Defeat of Hard and Deeply Buried Targets," submitted by the Secretary of Defense in conjunction with the Secretary of Energy in Response to Section 1044 of the Floyd D. Spence National Defense Authorization Act for FY 2001, P.L. 106-398," July 2001, 6.

31. Ibid., 18.

32. The *Nuclear Posture Review* reports that current conventional and single-yield nuclear weapons are inadequate to ensure the defeat of hardened and deeply buried targets. Accordingly, the Defense Department, in coordination with the National Nuclear Security Administration has been instructed to evaluate nuclear-weapon options to increase weapon-system effectiveness and flexibility and to limit collateral damage. Ibid.

33. Serious questions have been raised regarding whether a miniaturized nuclear weapon would have the limited effect that its proponents claim. See Robert Nelson, "Low Yield Earth Penetrating Nuclear Weapons," FAS Public Interest Report, *Journal of the Federation of American Scientists* 54 (Jan.-Feb.2001), accessed at www.fas.org/faspir/2001/v54n1/weapons.htm.

34. The Department of Energy labs have long held that the 1995 science-based Stockpile Stewardship program, the bureaucratic compromise negotiated by President Clinton in the wake of his decision to sign the CTBT in 1996, is inadequate to ensure the viability of the strategic arsenal. According to a growing number of administration and weapons lab officials, America's ability to design, build, test, and deploy a new nuclear weapon, and even verify the viability of the current stockpile, is increasingly at risk. An aging workforce and infrastructure, difficulties in recruiting and retaining the next generation of nuclear scientists and engineers, and low morale as a result of repressive security policies in the wake of the Wen Ho Lee affair have had a deleterious effect on America's nuclear capabilities. William B. Scott, "Aging Weapons and Staff Strain Nuclear Complex," *Aviation Week and Space Technology,* Aug. 20, 2001.

35. Nevada test site managers are currently conducting a review to determine what would be required to hasten the U.S. government's ability to resume underground testing should the president deem it necessary. Off-the-record interview by Brian D. Finlay, Feb. 2002.

36. Sam Nunn and Bruce G. Blair, "From Nuclear Deterrence to Mutual Safety: As Russia's Arsenal Crumbles, It's Time to Act," *Washington Post,* June 22, 1997.

37. Lachlan Forrow et al., "Accidental Nuclear War: A Post–Cold War Assessment," *New England Journal of Medicine* 338 (April 30, 1998).

38. Editorial, "Nuclear Trigger-Locks," *Boston Globe,* April 23, 2000, F6.

39. David Shambaugh, "Sino-American Strategic Relations: From Partner to Competitors," *Survival* 42 (spring 2000): 104–7; see also the somewhat alarmist "Cox Committee

Report," Report of the U.S. House of Representatives Select Committee on U.S. National Security and Military/Commercial Concerns with the People's Republic of China, available at www.house.gov/coxreport.

40. Cirincione, *Deadly Arsenals,* 142–45.

41. Ibid., 145.

42. For a full discussion of the Israeli nuclear program, see Avner Cohen, *Israel and the Bomb* (New York: Columbia University Press, 1998).

43. For a thoughtful discussion, see Sumit Ganguly, "India's Pathway to Pokhran II: The Prospects and Sources of New Dehli's Nuclear Weapons Program," *International Security* 23 (spring 1999): 148–77.

44. Samina Ahmed, "Pakistan's Nuclear Weapons Program: Turning Points and Nuclear Choices," *International Security* 23 (spring 1999): 192–99.

45. The draft Indian nuclear doctrine released in 1999 demonstrates the continued evolution of Indian strategic thinking and includes somewhat contradictory statements. Available at www.indianembassy.org/policy/CTBT/nuclear_doctrine_aug_17_1999.html.

46. Zafar Iqbal Cheema, "Pakistan's Nuclear Use Doctrine and Command and Control," in Peter R. Lavoy, Scott D. Sagan, and James J. Wirtz, *Planning the Unthinkable: How New Powers Will Use Nuclear, Biological, and Chemical Weapons* (Ithaca: Cornell University Press, 2000), 161–71.

47. Cirincione, *Deadly Arsenals,* 246–49.

48. Scott D. Sagan, "The Commitment Trap: Why the United States Should Not Use Nuclear Threats to Deter Biological and Chemical Weapons Attacks," *International Security* 24 (spring 2000): 85–115.

49. Cirincione, *Deadly Arsenals,* 49.

50. Bolton speech, Nov. 19, 2001. Available at www.usinfo.state.gov/topical/pol/arms/stories/01111902.htm.

51. In March 1992, under heightened criticism from the American intelligence community, Russian president Boris Yeltsin confessed publicly that Russia maintained a formidable though covert biological weapons research program in contravention of the Biological Weapons Convention of 1972. In the wake of the Gulf War, startling revelations were also revealed regarding the extent of Iraq's covert chemical and biological weapons program. Finally, the Japanese doomsday cult "Aum Shinrikyo" has also busied itself over the course of the past decade with attempts to acquire the capabilities to create and disseminate biological agents for destructive purposes.

52. Richard M. Price, *The Chemical Weapons Taboo* (Ithaca: Cornell University Press, 1997).

Chapter 3   The Proliferation of Conventional Weapons and Technologies

JO L. HUSBANDS

Because of the persistence of conflicts in many parts of the world, cold war policies and their legacies, and global trends in defense economics, vast quantities of military equipment have spread across the globe in recent decades. This hardware ranges from sophisticated high-performance weapons, such as destroyers and fighter planes, to the small, rugged "light weapons" that account for most of the casualties in conflict.[1] In parallel with the weapons has come the steady spread of technology and technical capabilities that enable an increasing number of countries to build their own weapons or to improve the quality of weapons they or others already have. And with the exceptions of ballistic missiles and antipersonnel land mines, throughout the 1990s most governments either ignored or actively encouraged various forms of this proliferation in the name of supporting allies and friends, promoting security in an insecure world, or maintaining their domestic military industries via exports.

The proliferation of conventional weapons and technologies is a significant security issue in the grave new world of the twenty-first century. To develop this argument, this chapter examines three major issues: the changing nature of the international trade in conventional weapons and technology and the forces driving these changes in the post–cold war world; the implications of these developments for international security and stability; and the prospects for national, regional, and international efforts to address these problems.

Arms Transfers during the Cold War

Arms transfers (sales and aid) functioned as a significant tool of both U.S. and Soviet foreign policy throughout the cold war, particularly in their competition for influence in the Third World. For the two superpowers, political factors provide the single best explanation of their arms transfers patterns. Open sales and military assistance, along with often significant covert supplies, supported dozens of countries as well as subnational groups on one side or another of conflicts across the globe. Particular sales or gifts of weapons were important symbols of commitment and friendship; just as a thoughtful guest might bring wine or flowers to dinner, an arms-supply agreement sweetened many a diplomatic mission. Advisors and trainers often came along with the weapons, providing a presence to further cement the relationship. Arms sales and military assistance also frequently provided the quid

62

pro quo for use of or access to overseas bases or facilities, particularly if it would not be politically acceptable to pay "rent."

U.S. arms transfers generally followed the shifting geographical focus of American security policy. In the 1950s military aid, largely in the form of used military hardware, flowed to Europe as part of the general reconstruction of the continent and the building of bulwarks against the Warsaw Pact threat. With the 1960s and the conflicts in Southeast Asia, most security assistance went to support U.S. friends and allies in Indochina. The end of the Indochina conflicts brought an increased interest in arms transfers. First, the Nixon doctrine promulgated in 1969 explicitly sought to substitute American weapons for American troops in supporting U.S. interests in overseas conflicts. Second, the enormous oil revenues available to Middle Eastern states led to an open U.S. effort to "soak up petrodollars" through sales of advanced military hardware that served both economic and political ends. Since the mid-1970s the bulk of U.S. arms transfers have been destined for the region stretching from North Africa to South Asia. At the same time, significant supply relationships, including transfers of technology and cooperative production arrangements, continued with key allies such as NATO, South Korea, Israel, and Japan.[2]

Soviet arms transfers, in keeping with their role as instruments to support the East-West competition, followed more or less the same shifts in geographic focus over the decades of the cold war. The Soviet Union began arms transfers in the 1950s as well, although on a more modest scale, with a captive market in Central and Eastern Europe and an aid program to friendly states and "forces of liberation" elsewhere in the world. Soviet military aid and even ostensible sales were frequently conducted with generous credit terms, which enabled countries such as Vietnam and Angola to rank among the leading international arms recipients. From the 1970s, however, the Soviets also cultivated sales relationships with wealthier states that could provide much-needed hard currency. The Soviets had a reputation for being less generous with supplies of spare parts than the Americans, presumably as a means of maintaining tighter control over how the weapons they supplied were used.[3]

Relative ranking was a source of often fierce political dispute, but most experts accepted the Soviet Union as the largest supplier, followed by the United States.[4] Other important arms suppliers during the cold war included European states such as Great Britain and France, as well as China. By the last decade of the cold war, the five permanent members of the UN Security Council provided around 80 percent of total arms agreements.

In part as a result of technology transfers and coproduction arrangements described further below, several dozen countries qualified as weapons exporters, although most offered a limited range of products.[5] Smaller suppliers such as East and West Germany, Israel, Italy, and Brazil provided important sources of weapons, in some cases specializing in a few highly valued systems. Countries such as South Korea and Brazil also saw high-tech defense industries as a leading edge in their development strategies. Only the United States and the Soviet Union could support their military industries with purchases for their domestic forces, so economic factors were essential to all the other suppliers. Arms exports generally accounted for significant shares of their production.[6]

Politics mattered as well, however; many European states were determined to maintain national defense industries as essential symbols of sovereignty, whether they made economic sense or not. Britain and France also frequently used their arms-supply relationships as another tie to former colonies where they sought to maintain influence. Countries such as Israel, China, and India developed their arms industries in part to escape dependence on foreign suppliers.

The amount of equipment transferred during the cold war numbered in the tens and sometimes hundreds of thousands of pieces. The U.S. Arms Control and Disarmament Agency reported, for example, that between 1972 and 1982 developing countries received more than 12,000 tanks, 3,500 supersonic combat aircraft, and 19,600 armored personnel carriers.[7] The comparable figures for 1984–88 were more than 7,200 tanks, almost 15,000 armored personnel carriers, and just over 1,700 supersonic combat aircraft.[8] The number of countries acquiring advanced weaponry rose as well. Missiles are a classic case. In 1970 fewer than thirty countries had some form of missile; by 1985 the figure had reached seventy-six countries.[9]

The pattern of proliferation was far from uniform, reflecting the uneven nature of global economic and political development. The Near East, broadly defined, received as much as 70 percent of the advanced weapons transferred in the 1980s and 1990s. East and South Asia were also significant recipients. By contrast, relatively limited numbers of advanced weapons reached Latin America and any part of sub-Saharan Africa except South Africa. Large quantities of light weapons reached conflicts in poorer regions such as Central America or the Horn of Africa, however, so in making generalizations one needs to distinguish between exports of major and light weapons.[10]

With an increasing number of weapons sales came agreements to transfer technology and production capacity. More and more buyers demanded—and

Table 3.1   Leading Arms Suppliers' Arms Transfer Agreements

Rank	1994–97	1998–2001	2001
1	United States	United States	United States
2	Russia	Russia	Russia
3	France	France	France
4	United Kingdom	Germany	Germany
5	China	China	Israel
6	Germany	United Kingdom	China
7	Israel	Sweden	United Kingdom
8	South Africa	Israel	Spain
9	Italy	Spain	Sweden
10	Ukraine	Italy	Brazil

Source: Richard F. Grimmett, *Conventional Arms Transfers to Developing Nations, 1994–2001* (Washington, D.C.: Congressional Research Service, 2002).

received—significant shares of the production or assembly process. The bulk of technology transfer arrangements were and remain among the Western nations and cover everything from licensed production of specific systems through co-development to genuine transnational production arrangements.[11] And with the exception of Eastern Europe and India, Soviet arms transfers did not generally include significant technology transfers or coproduction arrangements. But technology transfers nonetheless enabled the emergence of significant military industries in East Asia, particularly in Japan and South Korea, in Brazil, in Israel, in India, and in a number of developing countries. In 1988, for example, international licensing arrangements permitted India, Egypt, Indonesia, South Korea, Taiwan, and Brazil to produce forty-three major weapons.[12]

The Arms Market Today

The end of the cold war altered the fundamental characteristic of international arms transfers, its profoundly political character reflecting the role transfers played in the foreign policy of the dominant suppliers, the United States and the Soviet Union. Political motives still figure in key decisions but, as discussed below, economics rather than politics dominates much of arms transfers policy.

All arms-trade statistics need to be treated with care, as few governments provide comprehensive reports of their sales and assistance programs. Attempting to include light weapons sends one even further into the realm of speculation.[13] And the size of the black and gray markets that provide arms to nonstate actors, factions in internal conflict, and states subject to international embargoes is only a matter of experts' informed guesses.[14]

With all these cautions, it is apparent that the sheer volume of arms transfers today, at least of major military hardware, is significantly smaller than in the mid- to late 1980s. Then, the Iran–Iraq war—the most expensive in Third World history—added to the sales and assistance driven by U.S.-Soviet rivalry to push international arms transfers to an all-time high. With allowances for inflation, changes in reporting procedures, and the general vagaries of statistics that can imply false precision, today's arms market is probably not more than 50 to 60 percent of that total.

The report by the U.S. Congressional Research Service (CRS) estimates that in calendar year 2001 the total value of all *agreements* to transfer major conventional weapons to both developed and developing countries was $26.4 billion in current dollars, while the value of all *deliveries* was $21.3 billion.[15] The value of all agreements for transfer to developing countries in 2001 was $16 billion in current dollars, with deliveries at $14.4 billion.[16] Depending on what is included, estimates of the value of the legal trade in light weapons range from $3 billion to $6 billion in current U.S. dollars, with the illegal trade adding perhaps another $2 billion to $10 billion.[17]

The major arms suppliers have remained the same, although, as discussed further below, the ranking has shifted substantially (see Table 3.1, at left). In 2001, for example, the CRS report estimates that U.S. overall arms-transfer agreements accounted for $12.1 billion of the $26.4 billion total.[18] Russia was in second place, although with less than half the total dollar amount of U.S. agreements.[19] France, Germany, Israel, and China followed.

The broad regional patterns among recipients have remained the same since approximately the 1970s, although the Near East's share has declined to closer to half the market, with Asian nations accounting for another third of developing-country customers.[20] As already mentioned, neither Latin America nor Africa ever figured significantly in transfers of major weapons. The CRS report estimates that just over 60 percent of all arms transfers agreements in 2001 were made with developing countries. This is misleading, however, because a few developing countries account for the vast bulk of the sales of advanced weaponry captured by the CRS report. The top ten recipients account for anywhere from 70 percent to more than 90 percent of all these sales agreements (see Table 3.2).[21]

Other important trends are shaping the future directions of arms transfers, but any understanding of current conditions and prospects for policy must begin with four essential features of the post–cold war arms market.

The Primacy of Economic Forces

With the end of the cold war came an unanticipated "peace dividend": great over-capacity in military industries no longer needed to sustain the East-West arms competition. The deep declines in military spending, especially for weapons procurement, otherwise welcomed as a relief from an economic burden and competition with domestic priorities, left the military industries in the former Soviet bloc and the West in deep trouble. U.S. procurement spending, already being cut back in the wake of the Reagan administration's massive investment, entered the longest period of sustained decline since the end of World War II. Between 1985 and 1995 procurement spending fell by 67 percent.[22] The trends in Russia were stark,

Table 3.2   Leading Arms Recipients in the Developing World Arms Transfer Agreements

Rank	1994–97	1998–2001	2001
1	Saudi Arabia	U.A.E.	Israel
2	China	India	China
3	India	China	Egypt
4	U.A.E.	South Africa	Saudi Arabia
5	Egypt	Egypt	South Korea
6	Israel	Pakistan	U.A.E.
7	South Korea	Israel	India
8	Pakistan	Malaysia	Iran
9	Indonesia	Singapore	Singapore
10	Kuwait	South Korea	Kuwait

Source: Richard F. Grimmett, *Conventional Arms Transfers to Developing Nations, 1994–2001* (Washington, D.C.: Congressional Research Service, 2002).

exacerbated by disruption of key defense sectors with the breakup of the Soviet Union and compounded by the loss of the captive market in former Warsaw Pact states. By one informed estimate, Russia's military output fell by more than 80 percent between 1991 and the late 1990s.[23] European firms, which had never been sustainable on domestic consumption alone and whose governments most enthusiastically embraced the opportunity to invest in other priorities, faced a bleak future. Reduced military budgets also meant less trade among the developed states and fewer large new weapons programs.[24]

The affected states responded with various strategies. No nation was willing to abandon completely the idea of maintaining some military-industrial base, although a number of European states accepted that they would not be able to maintain the capacity to produce a full range of military hardware. U.S. Defense Secretary Les Aspin and Deputy Defense Secretary William Perry, in a 1993 meeting known in the trade as the "Last Supper," summoned the major American military manufacturers to the Pentagon, outlined the trends in spending, and advised them to consolidate or face extinction.[25] The Russians, as well as the Europeans and to a lesser extent the Americans, embarked on a number of efforts to convert their military industries to civilian production. Their success has been mixed at best. All of the countries embraced exports of weapons and technology as a way to sustain what remained of their defense industries. The result was ferocious economic pressure in all the major arms-producing states and intense international competition for sales. The "buyer's market" created by these pressures inevitably encouraged proliferation, including of the most advanced technology.

With the caveat that the political effects of the war on terrorism are still just beginning to make themselves felt, it appears that economics rather than politics will remain the driving force behind most of the world's arms transfers for the remainder of the decade and probably beyond.

The Shift in Rank: American Dominance, Russian Decline

The second significant post–cold war feature is the change in relative ranking between the United States and the former Soviet Union. Now the United States is by far the dominant supplier. Since the early 1990s the United States has accounted for close to 50 percent of all agreements and deliveries of major conventional weapons.[26] This includes transfers to both developed and developing nations; the percentage for developing nations alone is higher. The United States also maintains the only remaining military-assistance program of any significance, and that significance is growing as U.S. counterterrorism programs grow. This dominance is almost certain to remain unchallenged for at least the rest of this decade and probably longer.

In the immediate aftermath of the Soviet Union's demise, the new Russian Federation saw its arms transfers plummet. By one estimate, in 1993 total Russian agreements with developing countries totaled $1.8 billion; in 1987, the figure had been a record high of $27 billion.[27] By the end of the 1990s, however, Russian arms transfers had rebounded. Thanks to a strong finish, Russia actually ended up second to the United States in arms-sales agreements with developing countries in the latter half of the 1990s, although, as noted above, with less than half the total dollar amount of U.S. agreements.[28]

Two of the three major customers that have enabled Russia's return to the ranks of a major supplier—China and Iran—are sources of significant security and proliferation concerns for the United States. U.S. concerns are exacerbated because Russia has undertaken major technology-transfer arrangements as part of its agreements with China. The United States fears that this will enable China, which it regards as a less than completely responsible supplier, to export yet more advanced hardware to problematic destinations. Particular sales, such as that of Kilo-class submarines to Iran or advanced combat aircraft to China, have sparked sharp diplomatic exchanges. Russia's refusal to limit its sales to these countries remains an irritant in otherwise improved U.S.–Russian relations.[29] India is the third major Russian customer, and it has also received significant technology transfers as part of its continuing struggle to develop an indigenous arms industry. But U.S.–Indian relations have improved significantly in the wake of September 11, so much so that the U.S. arms transfers to India are now actively under discussion. This has cast some doubt on whether Russian transfers will continue to be significant now that they are in direct competition with U.S. weapons and technology.

An Excess of Firepower

The industrial overcapacity afflicting the former NATO and Warsaw Pact states has already been discussed, but when the cold war ended these countries also simply had too many weapons. Without the prospect of massive conventional war, there was no rationale for retaining the tens of thousands of pieces of military equipment that had accumulated over decades of East–West competition. The next section discusses the degree to which these overstuffed inventories have fueled an expanded black market in arms and technology, but it is important to note how much the major states cut their arsenals by simply and legally giving away or selling hardware at bargain-basement prices.

Ironically, a major arms-control agreement facilitated this process. After almost twenty years in negotiation, the 1990 Conventional Forces in Europe (CFE) treaty permitted states to transfer surplus military equipment to other states or parties as one method of achieving mandated reductions in treaty-limited equipment. Poorer NATO countries were the primary recipients. According to UN figures, between 1992 and 1995, as part of this "cascade," Greece received 940 battle tanks, 1,195 armored combat vehicles, 98 combat aircraft, and 12 warships. Turkey received 1,028 battle tanks, 773 armored combat vehicles, 60 combat aircraft, and 6 warships.[30]

The United States used other traditional military assistance channels to transfer millions of dollars' worth of additional equipment. South Korea, for example, received $66.6 million in excess defense items, including 275 old but certainly serviceable M48A5 tanks and 41,000 tons of excess ammunition and munitions.[31] Some of the hardware disposed of as surplus ended up in the secondhand market of private arms dealers, but much of the equipment slipped over the line to the world of illicit transfers.

The Increase in Shady Sales

Illicit arms transfers have always been part of the market for weapons and military technology, but the end of the cold war and the disintegration of the Soviet Union have apparently expanded trafficking significantly.[32] What cannot be known is how much this expansion of the black market is compensating for the end—or at least significant reduction—of the covert assistance that the United States, the Soviet Union, and others provided during the cold war. Much of that assistance went through black market channels, so this is also a likely case of perverse privatization. The actual size of the black market, such as the $2–10 billion figure cited above, is a matter of informed guesses.

A number of former Soviet republics and Eastern European states have becomes bases for the arms brokers that are essential middlemen in many legal but also the majority of illegal sales. Huge stocks of surplus military equipment, sometimes vulnerable to theft in poorly guarded facilities, and sometimes simply sold with little concern for the buyer's bona fides, have added a new source of proliferation concern.[33] The rise of sophisticated organized crime networks that include weapons and military technology in their inventory of drugs and other contraband cannot be blamed on the end of the cold war, but like the individual arms brokers, some of these networks thrive in and draw recruits from a number of former Soviet and Eastern bloc countries in the wake of a more general decline in law and order.[34]

The United States also bears responsibility for a share of the illicit arms market. As part of its effort to reduce U.S. military inventories to save costs after the end of the cold war, the Defense Department sold off millions of dollars' worth of surplus military equipment in the early 1990s. With responsibility for the sales delegated to the individual facility, controls were often lax, and a special investigation by *U.S. News and World Report* in cooperation with *60 Minutes* revealed numerous questionable cases of high-tech equipment reaching unintended foreign buyers.[35] Limited regulations in a number of U.S. states also means that large quantities of legally purchased firearms quickly end up in illegal channels. This is generally considered the major path for illicit weapons into Latin America; planes delivering illegal drugs to the United States, for example, return to their home bases with cargoes of military hardware.[36]

Light Weapons and the Development-Security Linkage

So far this section has focused largely on trends in the trade in major conventional weapons, but that is only one of two key parts of international arms transfers. In the early 1990s a number of governments and international organizations began to acknowledge the grim security situation in much of the developing world and the threat this posed to hopes of achieving sustainable development. This recognition came in part because the cold war's end permitted a new look at critical problems in developing countries and in part because sheer practical considerations would no longer permit avoiding the problems. Among the most disturbing facts developing countries faced are these:

• More than fifty countries have experienced significant periods of conflict since 1980. Civilians have accounted for at least 90 percent of the casualties. Fifteen of the world's twenty poorest countries experienced a major conflict between 1992 and 1997. In a number of cases these conflicts led to a complete breakdown of the state. Thirty countries have had more than 10 percent of their populations displaced by conflict, either internally or as refugees in other countries. In ten countries, more than 40 percent have been displaced.[37]
• Between 1990 and 2001 fifty-seven major armed conflicts took place in forty-five countries.[38]
• The humanitarian workers delivering relief are increasingly at risk. The UN reported, for example, that 180 of its workers have been killed since 1992; in 1998, for the first time, more civilian aid workers were killed than military peacekeepers.[39]
• Even after conflicts ostensibly end, violence continues in many societies where weak governments cannot provide basic security for their people.[40]

Most of the conflicts causing this devastation are civil conflicts and most are being fought with vast quantities of cheap, durable, and increasingly deadly light weapons. Much of the world is inundated with these weapons, many of which are rugged and durable, with long life spans. This has meant that automatic rifles left behind by U.S. forces in Vietnam have found their way to conflicts in Central America and the Middle East. In Africa and elsewhere, as one conflict ends weapons flow across porous borders for use in the next. Light weapons are also a standard part of the inventories of global organized crime syndicates, with insurgent groups or governments under international embargoes sometimes allying themselves with these syndicates to trade commodities from areas under their control for weapons.[41]

However uncertain the information available about transfers of major conventional weapons, data about the volume and values of light-weapons transfers and stocks are far worse. As already discussed, a significant portion of the trade in light weapons is illegal, and governments continue covert transfers of arms to other governments or to insurgent groups. Huge surplus stocks left over from the cold war and enormous quantities of weapons already in circulation further complicate efforts to make reliable estimates.[42] Dubious or distorted figures sometimes take hold and enjoy wide circulation.

With these caveats, important information is becoming available. The U.S. Arms Control and Disarmament Agency estimated that 13 percent of the international arms trade consists of small arms and light weapons and ammunition.[43] According to the 2002 edition of the Small Arms Survey, more than twenty countries now report their exports of light weapons. The survey identified a thousand companies in ninety-eight countries involved in some aspect of the production of small arms or ammunition, but thirteen of these countries dominate the market.[44] Estimates of the number of legal and illegal military and civilian-style firearms currently in circulation worldwide range from 500 million to more than 1 billion.[45] The reports produced by researchers and journalists in the field have added significantly to our understanding of the scope of light-weapons transfers.[46]

The process of making effective links between the problems of development and security is slow and often hesitant. The development and security communities reflect different cultures, different intellectual traditions, and frequently a history of mutual suspicion and even antagonism. The concrete, practical problems that light-weapons proliferation poses to sustainable development have made the issue a good place to focus initial efforts, as the international coalition of nongovernmental organizations (NGOs) now attempting to deal with the light-weapons issue illustrates.[47]

The Return of Security Assistance

After the end of the cold war, the United States was the only nation to maintain a security assistance program of any significance. Billions of dollars in aid continued to flow to Egypt and Israel, for example, as part of U.S. commitments from the Camp David accords. In as many as two dozen programs, the Clinton administration significantly expanded military and police training for forces overseas as part of its engagement with newly democratizing states, in support of peacekeeping and to assist international counternarcotics and anticrime programs. One critical study estimates that the United States trained 100,000 people annually in 180 countries.[48] But security assistance no longer played the central role it had enjoyed in U.S. policy during the long East–West competition.

In the wake of September 11, 2001, security assistance has returned to the center of U.S. policy as a critical instrument in the war against terrorism. In a speech marking the six-month anniversary of the attacks on New York City and Washington, D.C., President Bush said, "I have set a clear policy in the second stage of the war on terrorism. America encourages and expects governments everywhere to help remove the terrorist parasites that threaten their own countries and the peace of the world. If governments need training or resources to meet this commitment, America will help."[49]

The full range of the new security assistance program is still taking shape, but already the United States is expanding its training and engagement in countries it considers critical to the war on terrorism, including the Philippines, Georgia, and Pakistan. Many of its new allies are Central Asian states, such as Uzbekistan, Tajikistan, and Kazakhstan. How the Bush administration's strong statements in support of democracy will square with the authoritarian policies and dubious human-rights records of a number of its new friends and allies remains to be seen, but old problems may well be back on the agenda.[50]

Prospects for Controlling Light Weapons

One of the most interesting features of the light-weapons problem is that the leading actors in efforts to address the implications for international security are those most affected. The best-known example is probably the coalition of NGOs that achieved an international ban on antipersonnel land mines, discussed in greater detail below. The original members of the NGO coalition were human rights and humanitarian groups who came to the issue out of frustration that their basic humanitarian missions were being blocked by the indiscriminate use of land mines in areas of conflict.[51] Traditional peace and arms-control groups, though they ultimately made a significant contribution to achieving the ban on land mines, were still followers rather than instigators of this campaign.[52]

The international attention to light weapons reflects some of the lessons learned during the campaign that led to the 1997 ban on antipersonnel land mines.[53] It also reflects the commitment of a relatively small group of researchers, some in academia but many from NGOs, to raise awareness of the human toll the weapons were taking. In addition to the research conferences typical to any field, a self-conscious effort was made to build an international NGO coalition. As with the campaign to ban land mines, the groups included both organizations traditionally concerned with peace and security and humanitarian organizations. In August 1998 forty-five individuals representing thirty-three NGOs from eighteen countries held an initial strategy session in Canada. From that came a meeting in Brussels in October 1998, which attracted 180 participants from more than a hundred NGOs. The "International Action Network on Small Arms" created in those meetings was formally launched in May 1999 at the much larger Hague Appeal for Peace. The IANSA founding document, with its long lists of proposed actions for addressing both the supply and demand sides of the trade in light weapons, gives a good reflection of the diversity of interests within the coalition.[54] The effort to build as broad a coalition as possible has meant that essentially all ideas have been welcome. The IANSA founding document, for example, contains forty measures for controlling availability and access to small arms, and another thirty-two for reducing the demand for them. So far it has proved difficult politically to sort out the connections among the many proposals, identify issues of timing and sequence, and set priorities for action. It is hard to avoid the impression that there are more ideas than energy, resources, and effective strategies to carry them through.

The problems of illicit arms transfers—and their obvious links to other problems of transnational crime such as the drug trade—has brought in another set of actors from domestic, regional, and international law enforcement. This work is discussed below as well. Again, activities initiated by the countries most affected, using existing regional organizations where possible and building new coalitions where necessary, is one of the notable features of this effort.

On the international level, beginning in the late 1980s the United Nations embarked on a remarkable new course when it began paying attention to the weapons that were actually causing the casualties in the conflicts that affected many member nations. For years member states had demanded that the focus remain on weapons of mass destruction, in part out of genuine concern with the arms race between the superpowers and in part out of a desire to avoid international "interference" in their internal affairs. Now, led by afflicted countries such as Colombia, the countries most affected by light weapons brought the issue to the world body. In 1995 UN Secretary General Boutros Boutros-Ghali proposed a new focus on microdisarmament—"practical disarmament in the context of the conflicts the UN is actually dealing with and of the weapons, most of them light weapons, that are actually killing people by the hundreds of thousands."[55] As the UN group of experts he commissioned concluded in its pathbreaking 1997 report: "Accumulations of small arms and light weapons by themselves do not cause the conflicts in which they are used. The availability of these weapons, however, contributes toward exacerbating conflicts by increasing the lethality and duration of violence, by encouraging a violent rather than a peaceful resolution of differences, and by generating a vicious circle of a greater sense of insecurity, which in turn leads to a greater demand for, and use of, such weapons."[56]

The challenges facing relief and aid workers that drove Boutros Boutros-Ghali to call for microdisarmament have also led an increasing number of donor countries and even the international financial institutions to address security issues. The initiatives are taken most commonly in the context of postconflict reconstruction. In 1997, for example, the World Bank created a special postconflict unit devoted to these problems. The unit funded research as well as operational programs on the ground, with much of its work focused on demobilization and reintegration of combatants, an area that fits quite comfortably within the bank's mandate.[57]

The Post-Conflict Unit has now been renamed the Conflict Prevention and Reconstruction Unit, but the fundamental point of an unavoidable recognition of the links between development and security issues remains valid.[58] A number of the major donor countries, including Canada, Belgium, Sweden, and Norway, have become actively engaged in projects reflecting development-security linkages, in part through supporting the activities of NGOs. Under the leadership of Clare Short, the Department of International Development in Great Britain has put out a series of important policy statements.[59] This is part of a broader commitment to what has come to be known as "human security."

As attention focused increasingly on the light weapons issue, proposals have come from many quarters. As already mentioned, the first major effort focused on a single weapon, antipersonnel land mines. Along with land mines, considerable attention initially was paid to measures that put light weapons in the context of the conflicts in which they were used, and sought to identify policies suitable to a conflict's different phases.[60] This perspective remains important, particularly for the implementation of peace settlements. Over time, however, two other perspectives have gained prominence. The social devastation created by the "culture of violence" in many countries, facilitated by the ready availability of light weapons, has led to a broader concern with curbing illicit arms transfers and to important links to other efforts to restore basic security to citizens.[61] The focus on illicit arms also reflects growing concern with the power and global reach of organized-crime networks. A third approach, growing out of the practical problems for relief and reconstruction that attracted UN attention, emphasizes a development perspective to find measures that can affect the "demand side" for weapons.[62] All of the approaches are linked and the distinctions between them often blur, especially on the ground, in conflict-ridden countries. But they do represent different basic motivations for wanting to address the light-weapons problem and bring different constituencies into the process of developing and implementing policy.

The Case of Land Mines

Even if war seems uncontrolled and uncontrollable, people have long sought ways to limit its effects through the creation of a body of norms and international law: the "laws of war," also referred to as "international humanitarian law." Controlling or proscribing the use of certain weapons that are considered too indiscriminate or unnecessarily injurious is part of this effort. In 1868 the St. Petersburg Declaration outlawed the use of a newly invented bullet designed to explode and shatter on contact with a soft surface, such as the human body. The Hague Conventions of the early 1900s went on to ban other weapons.[63]

In the 1990s the primary focus of these efforts was on finding a way to cope with the millions of antipersonnel land mines sown in the course of conflicts around the world. The U.S. State Department has estimated that perhaps 60 to 70 million such land mines are still in the ground in countries such as Angola, Afghanistan, Cambodia, Nicaragua, and Somalia.[64] Parts of some countries are genuinely infested with mines, which are increasingly used as weapons of terror to make territory uninhabitable or to enforce "ethnic cleansing." Cheap to buy and easy to deploy, they are dangerous and expensive to clear, and they make it far more difficult for countries to rebuild and return to a normal life once conflicts are over. Returning refugees to their homes may become impossible if villages, roads, and fields are too dangerous to inhabit. Those who survive land mine explosions often lose limbs, placing additional burdens on already overloaded health care systems.

The 1980 "Convention on Prohibitions or Restrictions on the Use of Certain Conventional Weapons which May Be Deemed to Be Excessively Injurious or to Have Indiscriminate Effects" (otherwise known as the Convention on Conventional Weapons, or CCW) was the first international treaty to attempt to regulate the use of land mines in its Protocol II. A review of the CCW in 1996 led to an amended Protocol II, which, among other things, distinguished between the use of antipersonnel and antitank mines and restricted the uses of all antipersonnel mines. The United States has signed and ratified the CCW, including Amended Protocol II. Further measures to limit the use of land mines or ameliorate their effects are part of the regular process of periodic review conferences.

In an effort that ultimately earned them the Nobel Peace Prize, a group of

NGOs banded together in the early 1990s to form the International Campaign to Ban Land Mines. As mentioned above, this was the first example of the growing importance of NGOs in affecting national and international policy on arms transfers. The campaign, joined over time by a growing number of international organizations and governments, led to the "Convention on the Prohibition of the Use, Stockpiling, Production, and Transfer of Antipersonnel Mines and on Their Destruction" (the Ottawa Convention). Signed by 122 countries in Ottawa, Canada, in December 1997, the convention went into effect in March 1999. As of early 2003, 145 nations had signed or acceded to the Ottawa Convention.

The convention bans the use of all antipersonnel land mines, including those that are self-destructing and self-deactivating, whether alone or in mixed systems with antitank mines. Signatories are prohibited from developing, producing, acquiring, or stockpiling land mines; they also must not assist, encourage, or induce anyone else to undertake these actions. All land mines held by signatories must be destroyed within four years after the signatory becomes a full member of the convention.

Despite early support for a ban and continuing leadership in efforts to ameliorate the residual effects of land mines, the United States has not joined the Ottawa Convention. President Clinton stated in September 1997 that the United States would not sign the treaty until alternative technologies with capabilities similar to land mines had been identified and fielded. He announced an active research-and-development program to seek such alternatives. President Clinton also established as presidential policy that after 2003 the United States would no longer use land mines outside of Korea, where, the Department of Defense has argued, land mines play a particularly important role. If alternatives for Korea and for mixed systems could be found by 2006, the United States would sign the Ottawa Convention. In the meantime, the United States has destroyed 3 million non-self-destructing and non-self-deactivating mines. The possibility of a decision by the Bush administration to sign the convention is considered remote.

The ban on land mines was a remarkable achievement for international civil society, but it left scars within the U.S. government, where many still question the legitimacy of nongovernmental actors initiating and influencing the creation of an international treaty. It has also proved a difficult model to replicate; the consequences for civilians of the indiscriminate use of land mines long after war has ended makes them particularly easy to stigmatize. By contrast, other light weapons are the staple of military and police forces worldwide, so an outright ban is not a feasible policy goal. The Ottawa Convention is nonetheless a significant achievement in the creation of an international norm and, as already argued, represents the emergence of important—if not always welcome—new actors in the international security realm.

Illicit Arms Transfers

The growing concern with illicit arms transfers—and their obvious links to other problems of transnational crime—has resulted in initiatives at all levels, national, regional, and international. Although in principle these initiatives are not limited to light weapons, in practice this has been the primary emphasis. The Organization of American States (OAS) has undertaken two important actions:

• The OAS Inter-American Drug Abuse Control Commission (CICAD) used an expert group to create a set of Model Regulations to Control the Movement of Firearms, Ammunition, and Firearms Parts and Components. The regulations, adopted in November 1997, encourage regulation and licensing of firearms transfers by all OAS member states and seek to standardize practices throughout the hemisphere.
• At the initiative of the Mexican government, the OAS Permanent Council completed an Inter-American Convention against the Illicit Manufacturing and Trafficking in Firearms, Ammunition, Explosives, and Other Related Materials.[65]

The major supplier countries have also taken up the cause of curbing illicit arms transfers. In 1997 the European Union adopted a "Programme for Preventing and Combating Illicit Trafficking in Conventional Arms." The program makes explicit links between peace, security, and economic development and reconstruction. It seeks to combat illicit trafficking on or through EU territories, to provide capacity building in other countries, and to develop measures to reduce the number of weapons in circulation. Most of the EU effort is focused on Africa.[66]

On the international level, in May 2001 the UN General Assembly added a firearms protocol to the 2000 Convention against Transnational Organized Crime, declaring criminal such offenses as illicit manufacturing and trafficking in firearms, their parts, components, and ammunition, and falsifying or altering the markings on firearms. The purpose of the new instrument is to strengthen cooperation between states in order to prevent, combat, and eradicate illicit activities involving firearms and ammunition. Supporters argue that the new instrument creates a global standard for the transnational movement to prevent theft and diversion of firearms, while providing law enforcement officials with tools to effectively detect, investigate, and prosecute illicit manufacturing and trafficking offenses.[67]

Much of the UN's attention has been confined to illegal and illicit transfers, in part because of reluctance by the United States to address the domestically difficult question of limits on legal transfers. In July 2001 the UN Special Session on the Illicit Trade in Small Arms and Light Weapons in All Its Aspects almost foundered when the United States took strong positions against restrictions on civilian gun ownership or a ban on transfers to nonstate actors.[68] Many of the NGOs that had worked for months in preparation for the special session expressed strong disappointment. Nonetheless, the Programme of Action at the end of the conference did call for a review conference in 2006, thus further legitimizing continued UN engagement on the issue.[69] And in a further encouraging sign, in late August 2001 the UN Security Council made clear its continuing concern with the burdens that the light-weapons problem poses for carrying out its essential peace and security missions.

Conflict Process Measures

Very roughly, measures to stem the proliferation of light weapons that are linked to the stages of a conflict can be divided into those that apply before a conflict or in its early stages, those that apply while conflict is raging, and those that apply once a conflict ends. For example, tracking flows of weapons could offer early warning of potential outbreaks of violence and the opportunity for preventive action.[70] This would require significantly better information and more systematic analysis, as well as some expectation that the warning would be heeded.[71] In addition to initiatives for improved intelligence gathering and information sharing among governments, there are also proposals to use NGOs working on the ground in conflict-prone countries. Two NGOs in the United States and Germany, for example, cooperated to develop a basic handbook that would enable relief workers to identify the various types of light weapons that might be in use. The hope is that these workers would serve as field observers, providing early warning of new or increased weapons flows.[72]

While conflicts are underway, limits or outright embargoes on arms supplies are the obvious control mechanism. Access to supplies of weapons can be a significant factor in sustaining adversaries' abilities to continue to fight. Suppliers have long used controls on the resupply of weapons to affect the outcome of war, or even to force an early halt to fighting. Embargoes are controversial, however, because they may have only limited effectiveness or may convey a significant advantage to one side.

More research and experience have accumulated regarding the weapons left over when a conflict ostensibly ends. These measures seek to reinforce the peace settlements and also to prevent weapons used in one conflict from flowing to another. Here the measures include the formal disarmament provisions that may be part of peace settlements, disarmament measures that may be part of the demobilization and reintegration of former combatants, and collection—and, one hopes, destruction—of surplus weapons. It also can include programs to buy guns back from the civilian populations of war-torn societies. Some apparent early lessons include:

- For the peacekeeping operations of the post–cold war period, the timing of disarmament efforts is a critical issue.[73] Most of these assessments suggest that effective disarmament is best done early in a peace operation, but persuading deeply distrustful adversaries to turn in their weapons is often enormously difficult. Some peace settlements, such as that in Guatemala, provide detailed schedules for disarming combatants. Here the results of implementation have been mixed. In other cases, such as that of Northern Ireland, the only way to gain an agreement is to put off facing the issue until later; in this case the delay brought no relief.
- Concerted, serious attention to the problems of surplus weapons is relatively new, with as yet limited experience with efforts to collect and destroy stocks of excess weapons.[74]
- Studies of gun buy-back programs suggest that the most successful are those rooted in broader community development strategies that address the motives for gun ownership rather than those that only seek to purchase arms.[75]

Since the early 1990s, most of the energy of scholars and activists interested in arms transfers has gone to the problem of light weapons. The reasons are obvious: these are the weapons that, in miserable, grinding civil conflicts, on a day-to-day basis, account for thousands of casualties, mostly among civilians, and that, when wars do end, stand in the way of hopes for effective postconflict reconstruction and sustainable development. The achievements of just a few years—after decades of purposeful neglect—are significant, but what remains to be done is so enormous that it is easy to become discouraged. The policy tools available can appear woefully inadequate, successes small and infrequent, and governmental will for efforts at control hard to muster. Regional and international conflict resolution is not adequately developed, and once cycles of violence begin, breaking them is immensely difficult. The resources required to rebuild war-torn societies, including removing the arsenals accumulated in the course of conflict, too frequently fall short. Yet, looking ahead, this problem is going to remain on the international security agenda because the consequences of ignoring its toll have finally become too big to ignore.

Prospects for Controlling Advanced Weapons

With the exception of ballistic missiles, concern about controlling advanced weapons essentially disappeared after the mid-1990s. In the wake of the Gulf War, the revelations of the immense arsenal that Saddam Hussein had accumulated during the Iran-Iraq war sufficiently shocked the major arms suppliers into briefly attempting to negotiate restraint among the five permanent members (P-5) of the UN Security Council. (As mentioned above, the P-5 at the time accounted for about 80 percent of major arms exports.) But economic pressures to export and lack of uniform commitment to restraint quickly doomed the P-5 effort.

Restraint in the sale of arms has never been popular in the United States. In 1976 President Jimmy Carter made limits on U.S. arms exports a theme of his presidential campaign. In 1977 the White House announced a policy of restraint, listing eleven purposes that limiting arms sales would serve.[76] Four years later the Reagan administration put a different emphasis on arms transfers, reflecting its concern with the East–West conflict and the support that arms transfers could provide to Third World allies in that struggle. In 1981 the White House gave seven other reasons for using arms transfers as a foreign policy tool.[77] The Clinton administration gave economic considerations greater emphasis; for the first time, one of the five goals of its policy was "to enhance the ability of the U.S. defense industrial base to meet U.S. defense requirements and maintain long-term military technological superiority at lower costs."[78] Prior to September 11, 2001, the second Bush administration was still seeking to balance tensions on the subject; now, as already discussed, the security benefits of arms transfers in support of counterterrorism are receiving significant attention.

The impact of transferring advanced weapons is also subject to debate, as their proliferation has a number of apparently contradictory effects. As already noted, most of the casualties in conflicts since the end of World War II have resulted from relatively unsophisticated weapons. However controversial the sales agreements, relatively few of the advanced fighter aircraft exported to developing countries are ever actually used in combat. And with the exception of the Arab–Israeli conflicts, those aircraft that have seen combat generally performed below their advertised capabilities. This has led some to suggest that the trade in sophisticated weapons, although a drain on resources, has limited effect on most conflicts, particularly relative to the devastation wrought by light weapons.

The introduction of particular technologies may nonetheless have important effects. The devastating impact of Stinger missiles on the Soviet forces in Afghanistan is a classic example of such impact on the tide of battle or the outcomes of war. Technological sophistication and its impact are also relative. Allied air power completely dominated the Gulf War in 1991, yet the much-maligned Iraqi air force was then able to turn its helicopter gunships on its own rebellious citizens with devastating effect. And concern over the proliferation of ballistic-missile technology has led the United States to a multibillion dollar investment in defenses and withdrawal from a major arms-control agreement with the Russians that the Bush administration believed impeded the development of those defenses. The concern with ballistic missiles is in large measure driven by the fear of missile warheads carrying weapons of mass destruction, but there has been no comparable concern over the proliferation of advanced fighter aircraft that are also capable of delivering nuclear, chemical, or biological payloads.

Fostering Transparency: The UN Register

One of the first genuinely international measures to address advanced-weapons proliferation is modest in scope and ambition. The United Nations Register of Conventional Armaments is one of a number of international and regional efforts to foster transparency and openness about military spending, arms production, and arms imports and exports. Transparency is not control; instead, the hope is that greater openness and knowledge will build trust and encourage restraint. The work of the Organization for Security and Cooperation in Europe (OSCE) is perhaps the best example of creating a web of confidence-building measures as part of a regional security strategy.

The idea for an international register to report arms imports and exports emerged in the late 1980s. In 1988 the UN General Assembly passed a resolution to create a group of governmental experts to study ways to promote transparency and openness about conventional arms transfers. The end of the cold war and the revelations after the Gulf War about Iraq's arms programs increased interest in preventing weapons proliferation, and advocates thought increased transparency would support international nonproliferation efforts. The expert group's report formed the basis for a General Assembly resolution in December 1991 to create a register.

The register is a limited exercise, requiring countries to report their arms imports and exports for the preceding year in seven major categories: battle tanks, armored combat vehicles, large-caliber artillery systems, combat aircraft, attack helicopters, warships, and missiles and missile launchers. Its creators hoped this information would encourage governments to cooperate and coordinate their policies or would provide knowledge to the public so that citizens would become more active in urging their governments to limit imports or exports.

The register receives mixed reviews. About half of the total General Assembly membership submitted reports for the first year of its operation (1992), but the numbers have declined over the years. Some important countries—Saudi Arabia, Syria, and Iran, for example—do not submit reports. For some areas, in particular sub-Saharan Africa, the kinds of weapons reported in the register are irrelevant to the arms trade in the region. And the data provided by exporters and importers do not always match. Nonetheless, the register has so far succeeded in tentatively establishing a norm of transparency about international arms transfers, and has provided useful data for arms trade experts. Moreover, a number of countries also submit additional information about their arms-export policies or more detailed information about their purchases than required.

The issue now is the future of the register, especially of efforts to expand its scope to include other categories of weapons. Many observers believe that the register must grow or die, but there is only limited consensus on what direction the growth should take. Another problem is simply getting key nations to submit reports.

It is not clear how much the information the register provides genuinely enhances attention to arms transfers as a security issue. But getting the UN General Assembly to address arms transfers at all was a significant achievement. If, as intended, the register is coupled with other UN initiatives to promote regional and cooperative security, it could be part of important efforts to address the problems of arms transfers.

The Wassenaar Arrangement

The Wassenaar Arrangement on Export Controls for Conventional Arms and Dual-Use Goods and Technologies[79] was officially announced on December 19, 1995, and its founding document, the "Initial Elements," was issued in July 1996, with the first plenary session held six months later.[80] Technically the Wassenaar Arrangement is the follow-up to the Coordinating Committee on Export Controls (COCOM), created by NATO in 1949 to govern allied transfers to the Warsaw Pact and China. But Wassenaar is a very different kind of agreement. It differs from COCOM in at least three important ways:

• Wassenaar is *not* a control regime; like the UN register, it is a mechanism for information exchange and transparency. Decisions on exports remain solely the responsibility of each member country and its national regulations. There is no consensus decision making on transfers and there are no national vetoes of transfers.

• Wassenaar is *not* formally directed against any particular country or group of countries. Members are to inform one another about their transfers to nonmember governments. From the beginning, the Unites States made clear that it views Wassenaar as a mechanism to pursue controls on transfers of arms and dual-use goods and technologies to so-called "rogue" nations, but that view has never been accepted.

• Rather than being the object of controls, Russia and a number of former Warsaw Pact countries were among the founding members. Russia played a crucial role in shaping the agreement, although not always in ways the U.S. government appreciated.

The original twenty-eight members of Wassenaar included fifteen of the sixteen NATO countries (all but Iceland), plus Australia, Austria, the Czech Republic, Finland, Hungary, Ireland, Japan, New Zealand, Poland, the Russian Federation, the Slovak Republic, Sweden, and Switzerland. Since then, five other countries have joined: Argentina, Bulgaria, Romania, South Korea, and Ukraine. Two key suppliers, China and Brazil, are not part of the arrangement.

The stated purpose of the arrangement is "to contribute to regional and international security and stability, by promoting transparency and greater responsibility in transfers of conventional arms and dual-use goods and technologies, thus preventing destabilising accumulations." This language very much reflected the U.S.—and generally speaking the Western—response to the Gulf War and the revelation of the arsenal Iraq managed to acquire before it invaded Kuwait. The presumption is that the transparency provided by a regular exchange of information will promote export restraint and that trends can be recognized in time for the international community to respond.

The heart of Wassenaar is a series of data exchanges. All of them are confidential, although the lists of items to be controlled have been released. France and Russia, however, have formally stated that they view all of the Wassenaar control lists "as a reference list drawn up to help in the selection of dual-use goods which could contribute to the indigenous development, production or enhancement of conventional munitions capabilities."[81] Members may also provide other kinds of data or information on issues of proliferation concern and ask for additional data through regular diplomatic channels.

Wassenaar has two major lists of items about which members are to exchange data. The first is a munitions list that includes both major conventional weapons and light weapons. Members are to notify one another of deliveries to nonmember states every six months. Initially, data was exchanged only on the seven categories of arms included in the UN Register of Conventional Arms: battle tanks, armored combat vehicles, large-caliber artillery systems, combat aircraft, attack helicopters, warships, and missiles or missile systems. These are also the CFE categories.

Exchanging data only on the seven categories was probably the simplest way to begin these exchanges because countries are already reporting these data to the United Nations. For six of the categories, the Wassenaar data are more detailed, including information on model and type as well as quantities and recipients. But additional data on missiles are not to be provided and the arrangement thus perpetuates the UN register's flaw of not distinguishing between missiles and launchers. After more than two years of discussion, the members agreed in early 2001 to adopt nonbinding criteria to govern the export of man-portable surface-to-air missiles, such as Stingers.

The second Wassenaar list covers dual-use goods and technologies ("Tier 1"). Within that general list is a "Tier 2" list of sensitive items, which in turn has a subset of very sensitive items. There are several reporting requirements for data about dual-use goods and technologies. Members report:

- Denials of licenses for items on the Tier 1 list "where the reasons for denial are relevant to the purposes of the arrangement" twice a year on an aggregate basis;
- All relevant licenses issued and transfers made for items on the Tier 2 list twice a year on an aggregate basis;
- Relevant denials of licenses for items on the Tier 2 list, on an individual basis in a timely manner, that is, preferably within thirty but no later than sixty days.

The arrangement states that "Notification of a denial will not impose an obligation on other Participating States to deny similar transfers." But the U.S. government, prompted in part by U.S. industry, was concerned that this and other denial information could be used by other states to take advantage of the refusal to make a sale of their own. To avoid such "undercutting," members are to notify one another within thirty to sixty days if they issue a license for a Tier 2 item essentially identical to one denied by another member within the past three years. This is the only prior-notification provision in the arrangement. It is intended to avoid undercutting, but it also provides an opportunity for other members to try to persuade the country not to go through with the transaction.

At its plenary session in late 2001 the Wassenaar members adopted the first amendment to the initial elements, committing themselves to preventing terrorist organizations and individuals from acquiring conventional arms and dual-use goods and technologies that could be used for military purposes.[82] Without anything so formal, the members of the arrangement have used their plenary sessions for informal consultations about difficult situations, for example, reportedly to coordinate a ban on transfers to the Taliban when the implications of its rule for Afghanistan became apparent.

It is very easy to be critical of Wassenaar, even as a transparency measure. But one has to remember the lack of international consensus on the need for restraint on conventional arms or technology transfers, in contrast to that supporting efforts to prevent the proliferation of nuclear, chemical, or biological weapons. In addition, in today's ferociously competitive arms-export market, few countries have an incentive to turn aside an opportunity to make a sale. Transparency is certainly not restraint, but this is a potentially useful forum in which consensus might be created. When a group of West African states led by Mali undertook a moratorium on arms imports, they turned to the Wassenaar Arrangement as the one existing supplier forum; the Wassenaar members responded by endorsing the moratorium at their 1997 annual plenary.[83] Given the numerous prior failures to find a mechanism to restrain international arms transfers, the arrangement is probably best seen as "a glass half-full."

The Missile Technology Control Regime (MTCR)

Of all the advanced conventional weapons that are spreading throughout the Third World, ballistic missiles have received by far the greatest attention from policymakers. If one's concern is the potential threat to the United States or forward-deployed U.S. forces, then the attention to missiles is understandable. From the broader perspective of the proliferation of weapons that are most likely to be used in conflict or to cause the most casualties, however, the intense focus on ballistic missiles is less easy to accept.

Most experts emphasize three reasons for singling out ballistic missiles as a threat. The first is the lack of effective defenses. Of all the potential delivery vehicles, only ballistic missiles face few effective defenses at present. Second, ballistic missiles are significantly faster than other delivery vehicles, especially over middle-range and long distances. This offers the possibility of surprise and diminishes the chances that an adversary could mount effective civil defense. The latter is important for reducing the potential casualties from an attack using weapons of mass destruction. Third, missiles promise significant psychological and political effects. Ever since the German V-1 cruise missile and V-2 ballistic missile attacks in World War II, missiles have carried a special psychological power, sometimes exceeding their actual military impact.

The United States launched the Missile Technology Control Regime (MTCR) in 1987 in an attempt to curb the spread of ballistic-missile and missile technology. Modeled on other suppliers' arrangements to govern exports related to nuclear, biological, and chemical weapons proliferation, the MTCR focuses on controlling exports of missiles and missile technology for systems with payloads of more than five hundred kilograms and ranges of more than three hundred kilometers. The MTCR has grown from its initial seven members—the United States, Canada, France, West Germany, Italy, Japan, and Great Britain—to thirty-three full members.

The MTCR has been controversial from the beginning. First, in conception and initial operation the MTCR was a classic export-control regime based on denial by suppliers. As such, it was subject to the same dual criticisms of discrimination, on the one hand, and insufficient scope and effectiveness, on the other, that all such regimes confront. In addition, with the United States and some other industrialized countries increasingly interested in defenses against ballistic missiles, some critics charge that the MTCR is an effort to improve the chances that those defenses will be effective. This is the kind of arms control, they contend, that is designed primarily to make it safer and easier for the industrialized states to intervene in the developing world.

Other arguments over MTCR concern its effectiveness, particularly in response to the threat of weapons of mass destruction. Concentrating on missiles could give a false sense of security that one is doing something significant about this threat, especially if there is no comparable effort to address other potential delivery means.

The other critique of the MTCR's effectiveness centers on whether it can effectively inhibit the spread of missile technology. Some analysts argue that it has successfully dampened countries' efforts, particularly those indigenous production programs that depend heavily on imported technology. They cite successes such as the suppression of the joint Argentine, Egyptian, and Iraqi Condor II ballistic-missile program and of South African and Central European missile activities. Others respond that delay is the best that can be achieved, citing continuing programs by Iran, North Korea, and Iraq.

Finally, even if the MTCR works, critics question whether it is worth the strain it puts on relations between suppliers or between suppliers and recipients. Over the years the MTCR has caused tension in U.S. relations with a number of its European allies and with the former Soviet Union and China. As part of its efforts to counter U.S. proposals for national missile defenses, for example, Russia has proposed a "global control system" outside the MTCR. Others, however, regard the MTCR as the prototype of new arms-control approaches based on cooperative responses to emerging threats. Much of one's view of MTCR depends on whether one sees the effort as serving general international goals or U.S. national security interests, and what one thinks about the efficacy of nonproliferation efforts more generally.

Conclusion

To date, the record of attempts to control the spread of conventional weapons is mixed at best. The light-weapons problem is receiving significantly more attention and creative energy, but the small measures that are feasible simply do not seem to add up to enough in the face of the huge challenges posed by conflict-ridden regions. For major weapons, the economic pressures to export remain so strong for producers today that it is hard to imagine who would undertake the initiative for multilateral supplier restraint. Individual cases can frequently be justified within particular contexts in spite of the cumulative negative effects. And it is discouraging to remember that the drop in the total volume of the trade in advanced weapons in the 1990s reflected two major developments. The end of the cold war was the key factor. But the continuing economic troubles besetting developing countries, from the general recession of the early 1990s to lower oil prices through much of the decade to the Asian financial crisis of 1997, also depressed the market. This suggests that the decline in the international market for major weapons was the effect of broader political and economic forces rather than a drop in inherent demand. If so, then without other efforts to resolve fundamental conflicts or political motives to acquire arms, economic growth or revival in the developing world could be expected to restore high levels of arms imports.

More broadly, arms-transfers issues, for both light and major weapons, are intimately tied to international, regional, and national politics. The stigma associated with "weapons of mass destruction," which aids efforts for their disarmament and nonproliferation, does not apply.[84] In contrast, the right of national self-defense is enshrined in the UN Charter, and conventional weapons are the mainstay of military and police forces worldwide. Every nation in the world participates in the arms trade to some extent. And an argument can be made that in an anarchic world, where nations remain ultimately responsible for the security of their citizens, arms transfers serve the cause of peace and stability. If the resources of governments to pursue nonproliferation are limited, do conventional weapons deserve much attention?

In reality, the choices are not so stark. An international effort by suppliers to put significant restraints on their exports is unlikely in this decade unless some shock forces a substantial change in priorities. But individual suppliers will continue to regulate their exports to ensure that they meet national goals. In addition, there may be continuing efforts such as the MTCR to restrain the spread of particular technologies. Transparency measures such as the UN arms register may increase the amount of attention arms transfers receive. In recent years regional efforts, including those where many would have argued indigenous peace efforts were impossible, have become a significant force. The light-weapons issue is a fundamental part of the new and welcome recognition of linkages between security and development.

Notes

The views expressed in this chapter are those of the author. They do not reflect conclusions or recommendations by the National Academies.

1. "Light weapons," according to one leading scholar, include "all those conventional munitions that can be carried by an individual combatant or by a light vehicle operating on back-country roads." Michael T. Klare, "The Global Trade in Light Weapons and the International System in the Post–Cold War Era," in *Lethal Commerce: The Global Trade in Small Arms and Light Weapons,* ed. Jeffrey Boutwell, Michael T. Klare, and Laura W. Reed (Cambridge: American Academy of Arts and Sciences, 1995), 33.

2. Two examinations of U.S. policy from different perspectives are Michael T. Klare, *American Arms Supermarket* (Austin: University of Texas Press, 1984), and Paul Y. Hammond et al., *The Reluctant Supplier: U.S. Decisionmaking for Arms Sales* (Cambridge, Mass.: Oelgeschalger, Gunn & Hain, 1983).

3. Andrew J. Pierre, *The Global Politics of Arms Sales* (Princeton: Princeton University Press, 1982), 73–82.

4. See, for example, the statistics presented each year by the U.S. Arms Control and Disarmament Agency in its *World Military Expenditures and Arms Transfers* (Washington, D.C.: U.S. ACDA). As a candidate, Jimmy Carter declared that the United States should not be "both the world's leading champion of peace and the world's leading supplier of the weapons of war," and from the beginning his efforts at arms-transfers restraint were mired in controversy over who was "number one."

5. ACDA, for example, estimated that during the 1980s forty-one countries supplied

weapons to one side or the other during the Iran–Iraq war. It is worth noting that ACDA estimated that twenty-eight of them supplied both sides. U.S. Arms Control and Disarmament Agency, *World Military Expenditures and Arms Transfers 1988* (Washington, D.C.: U.S. ACDA), 22.

6. In the mid-1980s, for example, Brazil exported more than 80 percent of its military production, followed by Italy at more than 60 percent, Israel at more than 50 percent, and France at almost 50 percent. By contrast, the United States exported less than 20 percent of the arms it produced. The figures were compiled by the Office of Technology Assessment from reports by ACDA and SIPRI. U.S. Congress, Office of Technology Assessment, *Global Arms Trade: Commerce in Advanced Military Technology and Weapons* (Washington, D.C.: U.S. Government Printing Office, 1991), 6.

7. U.S. ACDA, *World Military Expenditures and Arms Transfers 1972–1982* (Washington, D.C.: U.S. ACDA, 1984), 99.

8. U.S. ACDA, *World Military Expenditures and Arms Transfers 1989* (Washington, D.C.: U.S. ACDA, 1990), 129.

9. Michael Brzoska and Thomas Ohlson, *Arms Transfers to the Third World 1971–85* (New York: Oxford University Press, 1987), 11.

10. Ibid., 15–16.

11. A good survey of the trends up to the early 1990s can be found in Richard A. Bitzinger, *The Globalization of Arms Production: Defense Markets in Transition* (Washington, D.C.: Defense Budget Project, 1993).

12. Office of Technology Assessment, *Global Arms Trade,* 8.

13. The Small Arms Survey, a project based at the Graduate Institute of International Studies in Geneva, Switzerland, is attempting to develop systematic data on light weapons production and trade. The project's website is www.smallarmssurvey.org/. Another important resource is the Norwegian Initiative on Small Arms Transfers; its website is www.nisat.org.

14. Black markets are the illegal trade, which may include covert transfers by governments through illicit channels. Gray markets refer to the trade in equipment and technology that may have both civilian and military purposes. The Norwegian Initiative on Small Arms Transfers compiles reports on illicit transfers.

15. Richard F. Grimmett, *Conventional Arms Transfers to Developing Nations, 1994–2001* (Washington, D.C.: Congressional Research Service, 2002), 3.

16. Ibid., 5. Whether to count—and emphasize—agreements or deliveries has long been debated among students of international arms transfers. Very broadly, agreements are best regarded as a political measure of the relationship between buyer and seller, while deliveries reflect the potential military impact of the arms acquired.

17. These figures are cited in Michael Renner, "Arms Control Orphans," *Bulletin of the Atomic Scientists* (Jan.–Feb. 1999): 24–26, available at www.thebulletin.org/issues/1999/jf99/jf99renner.html. The footnotes in Renner's monograph, *Small Arms, Big Impact: The Next Challenge of Disarmament* (Washington, D.C.: Worldwatch Institute, 1997) are a good source for the origins of various commonly cited statistics and estimates. The monograph is available online at www.secure.worldwatch.org/cgi-bin/wwinst/EWWP0137?7sVWkMTf;;40.

18. Grimmett, *Conventional Arms Transfers,* 71. Rankings, especially among second-tier suppliers, can shift dramatically from one year to the next. A single large sale can make a significant difference.

19. Ibid., 3, 71. The figure for Russian agreements in 2001 was an estimated $5.8 billion, or

22 percent of the total. The 2002 SIPRI Yearbook actually puts Russia in first place, but this is based on deliveries, and some Russian experts disputed the ranking because SIPRI assigns comparable weapons the same dollar value rather than attempting to determine the actual contract prices. Lyuba Pronina, "Report: Russia Is Top Arms Dealer," *Moscow Times,* June 14, 2002.

20. Grimmett, *Conventional Arms Transfers,* 10–11. The end of the Soviet military aid program did remove a number of major recipient states from the top ranks, however. In particular, Cuba, Vietnam, and Angola no longer figured in the "Top 10" among Third World arms recipients after the late 1980s. International arms embargoes then removed Iraq from the top rankings as well.

21. Ibid., 12.

22. Erik Pages, "Defense Mergers: Weapons Cost, Innovation, and International Arms Industry Cooperation," in *Arming the Future: A Defense Industry for the 21st Century,* ed. Ann R. Markusen and Sean S. Costigan (New York: Council on Foreign Relations, 1999), 209.

23. Igor Khripunov, "The Politics and Economics of Russia's Conventional Arms Transfers," in *Dangerous Weapons, Desperate States: Russia, Belarus, Kazakstan, and Ukraine,* ed. Gary K. Bertsch and William C. Potter (New York: Routledge, 1999), 135.

24. See, for example, David Gold, "The Changing Economics of the Arms Trade," in Markusen and Costigan, *Arming the Future.*

25. "Survey: Global Defense Industry," *The Economist,* June 14, 1997, 6.

26. Grimmett, *Conventional Arms Transfers,* 71.

27. Richard F. Grimmett, *Conventional Arms Transfers to the Third World, 1986–93* (Washington, D.C.: Congressional Research Service, 1994), 50.

28. Grimmett, *Conventional Arms Transfers* (2002), 71. The estimated value of Russian arms-transfers agreements between 1994 and 2001 was $39.9 billion, compared with $91.2 billion for the United States.

29. Presidents Clinton and Yeltsin had agreed in 1995 that Russia would not undertake new agreements with Iran after fulfilling its existing contracts, but the Russian government withdrew from the agreement in the fall of 2000. Wade Boese, "Russia to Bow Out of 1995 Deal Banning Arms Trade with Iran," *Arms Control Today* (Dec. 2000), available at www.armscontrol.org/act/2000_12/rusirandec00.asp.

30. Bonn International Center for Conversion, *Conversion Survey 1997* (Bonn: Bonn International Center for Conversion, 1997), 115.

31. Paul F. Pineo and Lora Lumpe, *Recycled Weapons* (Washington, D.C.: Federation of American Scientists, 1996), 14.

32. An excellent overview of the problem may be found in Lora Lumpe, ed., *Running Guns: The Global Black Market in Small Arms* (London: Zed Books, 2000).

33. Bonn International Center for Conversion, *Conversion Survey 1997: Global Disarmament and Disposal of Surplus Weapons* (New York: Oxford University Press, 1997), 124.

34. Phil Williams, "Drugs and Guns," *Bulletin of the Atomic Scientists* (Jan.–Feb. 1999): 46–47.

35. "Special Report: Weapons Bazaar," *U.S. News and World Report,* Dec. 9, 1996: 27.

36. Williams, "Drugs and Guns," 47–48.

37. World Bank, *Post-Conflict Reconstruction: The Role of the World Bank* (Washington, D.C.: International Bank for Reconstruction and Development, 1998), 2.

38. The figures are from the SIPRI website announcement of the 2002 Yearbook, www.editors.sipri.se/pubs/yb02/app01a.htmlreport.

39. Judith Miller, "UN Workers Become Targets in Angry Lands," *New York Times,* Sept.

19, 1999, A1, A6. For a discussion of the problems facing the International Red Cross, see Michael Ignatieff, "Unarmed Warriors," *New Yorker,* March 24, 1997, 54–71.

40. For a discussion of El Salvador, where by some reports civilian casualties have been as high in the postconflict period as during the twelve-year civil war, see Edward J. Laurance, *The New Field of Microdisarmament: Addressing the Proliferation and Buildup of Small Arms and Light Weapons* (Bonn: Bonn International Center for Conversion, 1996), 60.

41. The recent international attention to the problems of "conflict diamonds" is an example. An unusually candid UN report on the problems in Angola is United Nations Security Council, *Report of the Panel of Experts on Violations of Security Council Sanctions against UNITA* (March 10, 2000, S/2000/203), available online at www.un.org/Docs/sc/committees/Angola/AngolaSpecEng.htm.

42. For reports on surplus weapons, large and small, see the publications of the Bonn International Center for Conversion at www.bicc.de.

43. Cited in Renner, "Arms Control Orphans," 24.

44. Small Arms Survey, *Small Arms Survey 2002: Counting the Human Cost* (New York: Oxford University Press, 2002), 5.

45. Renner, "Arms Control Orphans," 24–26.

46. One of the pioneering sources of such analysis is the Arms Project of Human Rights Watch; a list of reports can be found at www.hrw.org/about/projects/arms/index.htm. Serious research on the problem began in the mid-1990s and there is now an international group of scholars and analysts in nongovernmental organizations producing a steadily growing volume of studies. One volume that offers a good reflection of the research available is Jeffrey Boutwell and Michael T. Klare, eds., *Light Weapons and Civil Conflict: Controlling the Tools of Violence* (New York: Rowman and Littlefield, 1999).

47. This is the International Action Network on Small Arms, currently including more than 500 organizations from almost 100 countries; for further information see the IANSA website at www.iansa.org.

48. Lora Lumpe, *U.S. Foreign Military Training: Global Reach, Global Power, and Oversight Issues* (Albuquerque: Foreign Policy in Focus, May 2002), 1.

49. Quoted in Lumpe, *U.S. Foreign Military Training,* 5.

50. The report by Lumpe and the monitoring by the Federation of American Scientists reflect this concern that "security" may come at the expense of reform and support for human rights.

51. The original members of the International Campaign to Ban Land Mines were Handicap International, Human Rights Watch, Medico International, Mines Advisory Group, Physicians for Human Rights, and the Vietnam Veterans of America Foundation.

52. For a case study of the effort to ban land mines, see Motoko Mekata, "Building Partnerships toward a Common Goal: Experiences of the International Campaign to Ban Landmines," in Ann M. Florini, ed., *The Third Force: The Rise of Transnational Civil Society* (Washington, D.C.: Carnegie Endowment for International Peace, 2000), 143–76.

53. The Florini volume examines the broader question of the new and enhanced role of NGOs in international politics.

54. The founding document may be found at www.iansa.org/mission/m1.htm. The IANSA website also contains links to a number of other organizations and sources of information about small arms and light weapons.

55. United Nations, *Supplement to an Agenda for Peace* (New York: United Nations, Document A/50/60-S/1995/1, 1995).

56. United Nations, *General and Complete Disarmament: Small Arms* (New York: United Nations, Document A/52/298, Aug. 27, 1997), 9–10.

57. Returning former soldiers to productive economic activity is considered an appropriate activity for the World Bank. In a similar way, its funding for humanitarian demining is undertaken to return land to productive use.

58. The description of the work of the unit may be found at worldbank.org. Then key into the Search option: Conflict Prevention and Reconstruction Unit.

59. See, for example, the 1999 policy statements by the department on *Poverty and the Security Sector and Conflict Reduction and Humanitarian Assistance*. The DFID website is www.dfid.gov.uk/.

60. For an early argument for this approach, see Jo L. Husbands, "Controlling Transfers of Light Weapons: Linkages to Conflict Processes and Conflict Resolution Strategies," in Klare, *Lethal Commerce*.

61. Jacklyn Cock, "A Sociological Account of Light Weapons Proliferation in South Africa," in *Light Weapons and International Security*, Jasjit Singh, ed. (Dehli: Indian Pugwash Society and British American Security Information Council, 1995).

62. See, for example, the World Bank report cited above and the founding document of IANSA, which may be found at www.iansa.org/mission/m1.htm.

63. The Chemical Weapons Convention and the Biological Weapons Convention can be seen as other examples of this approach.

64. U.S. Department of State, *Hidden Killers 1998: The Global Landmine Crisis* (Washington, D.C.: U.S. Department of State, Sept. 1998).

65. The text of the convention may be found on the IANSA website at www.iansa.org/documents/regional/reg5.htm. See also William Godnick, *The Organization of American States and the 2001 United Nations Conference on the Illicit Trade in Small Arms and Light Weapons in All Its Aspects: Tackling the Illicit Trade in Small Arms and Light Weapons* (London: BASIC, International Alert, Saferworld, and the Arias Foundation for Peace and Human Progress, Jan. 2002).

66. The text of the program may be found on the IANSA website at www.iansa.org/documents/regional/reg6.htm.

67. Information about the protocol and the convention may be found at www.odccp.org/crime_cicp_signatures.html.

68. For a statement of the ultimate U.S. policy toward the conference, see John R. Bolton, Under Secretary for Arms Control and International Security, "Plenary Address to the UN Conference on the Illicit Trade in Small Arms and Light Weapons," July 9, 2001 (online at www.state.gov/t/us/rm/2001/index.cfm?docid=4038).

69. United Nations Conference on the Illicit Trade in Small Arms and Light Weapons in All Its Aspects, "Programme of Action" (online at http://disarmament.un.org/cab/poa.html).

70. See Edward J. Laurance, *Light Weapons and Intrastate Conflict: Early Warning Factors and Preventive Action* (New York: Carnegie Corporation, 1998).

71. Alexander L. George and Jane E. Holl, *The Warning-Response Problem and Missed Opportunities in Preventive Diplomacy* (New York: Carnegie Corporation, 1997).

72. See, for example, the description of the light weapons field manual, a joint project of

the Bonn International Center for Conversion and the Program on Security and Development at the Monterey Institute of International Studies, at www.sand.miis.edu/about.htm.

73. See, for example, the multivolume series of the Disarmament and Conflict Resolution Project of UNIDIR produced in 1995–97, especially *Managing Arms in Peace Processes: The Issues* (Geneva: UNIDIR, UNIDIR/96/46, 1996), and Cindy Collins and Thomas G. Weiss, *An Overview and Assessment of 1989–1996 Peace Operations Publications* (Providence: Brown University, Thomas J. Watson Institute for International Studies, 1997).

74. David DeClerq, *Destroying Small Arms and Light Weapons: Survey of Methods and Practical Guide* (Bonn: International Center for Conversion, 1999). Many mandates for peace operations, especially in the early 1990s, did not include weapons collection or destruction. See the UNIDIR volumes for discussion of specific cases.

75. See Laurance, *The New Field,* 81–85.

76. United States Senate, Report to the Congress, *Arms Transfer Policy* (Washington, D.C.: U.S. Government Printing Office, 1977), 12–13.

77. Congressional Research Service, *Changing Perspectives on U.S. Arms Transfer Policy*, report prepared for the Subcommittee on International Security and Scientific Affairs of the Committee on Foreign Affairs, U.S. House of Representatives (Washington, D.C.: U.S. Government Printing Office, 1981), 127.

78. White House, *Fact Sheet: Conventional Arms Transfers Policy*, Feb. 17, 1995.

79. Wassenaar is the town near The Hague, Netherlands, where the arrangement was negotiated.

80. "Initial Elements," adopted by the plenary of the Wassenaar Arrangement to govern its operation, July 11–12, 1996.

81. This reservation is included in the "Initial Elements."

82. Wade Boese, "Wassenaar Members Amend Founding Document," *Arms Control Today* (Jan.–Feb. 2002), reported on the web at www.armscontrol.org/act/2002_01-02/wassjanfeb02.asp.

83. Joseph P. Smaldone, "Mali and the West African Light Arms Moratorium," in Jeffrey Boutwell and Michael T. Klare, eds., *Light Weapons and Civil Conflict: Controlling the Tools of Violence* (New York: Rowman and Littlefield, 1999).

84. Land mines are the obvious exception to this generalization.

Chapter 4   # Information Technology and Security

DOROTHY E. DENNING

Like many other technologies, information technology can be used both to promote stability and security and to threaten the same. On the positive side of the ledger, it can be used to disseminate and exchange ideas and strategies for security, to gather support for peace missions and security programs, and to implement and coordinate security plans and operations. It has played an important role, for example, in the international campaign to ban land mines and is used by governments and their citizens to foster peace and security throughout the world. It is a critical element of all government security operations, from intelligence collection to command and control. It is used to hunt down terrorists and implement border controls.

On the negative side, information technology can be attacked and exploited in ways that threaten stability and security. An adversary can jam or take down computer and communications systems with physical weapons such as bombs, missiles, and electromagnetic weapons; use mass media to propagate lies to the entire world; and penetrate or attack computer networks for the purpose of stealing secret information or sabotaging data and systems.

This chapter will focus on the latter aspect of information technology, specifically on cyber threats to computer networks. These threats involve operations that compromise, damage, degrade, disrupt, deny, and destroy information stored on computer networks or that target network infrastructure. They include computer intrusions and the use of network "sniffers" to eavesdrop on network communications. They include the use of malicious software, namely, computer viruses, worms, and Trojan horses. They include denial-of-service attacks that halt or disrupt the operation of networked computers, usually by flooding them with traffic, and web defacements that replace a site's home page with cyber graffiti, false information, and statements of protest.

Cyber attacks can be conducted to support a nation's defense. For example, a government might eavesdrop on network communications to gather intelligence about terrorists or others who threaten its security, or it might jam or disrupt an enemy's network during a time of conflict. In these cases, the attacks are employed to strengthen national security, at least of the state conducting the operations.

Because this chapter focuses on information-technology-related threats to stability and security, it will concentrate on attacks that threaten the security of the United States or its citizens or allies, or that more generally threaten stability and peace in the world. It will not explore U.S. government-sponsored cyber attacks conducted for the purpose of national security. This chapter will also focus on the Internet and private networks (intranets and extranets) that use the suite of protocols based on the Internet protocol. Although there are other types of networks, many of these have been or will be replaced by Internet-protocol networks to save costs and provide interoperability.

The chapter first reviews trends and developments in information security incidents, showing that the situation has been and continues to be a growing problem. It then examines information-technology trends and developments and how they are contributing to the growing rate of security incidents. Next, it considers the prognosis for the future. Finally, it considers policy recommendations for addressing the threat.

Incident Trends and Developments

Although data on cyber security incidents are sparse, by most if not all accounts, the number and severity of incidents is increasing. For example, the Computer Emergency Response Team Coordination Center (CERT/CC) based at the Carnegie Mellon Software Engineering Institute has published data showing a dramatic increase in incidents reported during the past few years. The number of incidents reported rose from 2,134 in 1997 to 21,756 in 2000. Almost 35,000 incidents were reported to CERT/CC during the first three quarters of 2001 alone.[1] The significance of these numbers becomes even more apparent when one realizes that many, perhaps most, incidents are never reported to CERT/CC, or indeed to any third party. Further, each incident that is reported corresponds to an attack that can involve hundreds or even thousands of victims. For example, when a hacker defaces hundreds of websites at once, or a computer worm invades several hundred thousand web servers as it propagates, this is regarded as a single incident.

The Department of Defense has indicated a similar increase in incidents reported to its Joint Task Force Computer Network Operations (JTF-CNO). The number of events against Defense Department systems rose from 780 in 1997 to 28,106 in 2000. Of the 28,106 events in 2000, 369 represented successful intrusions.[2]

Defacements of websites have increased dramatically. Attrition.org, which recorded mirrors of defaced web pages until spring 2001, received reports of thirty-seven defacements in 1997. By 2000 the number was up to 5,822. Like the CERT/CC data, these numbers do not represent all defacements, and the numbers in 2001 could easily be on the order of several hundred per day. A few incidents have involved mass defacements of thousands or even tens of thousands of websites.

Rather than modify a website directly, an attacker can apply a "DNS hack." This involves tampering with an Internet server that manages the domain-name service, which is responsible for mapping domain names (e.g., georgetown.edu) to Internet-protocol addresses (numbers). The attacker modifies the mapping so that Internet traffic is redirected to the attacker's own website, where the desired messages are displayed.

The prevalence of computer viruses and worms has been increasing for the past several years. Message Labs, which scans its clients' e-mail for viruses, reported that one in 1,400 messages had a virus in 1999. The infection rate doubled to one in 700 in 2000 and then more than doubled to one in 300 in 2001. ICSA.net (now TrueSecure) also has reported an increase in infection rate, from ten computers per thousand in 1996 to ninety computers per thousand in 2000.[3]

Denial-of-service attacks, which until a few years ago were relatively unheard of, are now commonplace. A study conducted at the Cooperative Association for Internet Data Analysis (CAIDA) at the University of San Diego Supercomputer Center observed about 12,000 attacks against 5,000 different targets during a three-week period in February 2001.[4]

Fraud and extortion are also common. In March 2001 the FBI announced that ongoing computer hacking by organized criminal groups in Russia and the Ukraine had resulted in the theft of more than 1 million credit card numbers. The numbers had been taken from forty U.S. computer systems associated with e-commerce and e-banking companies in twenty states. After successfully hacking into a company, the Eastern European groups than attempted to extort the company, offering services to solve the computer vulnerability.[5]

Many attacks are extremely costly. According to Computer Economics of Carlsbad, California, the ILOVEYOU virus and its variants, which crippled computers in May 2000, was estimated to have cost $8.5 billion in damages, vastly exceeding the damages from any previous virus. In July and August 2001, the Code Red worm infected about a million servers and caused another $2.6 billion in damages. In April 2001 the International Chamber of Commerce announced it had shut down an online banking fraud worth an estimated $3.9 billion. Victims were duped by bogus get-rich-quick schemes involving fake documents.[6]

Beginning in 1996 the Computer Security Institute and the FBI have conducted a survey of CSI's members about computer crime incidents. Each year about five hundred companies respond. In 2001 the reported losses were $378 million, up from $266 million in 2000 and $124 million in 1999. In all three years, the largest category of losses involved theft of proprietary information.

A global survey conducted by *InformationWeek* and PricewaterhouseCoopers LLP in 2000 estimated that computer viruses and hacking took a $1.6 trillion toll on the worldwide economy that year. The cost to the United States alone was an estimated $266 billion, or more than 2.5 percent of the nation's gross domestic product.

Computer-related security incidents threaten the national and global economy. In addition to causing direct financial losses, they can erode public confidence in e-commerce and technology in general. Attacks against military systems can affect national security, particularly if they compromise classified information or important military operations. Attacks against critical infrastructures, such as those used to provide power or water, can have potentially devastating consequences on our daily lives. Although cyber attacks against these infrastructures have so far been limited, the potential for serious harm is real.

Technology Trends and Developments

The growing threat from cyber attacks is mainly a function of trends and developments in information technology. Seven trends are especially important in this regard: the growing ubiquity of information technology, the increasing "groundedness" of cyberspace, the increasing mobility of information and information technology, the development of hacking tools, improvements in information technology performance, the emergence of new vulnerabilities, and mounting information security challenges.

The Growth of Information Technology

Information technology is becoming increasingly pervasive and connected. It is spreading throughout the world, in both our homes and workplaces. It is integrated into everything from appliances and vehicles to processes and infrastructures. Automation and connectivity are growing by leaps and bounds, aided by advances in computing and telecommunications technology. Much of the growth and connectivity is taking place on the Internet and the private Internet-protocol networks operated by organizations and their extended enterprises. This trend toward ubiquitous computing is increasing the challenges to information security. There are more perpetrators, more targets, and more opportunities to exploit, disrupt, and sabotage systems. There are more websites with information and tools for attacking information and systems.

The impact is partially illustrated by the rapid and widespread propagation of computer viruses and worms. The ILOVEYOU virus, mentioned above, infected the personal computers of tens of millions of users worldwide. All a recipient had to do to activate the virus was open an e-mail message containing the virus as an attachment. Once activated, the virus spread through e-mail to all of the persons listed in the user's address book.

The Code Red worm, which spread from one Internet computer server to another without any human intervention, reached hundreds of thousands of machines before its rate of proliferation slowed down. During a single fourteen-hour period on July 19, 2001, CAIDA observed the infection of more than 359,000 computers. While 43 percent of these were in the United States, countries all over the world were victimized.[7] The worm propagated itself by scanning the Internet for systems that had a particular vulnerability common to many machines. When it found one, it copied its code to the new victim. It also launched a denial-of-service assault against the Internet address for the White House by bombarding it with traffic (which the White House averted by changing its Internet-protocol address). Although many victims eradicated the worm and repaired their machines, others did not, contributing to its spread. Further, variants of the worm that exploited other vulnerabilities appeared, with the potential to cause even greater harm.

Another result of the spread of technology is that cyber attacks can come from almost anywhere in the world. Neither distance nor geography is a factor. An attacker in China, for example, can penetrate a system in the United States, and then use that system as a launching pad for attacking a system in Japan. It is not unusual for hackers to "loop" through computers in multiple targets on their way to their ultimate target. This conceals their tracks and makes investigations extremely difficult, because it requires cooperation from law enforcement agencies and service providers in all countries involved.

There have been numerous incidents of attackers gaining access to U.S. military computers. Before and during the Gulf War, for example, hackers from the Netherlands penetrated computer systems at thirty-four American military sites on the Internet, including sites that were directly supporting Operations Desert Storm and Desert Shield. They browsed through files and obtained information about the exact location of U.S. troops, the types of weapons they had, the capabilities of the Patriot missile, and the movement of American warships in the gulf region. According to some sources, the hackers tried to sell the pilfered information to Iraq, but their offer was declined.[8] A few years earlier, German hackers did successfully sell documents taken from Defense Department computers to the KGB.[9] More recently, hackers located in Russia have been snooping through Defense Department computers for the past several years. The investigation into this security breach, originally code-named "Moonlight Maze" but subsequently changed to "Storm Cloud," apparently has yet to determine whether the spies are operating on behalf of the Russian government or some other entity.

Although no break-ins have been attributed to terrorists, the *Detroit News* reported in November 1998 that Khalid Ibrahim, who claimed to be a member of the militant Indian separatist group Harkat-ul-Ansar, had tried to buy military software from hackers who had stolen it from Defense Department computers they had penetrated. Harkat-ul-Ansar had declared war on the United States following the August cruise-missile attack on a suspected terrorist training camp in Afghanistan run by Osama bin Laden, which allegedly killed nine of their members.[10]

Another effect of the spread of information technology is that many conflicts in the world now have a cyberspace component. For example, as Palestinian rioters clashed with Israeli forces in the fall of 2000, Arab and Israeli hackers took to cyberspace to participate in the action. According to the Middle East Intelligence Bulletin, the cyberwar began in October, shortly after the Lebanese Shi'ite Hezbollah movement abducted three Israeli soldiers. Pro-Israeli hackers responded by crippling the guerrilla movement's website, which had been displaying videos of Palestinians killed in recent clashes and called on Palestinians to kill as many Israelis as possible. Pro-Palestinian hackers retaliated, shutting down the main website of the Israeli government and the website of the Israeli Foreign Ministry. From there the cyberwar escalated. An Israeli hacker planted the star of David and some Hebrew text on one of Hezbollah's mirror sites, while pro-Palestinian hackers attacked additional Israeli sites, including those of the Bank of Israel and the Tel Aviv Stock Exchange. In addition to web defacements, hackers launched denial-of-service attacks against Internet service providers and other sites. The attacks continued for many months. In January 2001, iDefense reported that more than forty hackers from twenty-three countries had hit the websites of eight governments as well as numerous commercial sites.[11]

According to iDefense, some of the pro-Palestinian attackers had connections to terrorist organizations. One of these was UNITY, a Muslim extremist group with ties to Hezbollah. The hackers launched a coordinated, multiphase denial-of-service attack, first against official Israeli government sites, second against Israeli financial sites, third against Israeli ISPs, and fourth against "Zionist e-Commerce" sites. The other group, al-Muhajiroun, was said to have ties with a number of Muslim terrorist organizations as well as bin Laden. The London-based group directed their members to a website, where at the click of a mouse members could join an automated flooding attack against Israeli sites that were attacking Moqawama (Islamic resistance) sites. iDefense also noted that UNITY recruited and organized a third group, Iron Guard, which conducted more technically sophisticated attacks. According to a Canadian government report, the group's call for cyber jihad was supported and promoted by al-Muhajiroun.[12]

Hackers protesting the September 11 terrorist attacks against the United States have taken to the Internet to voice their rage. One hacker, "Fluffi Bunny," redirected tens of thousands of websites to one containing a rant about religion and the message, "If you want to see the Internet again, give us Mr. bin Laden and $5 million dollars in a brown paper page. Love, Fluffi B."[13] Another group, called the Dispatchers, with sixty members worldwide, has defaced hundreds of websites and launched denial-of-service attacks. Led by a twenty-one-year-old security worker, "Hackah Jak" from Ohio, the group announced that it would destroy web servers and Internet access in Afghanistan and target nations that support terrorists. Their targets have included the Iranian Ministry of Interior, the presidential palace of Afghanistan, and Palestinian ISPs.[14] A third group, called Young Intelligent Hackers against Terror (YIHAT), said it penetrated the systems of two Arabic banks with ties to bin Laden, although officials from the banks denied that any security breaches occurred. The group, which says that its mission is to stop the funding sources of terrorism, issued a plea to corporations to make their networks available to group members for the purpose of providing the electronic equivalent of a terrorist training camp.[15]

While condemning the September 11 attacks, one group of Muslim hackers, GForce Pakistan, said it stood by bin Laden. "Osama bin Laden is a holy fighter, and whatever he says makes sense," one of this group's web defacements read. The modified web page warned that the group planned to hit major U.S. military and British websites and proclaimed an "Al-Qaeda Alliance Online." Another GForce defacement contained similar messages, along with images of badly mutilated children who had been killed by Israeli soldiers.[16]

Web defacements and denial-of-service attacks have accompanied numerous other real-world conflicts and events, including the Kosovo conflict, the conflict in Kashmir, and various incidents involving China. The enthusiastic hackers may be motivated as much by their desire to impress their peers and by the fun and challenge of it all as by their patriotism. Often they direct their attacks against each other. Fluffi Bunny, for example, apparently defaced YIHAT's website. After suffering denial-of-service attacks as well, YIHAT announced that it was moving underground.

To date terrorists have been implicated in only a few computer attacks, and none was particularly damaging. In addition to the terrorist connections mentioned above, an offshoot of the Liberation Tigers of Tamil Eelam (LTTE) was said to be responsible for an e-mail bombing against Sri Lankan embassies over a two-week period in 1998. The group swamped Sri Lankan embassies with thousands of electronic mail messages, in what some intelligence agencies characterized as the first computer attack by terrorists. The messages read, "We are the Internet Black Tigers and we're doing this to disrupt your communications."[17]

Although terrorists have not engaged in many cyber attacks, they are using the Internet extensively to communicate and coordinate their activities. For example, some of the nineteen hijackers involved in the September 11 terrorist attacks against the World Trade Center and Pentagon exchanged e-mail messages in a mix of English and Arabic.[18] They also used the web to find information about crop dusters and to book airline tickets. As early as 1996 the Afghani headquarters of bin Laden was equipped with computers and communications equipment. Egyptian "Afghan" computer experts were said to have helped devise a communication network that used the web, e-mail, and electronic bulletin boards.[19]

The Increasing Groundedness of Cyberspace

Cyberspace, and the Internet specifically, is often viewed as a virtual world that transcends space and time, a world without borders or, by implication, border guards. This view has never been completely accurate, as computers reside in a physical world where laws apply, and many countries control access to the Internet or filter incoming e-mail and access to websites. Still, it has a ring of truth, as bits generally flow freely through the Internet without regard to physical geography. This was particularly true in the early days of the Internet (then ARPANET), when the net was used by researchers for e-mail, file transfer, and remote login to supercomputers.

Over time computer networks became increasingly integrated into real-world processes. Now these networks play a critical role in practically every sector of the economy and government operation. Thus attacks on these networks have real-world consequences. Governments are particularly concerned about terrorist and state-sponsored attacks against the critical infrastructures that constitute their national life support systems. The Clinton administration defined eight of these: telecommunications, banking and finance, electrical power, oil and gas distribution and storage, water supply, transportation, emergency services, and government services.

There have been numerous attacks against these infrastructures. Hackers have invaded the public phone networks, compromising nearly every category of activity, including switching and operations, administration, maintenance, and provisioning. They have crashed or disrupted signal transfer points, traffic switches, operations, administration, maintenance, and provisioning systems, and other network elements. They have planted "time-bomb" programs designed to shut down major switching hubs and have disrupted emergency 911 services throughout the Eastern Seaboard.[20]

In March 1997 one teenage hacker penetrated and disabled a telephone company computer that serviced the Worcester, Massachusetts, airport. As a result, telephone service to the Federal Aviation Administration control tower, the airport fire department, airport security, the weather service, and various private air-freight companies was cut off for six hours. Later in the day, the juvenile disabled another telephone company computer, this time causing an outage in the Rutland area, near Worcester. The lost service caused financial damages and threatened public health and public safety.[21]

Banks and financial systems are a popular target of cyber criminals. The usual motive is financial gain, and perpetrators have stolen or attempted to steal tens of millions of dollars. In one case of sabotage, a computer operator at Reuters in Hong Kong tampered with the dealing-room systems of five of the company's bank clients. In November 1996 he programmed the systems to delete key operating system files after a delay long enough to allow him to leave the building. When the "time bombs" exploded, the systems crashed. They were partially restored by the next morning, but it took another day before they were fully operational. However, the banks said the tampering did not significantly affect trading and that neither they nor their clients experienced losses.[22]

An overflow of raw sewage on the sunshine coast of Australia in early 2000 was linked to a forty-nine-year-old Brisbane man, who allegedly penetrated the Maroochy Shire Council's waste management system and used radio transmissions to alter pump station operations. A million liters of raw sewage spilled into public parks and creeks on Queensland's sunshine coast, killing marine life, turning the water black, and creating an overpowering stench. A former employee of the company that had installed the system, the man was angry after being rejected for a council job.[23]

Computer viruses and worms have disrupted the operations of systems used to coordinate and control the business processes associated with critical infrastructures. The Code Red worm, for example, was responsible for the delay of fifty-five Japan Airlines flights on August 9, 2001. The computer shutdown caused by the worm affected ticketing and check-in services for the carrier and its affiliates.[24] The FBI arrested a hacker in Houston for plotting to launch a worm that could have shut down 911 services by forcing the infected computers to dial 911. According to court documents, a quarter-million computers could have been infected in just three days.[25]

Increasingly, Internet-protocol networks are grounded in the physical world through network-connected sensors and actuators. Web-based portals are being developed for people, objects, places, events, and processes, as well as the usual document collections. These portals can provide access to cameras and other types of sensors, actuators, and controls, allowing one to view and alter the physical world, and to determine where devices are located. They can be used to control satellites, vehicles, robots, and other objects. According to *Federal Computer Week,* the U.S. Air Force is requiring that all command-and-control systems and weapons systems be web-enabled using commercial technologies.[26] The motivation is improved access to data and lower costs, but the requirement could expose these systems to greater risks.

Many other critical infrastructures are or will be controlled through networks that use Internet protocols. For example, a Midwest independent system operator (ISO) will use an Internet-protocol-based network to monitor and control the transmission of electrical power from independent power producers throughout a fourteen-state area in the Midwest.[27] Similar ISOs exist in other regions of the country, and in the spring of 2001, hackers penetrated the development system of the California ISO. Although the system was used only for testing and not production, the security breach, which lasted for seventeen days, raised concerns about the security of the networks used to control energy distribution.

The impact of all these developments is that cyber attacks that exploit vulnerabilities in Internet-protocol networks will have real-world consequences, beyond the basic costs and inconveniences they already involve. They could seriously endanger lives and the environment. Information security will become increasingly important, not only to protecting information and systems, but to protecting life itself. Most of the attacks today involve personal computers and Internet servers, but tomorrow's attacks could involve automobiles, wearable devices, and Internet appliances, with potentially more serious, even deadly, consequences.

The Increasing Mobility of Information and Information Technology

Information and information technology have become increasingly mobile. People and devices can be anywhere and they can move. Software and data can be stored and transmitted anywhere and at any time through electronic mail, the Web, and peer-to-peer sharing. Mobility has generally made the task of protecting information more difficult. It has extended an organization's network security perimeter from the workplace to homes, airports, and hotel rooms. Information once confined to office networks can make its way to home PCs, laptop computers, and hand-held devices, which may be less protected physically. Each year tens of thousands of laptops are reported lost or stolen, many with extremely sensitive information, including government classified information. After John Deutch retired as director of the CIA in 1996, for example, the CIA found classified information on the computer he had been given to use at home. The computer, which had been designated for unclassified use only, had been used to access the Internet, Deutch's bank, and Defense Department computers.[28] Although there was no evidence that any information had been compromised, the potential for compromise by a foreign intelligence service was certainly present.

Mobile software poses a major security challenge. Computer viruses, worms, Trojan horses, and other forms of malicious code can and do enter computers through e-mail, the web, and other Internet portals. They account for a substantial portion of all computer security incidents and can spread at alarming rates. Wireless communications allow small, battery-operated devices to tie into computer networks. These may be vulnerable to a new type of denial-of-service attack, namely, one that attempts to keep a device active (as opposed to in "sleep" mode) in order to drain its battery.[29]

The Development of Hacking Tools

The tools and methods used to attack computer networks have become more abundant. They are readily acquired from numerous websites in countries all over the world. Typing "hacking tools" into one Internet search engine yielded 42,012 hits in March 2000. By September 2001 the same search engine yielded 158,000 hits. By some estimates there are now more than 60,000 computer viruses alone. For a few dollars, anyone can buy a disk containing thousands of them.

Testifying before the House Science Subcommittee on Technology on June 24, 1999, Ray Kammer, director of the National Institute of Standards and Technology (NIST), said, "One popular site has over 400,000 unique visitors per month downloading attacks. We estimate that at least thirty computer attack tools per month are written and published on the Internet." The NIST also examined 237 attack tools and found that 20 percent of them could remotely penetrate network elements and that 5 percent were effective against routers and firewalls.[30]

Attack tools have become more powerful as developers build on each other's work and program their own knowledge into the tools. The Nimda worm combines features of several previous viruses and worms in order to create a powerful worm that spreads by four channels: e-mail, web downloads, file sharing, and active scanning for and infection of vulnerable web servers. The e-mail component automatically e-mails itself to addresses in the victim's address book.

The advanced distributed denial-of-service tools have sophisticated command-and-control capabilities. The attacker runs client software to direct the actions of server software running on potentially thousands of previously compromised "zombie" computers. In February 2000 a Canadian teenager calling himself Mafiaboy used zombies at universities in California and elsewhere to launch a costly denial-of-service attack against Yahoo, CNN, eBay, and other e-commerce websites. Computer worms like Code Red can be used to compromise potential zombies and install the server software needed for such attacks. Upon installation, they can "report in" to a central server and then await instructions to begin an assault.

Many attack tools are easy to use. "Script kiddies" and others with malicious intent but little skill can download the tools and launch destructive attacks without even understanding how the tools work. E-mail worms can be constructed with Windows-based software such as the VBS Worm Generator. All the attacker needs to do is type in a subject line and message body for the e-mail message carrying the worm and check a few boxes. Many of the tools support mass attacks against a single target or against multiple targets simultaneously. The computers involved in these attacks may be compromised themselves, as in the case of zombies.

Improvements in Information Technology Performance

Information technology is getting smaller, faster, cheaper, and more powerful. Processor speeds are doubling approximately every eighteen months according to Moore's law. This yields a factor-of-ten improvement every five years and a factor-of-one-hundred improvement every ten. Storage capacity is increasing at a somewhat faster rate, doubling about every twelve months, and network capacity is growing still faster, doubling approximately every nine months. One implication of these performance trends is that spies can download secret documents faster, and from repositories that are getting larger. Those with high-speed Internet access can acquire megabytes of information in just a few seconds.

Computer viruses and worms can spread quickly over high-speed Internet connections. During the peak of its infection frenzy, the Code Red worm infected more than two thousand computers per minute.[31] A researcher at the University of California at Berkeley showed how a "Warhol Worm" could infect all vulnerable servers on the Internet in fifteen minutes to an hour. Researchers at Silicon Defense took the concept further, showing how a "Flash Worm" could do it in thirty seconds.[32]

At the same time, high-bandwidth data pipes and increased network traffic can make it more difficult to monitor networks for intrusions and other forms of abuse and to intercept particular traffic in support of a criminal investigation or foreign intelligence operation. Similarly, it can be harder to scan disks for viruses and other forms of malicious code and to conduct computer forensics examinations if more data is stored.

The lag of processor improvements relative to those of storage and networks could aggravate the problem, although multiprocessor supercomputers and distributed computing can be used to compensate. A distributed approach is already used by many network-based intrusion-detection systems and to break encryption keys in criminal investigations. Breakthrough processor technologies such as quantum and DNA computing might also counter the lag, but these technologies represent long-term solutions and also give the opponent an advantage in code breaking. If network traffic grows faster than storage capacity, long-term retention of logs that record traffic could also be an even greater challenge than it is today.

The Emergence of New Vulnerabilities

Information technology is growing in complexity, owing to advances in technology and software development and the growing number of components to build upon. Systems are larger and have increasing numbers of components, features, and interactions. Many feature interactions are not anticipated. This growing complexity has made it extremely difficult to develop and deploy information technology products that are free of vulnerabilities. Even if a particular component is hardened against attack, the component may interact with new or upgraded components in ways that introduce new vulnerabilities. Experience has shown time and again that it is impossible to eliminate all vulnerabilities from computer systems despite our best efforts. Even our most trusted firewalls and other security products have been found to have weaknesses. Nothing seems to be immune.

Indeed, the number of vulnerabilities in software products reported to CERT/ CC has increased in recent years, from 262 in 1998 to 1,090 in 2000. In the first three quarters of 2001, CERT/CC received reports of 1,820 vulnerabilities, or more than six per day. Even if products are secure, they can be configured or used in ways that are not. Users can pick weak passwords and system administrators can fail to install security patches. In September 2001 the SANS (System Administration, Networking, and Security) Institute and the FBI issued a report identifying the top twenty Internet vulnerabilities.[33] At the top of the list was default installs of operating system and applications. Functions were enabled that were not needed and had security flaws. Second on the list was accounts with no passwords or weak ones.

The JTF-CNO found that the vast majority of reported intrusions into Defense Department computers exploited known vulnerabilities that were easily prevented. Major General James D. Bryan, commander of the office, noted that some employees failed to pick strong passwords, the most common password being "password."[34]

Many federal government systems remain insecure despite efforts to protect them from attack. Testifying before the Senate Committee on Governmental Affairs following the terrorist attacks against the World Trade Center and Pentagon, the General Accounting Office (GAO) noted that "independent audits continue to identify persistent, significant information security weaknesses that place virtually all major federal agencies' operations at high risk of tampering and disruption."[35] The GAO further noted: "An underlying deficiency impeding progress is the lack of a national plan that fully defines the roles and responsibilities of key participants and establishes interim objectives. Accordingly, we have recommended that the Assistant to the President for National Security Affairs ensure that the government's critical infrastructure strategy clearly define specific roles and responsibilities, develop interim objectives and milestones for achieving adequate protection, and define performance measures for accountability."

As information systems become "smarter" and more "like us," they may also become more vulnerable to attack. Humans are riddled with vulnerabilities. We can be deceived, bribed, robbed, and killed. Intelligent software agents may exhibit similar vulnerabilities as they mimic their human counterparts. There is no reason to believe that smarter systems will necessarily mean increased security.

The bottom line is that we will never have secure systems. The underlying technology will always have vulnerabilities and people will always make mistakes. Furthermore, insiders with access to information will commit intended acts of espionage and sabotage. Thus an important component of any security program is the capability to detect and respond to security breaches that do occur.

Mounting Information Security Challenges

Security technologies have advanced considerably in such areas as cryptography, biometrics, intrusion detection, antiviral protection, decoy environments, vulnerability scanning, and incident response. In addition, companies now offer managed security services, including remote monitoring for vulnerabilities and intrusions. While these advances have no doubt helped ward off numerous attacks, overall they have not kept up with the rising threat, as witnessed by the incident data presented earlier.

Security technologies, particularly those that hide information, have also been a boon to criminals and terrorists. In March 2000 George Tenet, then director of the CIA, reported that "terrorist groups, including Hezbollah, Hamas, the Abu Nidal organization, and bin Ladin's Al Qaeda organization are using computerized files, e-mail, and encryption to support their operations."[36] Ramzi Yousef, an associate of bin Laden and member of the international terrorist group responsible for bombing the World Trade Center in 1994 and a Manila Air airliner in late 1995, used encryption to hide details of further terrorist attacks, including plans to blow up eleven U.S.-owned commercial airliners in the Far East. Wadith El Hage, another bin Laden associate, who was convicted of conspiracy and perjury in the East Africa embassy bombings, sent encrypted e-mails to his associates in Al Qaeda. The Aum Shinrikyo cult, which gassed the Tokyo subway in March 1995, killing twelve people and injuring 6,000, also used encryption to protect their computerized records, which included plans and intentions to deploy weapons of mass destruction in Japan and the United States.[37]

Although authorities successfully decrypted the evidence in these cases, this does not always happen. Furthermore, when terrorists encrypt their communications, intelligence agencies may be unable to decrypt them fast enough to prevent a terrorist attack. In addition, other security technologies, such as steganography (which involves hiding the very existence of a message, often in an image) and the use of anonymity, can thwart authorities. In February 2001 *USA Today* reported that according to U.S. and foreign officials, bin Laden associates were "hiding maps and photographs of terrorist targets and posting instructions for terrorist activities on sports chat rooms, pornographic bulletin boards, and other Web sites." However, their use of steganography has not been confirmed and reports following the September 11 attacks indicated that at least the hijackers and their associates were sending their e-mail messages in the clear.

Although information security technologies can foil counterintelligence and counterterrorism efforts, they also play a key role in protecting these and other activities and in protecting critical information infrastructures. Like other technologies, they are two-edged swords.

Prospects for the Future

If current trends continue, the prognosis for the future is not encouraging. We can expect to see more attacks, and more mass attacks. In the area of e-mail viruses and worms alone, Message Labs, which observed an e-mail virus infection rate of one in three hundred messages in 2001, forecasts a possible rate of one in one hundred in 2004, one in ten in 2008, and one in two in 2013. If these predictions prove correct, the Internet could become unusable.

Many of the attacks will be financially motivated. They will be the work of or-ganized crime and lone criminals, as well as of terrorist groups seeking to fund their activities. The attacks may involve banking fraud, credit card fraud, extortion, stock manipulation, scams, and theft of intellectual property, all of which can be extremely costly. Besides the direct and indirect costs to the victims, these crimes can undermine confidence in the Internet and e-commerce, ultimately damaging the national economy.

The vast majority of attacks may continue to be the work of teenagers and young adults, motivated more by thrill, curiosity, challenge, and bragging rights than by money or the desire to cause harm. They may seek recognition in the hacking com-munity or the media. They may use hacking as a means of protest, defacing websites and attempting to shut down the computers of their targets. Even those that do not intend malice, however, can cause serious harm. Computer viruses and denial-of-service attacks can take an especially heavy toll on businesses and private users.

The more serious threats are generally considered to be cyber attacks conducted by nation-states and terrorists. With respect to the former, many governments have or are developing offensive information warfare programs. Russia, China, and Iraq are often cited, but other countries, including the United States, have them as well. Besides computer network attacks, these programs include other forms of information warfare, including psychological operations and perception manage-ment. The general consensus is that a nation-state with a well-developed computer-network-attack capability could potentially cause considerable damage to a target country's critical infrastructures. It might knock out power or the delivery systems for gas and oil, or shut down transportation or communications systems. Even more damage could result from a combination of cyber and physical weapons.

With respect to terrorists, less is known about whether and how they might pursue cyber terrorism. In August 1999 the Center for the Study of Terrorism and Irregular Warfare at the Naval Postgraduate School (NPS) in Monterey, California, issued a report that addressed the demand side of terrorism.[38] Specifically, the NPS assessed the prospects of terrorist organizations pursuing cyber terrorism, which it defined as "unlawful destruction or disruption of digital property to intimidate or coerce governments or societies in pursuit of goals that are political, religious, or ideological." The NPS concluded that the barrier to entry for anything beyond annoying hacks is quite high and that terrorists generally lack the wherewithal and human capital needed to mount a meaningful operation. Cyber terrorism, the study argued, was a thing of the future, although it might be pursued as an ancil-lary tool. The NPS study examined five types of terrorist groups: religious, New Age, ethno-nationalist separatist, revolutionary, and far-right extremist. Of these, only the religious groups were thought likely to seek the most damaging capability level, as it is consistent with their indiscriminate application of violence.

In October 2000 the NPS group issued a second report following a confer-ence aimed at examining the decision-making process that leads substate groups engaged in armed resistance to develop new operational methods.[39] They were particularly interested in learning whether such groups would engage in cyber terrorism. In addition to academics and a member of the United Nations, the participants included a hacker and five practitioners with experience in violent sub-state groups such as the PLO, the Liberation Tigers of Tamil Eelam (LTTE), the Basque Fatherland and Liberty-Political/Military (ETA-PM), and the Revolutionary Armed Forces of Colombia (FARC). The participants engaged in a simulation exercise based on the situation in Chechnya.

Only one cyber attack was authorized during the simulation, and that was against the Russian Stock Exchange. The attack was justified on the grounds that the exchange was an elite activity and that disrupting it would not affect most Russians. Indeed, it was felt, this might be popular with Russians at large. The group ruled out mass disruptions of e-commerce as being too indiscriminate and risking a backlash.

The findings from the meeting were generally consistent with the earlier study. Recognizing that their conclusions were based on a small sample, they concluded that terrorists have not yet integrated information technology into their strategy and tactics; that substate groups may find cyber terror attractive as a nonlethal weapon; that significant barriers between hackers and terrorists may prevent their integration into one group; and that politically motivated terrorists had reasons to target selectively and limit the effects of their operations, although they might find themselves in a situation where a mass-casualty attack was a rational choice.

The NPS group also concluded that the information and communication revolution may lessen the need for violence by making it easier for substate groups to get their message out. Unfortunately, this conclusion does not seem to be supported by recent events. Many of the people in bin Laden's network, including the suicide hijackers, have used the Internet but nevertheless engage in horrendous acts of violence.

Although cyber terrorism is certainly a real possibility, digital attacks have several drawbacks for a terrorist. Systems are complex, so controlling an attack and achieving a desired level of damage may be more difficult than using physical weapons. Unless people are killed or badly injured, there is also less drama and emotional appeal. In addition, terrorists may be disinclined to attempt cyber methods given the success they have had with bombs and other physical weapons.

In assessing the threat of cyber terrorism, it is also important to look beyond the traditional terrorist groups to those with considerable computing skills. As noted at the outset, some of these people are aligning themselves with terrorists such as Osama bin Laden. While the vast majority of hackers may be disinclined to violence, it would take only a few to turn cyber terrorism into reality.

Moreover, the next generation of terrorists will grow up in a digital world, with ever more powerful and accessible hacking tools at their disposal. They might see greater potential for cyber terrorism than do the terrorists of today, and their knowledge and hacking skills will be greater. Also, just as the September 11 suicide hijackers received flight training in American schools, terrorists could learn how to conduct cyber attacks through information security courses offered in the United States and elsewhere.

Terrorists might also see benefits to conducting cyber attacks against critical infrastructures. Just as the physical attack against the World Trade Center severely affected the financial and transportation sectors of the United States and elsewhere, so too might a cyber attack against critical computers supporting these sectors. The potential seriousness of such an attack is made all the more apparent by the considerable resources that the U.S. government is allocating to cyber defense of critical infrastructures and by the attention of the media. Terrorists have long targeted the infrastructure of countries, so a cyber attack may not be far-fetched. The Islamic extremist Ahmed Ressam, who attempted to place a bomb in the Los Angeles airport around January 1, 2000, testified that he was trained to target "such installations as electric plants, gas plants, airports, railroads, large corporations and military installations." He said that he chose an airport because it is "sensitive politically and economically."[40]

Cyber terrorism could also become more attractive as the real and virtual worlds become more closely coupled, with automobiles, appliances, and other devices attached to the Internet. Unless these systems are carefully secured, conducting an operation that physically harms someone may become as easy as penetrating a website is today.

Although there are no reports of Al Qaeda conducting cyber attacks against critical infrastructures or teaching methods of cyber jihad in terrorist training camps, there are some indications that cyber terrorism is at least on their radar screen. Following the September 11 attacks, bin Laden allegedly told Hadmid Mir, editor of *Ausaf* newspaper, that "hundreds of Muslim scientists were with him ... who would use their knowledge in chemistry, biology and [sic] ranging from computers to electronics against the infidels."[41]

In December 2001 *Newsbytes* reported that a suspected member of Al Qaeda said that members of the terrorist network had infiltrated Microsoft and attempted to plant Trojan horses and bugs in the Windows XP operating system.[42] According to the report, Mohammad Afroze Abdul Razzak told Indian police that the terrorists had gained employment at Microsoft by posing as computer programmers. Microsoft responded by saying the claims were "bizarre and unsubstantiated and should be treated skeptically." Regardless of whether the claim is true, the story is troubling for the simple reason that it shows that at least some terrorists are fully cognizant of the potential of cyber attacks and how such attacks can be launched with the aid of Trojan horses and access to the world's largest software producer. By planting malicious code in popular software, the terrorists could potentially steal sensitive information from Microsoft customers, including government agencies and operators of critical infrastructures, and use that information to facilitate physical or cyber acts of terror. They could sabotage data or networks, causing potentially enormous losses.

Although hijacked vehicles, truck bombs, and biological weapons still pose greater security threats than cyber terrorism does, the events of September 11 caught us by surprise. So too could a major cyber assault. The severity of the attack could be amplified by combining it with a physical attack. For example, terrorists might jam 911 services or shut down electricity or telecommunications after blowing up a building or releasing toxic gases.

Policy Initiatives

On October 16, 2001, President Bush issued an executive order on critical infrastructure protection in the information age. The order established a protection board and charged it with recommending policies and coordinating programs for protecting information systems for critical infrastructures. It assigned several areas of activity to the board, including outreach to the private sector and to state and local governments; information sharing; incident coordination and response; recruitment, retention, and training of executive-branch security professionals; research and development; law enforcement coordination with national security components; international information infrastructure protection; legislation; and coordination with the newly formed Office of Homeland Security. The chair of the board, designated special advisor to the president for cyberspace security, reports to the assistant to the president for national security affairs and to the assistant to the president for Homeland Security. Richard Clarke, who was already coordinating critical infrastructure protection efforts for the administration from his position in the National Security Council, was appointed chair.

Formation of the board followed a series of initiatives begun by the Clinton administration. These included the establishment of the president's Commission on Critical Infrastructure Protection, the recommendations of which led to presidential decision directive 63. PDD 63 created the Critical Infrastructure Assurance Office (CIAO) within the Department of Commerce and the National Infrastructure Protection Center (NIPC), housed at the FBI but with representatives from several agencies. The CIAO was established to coordinate national planning efforts related to critical infrastructure protection.

The NIPC serves as a national critical infrastructure threat assessment, warning, vulnerability, and law enforcement investigation and response entity. Its focus is as much on prevention as on investigation and response. To that end, it issues security assessments, advisories, and alerts, the last addressing major threats and imminent or in-progress attacks targeting national networks or critical infrastructures. In partnership with the private sector, it has also established InfraGard chapters at all fifty-six FBI field offices. The chapters provide formal and informal channels for the exchange of information about infrastructure threats and vulnerabilities. Several thousand organizations from industry, academia, and government have joined.

PDD 63 also encouraged the private sector to create information sharing and analysis centers (ISACs) in cooperation with the government. The centers would serve as the mechanism for gathering, analyzing, appropriately sanitizing, and disseminating private-sector information related to infrastructure vulnerabilities, threats, and incidents. So far ISACs have been established for several sectors, including banking and finance, telecommunications (operated by the National Coordinating Center), electric power (operated by the North American Electric Reliability Council), oil and gas, and information technology. In addition to the ISACs and InfraGard chapters, numerous other groups facilitate information sharing, including the CERT/CC and other computer emergency response teams, the Partnership for Critical Infrastructure Protection, the High Tech Crime Investigators Association, the New York Electronic Crimes Task Force, the Joint Council on Information Age Crime, and the Center for Internet Security. All of these efforts have helped strengthen the cyber-defense and crime-fighting capabilities of their members.

One of the challenges facing all of these groups is that industry has been reluctant to share information out of concern for its confidentiality. In particular, companies are concerned that sensitive information provided voluntarily might not be adequately protected, or that it could be subject to Freedom of Information Act (FOIA) requests or lawsuits. Industry is also concerned that cooperation with industry partners might violate antitrust laws. Bills have been introduced in the House and Senate to provide limited exemption from FOIA and antitrust laws, but they might not go far enough. Gary Fresen, an attorney working on information security issues, recommends giving companies a broader range of legal privileges consistent with that found in other industries, such as health care, railroads, and environmental protection. In addition to FOIA and antitrust protection, the privileges would include a peer-group privilege, a self-audit privilege, and a reporting privilege. Collectively, these would protect sensitive information that is acquired during vulnerability testing or that is shared with industry groups from disclosure through lawsuits.

The Justice Department has launched several initiatives aimed at strengthening the cyber-crime-fighting capability of the criminal justice community. The National Cybercrime Training Partnership provides guidance and assistance to local, state, and federal law enforcement agencies, with the goal of ensuring that the law enforcement community is properly trained to address electronic and high-tech crime. The Electronic Crimes Partnership Initiative is tackling a broader range of issues, including technology, technical assistance, legal and policy issues, education and training, outreach and awareness, and standards and certification. The partnership includes representatives from law enforcement, industry, and academia.

The commander of U.S. Strategic Command (USSTRATCOMM) has primary responsibility for computer network operations within the military. The Joint Task Force Computer Network Operations (JTF-CNO) within USSTRATCOMM serves as the operational component for all computer network operations, which include both computer network defense and computer network attack. In conjunction with the unified commands, services, and Defense Department agencies, the JTF-CNO coordinates and directs the defense of Defense Department computer systems and networks and coordinates and conducts computer network attacks.

One of the difficulties facing both the public and private sectors has been a shortage of people with expertise in information security. To remedy that situation, the Clinton administration began the Federal Cyber Service Scholarship for Service program, which seeks to increase the number of qualified students entering the fields of information assurance and computer security and to increase the capacity of colleges and universities within the United States to produce professionals in these fields. The program, which is administered by the National Science Foundation, offers scholarship and capacity-building grants to universities. Students receiving scholarships are required to work for a federal agency for two years as their federal cyber-service commitment. The NSF program ties in with another educational initiative operated by the National Security Agency. Its program promotes higher education in information assurance and security by designating qualified institutions "centers of academic excellence in information assurance."[43] As of December 2001, twenty-three institutions had been so named.

Research and development in information security technologies is also needed. In addition to programs in the private sector, the National Science Foundation, Defense Department, and other government agencies have R&D programs in information assurance and security. Given that many if not most security incidents can be attributed to faulty passwords and a failure to install security patches, innovations in these areas, including the use of biometrics to replace passwords, better tools for tracking and patching vulnerabilities, and methods and tools for developing systems with fewer vulnerabilities, can have a large payoff.

Increased customer demand has encouraged vendors of information technology to deliver products with better security than in the past. Another incentive that could lead to better security is the risk of exposure to liability lawsuits. In this regard, the Uniform Computer Information Transactions Act (UCITA) could have exactly the opposite effect, by allowing software vendors to absolve themselves of liability through licensing agreements. Fortunately, only two states passed the law. However, the issue of product liability is difficult, because developing fault-free software is all but impossible. Still, vendors should be liable for negligence, failure to use best practices in software development, and failure to respond to reported vulnerabilities in their products.

Because cyber crimes often cross national borders, international cooperation in fighting them is essential. To that end, the Council of Europe has adopted a Cybercrime Convention that aims to harmonize laws and address issues relating to mutual cooperation and evidence retention and sharing. Unfortunately, industry and other interested parties were not brought into the process until the draft convention was nearly finished. Although the final document resolved some of the issues relating to privacy and industry responsibilities and liabilities, others remain. An important lesson here is that the private sector should be involved in government efforts from the outset. Fortunately, other government initiatives have followed this strategy.

Conclusion

Information and information technology are becoming more ubiquitous, mobile, vulnerable, and grounded in the physical world. Security technologies are advancing, but so too are tools for hacking. The net effect has been an increase in the number and magnitude of cyber attacks, with a corresponding increase in losses to their victims. While few attacks have been attributed to terrorists or foreign governments, these threats are worrisome because of their potential to cause considerable damage, particularly if conducted against critical infrastructures. The U.S. government, alongside industry and academia, has initiated several programs to strengthen our cyber defense capability and thereby mitigate this risk. They are important steps forward.

Considerable work, however, remains to be done. We need more complete data about cyber security incidents, including prevalence and cost data; data showing the correlation of incidents with operating modes and particular cyber defenses; and data showing the return on security investment for different approaches. These data are essential if companies are to know what works and where to focus limited resources. We need to expand our education and research initiatives so that more people are capable of defending our networks and have better tools at their disposal, and so that new systems have fewer vulnerabilities and more mechanisms for limiting damages. We need to extend our international initiatives so that cyber offenses can be successfully prevented, investigated, and prosecuted, regardless of the locations of the perpetrators and victims. Finally, we need to make sure that our laws and regulations promote information security and accountability without overburdening industry or sacrificing privacy. Achieving these goals will not be possible without extensive collaboration between the public and private sectors. Cyber defense is not a task for governments alone.

Notes

1. See www.cert.org.
2. "JTF-CNO Battles Surging Tide of More-Destructive Computer Attacks," *Defense Information and Electronics Report,* Sept. 7, 2001, available at http://delphi.dia.ic.gov/admin/EARLYBIRD/010910/s20010910jjtf.htm.
3. See www.truesecure.com/.
4. David Moore, Geoffrey M. Voelker, and Stefan Savage, "Inferring Internet Denial-of-Service Activity," Proc. USENIX Security Symposium, Aug. 2001.
5. "FBI Warns Companies about Russian Hacker Attacks," *CNN,* March 8, 2001.
6. John Leyden, "$3.9 Billion Internet Banking Fraud Busted," *Register,* April 12, 2001.
7. David Moore, "The Spread of the Code-Red Worm (CRv2)," Cooperative Association for Internet Data Analysis, July 2001, available at www.caida.org.
8. For a longer account of this, see Dorothy E. Denning, *Information Warfare and Security* (Reading, Mass.: Addison-Wesley, 1999), 3–4.
9. Ibid., 205–6.

10. "Dangerous Militant Stalks Internet," *Detroit News*, Nov. 9, 1998.

11. "Israeli-Palestinian Cyber Conflict," *iDefense Intelligence Services Report*, Jan. 3, 2000.

12. "Al-Qaida Cyber Capability," Office of Critical Infrastructure Protection and Emergency Preparedness, Government of Canada, available at www.epc-pcc.gc.ca/emergencies/other/TA01-001_E.html.

13. Brian McWilliams, "Hacker Defaces Thousands of Sites in WTC Protest," *Newsbytes*, Sept. 14, 2001.

14. Jefferson Graham, "Hackers Strike Middle Eastern Sites," *USA Today*, Sept. 26, 2001.

15. Information was obtained from YIHAT's website at www.kill.net, which has subsequently been taken down. See also www.kimble.org and Brian McWilliams, "Anti-Terror Hackers Seek Government Blessing," *Newsbytes*, Oct. 17, 2001.

16. This defacement is mirrored at http://defaced.alldas.de/mirror/2001/10/20/www.dtepi.mil/.

17. "E-Mail Attack on Sri Lanka Computers," *Computer Security Alert*, no. 183, Computer Security Institute, June 1998, 8.

18. Kevin Johnson, "Hijackers' E-mails Sifted for Clues," *USA Today*, Oct. 1, 2001.

19. John Arquilla, David Ronfeldt, and Michele Zanini, "Networks, Netwar, and Information-Age Terrorism," in *Countering the New Terrorism*, ed. Ian O. Lesser et al. (Santa Monica, Calif.: RAND, 1999), 65. The authors cite "Afghanistan, Saudi Arabia: Editor's Journey to Meet Bin-Laden Described," *London al-Quds al-Arabi*, FBIS-TOT-97-003-L, Nov. 27, 1996, 4; and "Arab Afghans Said to Launch Worldwide Terrorist War," 1995.

20. National Information Infrastructure (NII) Risk Assessment, "A Nation's Information at Risk," prepared by the Reliability and Vulnerability Working Group, Feb. 29, 1996.

21. "Juvenile Computer Hacker Cuts off FAA Tower at Regional Airport," *Business Wire*, March 18, 1998.

22. "Reuters Staffer Sabotages Hong Kong Bank Dealing Rooms," *Financial Times*, Nov. 29, 1996.

23. "Sewage Hacker Jailed," *Herald Sun*, Oct. 31, 2001.

24. "Attack on Japan Airline Affected 15,000 Passengers," *Security News Portal*, Aug. 11, 2001.

25. Bill Wallace, "Next Major Attack Could Be over Net," *San Francisco Chronicle*, Nov. 12, 2001.

26. George I. Seffers, "Air Force Wires Weapons to Web," *Federal Computer Week*, Sept. 12, 2001.

27. "IP Network to Monitor Power Grid in Fourteen States," *Computer World*, Aug. 31, 2001, available at www.computerworld.com.

28. L. Britt Snider, "Improper Handling of Classified Information by John M. Deutsch," CIA Report, Feb. 18, 2000, available at www.fas.org/irp/cia/product/ig_deutch.html.

29. Frank Stajano and Ross Anderson, "The Resurrecting Duckling: Security Issues for Ad-hoc Wireless Networks," proceedings of the Seventh Security Protocols Workshop, lecture notes in computer science 1796 (Berlin: Springer-Verlag, 2000), 172–82.

30. Peter Mell, "Understanding the World of Your Enemy with I-CAT (Internet-Categorization of Attacks Toolkit)," proceedings of the 22nd National Information Systems Security Conference, U.S. Dept. of Commerce, National Institute of Standards and Technology, Gaithersburg, Md., 432–43.

31. David Moore, "The Spread of the Code-Red Worm (CRv2)."

32. Stuart Staniford, Gary Grim, and Roelof Jonkman, "Flash Worms: Thirty Seconds to Infect the Internet," *Silicon Defense*, Aug. 16, 2001.

33. See http://66.129.1.101/top20.htm.

34. "JTF-CNO Battles Surging Tide."

35. Homeland Security, United States General Accounting Office Testimony before the Senate Committee on Governmental Affairs, GAO-01-1158T, Sept. 21, 2001.

36. George J. Tenet, "Global Realities of Our National Security," statement before the Senate Foreign Relations Committee on the worldwide threat in 2000, March 21, 2000.

37. For more information about some of these cases and a general treatment of the use of encryption by criminals and terrorists, see Dorothy E. Denning and William E. Baugh Jr., "Hiding Crimes in Cyberspace," *Information, Communication and Society* 2, no. 3 (1999): 251–76. Also available at www.cs.georgetown.edu/~denning.

38. Bill Nelson et al., "Cyberterror: Prospects and Implications," Center for the Study of Terrorism and Irregular Warfare, Naval Postgraduate School, Monterey, Calif., Aug. 1999.

39. David Tucker, "The Future of Armed Resistance: Cyberterror? Mass Destruction?" Conference Report and Proceedings, Center for the Study of Terrorism and Irregular Warfare, Naval Postgraduate School, Monterey, Calif., Oct. 2000.

40. "Al-Qaida Cyber Capability," Office of Critical Infrastructure Protection and Emergency Preparedness, Government of Canada, available at www.epc-pcc.gc.ca/emergencies/other/TA01-001_E.html.

41. Ibid.

42. Brian McWilliams, "Suspect Claims Al Qaeda Hacked Microsoft," *Newsbytes*, Dec. 17, 2001.

43. See www.nsa.gov/isso/programs/coeiae/index.htm.

Emerging Technologies and Security

LOREN B. THOMPSON

It is impossible to make accurate predictions about the future of technology and its effects on human societies. And if we could somehow predict the future, we probably would not like the forecast. The most cherished institutions and values may one day fall by the wayside and, if and when they do, technology may be the main agent of their demise. Even something as seemingly immutable as human nature may soon be rendered elastic by the advances of technology.

James Gleick, a perceptive chronicler of technological change, describes a nascent world in which "we children go to sleep; our toys stay up and play."[1] He is referring to the convergence of wireless communication with portable computing, but his imagery captures the ethos of the information age. Technology is advancing so quickly on so many fronts that no one can fully grasp the intricacies of what is occurring. The material world now changes as much in a few generations as it did in the entire millennium following the collapse of Rome, and many experts believe that human knowledge and human skill are expanding at an ever faster pace.

A short essay cannot examine the full range of technological developments currently transforming international security and, more broadly, civilization itself. This chapter will focus on two clusters of emerging technologies—digital networking and genetic engineering—that are sure to have tremendous effects on security and stability, digital networking being the most important development for the immediate future and genetic engineering having potentially epochal effects in the long run. Although these two technologies are often discussed in the context of the social and political consequences of innovation, relatively little has been written about their impact on global security and stability, which is the subject of this essay.

The Allure of Utopia

Apprehension about technological progress has been a common theme in popular culture for centuries, from Mary Shelley's *Frankenstein* (1818) to Fritz Lang's *Metropolis* (1927) to Ridley Scott's *Blade Runner* (1982). But the dominant tradition in the United States—more than in any other country—has been to greet new innovations as certain progress, often with an eagerness that borders on the utopian.

In the 1920s many commentators saw radio as a powerful tool for peace, education, and democracy. A generation later television was said to offer the same potential benefits. A generation after that, some observers thought cable could revolutionize the "vast wasteland" that television had become. Yet another generation later—by which time the highest-rated programs on cable television were professional wrestling—the Internet was heralded as a new avenue for democracy.

Wilbur Wright predicted that airplanes would make war obsolete by making surprise attacks impossible. His contemporary, Margaret Sanger, saw similar promise in contraceptives, contending that "war, famine, poverty and oppression of the workers will continue while woman makes life cheap." She reasoned that "they will cease only when she limits her reproductivity and human life is no longer a thing to be wasted."[2] Even nuclear weapons have been presented as a force for peace, since the consequences of their use were alleged to be "unthinkable."

The persistence of American technological optimism is rooted in something more than ethnocentric naiveté. Many of the promises of technology really have come true. Electrification transformed everyday life, with huge social and economic consequences. The introduction of air conditioning after World War II, for example, is sometimes cited as the single most important factor in enabling the South to escape the agrarianism that had allegedly oppressed it since the Civil War. Automobiles remade cities and gave rise to suburbs, transforming both urban and rural life. Advances in medical science raised the average life expectancy in the United States by 60 percent over the course of the twentieth century. At the century's end two demographers calculated that without the gain in longevity, the U.S. population would have been half its actual size; half of the missing 137 million Americans would have died prematurely, and the others would never have been born at all.[3]

Having been direct beneficiaries of past breakthroughs, it is not surprising that many Americans harbor utopian expectations about the capacity of new technology to transform the human condition. They have been indirect beneficiaries, too: between 1900 and 1999, the Standard & Poor 500 composite-stock index rose from six to 1,417, with the greatest gains in equity value tied closely to the introduction of new technologies.[4] The 1920s witnessed one such surge, as huge fortunes were made from electrification. Another surge followed the end of the cold war, driven mostly by excitement about the Internet and digital communications.

During the latter period, many policymakers and academics followed Wall Street's example in embracing the revolutionary potential of emerging technology. New media and methods of transmission were said to be forging a global economy and culture characterized by open markets and democratic values. Every major institution, from the military to the clergy, rushed to assimilate the new technology, convinced of its promise and afraid of being left behind. Popular optimism persisted even after evidence began to surface that the high-tech hype had been overdone.

The Perils of Technology

On September 11, 2001, agents of the Al Qaeda terrorist organization seized control of four commercial airliners and used them to attack the nerve centers of

American economic and military power. Three thousand men, women, and children died. In the immediate aftermath of the September 11 atrocities, press reports noted the proficiency with which the terrorists had used new-age technology for distinctly unprogressive purposes.

The terrorists had communicated using cell phones and the Internet, possibly employing commercial encryption software to conceal their intent. They stored information about their operations and finances on computers. They may have purchased off-the-shelf simulation software to practice flying through the air space around their targets.[5] The first step they took after hijacking the planes was to shut off transponders, so that their movements within the air-traffic control network were harder to track. And once the attacks had been accomplished, Al Qaeda leaders used cable television to promote jihad in the Arab world—broadcasting images whose satellite feeds proved nearly impossible to suppress.

As if this were not enough of a blow to proponents of new technology, the September 11 attacks were followed within weeks by America's first experience with bioterrorism. Mysterious letters containing anthrax, an extremely lethal bacterium, began arriving at the offices of journalists and legislators. Here again, press reports noted the apparent facility with which unknown agents had used modern technology to culture, process, and disseminate the deadly pathogen. Because some of the letters originated in central New Jersey, home of many pharmaceutical companies, law-enforcement officials speculated that a rogue researcher had used commercial biotechnology to make the anthrax.

There was nothing new about biological warfare, just as there was nothing new about fanatics hijacking airliners. What was new in the autumn of 2001 was the widespread realization that modern technology was putting unprecedented destructive power in the hands of ordinary people. Policymakers had for some time expressed concern about the global diffusion of so-called "dual-use" technologies, meaning those with both commercial and military applications. But that concern waned after the collapse of communism, as the Pentagon was swept up in the high-tech enthusiasm of the 1990s. Emerging technologies were going to enable a "revolution in military affairs"—a revolution America would lead, just as it led the world in commercializing and marketing the new innovations. The terrorist attacks of 2001 restored some balance to the public discussion of new technology. The information revolution might have the potential to transform human relations, but there would be costs. Even before the attacks occurred, Washington was already embroiled in a heated debate about the ethics of biomedical research, a field witnessing rapid progress thanks largely to the use of information systems. The attacks fed a growing undercurrent of fear that new technologies were fostering new dangers, dangers that were hard to understand, much less resolve. Global security might be severely eroded before policymakers even grasped the nature of emerging challenges.

In American political parlance, "global security" tends to be synonymous with global stability, the natural preoccupation of a status-quo power. As the biggest beneficiary of the existing world order, the United States may lose as much as it gains from the technological ferment spreading across the globe. In the near term, the greatest changes will be wrought by various manifestations of the information revolution, a revolution driven by the networking of increasingly powerful computers. Over the longer run, similarly epochal changes may result from the biomedical breakthroughs this networking enables, most notably in the form of genetic engineering. U.S. and international policymakers have barely begun to consider the negative consequences that might arise from these twin revolutions.

Digital Networking

Digital networking is the communication of information between two or more electronic devices using binary computer language. Digital signals are conveyed electronically (as electrons) or optically (as photons). They differ from the analog signals traditionally employed for telecommunications in that they translate the original information into a series of ones and zeroes that can be decoded and processed by computers. Analog signals mimic the original information using amplitude or frequency modulation.

The basic idea behind digital networking is simple. It resembles the dot-dash exchanges between telegraph operators using Morse code. It has provided the foundation for a revolution in global communications because it enables high-speed transmission of data among increasingly powerful and pervasive computers used in nearly every realm of human activity. According to cybernetics authority Raymond Kurzweil, computing power has doubled more than thirty times since the first digital computer was devised during World War II, thanks primarily to the increasing density of integrated circuits.[6] As a result, computing power grew by a factor of at least 10 billion between 1950 and 2000.[7] During most of that time it was cheaper to process information in place than to transmit it, because computational power was growing much faster than the carrying capacity of telecommunications systems. That began to change in 1975 with the introduction of fiber optics, which offered greatly increased data rates.

George Gilder notes that it is now possible to carry a thousand different wavelengths simultaneously on a single optical fiber no thicker than a human hair, and to convey 10 billion bits of information per second on each of those wavelengths. Up to 864 fibers can be combined in a single cable, giving the cable transmission capacity of 8.6 petabits (quadrillion bits) per second. Gilder notes that "eight petabits per second is a thousand times the total average telecommunications traffic across the entire global infrastructure as recently as 1997." He concludes that this emerging technology "will make human communication universal, instantaneous, unlimited in capacity, and at the margins free."[8]

While such predictions may sound similar to the utopian claims made for other emerging technologies in the past, there is little question that networking really is transforming commerce and culture, and not just in the industrial world. The ubiquity of digital links within and between organizations, the range of means by which they can be accomplished, the volume of data that can be conveyed, and the diversity of content that can be received all point to a fundamental break with the past. The dominant feature of that past was the centralization of control over telecommunications according to political and economic interests. The dominant feature of the new environment is its unregulated, even anarchic quality.

Although hardly coterminous with the full breadth of networking technology, the Internet is the popular symbol of this revolution. Unlike telecom networks of the past, which concentrated expertise at the center and assumed low competence on the part of users, the Internet is simple and flexible at its core, facilitating expertise at its fringes. Anyone can use it to communicate anything, so long as they subscribe to the basic protocols that govern transmission. No one controls it, because it is not a unified network: it is thousands of separate networks linked in a loose technical confederation that defies borders or convention. Conceived in the 1960s by the Pentagon's Advanced Research Projects Agency, the Internet began to grow rapidly after introduction of the user-friendly World Wide Web in 1992. A medium that began in the 1990s with fewer than a million users ended the decade with more than 150 million users accessing nearly a billion web pages.[9]

The global proliferation of digital networks that elaborate, manipulate, or imitate the Internet has been accompanied by a profusion of new devices linked to those networks. Ranging from cell phones to satellite navigation aids to expert systems, these devices usually incorporate computing capability that leverages other elements of the network. Such networked devices are becoming embedded throughout the social and economic landscape in a trend that Michio Kaku calls "ubiquitous computing" and James Gleick calls "pervasive computing."[10] Whatever it is called, this trend marks a major change in global civilization. And like most such changes, it has drawbacks.

General Problems

Tom Standage observes, in *The Victorian Internet*, his history of early telegraphy, that "the potential of new technologies to change things for the better is invariably overstated, while the ways in which they will make things worse are usually unforeseen."[11] This insight almost certainly applies to digital networking, because many of the potential problems associated with the technology are inextricably linked to its much-touted benefits.

First, the technology will be diffused unevenly, both within and between nations. The fact that the Internet has grown from less than a million users in 1990 to 200 million today is impressive, but the latter number represents only 3 percent of global population. Other forms of networking are probably reaching an even smaller portion of the global community. Because there are a variety of methods other than hard-wired infrastructure by which networking can be accomplished (such as cellular and satellite links), the technology can spread in underdeveloped regions more rapidly than telephones initially did. But users will still require access to costly terminals, processors, and software that are beyond the means of most people.

Even though the price of such equipment will fall over time, the pace of innovation in economies where networking has made the deepest inroads is so rapid that by the time first-generation equipment reaches most of the developing world, fourth- or fifth-generation technology will be the norm in the developed world. For example, consumers in the United States will have broadband (1 million bits per second) access to the Internet and cellular service before most Indians or Indonesians have any access at all. Thus, rather than acting as an integrative force, digital networking may reinforce the existing stratification of the global economy. The less developed countries may never catch up to the global standard, and in fact may fall further and further behind due to the accelerated pace of innovation among those with access to the latest tools.

A second consideration is that as developing countries assimilate networking technology, the consequences of easy access to information and entertainment from anywhere in the world are likely to be profound for traditional societies. It is a common conceit among Western elites that the information age is giving rise to a global culture based on their own core values. Whether or not this is really the case, most human beings still live within the conventions of insular local cultures that dictate their beliefs and identities. They are barely aware of how life is lived in the cosmopolitan, secular, individualistic cultures of the West.

Television, radio, and other older forms of telecommunications had less impact on traditional culture than might be expected, because in most places, until quite recently, they were heavily regulated by political authorities. During the 1990s, though, the traditional media of many nations were deregulated while new media appeared that were far harder to control. As the U.S. government discovered to its dismay during the early stages of its global counterterror campaign, there is no easy way to turn off cellular networks, direct-broadcast satellite transmissions, or the Internet.[12] Even if there were, countries cannot shut down the networks without removing themselves from the mainstream of global commerce. So all the content of the entire global web will eventually be available to people unaccustomed to dealing with such heterogeneity. It is inevitable that this trend will occasionally lead to political instability, cultural frictions, and erosion of traditional institutions.

A third problem is that digital-networking technology empowers groups whose interests are incompatible with the existing alignment of political authority. Fifty years ago political scientists such as Karl Deutsch found that communications networks tended to reinforce state power, with the densest infrastructures and interactions concentrated within national borders and the thinnest exchanges occurring across frontiers. While it would be an exaggeration to say that the new technology is borderless, it certainly is less constrained by state power than the heavily regulated (and often state-run) networks of the past were. As a result, it is more easily accessed and exploited by groups that compete with the state for power.

In some cases the threat to state authority will be overt: disaffected groups will use the new technology to mount attacks on the existing order. The more pervasive problem, though, is that loyalties and identities will shift from the state to other frames of reference—economic, ethnic, religious, and so on. Even countries with long-established national traditions and institutions may see a marked diminution of their authority as competing affiliations are strengthened by the networking trend. More fragile states may see their legitimacy thoroughly undermined. It could be argued that networking technology merely provides a means for expressing the true alignment of popular sentiment, and thus hastens the transition to more durable political orders that meet the needs of their people. But that transition is likely to be accompanied by conflicts and dislocations that diminish global security in the near term.

A fourth problem is that the global community may become excessively dependent on a handful of core networks whose integrity cannot be assured. Digital networking is an emerging technology today, characterized by confusion and diversity. Over time, though, it will gravitate toward universal standards and economies of scale, just as every other mature technology has. Concentration and simplification are essential if the full integrative potential of networking is to be realized. Once global standards begin to coalesce, there will be strong economic incentives for users to abandon systems and applications that are incompatible. That will eliminate redundancy and waste, but it may also diminish resilience.

Even the most powerful and versatile networks will have vulnerabilities. Indeed, the very fact that they are powerful and versatile will make them attractive targets for some dissidents. Loss of continuous access to key networks could have catastrophic consequences for some types of activity, such as finance and the fighting of wars. Even if networks are sufficiently resilient to avoid upset, there is a high likelihood that they will be manipulated to the disadvantage of some users, particularly by countries and companies that have a leading role in maintaining them. It was precisely these concerns that led the European Union to initiate development of an alternative, called Galileo, to the U.S. Global Positioning System. European leaders were worried about being heavily dependent on an American satellite network for navigation and time synchronization, so they elected to make their biggest infrastructure investment to date a backup of GPS.[13] Whether that approach will prove feasible and affordable for other applications—and for less affluent countries—remains to be seen.

Specific Problems

In addition to these broad issues, a host of more specific security-related concerns will arise from the transition to what the military calls "network-centric" ways of doing business. Even though the digital networking trend is still in its infancy, several problems are already apparent.

First, global networks incorporating commercial standards and open architectures make it more difficult to enforce export controls for sensitive information technologies. Potential users of controlled hardware (such as supercomputers) who cannot obtain export licenses can use digital data links to access the equipment in third countries. The most complex software is routinely disseminated across international borders using such links. And the growing preference of Western militaries for "commercial off-the-shelf" information solutions further erodes the barriers that traditionally have protected defense-related technology. Thus, at precisely the time when information technology is becoming central to every facet of war, the ability to withhold it from adversaries is diminishing rapidly. A prestigious panel of former policymakers recommended in mid-2001 that most export controls on computers be scrapped, because they had become unenforceable.[14]

Second, digital networks have become the main conduit for disseminating computer viruses. Viruses are programs designed to erase, corrupt, or manipulate data in any computer meeting specified criteria. For example, a program can be written for invading and degrading any computer using Microsoft e-mail functions. Before the advent of open-architecture networks, it was hard to spread viruses to large numbers of computers. Rogue programmers had to corrupt software at its source or somehow penetrate private networks. But with many forms of computing now shifting to open networks with global reach, it has become much easier to quickly degrade huge numbers of machines. The potential for catastrophic damage will grow as diversity gives way to global standards, because more and more machines will share the same vulnerabilities. Not surprisingly, one of the few sectors that thrived during the 2001 downturn in demand for information products was companies that make security systems to protect computers from viruses.[15]

Third, digital networks have greatly increased the danger of espionage, theft, or other focused attacks on information systems. Unauthorized penetration of particular systems is referred to in the vernacular of the computer world as "hacking," and their perpetrators are called "hackers." Unlike the authors of viruses, who typically aim for mass effects, hackers seek to corrupt or manipulate specific computers and data bases. Most such attacks are little more than nuisances that can be repelled with simple fixes to software. But the increasing reliance on open networks of computers performing critical functions suggests that the potential for truly dangerous, destructive hacking is growing. Although frequently depicted in the media as a form of vandalism, hacking in its most sophisticated form is information warfare, a method of subverting systems that may be essential to a country's economy or military capabilities. The tolerance with which early instances of hacking met is gradually giving way to well-founded fears about the threat it poses to any society that relies on Internet information systems, as all advanced societies now do.[16]

Finally, even as new technologies are facilitating espionage and sabotage against the most network-centric societies, they are undercutting the capacity of Western intelligence agencies to keep track of potential enemies. When the cold war ended, about 90 percent of international telecommunications traffic was still being carried via copper cable, microwave relays, and satellite links. All such voice and data flows could be intercepted using various orbital, airborne, undersea, or ground-based eavesdropping systems. Today the ability to detect and interpret hostile information is eroding rapidly. The volume of traffic has exploded, so much more information must be searched. Fiber optics, the preferred means of transmission for the heaviest data flows, is difficult to tap because it has no electromagnetic emanations. When messages are intercepted, they may be indecipherable because of the use of unbreakable codes readily available on the Internet. And users of wireless communications may soon have the option of employing spread-spectrum (frequency-hopping) techniques to conceal their exchanges. It is no exaggeration to say that the cumulative effect of all these new technologies has been to produce a crisis in intelligence gathering.[17]

It should be noted that none of these developments is entirely new. The first telegraph codebooks appeared in the United States in 1845, at a time when the nation had only one experimental telegraph line running between Washington and Baltimore.[18] Every telecommunications technology that has appeared since then has been used by various rogue elements to commit espionage, break the law, or undermine the established order. The big difference between those earlier innovations and digital networking technology is that it is more capable and harder to control. At present, there is no easy solution to many of the security challenges posed by the new technology, because destructive potential is inherent in some of its most appealing features.

Genetic Engineering

Digital computers and networks are the most powerful information systems ever devised by man. They are not, however, the most powerful information systems known to man. That status is reserved for the biochemical processes of the body, most notably the brain and the genome encapsulated in the nucleus of every cell. The human brain conducts trillions of operations per second, far exceeding the performance of the most powerful supercomputer while using much less space and energy.[19] The human genome, encoded on microscopic strands of deoxyribonucleic acid (DNA), contains all the information needed to reproduce the brain and more than two hundred other specialized tissues that make up the body.

In the early decades of the twentieth century, breakthroughs in quantum physics provided the insights into atomic behavior necessary to construct today's complex digital devices. Those same insights illuminated the underlying biochemical dynamics of living organisms, and then enabled the development of analytical tools for sorting out the vast amount of information that had been unlocked. Thus the quantum revolution of the early twentieth century led to another revolution, in the life sciences, that is still gathering force at the dawn of the twenty-first century.

The most important product of the revolution in life sciences is genetic engineering, the deliberate manipulation of genomes. Genomes are the code of life of living organisms, the accumulated chemical instructions passed from generation to generation through reproduction, that define all the heritable characteristics of a species. In human beings the genome consists of 3 billion base pairs of nucleic acids arranged like the rungs of a ladder in six-foot-long helical strands of DNA. The nucleus of every cell in the human body (of which there are 100 trillion) contains such DNA strands, which provide chemical instructions for production of the proteins that make up the body. Instructions for specific functions are grouped in clusters called genes, which in turn are gathered on the twenty-three chromosomes that make up the genome.[20]

While the complexity of genomes varies among species—human beings have 30,000 genes, fruit flies 13,000—DNA encoding occurs in all known organisms. Moreover, higher forms of life tend to be constructed from the same genetic base as lower forms, with additional features added. For example, only about 1 percent of human genes are not shared with mice, and the human genome is nearly identical to that of chimpanzees. The realization that such overlaps exist led theoretical biologist Theodosius Dobzhansky to observe in 1973 that "Nothing in biology makes sense except in light of evolution."[21] In practical terms, the existence of shared genetic heritage means that material can be transferred between species to produce novel results.

That is precisely what scientists have begun to do, modifying the genetic code of various species to achieve targeted results. For example, crops have been engineered to yield more fruit, resist herbicides, and secrete their own organic insect repellants. Livestock have been engineered that grow faster, resist disease, and produce more nutritional output. And debate is growing about the potential benefits of applying genetic engineering techniques to human beings.

There are two basic types of genetic intervention: somatic and germline. Somatic interventions—modifications of any cells except those involved in reproduction—have consequences confined to the individual organism treated. Germline interventions alter reproductive cells, and thus are passed on to subsequent generations. Germline engineering of lower life-forms has become common in the pharmaceutical and agricultural industries but has never been attempted on humans. Somatic treatment of human beings has barely entered the experimental phase. Both types of genetic engineering will eventually be applied to humans, creating unprecedented policy dilemmas.[22]

General Problems

If digital networking is an emerging technology, genetic engineering is an embryonic one. Although opponents and proponents alike agree that it has revolutionary implications, there is no way of knowing how soon and how broadly specific applications will take hold. The technology is advancing rapidly, as indicated by the fact that the Human Genome Project, begun in 1990 to develop a precise blueprint of humankind's genetic endowment, accomplished its main goals five years earlier than expected. The basic mechanics of somatic and germline therapy are well understood. But genetic engineering is so controversial that legal and political obstacles to its progress are certain to arise. What follows, therefore, is merely illustrative of the issues that genetic engineering could pose for global security. Most of the discussion focuses on human germline manipulation, since it raises the most fundamental questions.

The most important issue raised by genetic engineering is that it may change the course of evolution, in the process redefining human nature. Any alteration of the germline produces permanent genetic changes that can gradually spread throughout the human race via reproduction. How quickly and widely a modification spreads will depend on the size and distribution of the population initially receiving the change, plus its robustness in terms of conferring competitive advantage in subsequent generations. In principle, though, any germline intervention is potentially a permanent shift in the vector of evolution. As Gregory Stock and John Campbell noted in the introduction to a series of conference papers on germline research published in 2000, "With germline engineering, we are beginning to seize control of our own evolution, and yet we have barely begun to grapple with the consequences. Ultimately, we will have to face the question lying at the heart of the emerging international debate about the application of molecular genetics to humans: How far are we willing to go in reshaping the human body and psyche?"[23]

Evolution as currently understood by most scientists is a random process that advances very gradually, partly due to natural selection and partly due to environmentally induced mutations. But research already underway in hundreds of biology labs is greatly accelerating the rate of change for many species of plant and animal, in some cases producing outcomes that might never have arisen naturally. Because all of human civilization is grounded in a genetic identity that may soon be subject to numerous alterations, the possibility of radical consequences within the current century is quite real. Sociologist James Hughes speculates that within a few generations after germline therapy becomes commonplace, many of the defining characteristics of human nature will begin yielding to genetic diversity. The consequences for the global community could be decidedly strange: "To preserve solidarity, we need a new model of collective identity, of 'transhuman' citizenship. Rights and citizenship need to be redefined around the abilities to think and communicate, not around human, version 1.0, DNA. As humanity subspeciates through germline therapy, it will be best if we can remain part of the same polity, a common society of mutual obligation and tolerance, for as long as possible."[24]

Hughes anticipates that this fantastic scenario will unfold within the twenty-first century. He may be underestimating the constraints imposed on genetic change by regulation, cultural pressure, and aesthetics. But the possibility of growing genetic diversity, cultural divergence, and even subspeciation cannot be dismissed, because the technology that could produce such results already, in large part, exists. Once the initial uneasiness about tampering with nature passes, few societies will be able to resist the appeal of enhancements that can greatly increase longevity, intelligence, sexual prowess, and the like. Major consequences for world order appear to be inevitable.

A second far-reaching issue for global security raised by genetic engineering concerns the potential demographic consequences of both somatic and germline therapy. During the twentieth century, average life expectancy in the United States grew by nearly 60 percent, due primarily to breakthroughs in medical science such as chemotherapy and antibiotics. If similar gains are achieved in the current century, then the average American can expect to live to about age 120 by the year 2100. Genetic engineering is likely to play a powerful role in extending average life spans. Not only can it be used to target genetic infirmities such as a propensity to cancer or heart disease; it may also be used to modify genes directly associated with aging. Some experts suspect that evolution did not reward longevity in humans because it played little role in species survival after the reproductive years. By modifying the genome, though, it may be possible to extend human life expectancy, just as scientists have already extended the life spans of simpler organisms such as roundworms.

There are good reasons why such ideas—heretofore the province of science fiction—should be taken seriously. About 20 percent of Americans who live beyond age 100 manage to avoid all age-related diseases up to that point, suggesting a genetic component in their longevity.[25] But, again, experience indicates that any mass alteration in natural demographic patterns will entail unforeseen problems. For example, much of the recent increase in global population is the result of gains in life expectancy, which have eclipsed the impact of falling birthrates in countries such as China and the United States. Access to prenatal sex-selection techniques in India has resulted in big gender imbalances among infant populations, because female fetuses are aborted at disproportionate rates. It is reasonable to assume that genetic interventions aimed at enhancing longevity could have serious negative consequences, particularly if longer life expectancy is not accompanied by a corresponding extension in productivity. Rapid population growth, increased pressure on limited natural resources, and the overburdening of social welfare systems are among the possible consequences.

A third major concern associated with germline engineering is the erosion of biodiversity in the natural environment. When new genetic properties appear that confer superior survival potential, they tend over time to crowd out organisms with less robust endowments. The weeding out of inferior organisms occurs both within and between species. Like Adam Smith's "invisible hand," by which the marketplace supposedly generates efficient results by its very nature, natural selection favors the most fecund and resilient organisms. But genetic engineering distorts the selection process by giving a short-term advantage to organisms whose genetic characteristics did not emerge naturally. The fact that such characteristics did not evolve spontaneously implies that they may not have long-term survival value even though they appear in the short term to meet human needs. The danger is that artificially engineered strains will crowd out naturally occurring organisms, only to prove far less resilient in the face of future threats.

This problem has already been noted in agriculture, where the growing use of "transgenic" plants is producing monocultures consisting of a single, artificially engineered crop. The tendency of hardier plants to crowd out weaker ones is accelerated for high yields and short growing cycles, even though such characteristics may not contribute to long-term survival. Many environmentalists believe that monocultures are excessively vulnerable to new diseases and pests because they lack diversity. If this is so, then they present the danger of catastrophic interruptions in food supplies over the long run, even though they satisfy a short-term desire for increased agricultural productivity.[26]

But the problem of diminished biodiversity does not end there. If germline engineering becomes as common among people as it already is among crops, there is a danger that vulnerabilities will be introduced (or reintroduced) into the human genome that diminish resistance to future biological challenges. Many of the germline enhancements currently being contemplated respond to the transient needs of individuals or cultures. Such needs may be incompatible with the longer-term requirements for a resilient, adaptable species. As Nobel laureate James D. Watson has observed, "evolution can be very cruel," but the continuous reshuffling of genetic cards from generation to generation is the best mechanism nature has devised to assure species survival.[27] While germline engineering has huge potential to enhance the human prospect in the near term, the interference with mankind's natural genetic diversity will probably have negative consequences over the long run that cannot be foreseen today.

Another general problem with genetic engineering, especially germline manipulation, is the challenge that it is perceived to pose to religious beliefs. Despite the apparent erosion of spiritual belief in Western civilization, religion remains a central force in many cultures. It legitimizes institutions, regulates social relations, and imparts meaning to the lives of adherents. But religion achieves its power by asserting influence over vital human matters, most notably reproduction and death. Since the Enlightenment of the eighteenth century, science has staked competing claims in these areas. Not surprisingly, every new advance in reproductive technology—from oral contraceptives to therapeutic abortions to in vitro fertilization—has met with religious objections. Efforts to "rationalize" the circumstances surrounding death have also engendered religious controversy.

Genetic engineering will exacerbate such frictions by further invading realms traditionally deemed sacred by many religions. At the very least, this promises conflict between prospective beneficiaries of the new technology and defenders of religious influence. But it could mean far more than that: the suppression of scientific progress or the waning of belief structures critical to social and political stability in some states. Religious objections are not likely to limit the spread of genetic research on plants and animals, because theologians usually are concerned only with the sanctity and dignity of human life. Indeed, traditional societies probably will embrace transgenic agriculture before the less needy countries of the European Union do.[28] But religious leaders in many regions may view human germline manipulation as an affront to their belief systems and resist it despite its manifest social benefits. Obviously, any such trend would generate tensions, perhaps even accelerating the fragmentation of human genetic destinies that James Hughes calls "subspeciation."

Specific Problems

The general problems described above will take some time to unfold. But genetic engineering also poses some short-term, focused challenges for global security. The most important is its potential use in fashioning biological weapons. The anthrax attacks that occurred in the United States in 2001 may be a harbinger of things to come, as terrorists and other aggressors increasingly apply biotechnology to the concentration and culturing of lethal pathogens. Like digital networking, genetic engineering is a dual-use technology; its greatest dangers are inextricably linked to its most promising applications. For example, many biologists are currently trying to develop viruses that can be used to implant artificial genes into the body. The techniques employed in creating these so-called "vectors" are indistinguishable from those required to build bioweapons.[29]

As genetic science advances, more options for tailoring the effects of biological weapons will become available. Pathogens could be developed that target specific demographic characteristics, such as race and gender. Or they could be fashioned to circumvent defensive measures. A team of Russian microbiologists disclosed in 1997 that it had engineered a strain of anthrax highly resistant to existing antibiotics. The danger such developments pose to global security is suggested by recent research on the outbreak of "Spanish flu" that occurred in 1918. Although influenza is a common virus to which humans usually have some degree of resistance, a random mutation may have resulted in the natural splicing together of genes from two preexisting strains into a new strain with no immunological history. The result was an epidemic that killed 20 to 40 million people worldwide, more deaths than occurred in the world war underway at the same time.[30] In the future, people working in laboratories around the world will be able to engineer similar mutations.

A second, related concern is that international trafficking in genetic engineering technology is nearly impossible to control. There are many peaceful uses of the technology, many producers of equipment such as DNA synthesizers and sequencers, and many users scattered throughout the world. The most demanding aspects of germline engineering may soon be within the control of a typical clinic that performs in vitro fertilization, which has become a common practice in all developed countries and in many developing ones.

Even if the technology were more heavily regulated, powerful financial forces will discourage the creation of control mechanisms. The United States has resisted implementing international conventions to regulate biotechnology in part because of fears that enforcement measures would facilitate industrial espionage against U.S. companies. Meanwhile, it has urged an end to European use of the so-called "precautionary principle," which blocks imports of transgenic products if there is a suspicion of adverse environmental consequences.[31] The European Commission in January 2002 reversed its opposition to genetically engineered products, warning that the global biotechnology industry would generate 2 trillion Euros in revenue by 2010 and that Europe needed to secure its share of the emerging sector.[32] With such strong incentives to embrace the new technology, efforts to limit its spread seem doomed to failure.

The vast size envisioned for the emerging biotechnology market leads to a third concern: that business interests will secure control over genetic innovations essential to economic competitiveness and social welfare. Although it is nearly impossible to regulate trafficking in the relevant technologies, it may be feasible for companies to win patents and other protections of intellectual property that give them lucrative global franchises in transgenic processes. That clearly is what some of the bigger companies, such as Monsanto, are hoping for. But, like the ongoing controversy over prices charged in the developing world by Western pharmaceutical companies, there is widespread fear that a few companies or countries will establish monopolies on humankind's emerging genetic destiny. Even if legal protections cannot be secured, companies may genetically engineer products to preclude easy replication, thus enforcing their rights in other ways.[33]

A final consequence likely to arise in the near term is that genetic science will be used to forecast the life potential of individuals, thereby consigning them to what Jeremy Rifkin describes as an "informal biological caste system" based on their genetic inheritance.[34] If genetic research could reliably project the behavioral propensities and longevity of individuals, that information would be of considerable value to political and business interests. Unfortunately, it would probably be used to discriminate against persons or classes exhibiting sub-par genetic potential. While Aldous Huxley's dystopian vision of a genetically engineered caste system will probably never be realized, some of the negative consequences of such a system could emerge spontaneously as a byproduct of increasing insight into individual genetic makeup. Of course, the new technology might also be used to enhance genes deemed to be deficient, but that capacity could emerge later than analytical techniques to determine levels of genetic potential.

Conclusion

If global security is defined in terms of political and economic stability, then every new technology is a threat. Technology is the principal means by which innate human limitations are overcome, and in the present century it may also become the means by which some of those limitations are entirely eliminated. But the transition to new competencies is often accompanied by the destruction of what came before. Sometimes the destruction is gradual and progressive, sometimes profoundly traumatic.

The two technologies discussed in this essay—digital networking and genetic engineering—will transform human relations within a few generations. Their proponents envision huge gains in economic wealth, social welfare, and cultural attainment. Skeptics foresee the potential for massive dislocations, the breakup of traditional institutions, empowered terrorists, and powerless peasants. Because there is no logical endpoint or central locus of technological change, all of these expectations, both good and bad, may be realized at different times and in different places.

Some of the technologies with which human beings are now experimenting are so powerful that they may overshadow the impact of all others. Imagine, for example, what nuclear war between the United States and the Soviet Union might have meant for the fate of Western civilization. Or what the rapid proliferation of gene-splicing techniques may yet mean for the consequences of global terrorism. Some proponents of the Internet compare its invention to the advent of movable type.

It is not surprising that many Americans still assume that technological change will produce positive results, because by and large that has been their experience. But it is essential for U.S. and international leaders to realize that there is nothing inevitable about progress. New technology needs to be understood, monitored, and in some cases regulated. On rare occasions, it may even need to be suppressed. It is not enough to leave technological developments to the marketplace, especially given the fact that many future users of new innovations will not share American values or aspirations.

The main reason political leaders resist closer scrutiny of emerging technology is that powerful economic interests benefit from their distraction. Scrutiny brings regulation, which in turn limits the potential for profit. Since government seldom shows much talent in shaping the innovative process, opposition to oversight appears reasonable. But if the world's leading innovator will not take a role in regulating emerging technology, then effective global regulation will not be feasible. That might be good news for free enterprise in the short term, but not for those who care about national and international security.

Notes

1. James Gleick,"Inescapably Connected: Life in the Wireless Age," *New York Times Magazine,* April 22, 2001.

2. Margaret Sanger,"Birth Control," excerpted in Richard Rhodes, ed., *Visions of Technology* (New York: Simon & Schuster), 1999, 68–69.

3. Kevin M. White and Samuel H. Preston,"137 Million Lives," ibid., 360–61.

4. Bill Dedman,"Portraying a Century of Changes in America," *New York Times,* Dec. 13, 1999.

5. Ben Webster,"Hijackers May Have Learnt To Fly Using £20 Software," *The Times* (London), Sept. 12, 2001.

6. Michael Shermer,"Shermer's Last Law," *Scientific American,* Jan. 2002, 33.

7. Michio Kaku, *Visions: How Science Will Revolutionize the 21st Century* (New York: Anchor Books, 1997), 28.

8. George Gilder, *Telecosm: How Infinite Bandwidth Will Revolutionize Our World* (New York: Free Press, 2000), 10.

9. Katie Hafner,"The Internet's Invisible Hand," *New York Times,* Jan. 10, 2002; National Research Council, *The Internet's Coming of Age* (Washington, D.C.: National Academy Press, 2001), 3–9, 29–39.

10. Kaku, *Visions,* 27; Gleick,"Inescapably Connected."

11. Tom Standage, *The Victorian Internet* (New York: Berkley Books, 1998), 104.

12. Seth Schiesel,"Stopping Signals from Satellite TV Proves Difficult," *New York Times,* Oct. 15, 2001.

13. Jennifer Lee,"Europe Plans to Compete with U.S. Satellite Network," *New York Times,* Nov. 26, 2001.

14. Reuters,"Report: U.S. Computer Export Controls Irrelevant," *New York Times,* June 8, 2001.

15. Ann Grimes,"Computer-Security Firms Post Strong Results on Robust Sales," *Wall Street Journal,* Jan. 21, 2002; Renae Merle, "Computer Attacks on Companies Up Sharply," *Washington Post,* Jan. 28, 2002.

16. National Research Council, "The Internet's Coming of Age," 84–85; Michael Ruane, "New Computer Technology Makes Hacking a Snap," *Washington Post,* March 10, 1999.

17. Neil King Jr.,"In Digital Age, U.S. Spy Agency Fights to Keep from Going Deaf," *Wall Street Journal,* May 23, 2001; William Broad,"Surge Of New Technologies Erodes U.S. Edge in Spying," *New York Times,* Sept. 20, 2001.

18. Standage, *The Victorian Internet,* 58, 111.

19. Kaku, *Visions,* 80.

20. Matt Ridley, *Genome: The Autobiography of a Species in 23 Chapters* (New York: Perennial, 1999), 4–22; Gary Zweiger, *Transducing the Genome: Information, Anarchy, and Revolution in the Biomedical Sciences* (New York: McGraw-Hill, 2001), 13–29.

21. Quoted in Lee M. Silver, *Remaking Eden* (New York: Bard-Avon Books, 1998), 24.

22. Gregory Stock and John Campbell, eds., *Engineering the Human Germline* (New York: Oxford University Press, 2000), 3–6.

23. Ibid., 4.

24. James Hughes,"Liberty, Equality, and Solidarity in Our Genetically Engineered Future," ibid., 132.

25. Mary Duenwald, "Discovering What It Takes to Live to 100," *New York Times,* Dec. 25, 2001.

26. Michael Pollan, "Genetic Pollution," *New York Times Magazine,* Dec. 9, 2001.

27. James D. Watson, quoted in Stock and Campbell, *Engineering the Human Germline,* 78.

28. Barbara Crossette, "Move to Curb Biotech Crops Ignores Poor, U.N. Finds," *New York Times,* July 8, 2001.

29. W. Wayt Gibbs, "Innocence Lost," *Scientific American,* Jan. 2002, 14–15.

30. David Brown, "Researchers Claim Clue to Deadly 1918 Flu," *Washington Post,* Sept. 7, 2001.

31. J. Raloff, "Treaty Nears on Gene-Altered Exports," *Science News,* Feb. 5, 2000.

32. "EU Fears of Biotech Are Costing It Jobs, Growth, Report Says," *Wall Street Journal,* Jan. 21, 2002.

33. Peter Huber, "Ecological Eugenics," *Wall Street Journal,* Dec. 20, 1999.

34. Jeremy Rifkin, *The Biotech Century* (New York: Tarcher Putnam, 1998), 3.

Part II Nonmilitary Aspects of Security

Chapter 6   Defense Economics and Security

THEODORE H. MORAN

The flow of high-performance capabilities from the civilian sector to defense-related systems and applications is increasing rapidly. Within the high-tech civilian industries on which defense suppliers depend—telecommunications, aerospace, microelectronics, data processing, propulsion, and special materials—economies of scale are growing and the pace of technological innovation is accelerating.

What are the consequences for defense-industrial-base strategy? This chapter begins by identifying the three purposes of defense-industrial-base strategy that can be justified with analytic rigor: to compensate for market failures in the development of new technology in the home country; to exploit market imperfections so as to extract rents and preempt competitors in other countries; and to avoid dependence on concentrated external suppliers who might delay, deny, or place conditions on the provision of inputs to key civilian or defense-related industries. It then asks to what extent these three purposes, defensible in theory, are feasible or desirable in practice.

What are the prospects for selective public sector interventions to manipulate market outcomes among the civilian components of the defense-industrial base—actions that were the subject of such earnest debate in the 1980s—in light of the experience of private sector behavior in creating new technologies and developing new products in the 1990s and early 2000s?

Can the dynamics of competition and innovation in civilian industries be harnessed to enhance American economic and political as well as military power vis-à-vis other countries? What options do Europe and Japan have to reinforce the performance and autonomy of high-tech civilian industries in their countries? What are the implications of growing economies of scale and more rapid cycles of technological change for their military suppliers? Might the increasing importance of scale economies and the more rapid pace of technological change across high-tech industries condemn European (or Japanese) defense companies to the role of subcontractors or, at best, coproducers of American military systems? What options will Russia and China have to reinforce the performance and autonomy of high-tech civilian industries in their countries? What are the implications of growing economies of scale and more rapid cycles of technological change for their military suppliers?

More generally, do the dynamics of high-tech industrial production point toward an era of U.S. "unipolarity" extending indefinitely into the future? Or might there be new threats to the defense-industrial base in the United States—to the performance and autonomy of high-tech civilian industries, and perhaps even to defense contractors that rely on them—looming just over the horizon?

Public Policy and the Defense-Industrial Base

Since the days of Adam Smith, debates about government policy toward civilian industries that are vital to national defense have swung back and forth between two main schools of thought. Some believe that governments should intervene selectively to protect and promote critical industrial sectors. Others believe that governments should rely on international market forces to determine the future of defense and defense-related industries.

Contending Schools of Thought

Advocates of National Self-Sufficiency. Alexander Hamilton and Friedrich Liszt were among the first to argue that some sectors of the defense-industrial base are too important for national defense to be left to the outcome of market forces. This school of thought contends that governments need to ensure self-sufficiency for defense-related civilian industries vital to the functioning of the country.

The impulse toward autarchy encounters immediate drawbacks, however. Policies aimed at self-sufficiency lose the benefits of international comparative advantage, of specializing in whatever economic activities a given nation does best, of capturing economies of scale in serving multiple national markets. Policies aimed at self-sufficiency retard the dynamic gains that result from international competition and from the associated pressure for continuous innovation and improvement in productivity (dynamic gains on the order of three times greater than the benefits of comparative advantage alone). Protection for favored industries provokes retaliation on the part of other nations.

A preference for relying on national producers rather than external suppliers requires the formulation of some kind of industrial policy through which government officials choose which sectors should be supported or protected and which should not. It obligates public sector planners, rather than the market, to pick winners and losers among individual technologies and companies, to determine whether industrial sectors are receiving too little or too much support in the aggregate, and to apportion the burden of supplying extra resources to some actors onto other unfavored parts of the economy.

The conduct of industrial policy also suffers from procedural hazards. However intelligent and insulated national industrial planners may hope to be, the process of choosing winners and losers is likely to fall prey to special pleading of and capture by powerful interests. In Europe, Japan, and the United States, the political power of "sunset" industries has almost always proved stronger than that of newer "sunrise" industries, and they have received more favorable treatment as a result.

Advocates of Market Forces. Others reject the idea that an industrial policy will enable a nation to rely on its "own" suppliers for vital goods and services. They argue that governments should rely solely on international market forces to determine the composition of activities within national markets. They contend that a country will be strongest if it uses whatever combination of economic actors can perform most efficiently.

Drawing on neoclassical economic analysis, this approach tends to ignore the nationality of producers and suppliers altogether. It answers the question "who are we?" by specifying that "we" are whoever can provide the best products and jobs within a given economy. Assuming perfect competition in national and international markets, this argument suggests that public sector protection of certain sectors or companies is almost certain to damage efficiency, subtract from maximum output, and—with rare exceptions (e.g., optimal tariff considerations when an economy produces a very large share of world output of a particular product)—detract from the welfare, and the power, of the nation-state.

Between these two poles, three analytically rigorous lines of argument coalesced in the 1980s to provide potential guidance in constructing national strategies for the civilian components of a country's defense-industrial base. All three derive their theoretical justification from the facts of market imperfections, market failures, and positive or negative externalities (positive or negative gains from the behavior of firms greater than what can be captured by the firms themselves), and from the potential for particular states to manipulate market imperfections, market failures, and positive or negative capabilities to their advantage.

Arguments for Public Support of Particular Defense Industries

Public Support for Civilian Research and Development. The first analytically rigorous argument for public sector intervention derives from the observation that the social returns from civilian research and development are greater than what can be captured by the firms that undertake the R&D.[1] These social returns may include political-military externalities that support the defense of the nation at large. The inability of the investors to appropriate all of the returns from R&D activity for themselves leads to suboptimal levels of private investment, particularly in defense applications where there is small civilian demand.

The market failure to supply socially optimal amounts of R&D can be remedied by subsidizing private companies, via an R&D tax credit, to augment their research where the payoff to them is highest. But this may still leave gaps in socially important activities with low private payoffs, and may therefore require special targeted programs—to create hyperefficient motors or promote "clean" propulsion technologies, for example, or to customize commercial technologies to meet defense needs such as designing miniature flat-panel displays for military aircraft, and so on. With special publicly funded programs, the question of whether foreign firms would be eligible to participate invariably arises. The answer depends on whether the top priority is to meet the objective as rapidly and effectively as possible, or to protect home firms over foreign firms.

While this rationale for public sector intervention can be defended analytically, the funding requirements still impose a burden on other sectors of the economy when resources are drawn away from them. If special programs are created, rather than simply using an R&D tax credit, this approach may suffer from other industrial policy ills as well, such as the favoritism associated with placing a demonstration project in a particular congressional district.

Strategic Trade Theory.   The second rationale for public sector intervention derives from "strategic trade theory" and suggests that individual states may have an interest in intervening in the marketplace to create, support, and preserve national companies in industries where there are market imperfections, dynamic learning, and first-mover advantages that generate (as above) economic or political-military externalities from the operations of those firms.[2]

The "strategic" in "strategic trade theory" does not imply any specific military importance for the sectors or companies involved but refers to the gaming strategy of the participants when economies of scale may be too large to support more than one actor, or more than a very few. Public sector support for a first mover may preempt the possibility of profitable entry for a follower company in another country. Not every country may end up having an aerospace industry, or a high performance microprocessor industry, or a computer-operating software industry. The successful pursuit of "strategic trade" policies allows the home government, where the champion is located, to extract economic "rents," or political-military advantages, from other countries that need its goods or services.

The second rationale for intervention still suffers from the disadvantages of conventional industrial policy (can government officials pick winners and losers better than the market? can they avoid favoritism?). But the advantages of strategic trade successes may, in theory, outweigh these disadvantages. In contrast to traditional trade theory, which predicts win-win outcomes for all participants, strategic trade theory predicts zero-sum outcomes and suggests tension, retaliation, and escalation among the participants.

Avoiding Dependence on Concentrated Suppliers.   The third guide to the management of the civilian-centered defense-industrial base is a mirror image of the strategic trade framework, aimed at avoiding dependence on external suppliers who may be able to deny, delay, or place conditions on the provision of products and inputs.[3] The "rigor" that distinguishes this approach from the primitive desire for self-sufficiency introduced earlier is that dependence only becomes worrisome if the suppliers are concentrated.[4]

If there are multiple alternative suppliers across many countries, it becomes less plausible that they or their home governments may collude to prevent needed goods or services from reaching a particular country. The rule of thumb is that if more than four firms, or nations, supply at least 50 percent of the output of a product, the prospects for collusion to delay, deny, or place conditions on provision of the product is very low.

Thus the traditional argument that the United States needs to protect a particular industry—say, the steel industry—for reasons of national defense disappears when the array of potential providers (including cross-border providers in friendly countries like Canada and Mexico) becomes so numerous that a coordinated attempt at deprivation is unfeasible.

At the same time, however, the prospect of dependence on one supplier, or on a very small number of suppliers located in a small number of countries, for a product crucial to the functioning of civilian or defense-related operations provides a rationale for public sector intervention. The prototype for the early postwar period was the U.S. denial of IBM computing capabilities to retard the development of de Gaulle's force de frappe. A more recent example, from the 1980s, was the fear that dovish Japanese political leaders would place conditions on the provision of advance ceramics from the Kyocera corporation that were used to house the Tomahawk cruise missile guidance system.

Faced with concentrated suppliers of goods and services crucial to the functioning of a nation's defense-industrial base, a government has limited options.[5] It may try to create its own home country supplier, running the risk that such a supplier may be competitively inferior to the foreign supplier. Or it may try to force the foreign supplier to build plants in the home country, in the hope that this will decrease the likelihood of delay or denial on the part of the parent company or its government.

Strategic Tasks. These three overlapping justifications for public sector intervention in the civilian components of the defense-industrial-base suggest, in theory, a formidable set of possible offensive and defensive tasks for government strategists. Offensively, these tasks include identifying promising but underfunded technologies and ensuring that they receive the resources they need to launch new products and processes. They include building "strategic trade" champions to use these new technologies where there are imperfect markets, dynamic learning, and large economic and political-military externalities, and helping them preempt the emergence of offshore rivals.

Defensively, these tasks include supervising the procurement decisions and corporate-alliance policies of U.S. companies to undermine the growth of quasi-monopolistic offshore rivals, and to prevent home country dependence on their products. They include preventing foreign acquisitions that might give other nations the potential to generate their own strategic trade players. They include backer-of-last-resort support if and when commercial markets turn against the fortunes of a national "strategic trade" champion.

That these tasks can be defended with analytic rigor does not mean, however, that they should be pursued or that they can be carried out in practice. Public sector intervention to support the creation of firms with a predominant or quasi-monopolistic position in high-tech civilian markets, combined with public sector actions to prevent or preempt the emrgence of rivals in other countries, especially in this era of global economics, carries a beggar-thy-neighbor dynamic that may generate antagonism among otherwise friendly nations. Moreover, whether public sector intervention can be carried out effectively is an empirical question that requires careful scrutiny. Sophisticated justifications for possible government action notwithstanding, the challenges of carrying out any industrial policy remain daunting. Defense-industrial-base strategists still have to pick winners and losers among individual technologies and companies better than the market does, still have to determine whether industrial sectors are receiving too little or too much support in the aggregate, still have to apportion the burden of supplying extra resources to some actors onto unfavored parts of the economy, and still have to avoid favoritism.

These offensive and defensive tasks were, arguably, feasible in the relative simplicity of the 1980s, when the rivalry of "strategic trade" champions such as Boeing and Airbus had high visibility and the growing dependence of the United States on Japanese semiconductors appeared preordained. Are these tasks feasible in the contemporary period, given growing economies of scale across many high-tech sectors and an ever-increasing pace of technological change? Are they feasible for the United States, feasible for Europe and Japan, feasible for Russia and China?

National Defense-Industrial-Base Strategies

The evidence from the 1980s and 1990s shows that an increasing portion of technologies with defense applications comes from the commercial marketplace. In 1980, according to the National Science Foundation, resources allocated to R&D in the noncommunist world equaled approximately $240 billion in 2000 dollars, split in equal amounts between the United States and the G-7 allies.[6] The U.S. Department of Defense funded approximately $40 billion, or one-sixth of the total amount. By 2000 this figure had increased by 50 percent, to $360 billion, with the United States again more than equaling the amount spent elsewhere. In 2000 the U.S. Department of Defense sponsored only half of its 1980 share, equivalent to one-twelfth of the total.

Of U.S. Defense Department spending on R&D, the proportion devoted to engineering improvements in existing systems or customizing applications for defense use (as opposed to developing new technologies) has been rising. In 1980 69 percent of Defense R&D spending went to development while 31 percent went to research. In 2000 88 percent went to development while only 12 percent went to research.

Overall, defense capabilities have increasingly been growing out of innovations developed by commercial companies for the commercial market in sectors such as telecommunications, aerospace, microelectronics, data processing, cryptography, special materials, and propulsion.[7] Not only have high-tech civilian sectors been growing at a rate significantly higher than the economy as a whole (thus increasing their role in the civilian economy) but their contributions to defense capabilities have been rising as well. The conduct of revolution-in-military-affairs operations depend directly on them. They undergird command, control, communications, and surveillance capabilities that allow military commanders to launch weapons and observe results in near-real time. They also provide the high performance, stealth, and precision of the weapons, delivery vehicles, and reconnaissance systems themselves. Countries with access to these capabilities will enjoy superior performance in both civilian and defense applications. Countries that might be denied access to these capabilities, or might find conditions placed upon their use, would suffer in both civilian and defense dimensions of their national activities.

What does the experience of the 1990s—a decade in which the pace of technological change accelerated and the importance of economies of scale increased— suggest about the need for public sector officials in the United States or other countries to conduct an offensive strategy to enhance the creation of national capabilities in high-tech sectors of importance for defense, or to devise a defensive strategy to avoid dependence on concentrated external suppliers in these sectors? What does the evidence from the 1990s and early 2000s suggest about the possibility that they can carry out such policies effectively?

Industrial-Base Strategy in the United States

Does the record of the late 1990s and early 2000s offer any indication that defense-industrial strategists might be able to pick winners and losers—firms and technologies—better than the market can, or that a defense-industrial strategy might be needed to ensure that particularly crucial sectors receive adequate resources?

Between 1995 and 2000 venture capital firms, angels, and investment banks in the United States provided funding to approximately 12,000 start-ups, of which almost 3,000 went public with a capitalization of more than $330 billion.[8] Roughly two-thirds were in the technology sector. Established firms almost doubled the aggregate amounts through internally conducted R&D to $160 billion per year in 2000, equaling approximately $800 billion over the 1995–2000 period.

Given such vigorous innovative activity, it is implausible to expect that a cadre of public sector planners would be able to outguess or outperform the universe of private sector venture capitalists, angels, and investment bankers, especially when the latter could attract and compensate individuals skilled in spotting valuable R&D initiatives far superior to that of government recruiters. Moreover, while it can be argued that, theoretically, appropriability problems could retard R&D, in practice the outcome in many high-tech industries (including telecommunications, microelectronics, and data processing) has been just the reverse.

Thus, whereas in the 1980s the complaint was that the private market was not supplying sufficient resources to the semiconductor, microprocessor, computer, and fiber-optic sectors, and that the U.S. government was ignoring the problem

("Microchips, potato chips: the market does not know the difference!"), the evidence from the late 1990s and early 2000s shows no such difficulty. To the contrary, hindsight makes clear that these sectors were being overbuilt, not underbuilt. The task for defense-industrial strategists would have been not just to make these sectors perform better than the investment bankers and venture capitalists did, but to muster the wherewithal to constrain—or even stop—their exuberance. Only in the case of bridging the gap between the civilian technology frontier and specific military applications (narrowly defined DARPA-like functions) might a role for government planners in directing the work of the private sector be justified. More broadly, the experience of the 1990s and early 2000s suggests a need for rethinking the relationship between enhancing capabilities within the national economy and enhancing the power of the nation-state.

Is the goal of defense-industry strategy to maximize relative capabilities that might be confined to national borders or to maximize overall capabilities that might not be amenable to national control?

The 1990s saw a new generation of U.S. companies with preponderant market positions emerge—much as Boeing and IBM had done in previous decades—without special government help. These spontaneous "strategic trade" champions included Intel (microprocessors), Cisco (Internet networking systems), Corning (optical fiber equipment), Qualcomm (Code Division Multiple Access technology), CDMA (wireless applications), and the ubiquitous Microsoft (personal computer software).

Strategic trade theory suggests that the home government should tolerate—and might want to bolster—the market position of these firms where first-mover advantages and barriers to entry into the industry might preempt the success of rivals abroad. But each of these natural national champions, to a greater or lesser extent, faced rivals among the ranks of U.S. and foreign companies: Intel (Advanced Micro Devices), Cisco (Alcatel, Ericsson, Nortel, Redback, Sycamore), Corning (JDS Uniphase, Alcatel, Nortel, Fujitsu), Qualcomm (LSI Logic and Philips), Microsoft (Sun Microsystems, Apple). The pace of innovation within these natural U.S. national champions was driven in large part by the need to meet and match the new approaches of these competitors.

The completion of the Uruguay Round of trade negotiations and the establishment of the World Trade Organization (WTO), enshrining the idea of most-favored-nation treatment among international suppliers, precluded the use of selective trade policy or preferential government procurement to bolster national firms and disadvantage firms of other nationalities, as contemplated in the "strategic trade" literature of the 1980s. But competition policy and selective antitrust enforcement still offer a possible means to build strategic trade national champions.

Should U.S. defense-industrial-strategy considerations reshape U.S. antitrust thinking and U.S. policies toward mergers and acquisitions, and lean toward accepting the risk of global domination, as long as a U.S. company is the dominator? Should U.S. defense-industrial-strategy urge the consolidation of Intel with Advanced Micro Devices, the acquisition of Redback and Sycamore by Cisco, the combination of

Corning with JDS Uniphase and of Qualcomm with LSI Logic? Should U.S. defense-industrial-strategy rewind the tape of the antitrust action against Microsoft (not just abandoning the demand for a breakup of the company but eliminating the imposition of any fines, penalties, or requirements to unbundled semirelated systems)?

The national champion route would give the United States a new array of mighty heroes—SuperIntel, SuperCisco, SuperCorning, SuperQualcomm, SuperduperMicrosoft—but much of the economic stimulus that kept them innovative would be lost.

The logical corollary of building up "strategic trade" national champions would be for public sector officials to supervise the corporate alliances or partnerships of home country firms on the basis of the nationality of the prospective ally or partner.

Should defense-industrial strategists limit or prevent alliances or partnerships between U.S. firms and foreign companies that might help foreign firms counter the dominance of the leading U.S. firms? Furukawa Electric has built up an ownership position in JDS Uniphase, making it the largest shareholder in the most rapidly growing rival to Corning in the production of advanced fiber-optic components and dense wavelength multiplexing (DWDM) modules. Sun Microsystems and Hitachi have cross-licensed each other's storage software, expanded their integration capabilities worldwide, and agreed to collaborate on the development of next-generation storage technologies to challenge the position of IBM. Intel, Advanced Micro Devices, and Motorola have teamed with Infineon of Germany and ASM Lithography of the Netherlands to develop "extreme ultraviolet" lithography to counter the all-American partnership of IBM and Lucent Technologies that uses ultrashort-wavelength X rays to etch microcircuits instead of light.

Should U.S. defense-industrial strategists supervise or pass judgment on such alliances and partnerships, with a view toward promoting all-U.S. outcomes and preventing the dilution of U.S.-based high-tech capabilities by foreign firms? Or should U.S. defense-industrial strategists accept the arguments of the participants that these alliances and partnerships are sources of strength for the U.S-based firms and that other firms would reproduce such alliances and partnerships if they did not?

The dynamics of high-tech innovation in the 1990s and early 2000s show that defense-industrial-base policies that might enhance the *relative* level of capabilities among nations (by encouraging the consolidation of competitors from a given country into a single national champion) run in the opposite direction of defense-industrial-base policies that enhance the *absolute* level of capabilities (by encouraging competition between national and extranational rivals). Any attempt to gain relative advantage on the part of the United States, moreover, would be sure to prick the sensitivities of America's allies, and provoke vigorous reactions.

An offensive defense-industrial-base strategy of building predominant market players in international markets would logically have propelled the U.S. government to support the proposed GE-Honeywell merger, for example, precisely because of the possibilities of "bundling" products, services, and financing in the aerospace industry that so frightened EU regulators.[9]

What actions the European Union (or others) might be able to take to counter the emergence of monopolistic external suppliers, like a SuperGE in the aerospace sector, is the subject of the next section of this chapter. But passive acquiescence is probably not the most likely option the EU would choose.

The experience of the 1990s and early 2000s, therefore, provides little evidence that public sector intervention is needed to make up for market failures in providing sufficient resources to civilian sectors with important defense-related applications, or that public sector strategists could perform this task better than private sector actors. The experience of the 1990s and early 2000s indicates, moreover, that any public sector effort to mold the behavior of potential "strategic trade" national champions in ways that might be used to extract rents or withhold capabilities from other nations would probably come at the expense of competitive pressures to keep improving their own performance. Finally, the experience of the 1990s and early 2000s suggests that public sector encouragement for the creation of predominant superfirms of U.S. origin would provoke energetic responses on the part of erstwhile U.S. allies.

Turning from "offense" to "defense," what is left of the role of defense-industrial strategy to counter the prospect that a nation may find itself at the mercy of external monopolists or quasi-monopolists in high-tech civilian sectors?

In the 1980s there seemed to be a potential need for the United States to bolster the position of American firms in the semiconductor industry when they appeared to be in irreversible decline in relation to externally concentrated suppliers. But the relative decline of the U.S. semiconductor industry turned out to be momentary, and in any case the number of alternative suppliers of memory chips at home and abroad multiplied over the course of the 1990s.

Perhaps more relevant for the contemporary era may be a potential need to serve as a backstop of last resort when a predominant U.S. firm stakes its future on a particular product or process and loses, leaving a preponderant international market position in the hands of a non-U.S. rival.

The experience of the 1990s and early 2000s showed that "next-generation" products or processes in some sectors are sufficiently costly, and sufficiently risky—with success or failure unknown until fixed capital of extraordinary proportions has already been committed—that a company may have to "bet the company" as it invests in the new endeavor.

Looking to the future, the aerospace industry might provide a relevant example for the United States (with mirror-image challenges for the Europeans, considered later). How should the U.S. government respond if Boeing decides to proceed with plans for a high-speed stratocruiser whose launch costs tens of billions of dollars, and discovers that the market will not support it? Should the U.S. government stand ready to help Boeing play catch-up if the market turns toward the rival Airbus super-jumbo (also costing tens of billions of dollars to launch) while Boeing has no product to match it?

The possible need for a "defensive" response springs not from the argument that Boeing (or Intel or Cisco) is "too big to fail," but more importantly that a company that occupies a predominant market position with important defense spillovers is "too singular to fail."

There could emerge a defensive task related to this, of blocking the hypothetical foreign acquisition of a strategic trade-like U.S. firm. Here U.S. defense-industrial strategists might want to join U.S. antitrust authorities in preventing an external takeover of Cisco, Intel, or Qualcomm, or any other company that enjoyed a predominant position within a small oligopoly of high-tech companies in international markets. The goal, once again, would be to prevent the United States from becoming dependent on an external quasi-monopolist for products and services vital to commercial and defense-related performance in the home economy.

As the last section of this chapter will point out, however, playing defense toward the defense-industrial base may turn out to be more problematic for the United States than might appear at first glance.

Industrial-Base Strategies in Europe and Japan

What does the experience of the 1990s suggest about the prospects for public sector authorities in Europe and Japan to ensure that civilian sectors crucial to national defense receive adequate levels of resources, to encourage the formation of "strategic trade" champions with preponderant positions in international markets, or to prevent their economies from being exposed to external monopolistic suppliers?

Looking first at technology creation along the frontier of international civilian industries, the generation of start-ups in high-technology sectors in Europe in the late 1990s and early 2000s reached a level no more than one-fifth of the amount of capital of the number of new ventures that emerged during the comparable period in the United States. In Japan the proportion was much lower than that. Within established European firms R&D expenditures amounted to less than half that within U.S. firms, and within established Japanese firms perhaps one-third (recalling that the Japanese domestic market was in a persistent slump during most of this period).

A majority of the start-up activity in Europe was launched under the auspices of U.S. venture capital firms and investment bankers. Indigenous start-up activity in Japan, while not nonexistent, appears to be a small fraction of what took place in Europe and the United States.[10] In both Europe and Japan, there is clearly a role for the design of public policies to augment the amount of resources flowing to high-tech civilian sectors. But the principal impediments to more vigorous R&D have not derived from appropriations problems; rather they have sprung from rigidities in labor and financial markets that make it difficult for new companies to be launched and to take off, and for innovative companies to succeed.

There is no evidence to suggest that public sector strategists could sort through the prospects for individual technologies or individual companies on the microlevel with any better chance of achieving superior results than their counterparts in the United States. On the contrary, government targeting—even for the once-revered MITI in Japan—has been shown to have had a problematic and often counterproductive impact on performance in the civilian sector.[11]

With regard to the creation of national champions that might extract rents and preempt rivals from other countries, the need to achieve economies of scale and to be close to the sources of rapid technological change pulled European and Japanese multinationals in the direction opposite to what "strategic trade" theory would propose, drawing them out of their home country and into the United States. As the preceding section indicated, many of these investments involved the European or Japanese multinationals' taking ownership positions in, or forming alliances with, the American rivals of predominant U.S. firms in high-performance computers, fiber-optics, semiconductors, microprocessors, and software development precisely to avoid their own corporate dependence on external monopolistic suppliers.

For European and Japanese firms seeking to compete with U.S. companies in industries with large economies of scale and a rapid pace of innovation, access to the U.S. economy and, increasingly, a presence in the U.S. economy have become critical to maintaining themselves at the cutting edge of high-tech civilian industries. Foreign direct investment by international companies with a European or Japanese origin duplicated the high points of the 1980s in 1995, 1996, and 1997, and more than doubled the high points of the 1980s in 1998, 1999, and 2000 (with flows equaling more than $250 billion per year).[12]

In the process, a hypothetical ability to formulate a "strategic trade" strategy that might harness indigenous companies to bolster the relative position of the European or Japanese home economy vis-à-vis other economies has dissipated as those indigenous companies globalized their own operations to keep themselves competitive in international markets. The high-tech civilian component of what might be called the defense-industrial base in Europe and Japan has taken on a transatlantic and transpacific character that thwarts control by authorities in the home country. At the same time, the prospect that defense-industrial strategists, or domestic politicians, in Europe or Japan could selectively delay, deny, or place conditions on provision of goods or services to American users—however worrisome in the 1980s—has receded toward the vanishing point.

Turning from offensive to defensive dimensions of defense-industrial-base strategy, the most assertive form of public sector intervention—in Europe, at least—has been the use of antitrust policy to minimize the risk of rent extraction or predatory behavior on the part of external firms. This has taken the form of newfound aggressiveness in EU scrutiny of proposed mergers between U.S. companies—first, the proposed merger of Boeing–McDonnell Douglas, and more recently the proposed merger of GE-Honeywell—to obviate a buildup of externally concentrated market power that would threaten EU producers as well as EU consumers. And, given the increasing importance of economies of scale of global dimensions, U.S. high-tech companies have discovered that their domestic merger-and-acquisition strategies require EU approval to become economically viable.[13]

For the future a corollary course of action, potentially justified on both antitrust and defense-industrial-base-strategy grounds, might come in the form of the presumption that authorities would block the takeover of an EU or Japanese company that would leave the acquirer in a position of market dominance. This might be complemented in a manner suggested earlier for the United States, with government support for a preeminent European champion like Airbus if the company were to bet the future of the firm on a new generation of products and lose. Despite Airbus's record of competitive success in recent years, its proposed super-jumbo jetliner threatens to bankrupt the company if the market does not support a large number of purchases. In Japan, however, public policy has been moving in the opposite direction—at least in some notable instances, like government approval for the takeover of Nissan by Renault—relying on new foreign owners and managers to restructure erstwhile keiretsu champions and return them to internationally competitive performance.

Industrial Base Strategies in Russia and China

What are the prospects for Russian or Chinese authorities to fashion policies to strengthen their own high-tech civilian sectors with defense-related applications, and to counter dependence on external firms with quasi-monopolistic market power?

Looking first at Russia, there is wide room for improvement in Russian public policy to enhance the performance of the country's high-tech business sectors. These include loosening the stranglehold on particular sectors by favored oligarchs, and instituting regulatory and tax reforms that make it easier for new entrepreneurs to enter the market.[14] The extent to which such measures can generate internationally competitive Russian companies in high-tech sectors without external alliances or partnerships, however, is problematic.[15]

Perhaps the most promising sector, as David Bernstein points out, has been space launch. Here the Russians have possessed fully developed, tested, and proven systems, including already manufactured inventory, that could be readily adapted for commercial satellite transport with low incremental costs. Russian performance compares favorably with the French, and very favorably with the United States. Russian companies have nonetheless had to rely on external companies not just for capital but for system integration, management, and quality control to enter international markets successfully. Khrunichev (builder of Proton boosters) and Energia (a major space company) have formed a joint venture with Lockheed Martin, called LKEI, to provide commercial space launches.[16] Energia has become a minority partner (25 percent owner) with NPO Yuzhoye (a leading Ukrainian aerospace company, maker of the Zenit rocket, 15 percent owner), Kvaerner (Europe's largest marine operator, 20 percent owner) and Boeing (40 percent owner), to create Sea Launch, offering sea-based platforms to boost satellites into orbit for commercial customers. Energomash's primary international operation to develop liquid-fueled rocket engines has been a joint venture, RD/AMROSS, with Pratt & Whitney, oriented toward Lockheed Martin as its principal customer.

Similarly, in other aerospace sectors, Ilyushin has chosen foreign subcontractors to build its IL-96T wide-bodied cargo plane, selecting Pratt & Whitney for engines and Rockwell International for cockpit instruments and controls. Tupelov Design

Bureau contracted with Boeing, under NASA auspices, for supersonic tests involving the TU-144LL with an eye toward creating a new generation of ultra-high-speed commercial aircraft. GE later became a member of this Boeing-led team. Outside of aerospace, Obukhov established a cooperative arrangement with FMC to jointly upgrade drilling equipment for oil and gas operations. The Karpov Institute of Physical Chemistry followed the same path with FMC for chemical-processing technology.

Software development illustrates some of the challenges of launching world-class competitive enterprises in Russia, according to Bernstein. Highly skilled Russian software engineering teams have been working together for years within various Russian enterprises (principally defense enterprises). Since software development is highly labor intensive, the costs of using Russian engineers are extremely favorable in comparison to U.S. or European equivalents. Foreign firms such as Intel and Boeing have used Russian expertise to good effect. Sun Microsystems contracted with MCST (the Moscow Center for SPARC Technology) to generate cutting-edge telecommunications applications. The reason this sector has been quite successful, however, is precisely that Russian and foreign entities have been able to join forces without having to go through the ordeal of reviving antiquated production plants or retraining Soviet-era managers.

Turning from reinforcing their own high-tech sectors to diluting the threat of dependence on monopolistic external suppliers, Russian strategy can try deliberately to ensure that the alliances, partnerships, and shared ownership between foreign firms and major indigenous companies and industrial groups be diversified as to nationality of participants.

Given the variety of competitors in high-tech sectors within the United States, Europe, and Asia, there is room for a Russian defense-industrial-strategy—if freed from the particularistic demands of Russian oligarchic groups—that can create a reasonable amount of buffer against external political pressures. The aerospace, telecommunications, advanced materials, and computer/electronics sectors of the Russian economy could come to be populated with a vibrant array of French, Italian, Swedish, German, Korean, Japanese—as well as U.S. and UK—partnerships, once reform of commercial and securities law creates a more viable business climate in Russia.

In the same vein, Chinese authorities have shown themselves to be rather adept at playing industrial giants of diverse nationalities off against each other in the aerospace, telecommunications, computer/electronics, and automotive sectors. They have a long history of pitting Airbus against Boeing, Mercedes Benz against General Motors, and Eastman Kodak against Fuji to avoid being dependent on single-source suppliers of goods, services, or technologies.

As for bringing the capabilities of indigenous Chinese producers of high-tech goods up to international competitive standards, the challenges of converting state-run companies into efficient modern enterprises may be even more daunting in the short run than in the case of Russia. But over the longer term the prospects may not be so problematic. Already there is interesting evidence, according to James Mulvenon, that in the telecommunications equipment sector, Chinese entrepreneurs, with preferential support from the government, have created "four tigers"—Huawei, Zhongxing, Datang, and Julong—with significant competitive potential both domestically and in international markets.[17] Recruiting the best talent from Chinese universities and offering them attractive compensation and superior working facilities, these companies have established themselves as credible rivals to international providers of routers, mobile communications, and narrowband/broadband integrated switching devices, optical systems, and Internet access.

The civilian prowess of these four companies clearly has defense-related applications. The U.S. Department of Defense pointed the finger at Huawei Technologies as being responsible for constructing a fiber-optic network among Iraqi antiaircraft batteries, radar stations, and command-and-control facilities.[18] Zhongxing was the supplier of the replacement for the wireless system in Yugoslavia destroyed by NATO bombing. Julong has sold telecommunications systems to Russia, North Korea, Pakistan, Vietnam, and Cuba. While these Chinese companies, like their Russian counterparts, do rely on external suppliers for hardware and software inputs—from Intel, Qualcomm, and Motorola—Mulvenon characterizes these four firms as largely indigenous "national champions" in what the state has designated as a strategic sector.

Over the longer term, the prospects for the development of related high-tech sectors in China may be more promising than appears to be the case for Russia. If "greater China" comes to include most of the offshore Chinese capabilities now located in Taiwan, China may enjoy the possibility of creating autonomous or predominantly Chinese national champions in other areas, such as high-performance microelectronics and data processing.

The Perils of National Autonomy and Transborder Integration

What are the implications of growing economies of scale and a more rapid pace of technological change for defense contractors and suppliers of military equipment?

Military Suppliers in the United States, Europe, and Japan

Since the end of World War II, the size of U.S. Defense Department demand for military equipment has favored American defense contractors in comparison to their counterparts in Europe and Japan. But U.S. defense contractors have not been immune to pressures to capture the cost benefits that come from greater production runs and to tap the most advanced international sources of technology from around the world.

Beginning with the "competition of the century" between General Dynamic's F-16 and the Mirage F-1 to provide the next generation of fighter aircraft to NATO, in 1975 U.S. defense firms sought to maximize sales to allies by subcontracting major components to countries that purchased the final products. General Dynamics won support for the F-16 among NATO member states not just by offering what it considered to be a superior product, but by agreeing to allow European buyers to supply 40 percent of the content of the European version of the F-16, 10 percent of the content of the planes bought by the United States, and 15 percent of the content of planes purchased elsewhere.[19]

Since then allied defense contractors and their home governments—principally the Europeans rather than the Japanese, since the legacy of World War II has moderated periodic Japanese aspirations to create prime system-integrating defense contractors—have faced a dilemma: should they try to remain autonomous in supplying their own military needs, or would such an effort condemn them to second-class capabilities? How should they respond to the attractions of becoming coproducers and subcontractors of first-tier systems with American primes? In the future, to what extent will they be able to match the United States in building the integrated capabilities and the "systems of systems" involved in C3I operations and operations related to revolutions in military affairs?

Looking first at Europe, the EU members of NATO spend, in the aggregate, approximately 60 percent of the U.S. total on defense. Their R&D and procurement allocations are significantly smaller than this.[20] Approximately one-third of the U.S. defense budget is devoted to equipment expenditures and R&D combined (and Secretary of Defense Rumsfeld has indicated he would like this proportion to rise). For Britain and France, the corresponding share is about one-fourth; for Germany, 14 percent; for Italy and Spain, 12 percent. The research and procurement efforts of the European national forces, moreover, are not closely coordinated or integrated among themselves.

When they have tried to operate as prime suppliers of military products, European defense contractors have a record of creating systems that are quite proficient but nonetheless operate well behind the cutting edge of military capabilities by the time they appear (Tornado, AlphaJet, Eurofighter, Typhoon, and Tiger helicopter). At the same time they have found themselves pulled in a transatlantic direction by the allure of becoming coproducers or subcontractors to U.S. prime defense companies. Following the model of General Dynamics with the F-16, Boeing diverted interest from the British Nimrod, for example, by dangling aerospace and avionics coproduction contracts for Airborne Warning and Control System (AWACS) in front of potential purchasers.

The schizophrenia of European military firms about whether to maintain their autonomy or join American defense contractors in joint projects has been exacerbated by the tendency of the members of their ranks closest to the Americans—the British—to side with the United States rather than with the Continent. British Aerospace and GEC/Marconi (now combined in BAE Systems) have a record of "betraying" the goal of building an autonomous European defense capability by turning regularly in the direction of their American cousins. The new German-French EADS (the European Aeronautic, Defense, and Space Company, from the merger of Aerospatiale Matra and Deutsche Aerospace) has announced its intention to move closer to U.S. primes such as Lockheed Martin, as well.[21]

The rival contractors for the Joint Strike Fighter—both Lockheed Martin (the winner) and Boeing (the loser)—enlisted Britain, led by BAE (British Aerospace), to be a "level-one" partner in the project, agreeing to contribute $2 billion in return for responsibility for 8 percent of the development portion of the program.[22] Italy, Turkey, and the Netherlands have considered becoming "level-two" partners, contributing $1.2 billion each for a role in avionics, or propulsion. Canada, Denmark, and Norway have positioned themselves to become "level-three" partners, with an investment of $250–$500 million and a smaller role as subcontractors. Singapore and Israel have sought some smaller degree of participation.

Commercial and military considerations reinforce each other from the point of view of the participants. "If you are interested in coalition warfare any time in the next fifty years, this is the airplane you need to buy," has been the selling point used by Lockheed Martin.[23]

The relative sizes of the U.S. and EU procurement and R&D budgets, and the attraction of working on the most advanced projects with U.S. partners, may propel European defense firms in the direction of becoming perpetual subcontractors to the Americans.

The NATO action in Kosovo has often been characterized as the "wake-up call" that alerted the Europeans to deficiencies in their ability to conduct sophisticated military operations. Of the thirty-five satellites positioned over Kosovo, only two were European. In launching air strikes, the Europeans depended on American military infrastructure for battle control, refueling, and jamming and destroying Serbian radar, and had few precision-guided munitions, limited ability to communicate rapidly or securely with allied forces, paucity of all-weather/day-night assets. With regard to force projection more generally, the Europeans have meager fast sealift and heavy airlift capabilities.[24]

The more fundamental question from the point of view of defense-industrial-base dynamics may be whether Kosovo was a call waking Europeans up to the prospect of a robust new era of intra-European military procurement, or to the vision of a second-class and possibly subordinate status stretching far ahead in time.

If Japan were to combine resurgent political-military aspirations with the industrial recovery that surely will come when the country finally emerges from the economic doldrums, Japanese high-tech firms would be subject to similar cross-pressures.[25] And the precedent of the FSX—a Lockheed-Mitsubishi project that ended up "grossly over budget" and not much more capable than the original F-16 model on which it was based—is not likely to inspire strong support for indigenously produced military equipment.[26]

Military Suppliers in Russia and China

The policy dilemmas are similar for Russia and China. The amount of domestic resources that might be devoted to procurement of advanced military systems (and development of improved models) in Russia, while not negligible, is certain to be constrained until the growth path of the home economy continues on a steady upward course for some time. The export of military equipment to other countries has assisted Russian defense companies, however, in keeping their production lines and design teams in operation.

In the meantime, as indicated previously, most if not all of the high-tech defense suppliers are developing foreign partnerships to help them keep on the cutting edge of technologies and business practices, to help with system integration, and to penetrate external markets for civilian products, including Ilyushin, Tupelov Design Bureau, Khrunichev, Energia, Energomash, and the Karpov Institute of Physical Chemistry.

The Chinese conglomerates that supply military equipment have also been aggressive in lining up foreign partners and suppliers, sometimes using commercial connections to gain militarily useful assistance, perhaps best illustrated in the case of Loral. In the telecommunications sector, however, as indicated earlier, the "four tigers"—Huawei, Zhongxing, Datang, and Julong—have given the PLA (People's Liberation Army) some freedom from relying on foreign suppliers for information-technology equipment. Their success also has provided China with the capability to transfer critical systems, such as fiber-optic networks, to countries of concern such as Iraq.

When China has maintained its traditional approach of "self-reliance" ("ti-yong") with regard to military equipment suppliers in ordnance, shipbuilding, and aircraft, Chinese military firms, in the estimation of James Mulvenon, have not been able to keep up with performance standards elsewhere. Looking beyond the performance characteristics of individual weapons, however, the larger question—for both Russia and China—is the extent to which the increasingly privatized civilian components of each country's defense-industrial base will be able to provide the complex system integration that is needed to conduct sophisticated modern military operations, independent of foreign inputs, foreign corporate alliances, and foreign management assistance.[27]

A key question for the analysis of "asymmetric threats" is whether China or Russia can exercise power as regional hegemons and deter U.S. intervention in local conflicts, if their own forces lack cutting-edge capabilities, including advanced information warfare, reconnaissance, target acquisition, stand-off, and precision strike competencies.[28] Will second-best, or third-best, be good enough to offset first-best U.S. capabilities in an era of rapid technological change and steeply rising unit costs due to large economies of scale?

The Prospects for American Unipolarity

The preceding sections have shown that there do not appear to be noteworthy "market failure" problems in providing adequate resources to those high-tech civilian sectors that have important defense applications in the United States. The industrial dynamics of high-tech industries in which there are large economies of scale and a rapid pace of technological innovation—in both civilian and defense applications—favor firms with a large presence in the United States.

This means that high-tech firms with preponderant market positions are more likely to emerge in the United States, and that their foreign counterparts are more likely to establish a large presence here, than models of strategic trade battles across the Atlantic or the Pacific among exclusive home country–based firms seem to predict. The process may reduce the likelihood that the United States will be denied access to high-performance capabilities of importance to both civilian and defense sectors. Economies of scale and pressures from the pace of technological innovation may give an edge to defense contractors and producers of military systems in the United States, and to those non-U.S. firms that become coproducers and subcontractors to them.

But a new and unaccustomed challenge is already emerging on the horizon: Who is going to own the U.S. high-tech companies, including prominent commercial participants in the defense-industrial base? The answer to this question is being driven by forces much more profound than the nervousness about Japanese and other foreign acquisitions during the 1980s. The outcome will be determined not just by corporate preferences in the area of mergers and acquisitions, or by individual preferences about what investor would like to buy the stock of this or that American company, which have traditionally preoccupied defense-industrial strategists in the United States. Rather, the outcome will be determined by a macroeconomic tidal wave largely overlooked in the analysis of defense-industrial-base strategy precisely because it has seemed so mundane—a macroeconomic tidal wave springing from the ratio between consumption and savings in the United States, from the consequent trade deficit, and from the buildup of aggregate foreign claims on American assets.

The U.S. household savings rate has dropped from half that of Europe and one-third that of Japan (and Korea) to near zero, sometimes even to a net negative figure. Traditional nonfinancial forms of savings—principally private home ownership—have actually been drawn down, as Americans have used home equity loans to finance current consumption. This performance in the private household sector was momentarily offset by U.S. public sector balances that moved upward at the end of the 1990s from deficit to surplus. But now U.S. public sector surpluses have disappeared, and projections for the future show renewed deficits. With the demographic transformation of the U.S. population, in which older citizens consume their accumulated savings (to the extent that they have accumulated savings)—selling the stock in their 401k plans to provide money to live on, and so on—who will be the new buyers of the stock and the new providers of capital to the U.S. economy?

The low savings in the public and private sectors combined has been reflected in the growing balance-of-payments deficit for the United States, which reached 4.5 percent of GDP in 2000. A balance-of-payments deficit occurs when a country spends more than it earns, purchases more than it produces, or invests more than it saves. A balance-of-payments deficit essentially means that a nation is buying goods and services from abroad on credit. A balance-of-payments deficit generates an accumulation of claims on U.S. assets in the hands of foreigners. "Do the math," to use a popular phrase, to predict the outcome from balance-of-payments deficits on the order of 4 percent of GDP each year for the next ten or fifteen years.

There are reasons to claim, as the *Economic Report of the President* of January 2001 did, that the record balance-of-payments deficit was a sign of American strength, not American weakness: foreigners wanted to invest in America, foreigners wanted to hold American assets, foreigners wanted to participate in the high growth rate and innovation of the U.S. economy.[29]

International macroeconomics have self-equilibrating features, in particular an eventual decline for the dollar. But devaluations have no long-term impact unless they are simultaneously accompanied by changes in the ratio between consumption and savings in the home economy. As long as a country (like an individual) spends more than it earns, purchases more than it produces, and invests more than it saves, that country will experience an increase in the claims against domestic assets held by outsiders.

Between 1995 and 2000, foreign-owned assets in the United States doubled, from $4.3 trillion to $8.6 trillion.[30] By 2000 foreign direct investment in the United States had climbed to $1.2 trillion (including 1,202 acquisitions of U.S. companies in 1998 and 1,701 acquisitions of U.S. companies in 1999, for a total of 6 percent of U.S. equity markets), foreign ownership of U.S. corporate stock had climbed to $1.4 trillion (7 percent of U.S. equity markets), together totaling 13 percent of the aggregate ownership of all U.S. firms. Foreign holdings of U.S. corporate bonds amounted to $1 trillion, and foreign ownership of U.S. Treasury bonds, other agency securities, and other assets amounted to $3 trillion.

Over the same 1995–2000 period, the proportion of foreign claims devoted to instruments of foreign corporate ownership (foreign direct investment, acquisitions of U.S. companies, acquisition of corporate stock), rather than purchases of U.S. Treasury bonds and corporate bonds, has been climbing, from 48 percent to 61 percent of all foreign assets.

For the latest figures that are available (1999), 25 percent of the augmentation of foreign-owned assets took the form of increases in foreign direct investment (including mergers and acquisitions of U.S. companies) and 44 percent took the form of foreign ownership of U.S. stocks. Thus, at the margin, 69 percent of all new foreign claims on U.S. assets have resulted in some kind of external control over companies based in the United States, rather than the traditional preference for government and corporate bonds and bank deposits. This increase in foreign ownership of companies based in the United States is growing at a rate that equals almost one percent of the entire stock of corporate securities each year (0.08 percent per year).

Projecting U.S. current account deficits into the future, even to 2010 or 2015—well before the great demographic transition—soon produces foreign portfolios of corporate assets in the United States of dimensions well beyond the historical experience of the United States. A simple projection of the buildup of foreign ownership of corporate assets using the growth rate of 0.08 percent per year shows the proportion growing from 13 percent in 2000 to 24 percent in 2015. Alternatively, a more complicated model of the evolution of obligations owed to foreigners as a result of the balance-of-payments deficits, constructed by Catherine Mann, suggests that foreign ownership of U.S. corporate assets could grow to 35 percent of the total over the same period (this is in addition to foreign ownership of U.S. Treasury and agency bonds and corporate bonds).[31]

If foreign ownership were concentrated in high-tech sectors, it would not be far-fetched to suggest that the figure could reach 50 percent in the foreseeable future. An ownership stake of 50 or 51 percent is not needed to exercise control over a corporation, however. The U.S. Securities and Exchange Commission requires a purchaser to notify the SEC upon obtaining 5 percent of the stock of a company, and percentages of ownership between 10 percent and 20 percent are commonly taken to represent effective control of the corporation.[32]

The result is that the presumed dominance of the United States as an economic power—and hence as a political power—free from external constraints and influences rests on surprisingly fragile foundations. Unless the United States reverses what has now become a decades-long record of weak public and private saving, the claims of foreigners on the assets of corporate America will climb to unprecedentedly large proportions quite rapidly. The outcome is perfectly consistent with the dynamics of comparative advantage: the United States excels at generating new technologies and at allowing competitive forces to determine which thrive and which perish; other countries excel at saving their resources and acquiring a stake in the surviving companies.

What would this mean for the power and influence of the United States in the international system? Most scare stories about foreign direct investment in the United States turn out to be quite wide of the mark.[33] Foreign investors do not come in, like the Soviets in post–World War II Germany, dismantle plants and laboratories, and cart them off. Foreign investors do not even come in and transfer high value-added activities and leading management functions back to the home country (the so-called "headquarters effect"). Quite to the contrary, they usually leave the most valuable activities and management functions where they are—that is why they bought the assets in the first place—and bring new resources to improve the performance of existing plants and laboratories.[34] Thus the rising share of foreign ownership in the U.S. economy might well be expected to bolster the capabilities and competitiveness of firms based in the United States.

However, the rising share of foreign ownership—on the part of a diverse array of Asian, European, and other participants—is likely to diminish the ability of U.S. authorities to confine high-tech technology capabilities to the United States or to deny them to others. Even in the case of military capabilities and dual-use or classified technologies, the thrust of cross-national ownership pressures is likely to push the United States toward a narrower and narrower domain in which American authorities can restrict and control the spread of products and processes abroad. Multinational companies in high-tech commercial sectors with substantial multinational ownership and substantial presence in all of the major industrial economies will be less and less able to confine dual-use production capabilities to any one market. Co-producers and subcontractors from the ranks of U.S. allies may increasingly become partner-owners, complicating compartmentalization of sensitive activities. Indeed, it is difficult to see how defense-industrial strategy could even "play defense" effectively over time, trying to avoid dependence on preponderant market players in high-tech industries increasingly owned by outsiders.

Instead of an era of assertive U.S. "unipolarity," the future may hold increasing interpenetration and integration of the major industrial states. This may impose constraints on policies that the United States can deploy, unilaterally, toward Russia and China and various "rogue states," as the exercise of control over the activities of even those members of the multinational corporate community headquartered in the United States increasingly eludes the grasp of the U.S. authorities.

Notes

1. David C. Mowery, "Survey of Technology Policy," in *Science and Technology Policy in Interdependent Economies,* ed. David C. Mowery (Boston: Kluwer Academic Publishers, 1994).

2. Paul R. Krugman, *Strategic Trade Policy and the New International Economics* (Cambridge: MIT Press, 1986).

3. Laura D'Andrea Tyson, *Who's Basing Whom? Trade Conflict in High-Technology Industries* (Washington, D.C.: Institute for International Economics, 1992).

4. Theodore H. Moran, "The Globalization of America's Defense Industries: Managing the Threat of Foreign Dependence," *International Security* 15 (summer 1990).

5. Theodore H. Moran, *American Economic Policy and National Security* (New York: Council on Foreign Relations, 1993).

6. These figures come from the National Science Board, *Science and Engineering Indicators—1998*, NSB 1 (Arlington, Va.: National Science Foundation, 1998), and Ashton B. Carter, with Marcel Lettre and Shane Smith, "Keeping the Technological Edge," in *Keeping the Edge: Managing Defense for the Future,* ed. Ashton B. Carter and John P. White (Cambridge: MIT Press, 2000).

7. *Final Report of the Defense Science Board Task Force on Globalization and Security* (Washington, D.C.: Department of Defense, Office of the Under Secretary of Defense for Acquisition and Technology, Dec. 1999).

8. *New York Times,* Dec. 9, 2001. The number of start-ups that did not go public is, by necessity, an estimate.

9. A U.S. approach along these lines would simultaneously disadvantage other U.S. aerospace firms, such as Pratt & Whitney.

10. "In Japan, Start-Up and Risk are New Business Watchwords," *New York Times,* April 22, 2001; "'Internet Tsunami' Draws Foreign Cash, Stirs Up Long-Stagnant Venture Climate," *Washington Post,* Feb. 13, 2000.

11. Daniel I. Okimoto, *Between MITI and the Market* (Stanford: Stanford University Press, 1989); Richard Beason and David Weinstein, "Growth, Economies of Scale, and Targeting in Japan (1955–1990)," (discussion paper 1644, given at the Harvard Institute of Economic Research, 1994).

12. *Economic Report of the President* (Washington, D.C.: U.S. Government Printing Office, Jan. 2001), table B-107, 397.

13. "U.S. Businesses Turning to European for Antitrust Help," *New York Times,* June 19, 2001.

14. Anders Aslund, *How Russia Became a Market Economy* (Washington, D.C.: Brookings

Institution, 1995); McKinsey Global Institute, *Unlocking Economic Growth in Russia*, (Moscow: McKinsey & Co., 1999).

15. I am indebted to personal communications from David Bernstein of Stanford University in constructing this section on Russia.

16. David Bernstein, *Commercialization of Russian Technology in Cooperation with American Companies* (Stanford: Stanford University Press, 1999); David Halloway, ed., *The Anatomy of Russian Defense Conversion* (Stanford: Stanford University Press, 2001).

17. I am grateful to James C. Mulvenon of the RAND Corporation, who has shared his most recent research in this area.

18. Colum Lynch, "Chinese Firm Probed on Links With Iraq," *Washington Post*, March 17, 2001.

19. These figures come from the National Science Board, *Science and Engineering Indicators*, and Carter, Lettre, and Smith, "Keeping the Technological Edge."

20. Gordon Adams, "Convergence or Divergence? The Future of the Transatlantic Defense Industry," draft, Feb. 2000, 5.

21. Ibid., 24; remarks of Jean-Luis Gergorin, group managing director for strategic coordination at Aerospatiale Matra.

22. "Allies Enlisted to Pay for Jet," *Washington Post*, March 11, 2001.

23. William S. Harrell, of Lockheed Martin, quoted ibid.

24. Gordon Adams, "Convergence or Divergence?" See also his "Fortress America in a Changing Transatlantic Defense Market," in *Between Cooperation and Competition: The Transatlantic Defense Market*, ed. Gordon Adams, Christophe Cornu, and Andrew D. James (Paris: Institute for Security Studies, Western European Union, Jan. 2001).

25. Michael J. Green, *Arming Japan: Defense Production, Alliance Politics, and the Postwar Search for Autonomy* (New York: Columbia University Press, 1995); Michael Mastaduno, "Do Relative Gains Matter?" *International Security* 16 (summer 1991).

26. "Concern over 'Menace' Dissipates as Japan, U.S. Unveil Fighter Jet: Lockheed, Mitsubishi Project Is Late and Over Budget," *Wall Street Journal*, March 22, 1996.

27. Bates Gill, "Chinese Military-Technical Development: The Record for Western Assessments, 1979–1999," (Washington, D.C.: Brookings Institution, draft, 2001); Larry M. Wortzel, *China's Military Potential* (Carlisle, Pa.: Strategic Studies Institute, U.S. Army War College, Oct. 1998); Wendy Frieman, "Arms Procurement in China: Poorly Understood Processes and Unclear Results," in *Military Capacity and the Risk of War: China, India, Pakistan, and Iran*, ed. Eric Arnett (New York: Oxford University Press, 1997).

28. Michael Pillsbury, ed., *Chinese Views of Future Warfare* (Washington, D.C.: National Defense University Press, 1997); Mark Stokes, "China's Strategic Modernization: Implications for U.S. National Security" (paper prepared for the Project on the New American Century, July 1999).

29. *Economic Report of the President*, Jan. 2001, chap. 4.

30. Ibid., table B-107, at 397; and IMF, International Capital Markets Report (original data from Federal Reserve Board updates of Treasury/FRB Portfolio Survey and Treasury TIC data, 2001).

31. Catherine L. Mann, *Is the Trade Deficit Sustainable?* (Washington, D.C.: Institute for International Economics, 1999 and 2001 update).

32. J. Fred Weston, Kwang S. Chung, and Susan E. Hoag, *Mergers, Restructuring, and Corporate Control* (Englewood Cliffs, N.J.: Prentice Hall, 1990), chap. 21.

33. Edward M. Graham and Paul R. Krugman, *Foreign Direct Investment in the United States* (Washington, D.C.: Institute for International Economics, 1989 and 2000 revision).

34. Theodore H. Moran, "Foreign Direct Investment and Good Jobs/Bad Jobs: The Impact of Outward Investment and Inward Investment on Jobs and Wages," in *Growing Apart: The Causes and Consequences of Global Wage Inequality,* ed. Albert Fishlow and Karen Parker (New York: Council on Foreign Relations, 1999).

Chapter 7   Energy and Security

MARTHA HARRIS

Energy markets have become more globally integrated and more open since the end of the cold war. This trend will likely continue and deepen in the next twenty years. Globally integrated energy markets offer opportunities for fuel substitution, lower-priced energy, and improved energy efficiencies. More integrated global markets, however, present new security challenges that must be addressed. The risks stem from the incomplete transition to open markets and the unintended consequences of increased reliance on market forces in the context of new threats to security.

The transformation of energy markets has provoked a debate about whether market forces or geopolitics are more important in determining energy futures, and about what policy approaches are most useful for ensuring energy security in the century ahead. Daniel Yergin and Robert Manning emphasize the expansion of market forces and interdependence as nations link their fates to one another through pipelines, grids, and cross investment.[1] But in order to deepen global energy trade, technology transfer, and investment, nations and private sector firms will need to ensure that investment requirements for infrastructure expansion and transportation are met.

In contrast, Michael Klare and Kent Calder see unequal energy and resource endowments as sources of conflict, particularly in Asia, where the emergence of big energy users like China and India suggests a likely intensification of competition among importing countries for oil from the Middle East and for sovereignty over energy resources in Asia.[2] Terrorist attacks and growing piracy in Southeast Asia underscore the vulnerability of infrastructure and citizens to new types of threats that may jeopardize energy supplies. Observers stress the need to deal with competing national claims and differing threat perceptions in order to address the new security challenges.

While energy market interdependence is growing, it is uneven, and governments are still striving to expand "independent" supplies by building special relationships with supplier countries. In the current period of partial transition to market-oriented approaches, both government and private sector leadership is needed to address security challenges and thereby ensure that market-oriented approaches will be strengthened in the years ahead. The most important question is what can be done to mitigate the energy security risks so that open markets can be widened in the confidence that security will not be jeopardized.[3] A central argument of this chapter is that the United States must develop new ways of fostering multilateral cooperation in order to promote energy and security interests in the century ahead.

157

This chapter begins with an overview of evolving relationships between energy and security in the twentieth century as background for analyzing implications for energy security in the twenty-first. It then draws on forecasts of energy trends for the next twenty years as a foundation for developing general policy recommendations for dealing with the challenges ahead. Through an examination of competing U.S. priorities for obtaining adequate supplies of energy and for achieving economic integration and efficiency and environmental protection, this chapter argues that the tensions among these different goals must be reconciled through U.S. commitments to restraining the demand for energy and promoting environmental protection in order to ensure multilateral cooperation in energy security. Those who advocate opening energy markets, in other words, have an obligation to address security concerns from a global perspective in order to promote real energy security in the century ahead.

Trends

Perspectives on the relationship between energy and security evolved during the twentieth century, as the global strategic context changed from great-power competition to the superpower tension of the cold war and, at the end of the century, to a U.S.-centered system of alliances and multilateral cooperation on specific issues.[4] In terms of energy and security, the history of the twentieth century can be seen as a quest for oil, money, and national power.[5] The focus has traditionally been on expanding national control of energy resources in order to ensure national security. In the early twentieth century this drive for national control of energy resources gave way to limited practical cooperation among wartime allies necessary to ensure victory in the two world wars. Although cooperation among Western nations has grown in times of crisis—such as the oil shocks of the 1970s and the Persian Gulf War in the early 1990s—it remains uneven. The developing world, Russia, and the states of the former Soviet Union remain largely outside the emergency response mechanisms established by the International Energy Agency. Securing autonomous national control continues to be a major theme of national policies in China, the United States, and other countries. Although energy policy has been categorized as a "nonmilitary" component of national security, achieving stability in the oil-producing states of the Persian Gulf and defending the sea-lanes through which oil travels are major U.S. military goals that increasingly require international cooperation.

Global integration of energy markets was another key trend of the twentieth century, given impetus by the end of the cold war and by the growing acknowledgment of the benefits of free markets in the 1980s.[6] As a result, by the end of the century Western nations had moved toward more constrained roles for government in the regulation of energy industries. For a time in the late 1990s, interest in energy security all but disappeared in many countries. Oil being cheap and plentiful, oil producers seemed more dependent on their customers than vice versa. Recent experience with "deregulated" energy markets, however, has exposed risks such as price spikes and problems with reliability and market power that require continued government oversight and regulation.[7]

By the end of the century, environmental protection had become a key theme in debates about energy policy around the world. But developing and developed nations have different perspectives on the question of how to assess the costs of environmental damage and who should bear them. The U.S. withdrawal from negotiations over the Kyoto Protocol, which sets limits on emissions of greenhouse gases, shows the difficulties of reconciling diverging national interests. Like the new challenges stemming from piracy, ethnic unrest, and terrorism, which also jeopardize energy security through potential disruptions in supply and damage to infrastructure, these transnational problems can be addressed only through new forms of cooperation among nations and private sector actors.

These three dimensions—security, economics, and the environment—are all critical elements of energy policy, but their relative salience has shifted over time, reflecting changes in the global security context. In the early twentieth century, as military operations were transformed by the use of petroleum-powered land vehicles and aircraft, nations attempted to create "national champion" oil companies in order to ensure adequate national energy supplies from around the world. Later in the century, the oil shocks of the 1970s led many nations to attempt to reduce imported oil and diversify supplies in order to promote "energy security." But by the end of the century, more open energy markets, low energy prices, and corporate mega-mergers dominated attention. In Europe, Japan, and the United States, environmental concerns deepened in the wake of major oil spills, nuclear accidents, and global warming.

Each of the three dimensions of energy policy forms a continuum along which policies shift over time. In the security realm, reliance on national policies and efforts to promote multilateral cooperation represent opposite ends of the spectrum. Despite a central focus on securing national supplies of oil and other energy resources, there was a gradual evolution in the twentieth century toward increased multilateral cooperation, particularly during wartime. Confronted with situations like the Suez Canal Crisis of 1956 and the 1973 "energy crisis," Western nations were moved to compete for supplies. In each case, however, they eventually found ground for practical cooperation; the establishment of the International Energy Agency is one example. More recently, in the Persian Gulf crisis of 1990, the United States succeeded in building a broad-based international coalition to deter Iraqi aggression and liberate Kuwait. Today the inability of powerful countries like the United States to rely on indigenous supplies of energy is pushing U.S. policymakers toward a global definition of energy security, transforming the definition of "national interest" to include stable global energy markets, open transportation channels, and security of infrastructure. These themes are evident in the Bush administration's energy policy outline of May 2001, which includes recommendations to promote international cooperation but focuses centrally on developing U.S. and North American energy supplies.

The economic dimension, which exists on a continuum with laissez-faire policies at one end and extensive government regulation at the other, appeared to dominate energy policy in the late 1990s. Although one might draw analogies to the early days of the oil industry, when huge corporate monopolies like Standard Oil expanded through ruthless competition, the federal antitrust laws that were passed in response, and the recognition of the importance of energy to society and economic growth, led over time to extensive regulatory regimes that can not be easily dismembered. Recent experience with failed attempts to restructure electricity in California and the fall of the corporate giant Enron illustrate the need for ongoing government regulation.

The environmental dimension of energy policy, all but nonexistent in the early years of the twentieth century, has become much more important. There is greater consensus in Europe, however, than in the United States about how to define environmental-protection goals and the need for transition to a different and more environmentally friendly fuel mix. Japan has sought to reduce carbon dioxide and other emissions by putting nuclear power at the center of its energy policy. Only a few other developed countries, among them France, have pursued a similar course, and even Japan's plans to expand nuclear power generation have been curtailed by public resistance. Because the environmental dimension of energy policy has many facets (pollution control, fuel mix, promotion of alternative fuels and energy conservation, as well as global warming and the contested role of nuclear power), there is no simple formula for incorporating it into a successful strategy for energy security. But if security is fundamentally about reducing the risks to national and global prosperity, the grave potential for environmental damage from power generation, damage that lasts for generations and crosses national borders, will make environmental concerns increasingly important in the future.

Changes in the relative salience of the security, economic, and environmental dimensions of energy policy have involved shifts in priority and in preferred policy instruments over time. In the security realm, the pendulum has swung between achieving national autonomy through favoring domestic energy producers and multilateral cooperation through burden sharing. In the economic realm, state-led ownership and extensive regulation of energy enterprises has given way in recent years to private sector leadership, experiments with self-regulation, and expanded competition. In the environmental realm, early neglect gave way to the protection of public lands and later to mitigation of pollution and public health hazards, and more recently to global environmental security issues like global warming and the long-term impact of energy development and use.

Implications for Energy Security

Although the challenge for policymakers has sometimes been described as balancing the security, economic, and environmental dimensions of energy policy, there is no simple way to do this.[8] Policymakers do need to take these different interests into account, but they must also consider the larger security and market contexts in assessing risks and developing priorities. Wartime mobilization, market reform in developing countries, and major environmental disasters all call for study and corrective action. In setting priorities for action, however, policymakers need to clarify the costs as well as the benefits of achieving reliable energy supply, economic efficiency, and environmental protection in the long term. Typically, however, the complex array of competing interests makes it impossible to formulate a truly comprehensive policy, and the outcome is dictated by a series of political compromises that include disparate and even contradictory measures.

The availability of energy resources is one of the most important factors in the larger security context. While the United States was the world's largest oil producer early in the twentieth century, U.S. demand rose sharply during the post–World War II period, causing the country to become a net importer of oil. By the 1970s the Middle East held the cards in terms of oil supply, a shift that made the United States and Europe particularly vulnerable to the oil embargo.[9] Today other Organization for Economic Cooperation and Development (OECD) countries, as well as large developing countries like China, also depend on imported fossil fuel for a significant portion of their energy supply.

The nature of energy markets is another important factor. The major oil companies were able to allocate scarce resources during the 1973 oil shock and thus effectively manage the crisis, and the power of OPEC producers to dictate prices and set production levels declined over the next three decades. Today there are many more players in energy markets and lines are blurring both within the energy industry and between it and other sectors such as telecommunications. Although long-term contracts have been the norm for many years, more flexible forms of energy trading (including futures trading, shorter-term contracts, and spot markets) have expanded. A whole new breed of energy traders has entered the electric-power market. Cross-investment grew substantially in the 1990s as "foreign" firms moved to acquire generation assets in countries where ownership had for years been reserved for "national" or public firms; this development has hastened the trend toward globalization. The information intensity of the energy sector has increased markedly, but market transparency remains partial and expert knowledge provides a significant asset for those involved in large-scale energy trading.

At the same time, infrastructure and transportation are key factors in influencing the reliability of supply and prices. While oil, for example, makes up a smaller share of total GDP and global trading than it did in the 1970s, modern economies require substantial investments in the "hardware" of the energy sector in order to provide adequate supplies of energy. Because investments in infrastructure and new technologies increase with rising prices and fall with declining demand and lower prices, the backbone of energy-security infrastructure typically lags behind the market. Where energy markets have been reformed to increase competition, problems with reliability of supply have often been an unintended consequence. Traditionally the energy sector (particularly the oil sector) was dominated by large firms that built in redundancy and were permitted by regulators to cover the associated costs. Today reliability of energy supplies is a key issue because markets do not necessarily value it or provide incentives for new investments that incorporate new, environmentally beneficial technologies.

The larger security context also frames choices for energy policy. With the end of the cold war and the breakup of the Soviet Union, the United States today faces a broad range of threats and a great degree of uncertainty about which ones will turn out to be most serious in the years ahead. Terrorism, environmental degradation, weapons of mass destruction, ethnic conflict, not to mention economic recession and poverty, all threaten U.S. security and stability, in terms of energy and in many other ways as well. But policies that emphasize military preparedness are easier to sell to Americans today than are measures that involve restraint or foreign assistance. The multifaceted nature of global security challenges inextricably links the well-being of nations and regions to choices and trends beyond their immediate control.

In this context of multiple and shifting threats, governments and politicians can still exercise leadership in forming energy policies, but the process of decision making is more complex, as competing interests lobby government and private sector actors make key decisions that affect national security. These complexities are magnified because experts on security, trade, and environment come from different intellectual traditions, work for different organizations, and often differ in their agendas. At the international level, security alliances to deter aggression are slowly evolving into frameworks for new kinds of cooperation. Energy, however, has not been a major theme except in U.S.–Russian relations, where the legacy of the Soviet arsenal has necessitated programs that prevent the proliferation of weapons technologies. In U.S.–Japanese relations the agreement on new defense guidelines lacks a framework for cooperation on energy security, although the war against terrorism is providing opportunities for Japan to play a larger supporting role. International trade and environmental negotiations run on separate tracks, and the critics of globalization see environmental neglect as an Achilles heel of market integration. As a result, developing a comprehensive energy policy that addresses all three dimensions has proved difficult at both the national and international levels.

The question is whether in the century ahead it will be possible to transcend what now is a clear history of shifting, reactive, and partial energy policies. In order to address this question it is necessary to anticipate the threats and risks that will present key challenges, both to the United States and to global security. We must think beyond the immediate present and ask how energy policies can be developed that will contribute to national and global security in the future. We need to think about energy and security in new ways that take account of the new threats and new requirements for multilateral responses. In today's increasingly interconnected world, all countries are affected when oil crises occur. National energy autonomy is an inappropriate goal in an era of interdependent markets and expanded access to global resources.

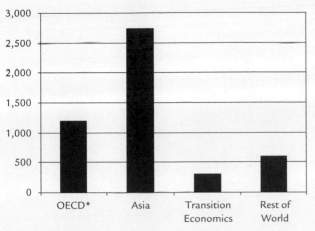

*Organization for Economic Cooperation and Development

Asia=2,737 million tons of oil equivalent or 55.1% of total demand increase

Source: International Energy Agency

Figure 7.1   Increase in Energy Demand by Region, 1997–2020

Prospects for the Future

Most forecasts anticipate that world energy consumption will grow by two-thirds, while the world economy will double, in the next twenty years. World energy demand will double in Asia and parts of Central and South America, accounting for more than half of the total growth in energy demand worldwide. China's energy demand will more than double (see Figure 7.1).

While some forecasts see oil's share of primary energy declining during this period, the Department of Energy's world energy outlook sees it remaining stable at roughly 40 percent of total energy consumption, with total world oil demand increasing from 75 million barrels a day to 120 million barrels a day annually (see Figure 7.2).[10] Oil demand in the transportation sector, in particular, is expected to grow rapidly in developed countries. Oil demand in developing countries will come to equal that of the industrial countries, with rapid increases in the transportation sector and shifts from noncommercial to commercial fuels for power generation.

According to most projections oil prices will remain relatively stable and supplies will be adequate. U.S. Department of Energy projections show that OPEC suppliers will provide two-thirds of the additional 45 million barrels a day needed by 2020 and OPEC exports to developing countries will increase by more than 18.6 million barrels a day over the period, with more than half going to Asia (China alone is expected to import 5.3 million barrels a day from OPEC by 2020).[11] Although non-OPEC oil supply has grown in recent years in Russia and other countries, the central role of OPEC is likely to continue in this period (see Figure 7.3).[12]

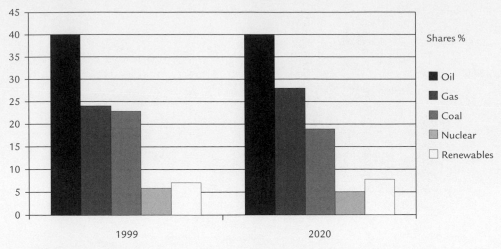

Source: U.S. Department of Energy, Energy Information Agency, World Energy Projections Systems

Figure 7.2   World Energy Consumption Shares, 1999 and 2020

During the period to 2020, even though prices may be relatively stable, in the short term volatility will be likely as producers attempt to constrain production in order to avoid price dips. Thus, even if half of U.S. imports in 2020 come from the Atlantic Basin, OPEC will continue to dominate the global oil market and developing economies will be particularly vulnerable to price increases. All countries will be affected if a supply disruption occurs, no matter how far away. If, on the other hand, OPEC and other suppliers do not succeed in regulating production to meet demand and oil prices fall, incentives for investment in new exploration and technology will be jeopardized. In the United States, a desire to maintain low energy prices (and energy taxes) in order to ensure international competitiveness undermines incentives for investment in transmission infrastructure and in redundancy that guarantees reliability.

These twenty-year forecasts highlight the risk of oil and liquified natural gas (LNG) supply disruptions. More than 9.5 million barrels of oil flow daily through the Strait of Malacca to Japan, China, South Korea, and other countries in Asia, making it second only to the Strait of Hormuz in importance as an oil chokepoint. According to some projections, oil and gas tanker traffic may more than double in the next decade.[13] A number of other factors (quite apart from the situation in the Middle East), including the growing potential for accidents due to increased shipping traffic, make freedom of transit a key issue for future energy security. Because the critical sea-lanes intersect with disputed territorial claims (for example, in the South and East China Seas), the transportation challenge looms large. Declining oil stocks and the lack of an emergency response architecture accentuate the risks of supply disruptions.

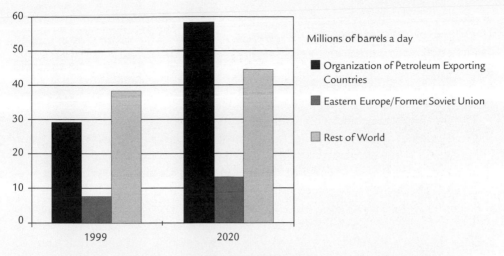

Source: U.S. Department of Energy, Energy Information Agency, World Energy Projection System

Figure 7.3   World Oil Production by Region, 1999 and 2020

The security of energy infrastructure is also a growing concern. Energy pipelines, LNG terminals, transmission grids, and power plants are critical components of national infrastructure that are vulnerable to terrorists, hackers, disaffected local groups, human error, and natural disasters like earthquakes. Twenty thousand miners rioted in northwest China in early 2000 in reaction to restructuring plans. Civil unrest in Aceh, on the western coast of Sumatra, where two-thirds of Indonesia's LNG exports originate, forced Exxon-Mobil to close its Arun gas field for four months.[14] In Nigeria, Mexico, and other developing countries, thieves routinely tap into pipelines and electric power lines to steal energy, causing the risk of explosions and accidents.[15] In the United States in the wake of September 11, 2001, the security of the nation's nuclear power plants has become a concern. The information intensity of modern energy infrastructure such as power grids also makes it vulnerable to cyber warfare.

Environmental degradation is a major risk closely related to transportation challenges and growing energy requirements. Global warming from the buildup of carbon dioxide and greenhouse gases emitted from fossil-fuel-fired power plants, transport vehicles, and other sources is predicted to cause rising sea and temperature levels and changing patterns of precipitation and soil moisture. According to the International Institute for Strategic Studies, nineteen cities in Asia will be at risk of flooding from rising sea levels. Environmental concerns must be addressed in every energy project, and mitigating environmental risk typically means paying higher costs in the near term. Pollution is a major issue for megacities like Delhi, where diesel vehicles contribute to 65 percent of particulate production. A concerted effort to switch to compressed natural gas fuel, however, has put pressure on taxi drivers to shoulder higher costs of limited supplies. Environmental effects of exploration and development of oil and gas in offshore waters have had a major influence on resource development from the Gulf of Mexico to the Sea of Okhotsk. In order for many non-OPEC producers like Russia to play bigger roles in world oil and gas markets, industrial reform and an expanded role for civil society will be needed to address environmental challenges.

These mainstream energy forecasts for the next twenty years (compiled prior to the Iraq crisis of 2003) thus point to significant security challenges ahead. Royal Dutch/Shell, a major energy company that has developed scenarios for the next thirty years, released a study in 2002 that anticipates radically different future possibilities. The "business-class" scenario involves increasing globalization under the U.S. banner with a shift to gas, while an alternative scenario sees a backlash against globalization in the U.S. and elsewhere. In this alternative scenario, oil price increases, disappointment with U.S. economic performance, and deepening connections to local culture and social needs in poor developing countries lead to a period of regionalism, expanded government regulation to ensure energy security, social equity, and environmental protection. In this scenario, large developing countries like China play dominant roles after they experience economic derailment following the introduction of partial reforms.[16]

The backlash that characterizes the second scenario is directed against the dominance of American-style globalization. In this scenario, however, governments and citizens do not believe that markets will provide energy security, a clean environment, and energy for all. The backlash scenario reminds us that the globalizing trends of the past decade can still be reversed.

Both scenarios present significant challenges for energy security. In the first case, oil price increases threaten large developing economies like China, causing the United States to pressure OPEC to reduce prices and ultimately persuading the United States to implement carbon dioxide emissions trading. These developments eventually lead to the benign outcome of a transition to natural gas and the development of new, cleaner technologies such as fuel cells. The antiglobalization scenario involves increasing government regulation of the regional energy infrastructure in developing countries that have experienced the adverse effects of oil crises.

The next twenty years will undoubtedly bring surprises; the scenarios just outlined caution against assumptions that current trends will necessarily prevail and highlight social and nonquantitative factors that may help to shape the future context. For policymakers developing strategic approaches to energy and security in the next century, a wide range of potential outcomes must be taken into account in assessing risks and priorities.

Regardless of what shape the future takes, multilateral efforts will be needed to promote energy security in the century ahead. In the globalization scenario, private sector organizations (energy companies, NGOs, and expert advisors) will play larger roles in forging new forms of cooperation that take advantage of the opportunities markets provide for developing new technologies, providing new services to consumers, and improving efficiency. In the backlash scenario, governments push to create regional blocs in an effort to shore up communities of interest among neighbors. Although the United States, as the dominant power in a globalization scenario, can exercise leverage vis-à-vis OPEC and promote global energy cooperation, the private sector is the driving force in the marketplace, where the deals are actually made.

Whether the globalization scenario will prevail depends in large part on whether the record of good U.S. economic performance continues and whether market reform in developing nations brings anticipated benefits in terms of improved living standards and economic growth. From an energy policy perspective, the California electricity crisis and the Enron collapse must be shown to be defects in the market-reform program and in corporate management, rather than evidence of systemic liabilities associated with restructured and more competitive energy markets. In addition, the opening of energy markets in developing countries must bring tangible benefits, such as rural electrification to the poor in China, India, and other developing countries that have so far experienced uneven effects of globalization and only partial market reforms. In developing countries where the institutional infrastructure (a robust legal and regulatory system and an open decision-making process) is not in place and where subsidies have traditionally insulated consumers from market forces, the transition to a more competitive energy market is very challenging and may require a multistage approach.

From the perspective of the oil producers, major concerns include the potential for economic slowdown because of stagnant revenues in a prolonged global economic recession and domestic opposition to policies that promote stability through cooperation with the United States and other consumer nations, particularly in the context of the Iraq crisis. Saudi Arabia's role will continue to be critical, but Russia and other non-OPEC producers have also emerged as key players. Russia is now a major oil producer, and its decision late in 2001 to cooperate with OPEC in production cuts forestalled a potential price war. According to the European Commission, Russia could be providing the European Union with 45 percent of its gas imports by 2020.[17] Russia needs oil and gas revenues to finance social spending and reform programs that will open the market for competition and more efficient production. For the producers that rely heavily on energy export revenues, avoiding price plunges and cycles of unpredictable boom and bust is essential to their domestic political support and to their ability to participate constructively in international energy markets.

Energy forecasts for the next twenty years indicate serious environmental challenges ahead. By 2020 China and India will increase their coal-fired power-generating capacity by at least 220 gigawatts (GW) and 60 GW, respectively.[18] Burgeoning energy requirements of large developing countries like China and India, where coal is locally available and comparatively cheap, indicate that coal will remain a major element in their energy futures during this period. According to the Energy Research Institute of China's State Development Planning Commission, fifteen of the twenty most polluted cities in the world are in China.[19] China is attempting to promote a shift from coal, which currently provides almost 70 percent of primary energy consumption, to natural gas. Demand for gas could reach more than 200 billion cubic meters by 2020, with the power-generation sector making up the largest share; demand may grow by 5.5 percent annually. Total power demand will more than double, according to Chinese estimates, reaching 2,221 billion kilowatt hours by 2020. If a quarter of the new generation capacity uses gas as a fuel, China will need 35 billion cubic meters.[20] Achieving these ambitious goals will require huge investments in infrastructure, as well as robust implementation of environmental regulations at the national and local levels. An array of projects, including the West–East pipeline (for which estimated construction costs alone total $15 billion), LNG terminals, and new power stations, are planned. The world has a stake in China's efforts to make these shifts, not only because of the significant potential environmental impact but also because of the implications for global trade in fossil fuels. In addition, a China determined to establish sovereignty over resources could resort to old-style "oil diplomacy," rather than open markets, by pursuing oil-for-arms relationships with Middle Eastern countries like Iran and Iraq.[21]

Oil today provides 95 percent of the fuel for transportation globally, a sector that accounts for almost half of today's oil consumption and is a major source of emissions. Demand in the transportation sector is likely to increase by 57 percent in the next two decades. Growth in demand for oil in the transportation sector is projected to make up half of this expected increase, according to forecasts by the U.S. Department of Energy, the International Energy Agency, and the European

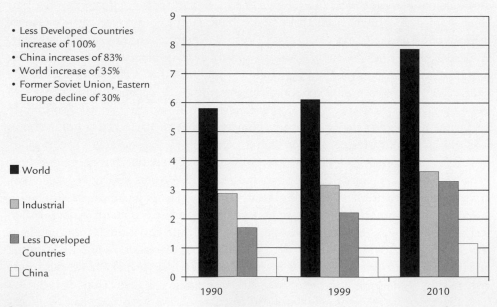

- Less Developed Countries increase of 100%
- China increases of 83%
- World increase of 35%
- Former Soviet Union, Eastern Europe decline of 30%

■ World

▨ Industrial

■ Less Developed Countries

☐ China

Source: U.S. Department of Energy

Figure 7.4   Carbon Dioxide Emissions, 1990–2010

Community. Because North America makes up 40 percent of the total energy used in transportation worldwide, policy choices for this sector can have a significant impact on energy use and environmental effects. U.S. energy demand in the transport sector slowed in the 1980s, reflecting higher prices and stringent emissions standards. In the past decade, however, U.S. demand for larger vehicles, which emit more pollution, has grown. Many of the new, lower-emission technologies for transport, such as fuel cells, are not likely to achieve broad market penetration until late in the period. In contrast to Europe, where high fuel taxes account for 80 percent of the price, the United States has an opportunity to examine policy approaches, including raising the corporate average fuel efficiency (CAFÉ) standard in order to control emissions and reduce oil imports.[22]

Redefining Energy Security in the Twenty-first Century

The forecasts of growth in energy demand for the next twenty years indicate the need to broaden our definition of "energy security." The oil shocks of the 1970s encouraged us to think of energy security as something that minimizes national vulnerability to oil-import disruptions. But the growing integration of global energy markets and the rising demand for energy worldwide call for a *global* approach to energy security, based on a realistic assessment of differing national interests.

The contrasting policies of the nations of the world reveal these differing national interests and priorities. The developed countries have pushed for more open energy markets so as to promote more efficient industries, lower prices, and better trade and investment opportunities. At the same time, U.S. leaders have called for a reduction in U.S. dependence on foreign oil by developing indigenous or North American resources. Western Europe and Japan are attempting to establish limits on greenhouse gas emissions, while developing countries are more concerned about adequate oil supplies and the high costs of clean-energy technologies. The United States has borne the major military burden of ensuring Persian Gulf security and freedom of the seas, but other countries have provided more foreign assistance to countries that have the potential to develop energy resources. The United States and Russia are vying for control of the oil-rich Caspian Sea.

Although the United States is the only superpower today, its approach to energy policy has been uneven at best. The United States has succeeded in forging coalitions to meet military threats to oil resources such as the 1990 Iraqi invasion of Kuwait. But resistance to the liberalization of markets and anger over U.S. opposition to the Kyoto Protocol suggest that there are significant limits to U.S. leadership in the area of global energy policy. The war on terrorism, at least in its current stage, only reinforces the perception that the United States gives much higher priority to the stability of its oil supply than to global environmental protection.

Integrating the diverse national interests and social values at stake in one comprehensive approach is a daunting task, even for a superpower. As a first step, it would be useful to define objectives for "energy security" that take account of the trends and challenges we have identified. Looking ahead to the next twenty years, energy security requires that all nations have adequate supplies of energy from global markets and that they establish policies that protect the environment and ensure effective response to emergencies like disruptions in oil supply. No country can achieve energy security independently today. Energy security and open markets must be directly linked in policies. In order to gain support for open energy markets, the United States will need to address concerns about tightening energy supplies in Asia and other developing countries. To promote real energy security, the global environmental impacts of fossil fuel use must be also be addressed.

Costs and benefits will have to be assessed and difficult choices made. One option would be for the United States to develop a policy that makes conservation a centerpiece of its energy policy and demonstrates willingness to take global environmental concerns into account. This could be accomplished through a variety of approaches, among them raising the CAFÉ standard or increasing taxes on energy. In either case energy consumers and U.S. businesses would bear the burden of adjustment. Of the two approaches, raising the CAFÉ standard appears to be more feasible politically. The popularity of SUVs and other fuel-inefficient vehicles, as well as opposition from U.S. automobile manufacturers, will make this a difficult choice, and indeed the U.S. Senate rejected legislation in 2002 that would have raised the CAFÉ standard. The experience of the 1970s, however, when the CAFÉ standard was first introduced, shows that companies can win competitive advantages in global markets by developing fuel-efficient vehicles. If the U.S. government were to introduce the higher standard immediately and set a target date for implementation, auto manufacturers would have a clear incentive to invest in fuel-efficient technology.

An increase in the CAFÉ standard could be announced as a contribution to energy security by reducing demand for foreign oil and as a contribution to environmental protection. Unlike calling for conservation on the part of American consumers, raising the CAFÉ standard could also establish more equitable energy use in the transportation sector worldwide. Technological innovation could contribute to the needs of the developing countries, where motorization will grow rapidly in the next two decades. Although raising the CAFÉ standard would not transform patterns of high per-capita energy use in the United States, it could help to reduce demand for oil and send a message that the United States is willing to exercise restraint in the interest of global environmental and security objectives.

In order to address the concerns of developing nations about adequate energy supplies, the United States will need to do more than guarantee security in the Persian Gulf. The obvious solution to the problem of growing Asian dependence on Middle Eastern oil is to develop local energy resources. This would allow for diversification of suppliers and fuels, particularly the expanded use of gas to offset declining oil production in Asia in the decade ahead.

In Asia large prospective gas projects (e.g., the West–East pipeline project in China, a pipeline from Kazakhstan, and a number of proposals for developing Siberian energy resources) compete for investment. The investment requirements of all the projects under discussion for the next decade far exceed the capabilities of the international community. China hopes to boost the share of gas from 2.2 percent in 1998 to 10 percent of its primary energy supply by 2010 and thereby address serious environmental problems. Estimates of China's proven gas reserves, however, vary widely. Recent Chinese estimates indicate that the northwest holds almost 3 trillion cubic meters of recoverable reserves, but proven reserves for the region are estimated at only 372 million cubic meters.[23] Widely varying estimates reflect the reality of limited exploration. Ideally, international teams would conduct exploration throughout the region and publish results that better inform investment choices. Both governments and private sector actors can contribute to developing common approaches to the regulation of foreign investment, transit rights, and industrial standards. The United States could also participate actively in negotiations to implement the Energy Charter, thereby building a framework for global cooperation in energy development.

One of the key issues that must be addressed is the role of Russia in future energy markets and in development of resources in the Caspian Sea area. The United States and U.S. companies can assist countries in Central Asia to resolve competing claims in a way that allows all countries bordering the sea to participate.

In addition, the U.S. could signal support for Russian energy development by more actively supporting offshore oil and gas development near the island of Sakhalin, through loans and guarantees and technical assistance for environmental monitoring and emergency response. Sakhalin could provide gas for Korean and Japanese markets. The Russian delay in passing needed implementing legislation for production-sharing agreements, and difficulties in building pipelines in Japan, represent significant hurdles that need to be overcome. But Sakhalin energy development could become a model for multilateral cooperation in the development of Russia's energy resources. Cooperation with Russia in environmentally sound development of energy resources at home and in the Caspian region could help to build a new understanding of the requirements for global energy security.

Freedom of transit through the sea-lanes, particularly the Strait of Malacca and the South and East China Seas, is essential for global energy security because of the rapid increase in oil and gas trade projected for the next twenty years. A number of threats to free transit stem from regional problems. China has claimed the South China Sea as its national maritime area and reserves the right to use force there, despite the conflicting claims of Taiwan, Vietnam, Brunei, Malaysia, and the Philippines. In the past decade China has upgraded structures on Mischief Reef in the Spratly Islands, exchanged gunfire with the Philippines over Scarborough Shoal, and sent "research vessels" into areas near the Senkaku Islands, claimed by Japan as part of its exclusive economic zone.[24] China and an ASEAN Regional Forum (ARF) working group exchanged views on a code of conduct for the South China Sea, but settling the competing national claims is a difficult and complex problem unlikely to be resolved for many years.

The United States could take advantage of the new climate of cooperation in the war on terrorism to promote discussions of maritime cooperation to protect the sea-lanes involving China and Japan as well as other countries in the region. Small steps toward cooperation have already been initiated through joint exercises for rescue at sea.[25] Participation by military and nonmilitary organizations (such as the Coast Guard and customs agencies) would be necessary to develop protocols for monitoring transit, reporting, and response to incidents and accidents.

The growth of piracy in the South China Sea in recent years is a related threat that requires private sector as well as government action.[26] The International Maritime Bureau reports that piracy and hijack attempts are at a ten-year high, with one-third of all incidents occurring in the Straits of Malacca, through which more than two hundred ships pass daily. The South China Sea has the heaviest concentration of piracy of any body of water in the world, according to the International Institute for Strategic Studies (IISS). Indonesian pirates have been involved in many of these incidents, but the Indonesian navy is ill equipped to deal with these problems. The U.S. Department of Energy has identified the resource-rich islands of Indonesia as a global energy hot spot. Tackling the growing threat of piracy raises complex issues of overlapping jurisdiction and conflicting legal interpretations. Governments could begin by implementing the draft guidelines for cooperation against piracy developed by the International Maritime Organization of the United Nations.

One of the biggest obstacles to combating piracy is the reluctance of shipping firms to report incidents, because this takes time and resources. Private sector interests could do much more to improve the information base on transportation security problems. Maritime security is a threat not only to smaller ships but also to oil tankers and other large ships. The International Maritime Bureau has recommended that ships expand their security personnel and has pointed to the need for greater cooperation. Joint patrols involving Indonesia, Malaysia, and Singapore have been effective in reducing incidents in the Malacca Strait. Shipping firms and those who charter ships could also support joint training programs to establish best practices, workshops involving experts from the region, and aid to coastal states, including technology transfer and information systems. Private sector initiatives can lay the groundwork for deeper cooperation among governments in areas such as maritime patrols and enforcement of security of transit.

Ensuring freedom of transportation can also help to address serious potential environmental damage. A major shipping accident in the South China Sea, for example, could cause environmental havoc. Most very large supertankers are unable meet the 3.5-meter clearance required by Malaysia and Indonesia and barely meet the industry minimum standard of one meter.[27] Increased traffic in the shallow and congested Strait of Malacca heightens the danger of oil spills and other environmental problems, including the release of other substances, both from collisions and from normal operations such as tank cleaning and bilge pumping.[28] One good example of private sector cooperation is East Asia Response, Ltd. (EARL), a nonprofit venture established by six major oil companies to respond quickly to oil spills. Private sector leadership is needed to improve ship maintenance, crew training, and contingency planning for a broader range of potential negative environmental effects associated with shipping.

The vulnerability of developing countries to oil crises such as supply disruptions is a global risk. In Asia, only Japan and South Korea are members of the International Energy Agency (IEA) and hold the required ninety-day oil stocks of net imports. The IEA and Japan have been working with nonmember countries like China to provide technical information about stockpiles and to develop common approaches to energy security, including improved data collection and analysis. Stockpiles and emergency response programs are costly and difficult for many developing countries in Asia. Joint stockpiles and other schemes would be a logical approach, but difficult to implement in the near term.

The IEA could consider admitting associate-member states that are not yet capable of fulfilling all requirements but are working to do so. In addition, donor countries and international financial institutions could establish programs to support the development of stockpiles and emergency response programs through development assistance. Oil, gas, and transport companies can also help to build technical expertise and share facilities. Providing grants and loans for stockpiles and emergency preparedness would involve a trade-off with other projects, including those supporting renewable energy and conservation.

Developing a multifaceted approach to global energy security that includes curbed energy demand in the United States, joint efforts to ensure freedom of transit, cooperation with Russia and China in energy resource development, and improving the emergency response capabilities of developing countries would address many of the concerns of key players and make it more likely that other countries would continue to open and liberalize their energy markets rather than retreat into protectionism.

This type of approach would not eliminate Middle East conflicts, price volatility, reliability problems, or global warming. It would, however, provide a foundation for a more robust and global energy security strategy, one that involves governments and private sector actors in new forms of cooperation. If successful, these policies would reduce the risks of competition for energy resources and supplies by integrating China, Russia, and other new producers into the global security and energy market frameworks. Restraint in U.S. gasoline use (through tightened CAFÉ standards) could send a signal that the United States is committed to a broader global definition of energy security that could lead to further cooperation in environmental policies. In addition, this approach would limit the negative impacts of oil- and gas-supply disruptions by spreading the safety net of emergency response programs and maritime security.

The United States will need to maintain its commitment to security in the Persian Gulf, a region that will continue to be a major oil supplier. But through the development of energy resources in other regions and alternative energy sources, the risks could be diversified and gradually diminished. There is no guarantee that joint development of resources and infrastructure would preclude attempts to exert unilateral control of resources or infrastructure, but multilateral approaches would limit the capabilities of any one player to do so. Shared investment and experience in addressing the energy security needs of other countries would enhance the prospect for international cooperation to counter terrorist and other threats to seize energy resources or assert unilateral control of infrastructure, transit, or markets.

Conclusion

In the context of globally integrated energy markets, the United States can best secure its own energy future by fostering multilateral cooperation among governments, international agencies, and private sector actors. Cooperation will necessarily be issue-specific, but in many cases it will provide overlapping benefits. For example, programs for dealing with piracy, emergency response to incidents in sea-lanes, and environmental problems like oil spills are mutually reinforcing, even though they may involve different actors and organizations. The United States can promote such efforts by demonstrating a willingness to address the environmental and energy security concerns of other nations, in the process mitigating anxieties about national vulnerabilities that lead to protectionism, stalled reform programs, and exclusive agreements. In the century ahead, the United States will need to ensure a secure energy future by taking a global approach.

In the twentieth century energy policies were shaped by national competition for resources, as well as by the integrating effects of market globalization and environmental concerns. At the beginning of the twenty-first century we are in the midst of a transition where both geopolitics and market forces influence policies. The question is whether the United States and other leading energy-consuming countries build policies that look more to the future than to the past. While it may be easier for politicians to call for energy "independence" than to advocate policies of conservation, alternative energy development, and support for energy development around the world, the United States will not be secure if competition for control of energy resources around the world leads to conflict, market disruptions, and environmental disasters.

In developing a global approach to energy security, the United States will need to foster multilateral approaches. In some cases, it will need to lead in building coalitions, particularly where military threats to energy security arise. In other cases, where other countries are capable, the United States can support their lead in addressing problems like piracy and maritime accidents in Asia. In still other cases, the United States will need to make decisions independently to curb its own energy use.

In the process, different countries will continue to take distinctive approaches to energy policy. Such differences notwithstanding, commitments to open markets, environmental protection, and cooperative approaches to energy security will be critical. The United States, as the leading energy-consuming nation and only global superpower, has both the opportunity and the responsibility to shape energy security in the century ahead. While a comprehensive strategy cannot be developed overnight, concrete actions that show American resolve will help to assuage energy insecurities elsewhere and increase the prospects for cooperation rather than conflict over energy in the twenty-first century.

Notes

1. For a broad analysis of the movement toward open markets and away from extensive government regulation, see Daniel Yergin and Joseph Stanislaw, *The Commanding Heights: The Battle between Government and the Marketplace That Is Remaking the Modern World* (New York: Simon & Schuster, 1998). See also Robert A. Manning, *The Asian Energy Factor* (New York: Council on Foreign Relations, 2000).

2. Michael T. Klare, *Resource Wars: The New Landscape of Global Conflict* (New York: Metropolitan Books, 2001), and Kent E. Calder, *Asia's Deadly Triangle: How Arms, Energy, and Growth Threaten to Destabilize Asia-Pacific* (London: Nicholas Bealey Publishing, 1996).

3. Martha Caldwell Harris, "The Globalization of Energy Markets," in *The Global Century: Globalization and National Security,* ed. Richard L. Kugler and Ellen L. Frost (Washington, D.C.: National Defense University Press, 2001), vol. 1, 271ff.

4. G. John Ikenberry notes that divergent impulses toward unilateralist approaches and expanded, pragmatic multilateral cooperation exist within U.S. foreign policy today, but argues that requirements for a cooperative approach to terrorism will probably push U.S. foreign policy toward a centrist position. See his "American Grand Strategy in the Age of Terror," *Survival* 43 (winter 2001).

5. See Daniel Yergin, *The Prize: The Epic Quest for Oil, Money, and Power* (New York: Touchstone, 1992).

6. Global energy markets are not new. The expansion of the U.S. oil industry depended on sales in foreign markets, and in 1892 the Suez Canal opened a new era of global oil trade with the Far East. Globalization today is deeper, with complex networks of interactions among developers, producers, traders, and consumers around the world playing larger independent roles.

7. The term "deregulation" is a misnomer when applied to energy-market restructuring, since it typically involves new forms of pro-competitive regulation, rather than elimination of the government role.

8. See David Gamson, "The California Conundrum: Rates, Reliability, and the Environment under Electric Restructuring in California," in *Energy Market Restructuring and the Environment* (Lanham, Md.: University Press of America, 2002). Gamson analyzes California's dilemma in terms of attempting to ensure low rates, reliability, and environmental protection all at the same time. He shows how California lost on all three dimensions in response to the electricity crisis of 2001.

9. U.S. policies also played an important role. Restrictions on imported oil led to a depletion of domestic resources and reduced incentives for energy efficiency. See Edward L. Morse, "A New Political Economy of Oil?" in *Fueling the 21st Century: The New Political Economy of Energy,* special issue of the *Journal of International Affairs* 53 (fall 1999).

10. See Dept. of Energy, Energy Information Agency, *World Energy Outlook,* available at www.eia.doe.gove/oiaf/ieo/index.html; and John Mitchell, *The New Economy of Oil: Impacts on*

Business, Geopolitics, and Society (London: Royal Institute of International Affairs, 2001), chap. 1.

11. U.S. Dept. of Energy, *World Energy Outlook,* chapter on oil markets. Non-OPEC sources of oil are also projected to increase, but OPEC remains the major source of oil for the period.

12. The Exxon-Mobil long-range energy outlook (2001) anticipates a lower global oil demand in 2020 (110 million barrels per day) and a stronger role for non-OPEC suppliers, as reported by Mark A. Schwartz, IEEP Energy Seminar, Jan. 23, 2002, Johns Hopkins University, SAIS, Baltimore.

13. See Donald Urquhart, "Tankers Prime Target in Strait," *The Straits Times,* April 30, 2002.

14. President Megawati's special autonomy proposal has been viewed skeptically by the rebels, despite official apologies for years of human rights abuses.

15. Royal/Dutch Shell pulled out of the oil-rich Ogoniland region of Nigeria in 1993 after vandalism to the infrastructure and resentment of the company grew.

16. See *People and Connections: Global Scenarios to 2020* (Public Summary), available at www.Shell.com.

17. Overall EU import dependence is projected to rise to almost 70 percent for gas, 80 percent for coal, and 80 percent for oil by 2020. See *Directorate-General for Energy, European Commission, Energy in Europe: Economic Foundations for Energy Policy* (special issue, Dec. 1999), 88.

18. U.S. Dept. of Energy, *International Energy Outlook,* 1999. The Nautilus Institute anticipates that China will increase its electricity-generation capacity to 740 GW by 2020, 905 GW of it in coal-fired plants.

19. Zhou Fengqi, "Environmental Protection and Natural Gas in China" (paper presented at Economic Research Institute for Northeast Asia workshop on Energy Security and Sustainable Development in Northeast Asia, Niigata, Japan, June 2000).

20. Ibid., 20.

21. See Amy Myers Jaffe and Stephen W. Lewis, "Beijing's Oil Diplomacy," *Survival* 44 (spring 2002).

22. During the twenty-two years of its existence the U.S. CAFÉ standard has reduced oil imports over what they might have been. Oil imports in 2001 would have been 2.8 million barrels a day (14 percent) higher, according to the National Academy of Sciences. See NAS, *Effectiveness of Corporate Fuel Efficiency Standards* (Washington, D.C.: National Academy Press, 2001).

23. Fengqi, "Environmental Protection and Natural Gas in China."

24. Ji Guozing notes that Chinese naval strategy has changed from defense of coastlines to offshore defense. See "SLOC Security in the Asia Pacific" (paper given at the Asia-Pacific Center for Security Studies, Honolulu, Feb. 2000).

25. According to the International Institute for Strategic Studies, Japan's Maritime Self-Defense Force participated with the United States, South Korea, and Singapore in October 2000 in a submarine-rescue exercise in the South China Sea, the first time since the end of World War II for the JMSDF to participate with countries other than the U.S. in such an exercise. The IISS predicts that the JMSDF will carry out more combined training exercises with regional navies, particularly those of Singapore and South Korea, in areas such as merchant ship protection and search-and-rescue. See International Institute for Strategic Studies website at www.iiss.org/pub/sp/sp01012.asp.

26. The definition of "piracy" is a matter of debate. The law of the seas limits piracy to

acts in the high seas undertaken for private ends, but a broader definition of "armed robbery at sea" captures acts in territorial waters, including those by terrorists. The International Maritime Bureau, a private organization established under the International Chamber of Commerce, reports that two-thirds of all reported cases of piracy occur in Southeast Asia.

27. John H. Noer, *Chokepoints: Maritime Economic Concerns in Southeast Asia* (Washington, D.C.: National Defense University Press, 1996).

28. Transportation of mixed-oxide fuel and nuclear waste between Europe and Japan is another area of concern. Protests by Malaysia, Indonesia, and Singapore over the plan to use the Strait of Malacca led to a rerouting of the *Akatsuki Maru* in 1993.

Chapter 8   Environmental Change and Security

J. R. McNeill

"Had I been consulted at the moment of Creation, I would have recommended something simpler."

—Alfonso El Sabio, King of Castile and León (1221–84)

In the seven centuries since King Alfonso's lament, creation has grown no simpler. Indeed, if evolutionary biologists are correct, the biosphere should have gotten slightly more complicated since the thirteenth century, as the usual direction of biological evolution is toward greater complexity—punctuated by catastrophic simplifications of the sort not recently seen on earth. The march of science (which the king did his share to promote) has resolved many mysteries since the thirteenth century, but has only deepened our sense of nature's complexity.

International relations and international security are almost as tangled and inscrutable as the natural world. While there is no shortage of rigorous theory (as in biological evolution), everything of importance on the human scale is contingent and unpredictable. In the study of international affairs, as in environmental matters, there are too many mutually interactive variables, and too many nonlinear effects, for human brains to understand how things work until they have happened and can be observed in detail.

Lately an interdisciplinary inquiry has grown up that tries to link the fields of environment and international relations. It is not, as fields go, highly theoretical, but is more often based on case studies.[1] Drawing useful lessons from these cases is no easy business, however, in part because they combine the uncertainties and complexities of these two very uncertain and complex fields.[2] It is, therefore, an unpromising intellectual enterprise to seek connections between environment and security. This chapter, however, aims to do just that for the twentieth century and, to a very limited extent, the twenty-first. It argues that such connections existed in the past and will exist with greater force in the future, but that they have been and will remain modest in comparison to the traditional concerns of international security.[3]

Environmental Change in the Twentieth Century: A Brief History

One of the distinguishing features of the twentieth century was its tumultuous environmental change. While earlier periods in earth's history contained moments far more disruptive, these invariably were the work of volcanoes, asteroids, or other

178

purely natural forces. In recent millennia humankind has proved the most ecologically disruptive force on the planet, and never more so than in the last hundred years. From forests to fisheries and from soils to the stratosphere, humankind had never before altered ecosystems so comprehensively. A very rough appreciation of the magnitude of the process emerges from the following table, which seeks to give some measure to this proposition.

Table 8.1 is less than thorough. It presents only data that are fairly easily retrieved, for example, bird and mammal species but not fish and insects. It neglects variables for which the coefficient of growth in the twentieth century would be astronomical, say, automobiles or organic chemicals, and those for which the coefficient would be infinite, such as chlorofluorocarbon emissions, which were zero prior to the 1930s. Its figures are all global ones, whereas most environmental effects—not all—are local or regional in scope. Nonetheless, it conveys the right impression and gives some precision, where that is feasible, to the proposition that twentieth-century environmental change was both broad and deep, comprehensive and thorough.

As a heuristic exercise, it may be helpful to imagine a single index of human-induced environmental disruption, conflating all the variables, and consider its history. If one did, one would find that environmental disruption on some scale existed from the dawn of human history, grew extremely slowly, roughly in step with human population growth, and then around 1800 or so sped up slightly. This modest acceleration came as a result of faster population growth and faster economic growth, although both were still very slow by recent standards. Technical change, in particular the emergence of coal-powered steam engines, helped too.

Table 8.1   Measures of Environmental Change, 1890s–1990s

Environmental Indicator	Coefficient of Increase, 1890s–1990s
Energy use	13–15
Population	4
Urban population	13
World GDP	14
Industrial output	40
Freshwater use	9
Cropland	2
Irrigated area	5
Cattle population	4
Marine fish catch	35
Lead emissions to atmosphere	8
Carbon dioxide emissions	17
Air pollution in general	2–10
Forest area	0.8 (20% decrease)
Bird and mammal species	0.99 (1% decrease)

Source: J. R. McNeill, *Something New under the Sun* (New York: Norton, 2000), 360–61.
Note: Some of these figures deserve more confidence than others. For details, see McNeill 2000, *passim*.

A much more marked acceleration came around 1950. This one too resulted from faster (this time much faster) population growth, but also from the emergence of more energy-intensive economies, made feasible in particular by the arrival of cheap oil, about which more below.

Throughout the period since 1800 and especially since 1950, the human relationship with the rest of nature has been very much in flux. Ecologically, and without much awareness of the process, we have created a regime of constant disturbance. This regime is itself both a result of and a contributor to rapid social and economic change. Our modern social regime and our modern ecological regime coevolved, adjusting to each other while shaping each other.

This, in very general terms, is the trajectory of modern environmental history. Let us now look more closely at two components of it, water and energy, chosen for their relevance to contemporary security concerns.

A Brief History of Freshwater Use

The world has always had plenty of fresh water, but it is often inconveniently distributed in time and space for human designs. Getting just the right amounts of water in the right places at the right times is an ancient art, at least 9,000 years old. Success or failure in the art of water management was crucial in the distant past. Irrigation made crops grow where they otherwise would not, allowing states greater population, revenues, and power. Urban life depended on the ability to assure a supply of clean drinking water and to provide a means to disperse wastes. Failure to segregate drinking water from waste water assured a heavy burden of gastro-enteric diseases and made urban life all but unsustainable. The great civilizations of the ancient world, in Mesopotamia, Egypt, the Indus valley, and north China, all rested on sophisticated water management, as did the great pre-Columbian empires of the Americas. With the exception of the transitory Mongol Empire, no great states of the past existed without great cities at their core, and all great cities required careful water management. In the modern world water management remains fundamental. One of the differences between rich and poor societies is their ability to provide adequate clean water, and thereby to minimize the burdens of disease (and the time spent in fetching water).

Irrigation remains the most important use of freshwater, accounting for about two-thirds of global water use, down from 90 percent a century ago. Roughly a sixth of the world's cultivated acreage is irrigated, and it produces about a third of the world's food. The tenth of the world's freshwater usage that goes to cities is responsible for the comparative good health of 1 or 2 billion people (of the 3 billion in all who live in cities). The enormous expansion of water use in modern history (see Table 8.2) has generated inestimable benefits to human health and nutrition, and sizeable ones to industry and routine household life. Table 8.2 outlines the quantities of fresh water withdrawn from lakes, rivers, and aquifers, and the uses to which they have been put over the past 300 years.

While the benefits of this enormous replumbing of the planet have been great, they have come at a cost. Irrigation everywhere leads to the salinization of land, although at widely divergent rates. Today the accumulation of salts forces the abandonment of farmland at about the same rate as engineers bring new land under irrigation. So, in effect, irrigation amounts to a short-term maximization strategy. It is also notoriously wasteful, although again to widely varying degrees. Half the water diverted for crops never reaches a root or leaf. In some of the more poorly designed irrigation schemes in high-evaporation zones, the proportion wasted reaches 90 percent. Probably the most costly irrigation scheme is that of Central Asia, planned by Soviet engineers in the 1950s, a region-wide project far more ambitious than anything previously tried in the long history of Central Asian irrigation. The plan diverted the snow-melt waters of the Syr Darya and Amu Darya rivers into the cotton fields of Soviet Central Asia, principally Uzbekistan. Since 1960 it has strangled the Aral Sea, killing off its fishing industry and most of its fish and exposing the salt-encrusted seabed to steppe winds, which distribute airborne salt throughout Central Asia. The Aral, now about one-half its 1960 area, now has a weaker moderating effect on the Central Asian climate, which is getting hotter in summer, colder in winter, and drier, so that the Himalayan snowmelt that feeds Central Asia's rivers is declining. The usual curses of irrigation, rising groundwater and salinization, affect much of Turkmenistan's and Uzbekistan's best soils. All this in order to make the USSR self-sufficient in low-quality cotton, unmarketable anywhere outside the Soviet bloc.[4]

The Soviet experience with the Aral Sea was unique in its severity but typical in its origins. While water manipulation had been a part of state efforts for millennia, in the twentieth century new skills and technology, and a new ambitiousness, raised the ceiling on what states might attempt. From the end of the nineteenth

Table 8.2   Estimated Global Freshwater Use, 1700–2000

Year	Withdrawals (km2)	Withdrawals per capita	Uses (percent of total)		
			Irrigation	Industry	Municipal
1700	110	0.17	90	2	8
1800	243	0.27	90	3	7
1900	580	0.36	90	6	3
1950	1,360	0.54	83	13	4
1970	2,590	0.70	72	22	5
1990	4,130	0.78	66	24	8
2000*	5,190	0.87	64	25	9

*A projection, which may be too high.
Source: J.R. NcNeill, Something New under the Sun (New York: Norton, 2000), 121, elaborated from I. A. Shiklomanov, "World Fresh Water Resources," Water in Crisis, ed. Peter Gleick (New York: Oxford University Press, 1993), 13–24, and Mark L'vovich and Gilbert White, "Use and Transformation of Terrestrial Water Systems," in The Earth as Transformed by Human Action, ed. B. L. Turner et al. (New York: Cambridge University Press, 1990), 235–52.

century it was possible to generate electricity from water-powered turbines. With improvements in engineering and construction techniques beginning in the 1930s it became possible to build gigantic dams across all but the largest rivers. Large dams in particular acquired a certain totemic quality for ambitious states and their leaders: Nehru called dams the "temples of modern India." Like Franklin Roosevelt, Franco, Stalin, Nasser, Mao, Deng, and a legion of lesser leaders, Nehru saw in big dams a mighty symbol of an energetic, modernizing state, tangible evidence of a commitment to improve life for the masses. That some of the costs of dam-building could often be shunted onto the poor and powerless, foreigners, or the future, made dam projects all the more appealing.[5]

Two notable examples of large-scale rerouting of waters in the interests of state power are Italy and the United States. When, by the 1890s, it had become clear that the basis of military power had shifted away from cannon fodder, horseflesh, and heroism to heavy industry, Italy appeared to be in a particularly unenviable position. It had almost no coal. Imported coal was expensive, and unreliable in time of war. The Italian solution lay in turning the alpine lakes and rivers into sources of electric power on which to construct an industrial base on the northern rim of the Po Valley. Italy built its first hydroelectric power station in 1885 and by 1905 led all Europe in hydropower. Further electrification became a major goal of fascist Italy (1922–43), which was intent on building a self-sufficient military-industrial complex. This it never quite achieved (Italy still imported coal through World War II, from Germany and Poland), but by the 1930s Italy had built up its metallurgical, shipbuilding, aircraft, rail, and armaments industries to the point where Mussolini could field a semi-industrialized military in wars in Ethiopia and Spain, and could seriously rival Britain's Royal Navy as top dog on the Mediterranean Sea. Without the harnessing of alpine hydropower, fascist geopolitical ambitions would have been impossible rather than merely impractical.[6]

The United States recast its waterways too, and on a much larger scale. The state was deeply involved from the 1930s, building dams, channelizing rivers, subsidizing irrigation and hydropower. The agricultural development of arid regions in the Southwest, in California, and in Washington and Oregon depended fundamentally on government enterprise. So too did the vast hydropower schemes on the Columbia River. These were not deliberately built in order to construct a military-industrial complex, but the fact that the United States was able to construct one in a single year, 1942, required as a precondition the cheap hydropower just recently made available.[7] Without it, the aircraft industry in Seattle and the shipyards of the Pacific coast could not have been as enormously productive as they were. One cannot weld a ship together every eight days without plenty of electricity.[8]

The vast effort to reorganize rivers and lakes for human purposes had, as always, state power as well as social welfare among its motives. State ambition and security anxiety played an equal role in shaping the energy regime of the twentieth century. Only a small part of the modern energy regime derived from hydropower. The lion's share came from fossil fuels.

A Brief History of Energy Use

Energy is essential for making things, for transport, and for mere survival. Before the use of fossil fuels, people could use only the tiniest fraction of the energy available on earth. By eating plants people acquired chemical energy that photosynthesis had captured from sunlight. By eating animals, or using the muscle power of draft animals, humans tapped further energy. Wind and water power, available only in favorable locations, also harnessed a fraction of the annual energy delivered to the earth from the sun. Each of these methods tapped only the annual flow of energy generated by the sun, which, although abundant, was very inefficiently converted into useful forms. By burning wood or charcoal people could tap energy stocks accumulated in trees over a century or two. But ultimately all these methods provided a very limited energy harvest, which meant that almost all people would always be poor, dependent on grinding toil for their daily rice or bread.

Fossil fuels changed all that. The Dutch were the first people to make them central to their economy. They burned peat to heat their homes and fuel industries such as brewing, brick making, sugar refining, and glass making (but not metallurgy, for which a peat flame was not hot enough). Peat is accumulated vegetable matter, preserved by water. The Dutch cut it out of bogs, dried it, and burned it to harvest energy that plants had captured over millennia. This delivered more concentrated energy than wood or charcoal and gave the Netherlands a unique advantage (until coal) in energy-intensive industries. To a considerable extent, the prosperity of the Dutch in their golden age (c. 1580–1700) depended on low energy costs.[9]

While wood allowed access to stores of energy captured over centuries, and peat to energy captured over millennia, coal represented eons of accumulated energy stocks. People around the world had known of coal's uses for a long time, and medieval China had used it on a large scale in its iron industry. London had burned coal for home heating from at least the thirteenth century. Britain had plentiful coal deposits, part of a "carboniferous crescent" that stretched from the Scottish lowlands through England to northern France and Belgium and on to the Ruhr region of Germany. This would become the industrial heartland of Europe, as important for modern history as the Fertile Crescent was for ancient history. By 1815 annual British coal production yielded energy equivalent to the yield garnered from a hypothetical forest equal in area to all of England, Scotland, and Wales, twenty times what the actual woodlands of Britain could then produce. Steam engines did the work of perhaps 50 million vigorous men, far more than Britain actually had.[10] Britain was on its way to becoming the first high-energy society. Table 8.3 shows the difference in energy use before and after fossil fuels.

The harnessing of fossil fuels ratcheted up the energy supplies available for human use, thereby permitting a vast increase in human numbers and wealth. Between 1800 and 2000 the total increase in energy use was about sixty- or eighty-fold. The expanded energy harvest meant that for the first time in history mass poverty became unnecessary. It had other implications as well.

Table 8.3   Average Annual Per Capita Energy Use (in gigajoules)

Basic Requirements of the Human Body	3.5
Hunting and gathering societies	10.5–21
Agrarian societies	63–84
Industrial societies	245–280

Based on Rolf-Peter Sieferle, *Der Europäische Sonderweg: Ursachen und Faktoren* (Stuttgart: Breuninger Stiftung, 2001), 18–19.

The most pertinent ones are the geopolitical and environmental. The wealth generated in the Netherlands through the use of peat in select industries helped underwrite Dutch imperial ambitions in the seventeenth century. But peat conferred no direct military advantages. Coal was different. It made cheap iron possible, and eventually steam-powered ships. Whereas in 1793 a British embassy to China was dismissed peremptorily and the Qianlong Emperor (reigned 1735–95) could suppose that Britain was of no consequence, in 1840 British gunboats could sail up rivers 10,000 miles from home and British diplomats could therefore dictate terms even to the most populous country on earth. The ships and weapons made possible and affordable by coal also tipped the balance in Britain's favor in India and Africa in the nineteenth century.[11] Britain was the first state to adjust, economically and militarily, to the potential of coal, and its geopolitical position in the nineteenth century reflected this. By the 1890s Germany too had converted its abundant coal and ore deposits into cheap metals and good weaponry, and thus also fielded a formidable industrialized military.

In the twentieth century the United States revamped the world's energy regime by developing oil as a primary fuel. Large-scale oil production began on the shores of the Caspian Sea late in the nineteenth century. America's first big gusher, in Spindletop, Texas, came appropriately in the first month of the twentieth century, January 1901. Thereafter Americans led the way in the technologies necessary for drilling, transporting, refining, and burning oil. They led the world in oil production for much of the twentieth century, and in oil consumption for all of it. This was crucial to the emergence of the United States as a great power, because the mobile warfare—on land and sea and in the air—that characterized the twentieth century after 1918 was an extremely oil-intensive business. So the United States, like Britain a century before, profited handsomely in geopolitical terms (as in economic terms) by being the first to adapt thoroughly to a new energy regime.

The transition to fossil fuels was just as consequential in environmental terms. Coal created urban air pollution of a new intensity and lethality. By 1900 air pollution caused or exacerbated respiratory diseases that killed hundreds of thousands annually in coal-burning cities around the world. At its worst coal smoke and associated sulfur dioxide and particulates could kill 4,000 people in a week, as in London in December 1952.[12] Through railroads and steamships, coal made it feasible to open up agricultural frontiers around the world, producing cotton, coffee, wheat, and, after the 1880s, meat and butter, for shipment to growing cities. This led to very wide-spread conversion of grassland and forest into farmland and pasture in the Americas, South Africa, Siberia, Australia, and New Zealand. Oil led to still greater changes.

Oil burns more cleanly than coal. But because oil is a useful fuel in a broad range of applications, its emergence sharply raised the total amount of fossil-fuel combustion, increasing total air pollution loads. In Mexico City, for example, by 2002, air pollution, mainly from vehicle tailpipes, killed 35,000 people annually according to the municipal government. Oil also made possible machinery that revolutionized extractive industries—mining and lumber, for instance. By the late twentieth century humankind had become a major geological agent, moving ten times as much earth and soil as all the world's glaciers and almost as much as all the world's streams and rivers. Oil-powered machines made this possible. They also enabled people to cut timber far faster than had hitherto been possible, helping to propel the dramatic surge in deforestation since 1960. Of all the factors underlying the tumultuous environmental changes of modern times, high energy use, and especially the liberal use of oil after 1950, is probably the most important.[13]

Environment, Security, and Resources: A Brief History

The chief contentions of the environmental security literature are that environmental changes may prove so destabilizing as to create security problems and that resource scarcity may lead to war. I will review these contentions in light of twentieth-century history, and add a third: that a scarcity of security led to greater environmental change.

The first proposition is a weak one in the sense that of all the security problems and conflicts observable in history, almost none of them may confidently be put down to environmental changes. That is because until recent centuries major environmental changes happened so infrequently and proceeded so slowly that they normally gave societies ample time to adapt. The likeliest exception to this is climate change, which until about 150 years ago took place for exclusively natural reasons. It is plausible, although uncertain, that cycles of drought helped to propel migrations that set pastoral peoples of the Eurasian steppe (Xiongnu, Turks, Mongols, for example) against settled populations in China, Iran, or eastern Europe. Equally plausibly, drought may have led to intensified slave raiding and concomitant warfare in Angola and the West African Sahel. These are only speculations: in general, the propensity to award climate change a causative role in large-scale political events (the collapse of the ancient Indus civilization, or the classic Maya, for example) is inversely proportional to our knowledge of these events. This should encourage skepticism.

In the twentieth century, the strongest case for this first proposition is the drought cycle that befell much of Africa after 1967, hitting the Sahel belt from Senegal to Somalia hardest. After more than fifty years of broadly favorable rains, which roughly coincided with the colonial era in Africa, killing drought returned in 1968. Its impact was probably greater than the previous severe drought, because in the interim population and herds had grown, and colonial policy had purposely reduced the mobility of the population to make it more manageable and taxable. In the six years after 1967, desiccation, starvation, and related diseases killed 1 percent of the population of the Sahel, and 30 to 40 percent of the cattle, a severe blow in cattle-keeping societies. This catastrophe probably played some role in bringing on a spate of political coups in the 1970s, ushering in some of modern African history's most unsavory regimes.

However, a note of caution is in order. The area in which the coups took place does not correlate perfectly with the area of most intense drought. The 1970s were politically turbulent in parts of Africa least affected by drought, such as South Africa and Rhodesia/Zimbabwe, as well as in the regions hardest hit. Independent African states in the late 1960s were, most of them, fully laden camels, needing only a single straw to break their backs. The hike in oil prices in 1973 might have been that straw just as plausibly as drought. So might some less-conspicuous events. The most one can reliably say is that the drought, while extremely disruptive environmentally, socially, and economically, probably helped bring about the dissatisfactions, instability, and coups that affected Niger, Chad, Ethiopia, and Uganda, among other countries. That is a modest and guarded claim made for an extreme environmental event. Less extreme environmental events or trends presumably cannot carry heavier explanatory loads or support stronger claims.

All of this is not to say that this first proposition is uninteresting. It is, rather, to say that it has very little use for making sense of the conflicts and security dilemmas of history. But the future is a foreign country, and things may be different there.

The second proposition concerns resource scarcity, resource competition, and warfare. This has a firmer base in modern history, indeed in all history. If one adopts a broad enough definition of the term "resources," then most wars have been over resources. Prior to the Industrial Revolution, most states had a keen interest in both land and labor, because these, when combined, were the main source of revenues on which states subsisted. Labor must be included as a scarce resource in most contexts prior to 1800, especially where disease burdens were heavy, death rates high, and the demand for labor great. In such contexts rulers frequently made the capture of people a primary objective of warfare. They also did so in contexts where they could easily strike against ill-defended populations, that is, where the supply of captives could be cheaply acquired. All of these conditions obtained in tropical Africa before 1850, and in southeast Asia as well, both scenes of extensive slaving. Wars and raids undertaken, at least in part, to secure captives took place wherever slaving and forced labor was a way of life: in the Mediterranean before 1600, in colonial Latin America, in pre-Columbian America, for example. Mongol captains consciously sought to capture skilled personnel to distribute as war booty among their supporters.[14] In the Turko-Persian military tradition, which featured slave soldiers, conquerors had among their explicit goals the capture of skilled military personnel and the capture of youths who could be trained as warriors. After 1850 the logic of forced labor declined quickly, mainly because of the onset of rapid population growth, but also because of the development of fossil fuels. The capture of labor as a motive for war quickly became vanishingly rare, although even today it is not entirely absent from, for example, the calculations behind the civil war in Sudan.

Land of course always figured as a motive in warfare wherever land rather than labor was the scarcer factor in producing revenue. This means, chiefly, the historically thickly populated regions of the world, Japan and China, North India, and Europe. Some lands were so rich that they were routinely fought over—Egypt or the Gangetic Plain, for example. As these two examples suggest, it was often land in combination with water that made control of a given territory worth warring over. Egypt without the Nile's irrigation system was as unprepossessing as Arabia before oil. Nonetheless, whether the prize was land alone or land together with water, the conquest of territory routinely figured as a central motive for warfare. It still does, although on a reduced scale. Only in a few places does land remain the basis of revenue. What is on or under the land is now usually more valuable. That brings us to a narrower definition of resources.

Occasionally a quest for other sorts of resources served as a *casus belli*. Just what counts as a resource changes over time. Pharaonic Egypt undertook the occasional campaign in Lebanon to secure ship timber. Ship timber, like saltpeter and flint, is no longer a strategic resource and is therefore not worth fighting over. In the modern world the only resource worth the risk of war has been oil.

Oil became a strategic resource suddenly after 1912, when the British admiralty began to convert the Royal Navy from coal to oil. When World War I began, the British expeditionary force in France had fewer than 1,000 motor vehicles. Before the war was over, it had 110,000 trucks, cars, and motorcycles—and several hundred tanks. The Allies also used upwards of 100,000 airplanes in the war effort. All these engines needed fuel, which oil provided. Georges Clemenceau at the outset of the war allegedly said that if he wanted oil he would find it at his grocer's; by 1917 he thought "every drop of oil is worth a drop of blood." In World War I the quest for oil motivated modest campaigns (German offensives in Rumania and toward Baku), but no more. But the rapid mechanization of warfare, and the general reliance on oil in industry, soon made oil worth fighting wars over.[15]

The best examples are the Pacific war of 1941–45 and the Gulf War of 1991. In the first case, Japan had embarked on an empire-building program in Asia after 1931 and a war in China after 1937. The Japanese navy and, after 1937, the army, needed oil, of which Japan had none. The nearest source lay in the Dutch East Indies (now Indonesia). In January 1941 the Japanese demanded access to that oil but were refused; in August the Dutch, British, Chinese, and Americans organized oil sanctions against Japan. This obliged the Japanese either to surrender their imperial ambitions, a course unacceptable to the military, or to attack and seize the oilfields of Sumatra and Borneo. Attacking the Dutch islands implied war with the United States, so it required a prior attack on American installations in the Philippines and Hawaii, begun on December 6–7, 1941. Had the Japanese not needed oil for their war in China, they could have avoided the Pacific war that brought their defeat, which would have led to a very different recent history for East Asia.

Sometimes timing is everything. Had the great Siberian oilfields, the world's second-largest after those of the Persian Gulf, been opened prior to 1941 (they were opened in the early 1960s), the Japanese would have had a much more palatable option at hand. From their base in Manchuria they could have attacked the USSR, which after June 1941 was reeling under German assault. There would have been no Pearl Harbor, no Pacific War, no external constraints on Japanese imperialism in China, and, very quickly, no USSR. That of course is what did not happen: let us return to what did.

The Gulf War of 1991 was also mainly over oil, specifically how much of the gulf region's supply should be in the hands of Saddam Hussein, who invaded and occupied Kuwait late in 1990 and threatened Saudi Arabia, the world's largest oil producer. At the time American officials marketed the war to the public as one over jobs (James Baker) or principle (George H. W. Bush). It was certainly not about principle: had Mozambique invaded Malawi the Americans would not have launched a war to undo it. It was about jobs in the sense that the American economy, and that of the industrial world generally, floated (and floats) on oil. Allowing a high proportion of the world's oil to be controlled by someone as unbiddable as Saddam risked recession and many jobs. Indeed, American policy toward the Middle East since the 1940s has recognized that oil is a vital economic and military resource for the United States. It is even more vital for Japan: when the Japanese agreed to pay a goodly share of the costs of the Gulf War they understood they were paying for continued access to cheap oil. They did not suppose they were paying for a principle. American leaders have felt it necessary to invoke principle only because in the modern world fighting over resources is deemed crass and morally dubious, and thus candor on this point might undermine popular support for a given war. This is perhaps a reaction in part to Hitler's justification for his war in terms of *Lebensraum*. The ancient Athenians—at least Thucydides—had no compunctions about saying that the value of Amphipolis (in Thrace) lay in its timber.

In a sense, wars over oil have replaced wars over people. Before fossil fuels a ruler's most practical way to amass energy for any given task was to amass people, which was most quickly done by enslaving them. Human beings are considerably more energy-efficient than horses, oxen, llamas, elephants, or any other work animal. But in the past 150 years machines and fossil fuels provided a cheaper way to build monuments or fortresses, and the usefulness of massed, unskilled labor has plummeted accordingly.

In general, wars over environmental resources occur when valued resources are somehow made to seem more scarce or when wide differentials in power make seizure of resources easy and tempting. A sense of heightened scarcity can occur with a technological shift that suddenly makes something indispensable. Before 1910 no state needed reliable access to oil. By 1930 all great powers did, because the technology of war had changed. Heightened scarcity may also come with shifts in patterns of distribution and supply: in the 1860s the American Civil War created a shortage of cotton, which made it seem important to the Russians that they should control the oases and river bottomlands of Uzbekistan, where they might grow their own cotton; the Russian push there began in 1864. States (and societies) may also feel the pinch of resource scarcity in times of rapid population growth. This often took the form of land hunger and provoked ambitions of territorial conquest, as in the case of the U.S.–Indian wars of the nineteenth century, the Chinese and Japanese pushes into Manchuria, and in other cases too numerous to mention.

The United States also fought its Indian Wars because they were so easy to win. Seizing resources becomes more tempting when it appears cheap and easy to do so. Farmers have routinely displaced hunting-and-gathering peoples from potential farmland because their technological and numerical edge made it simple to do. The Russians acquired Siberia and the Japanese Hokkaido because resistance was so feeble as to make the resources of those lands seem cheap to acquire. In the first decade of the twentieth century, the Germans fought colonial wars of conquest in what are now Tanzania and Namibia on the unconfirmed (and ultimately disappointed) hopes of finding useful natural resources. In short, wars over scarce resources are most likely when circumstances conspire to make the specific resources in view suddenly seem more valuable, or make the cost of taking them seem low. Such circumstances are most likely to arise in times of rapid and uneven population growth (or decline) and times of technological dynamism (when hitherto unvalued items suddenly become resources).

A third proposition, not prominent in the environmental-security literature, is that security anxiety affects environmental change. Some researchers have shed light on the environmental effects of war itself, generally aiming to show that combat is bad for all life and land.[16] It usually is, although there are some exceptions, such as the flourishing of North Atlantic fish populations during World War II while fishing fleets were stuck in port. More important than combat, however, is the business of preparing for war. This is because more states prepare for war than actually fight wars, and because war itself is usually briefer than periods of preparedness.

States have long altered environments in the interest of security. They sometimes pursued forest conservation for strategic reasons. Qing China in the seventeenth and eighteenth centuries tried to maintain a wooded blockade ("the willow pallisade") between Chinese cultivators and steppe pastoralists in Manchuria. Naval powers from the thirteenth century, if not before, sought to conserve forests for ship timber; Venice perhaps took this the furthest. More recently, after the shocking defeat of 1870, the French army won the power to preserve public and private forests in eastern France so as to channel any future German invasion along well-fortified corridors. (The next German invasion came via Belgium in 1914).[17]

States also brought on environmental change by seeking to stockpile strategic resources, whether food, rubber, oil, or soldiers. Mussolini, for example, wanted Italy to become self-sufficient in food so as to be less vulnerable to blockade of the sort he had seen weaken Germany in World War I. So he mounted the "Battle for Wheat," encouraging Italians to clear forests and plant wheat on sloping and other marginal lands, inviting a surge of soil erosion. Crash programs of this sort proliferated in the twentieth century when susceptibility to the interruption of international trade made autarky appealing, especially when war loomed. The USSR and China after 1949—for ideological as well as strategic reasons—undertook several such campaigns, of which the most famous example is the backyard steel furnaces of the Great Leap Forward (1958-60), a great leap backward for Chinese forests, which provided fuel for the inefficient furnaces. Such programs amounted to a form of environmental roulette, but states willingly played because the ecological bills, poorly understood in any case, seemed likely to fall due much later than would the political and military bills of unpreparedness.[18]

The most obvious connection between security anxiety and environmental change is the nuclear weapons programs organized after 1942. In the United States and especially in the USSR these led to the contamination of sizeable areas, to numerous health problems and premature deaths. The hair-raising risks taken, normally secretly, with their own populations show the lengths to which security anxiety during the cold war drove both the Americans and Soviets. The plutonium buried at Hanford Engineering Works in the state of Washington or dumped in Lake Karachay (in the southern Urals) will remain deadly for about 24,000 years, a long lien on the future. Cleaning up after the nuclear weapons programs will prove much more expensive than building the warheads and missiles in the first place, and will never be done completely.[19]

Less directly, states helped shape ecological change by building transport infrastructure in the name of military preparedness. New roads and railroads, aside from their immediate environmental impact, invariably change land use and human settlement patterns, especially in thinly populated areas. The trans-Siberian railroad is a case in point. Built mainly for military reasons, it opened the gates to settlement and cultivation in the southern Siberian forest and northern steppe. It also made practical numerous mining and logging enterprises. The highways built in Brazilian Amazonia after 1960 also had strategic reasons behind them, and also led to waves of migration, settlement, forest clearance, and otherwise unimaginable mining and logging businesses. Even the U.S. interstate highway system begun in the 1950s, which strongly affected land-use and settlement patterns, featured military considerations prominently among its justifications.

Last, and perhaps least directly, states have often sought (and occasionally still seek) to maximize their supply of soldiers by various pronatal policies. Insofar as these are successful (which is rarely) they affected environments by raising population. Third Republic France, Fascist Italy, Nazi Germany, and Stalinist Russia all encouraged women to bear more children, with modest success. In Europe the only pronatalist effort that produced a real surge in births was that of Ceauçescu's Romania, which doubled its birth rate in 1966. Ceauçescu, who was interested in pursuing an independent foreign policy that carried serious risks, set a goal of 30 million Romanians by the year 2000. He outlawed all forms of birth control and assigned the secret police the duty of making sure that Romanian women did not shirk their duty. Mao, too, thought that millions of additional Chinese would enhance the military security of China, and, with brief exceptions, resisted efforts to curtail population growth in his country.[20]

Of course, in most cases these population and transport policies had many motives behind them, of which security anxiety was only one. The point here is simply that historically, and especially in recent history, the ordinary business of preparing for war has helped drive states to actions that carried profound environmental consequences. Normally these consequences went unconsidered, but when they were taken into account they were underestimated.

Prospects

The prospects for security problems to arise from environmental changes are better than ever. That is not to say that they outrank more traditional causes of conflict. They do not, nor will they any time soon. But they are real enough to merit attention, and indeed do now command attention in places such as the Pentagon.

The chief reason that environmental changes are more likely to play a larger role in security issues in the future than they have in the past is that ecological pressures of the sort most relevant to international competition are higher than ever before. Many of the reserves and ecological buffers—forests, unexploited fisheries, unpolluted fresh water—have been pared down. Put another way, there is less slack in the human environment system now.

Against that is the welcome fact that the technological, and perhaps administrative, capacity to deal with environmental shocks and problems is also greater than ever before. The power of technology and political will to check conflict, however, is limited by the unwelcome fact that they are so unevenly distributed around the world, and by and large are weak in places where the need for them is strongest.

Let us return to water and energy. At present some thirty or forty countries in southwest Asia and North Africa are, by the conventional measures of hydrologists, short of water. They are also, as it happens, countries with population growth rates among the highest in the world, so that their scant water will have to be shared more widely in the years to come. Ethiopia and Sudan could make very good use of the Nile water that makes Egypt viable, and the temptations and pressures to do so will rise with growing populations. Similarly, Turkey, in its quest to develop the poorer and politically disaffected southeast, could find uses for the waters of the Tigris and Euphrates, the lifeblood of Syria and Iraq. Indeed, the Turks have built a series of dams that give them the option of impounding the water of those rivers. In a severe drought, Ethiopia and Turkey would feel the urge to take a larger share, despite the clear threats voiced by neighbors downriver. The likelihood of friction over these rivers is high, but the likelihood of war is governed by other factors. This is true of all the other international river basins over which conflict might break out, among which the leading candidates are probably the Indus and the Jordan, where frictions are great for other reasons.

There are other ways in which water might affect security besides quarrels over supply. The economic strength of every society depends on (among many other things) its water. This will presumably be less true in the future, as sectoral shifts in the world economy emphasize agriculture and industry less and services more. But that process is slow and less than universal. To take only two large cases, both the United States and China face adjustment to looming shortages of groundwater. The cattle and wheat economy of the high plains in the United States has rested in recent decades on a large aquifer called the Ogallala, which stretches from north Texas to South Dakota. Cheap energy allowed farmers to pump up Ogallala water at great rates since the 1940s, and now about half of it is gone. The aquifer recharges slowly, over thousands of years, so in effect this is water mining. In twenty or thirty more years the water will be gone, and the United States will have to find another source for beef and wheat—or find some more water somewhere, an idea that worries Canadians and residents of Great Lakes states.

Moving water rather than shifting patterns of production appeals to the Chinese leadership, which faces a broadly similar problem in north China. There too water is short, and agriculture and industry must either find more, become more efficient in their use of water (there is plenty of room for that), or cut back operations. The current preferred choice is to reroute some of the water of the Yangzi to the north, a gigantic project that recalls in its towering ambition the Soviet plans to redirect some of the flow of the Siberian rivers from the arctic to Central Asia. Whether or not the Chinese will carry through with the "southern waters north" scheme remains to be seen. Without it they face limits on production. With it, they need massive capital investment (that other infrastructure projects would lose) and create another source of vulnerability in the form of water pipelines, sitting targets for missiles or terrorists.

In the past, while water has motivated countless quarrels and much small-scale violence, it has yet to serve as a cause for war. It is somewhat more likely to do so in the future, but only in contexts where frictions are already high and war, should it break out, would have, as it normally does, many causes. In the meantime water shortage will continue to constrain the economic development of dozens of countries, confining their military potential below what it otherwise might be. Climate change, should it continue on the path of the past twenty years, will exacerbate the trends in most cases by making most dry regions a bit drier.

Although the economies of the rich and powerful countries of the world are growing less energy-intensive, the overall demand for energy will continue to increase and fossil fuels will for some time remain the heart of the world's energy system. Thus the uneven match between the geography of petroleum production and the loci of oil consumption will continue to bedevil world politics for decades to come. In just which ways, of course, remains quite unpredictable, especially as the emergence of Central Asian oil and gas has begun to shift the balance. Control of these resources, and of the offshore oil of the South China Sea, are plausible candidates as sources (or intensifiers) of international conflict. As natural gas slowly acquires a larger place in the world's energy mix—as it has been doing for decades and will almost surely continue to do—the geopolitics of fossil fuels will perhaps become less volatile, because gas fields are distributed much more widely around the planet than oilfields. No single country can have the power in that market that the United States had in the oil market early in the twentieth century, and no combination of countries could easily acquire the power that OPEC had in the late 1970s.

Looking further forward, the fossil fuel energy regime will one day come to an end. Just what will replace it, when, and how, is up in the air. Some authorities think the world's oil supply will begin to run short very soon (between 2004 and 2008), but this is a minority opinion.[21] Nonetheless, it will happen one day and someone will take advantage of the shift in ways analogous to the deft exploitation of coal undertaken by Britain 200 years ago or the quick and canny adaptation to oil that the United States achieved eighty years ago. The future energy regime may or may not be as easy to turn to geopolitical advantage as those of coal and oil were, but it is sure that there will be winners and losers in the transition, and the winners will be selected from among those who pioneer the shift. On the strength of historical evidence, one should not expect the United States to be among the pioneers: typically beneficiaries of the old regime try to prolong it. Current American energy policy is fully consistent with this observation.

Perhaps substitutes for oil will emerge soon enough to prevent serious conflict, and (less plausibly) perhaps efficiency and conservation in water use will mitigate any potential international crises over water. Even should both these things happen, environmental considerations will impinge on international security. That is because environmental change in almost any form amounts to environmental degradation for someone, and environmental degradation leads to environmental refugees, that is, people who migrate because of deteriorating ecological circumstances at home.

The coming decades look to be another age of migration. This is true for many reasons, only one of which is environmental degradation. But in places where peasant populations are large and growing, and the material basis (soils, water, forests) for their livelihoods is wearing thin, the pressures and temptations to uproot and try to get to a richer country will intensify. Richer countries have shown wide variability in their willingness to accept migrants, an issue of some importance in rich-country politics now and surely of yet greater importance in the decades to come.

By far the most volatile relationship in this respect is that between Europe and Africa, including North Africa. Demographers expect that the world population will grow to about 9 or 10 billion by 2050, that more than 95 percent of the growth will take place in poor countries, and that African countries will grow fastest. This means that adding the next 3 billion people to the global population will be a more difficult business than was adding the last increment of 3 billion (which happened between 1960 and 2000). A much larger share of the next 3 billion will be born into circumstances of greater shortage of soil, water, and forest, and will see migration as their best option. Because Europe is easily accessible from Africa, especially North Africa, because Africa will probably continue to have the highest rates of population growth, and because many African environments are fragile and already heavily stressed, the likelihood is strong that the greatest pressures will emerge between Africa and Europe. Sometimes location is everything.

How European countries will react is an open question, but it is likely that they will not all agree, that their capacity to enforce their (or EU) policy will be unequal, and that anti-immigrant politics will have a strong future. This implies a resurgence of European nationalisms with attendant pressures on the integrating and globalizing trends of recent decades. Almost inevitably this will add fuel to the fires of religious chauvinism, both within Europe and probably among Muslims suffering backlash effects in Europe and among their sympathizers elsewhere. Developments along these lines are likely to complicate the security picture, especially in Europe, but also in North Africa and the Middle East.

Ethnic and religious tensions deepened by currents of migration may also affect other regions, but probably less acutely. The flows from Mexico, Central America, and the Caribbean to the United States and Canada will probably not grow quickly, because population growth in the sending countries is slowing down fast. In any case, environmental refugees are not likely to figure prominently in this migration.

Conclusion

In the spirit of King Alfonso, this chapter has sought to simplify the very complex nexus between environment and international security. It offers four main ideas, all based on historical perspectives.

First, in modern times environmental perturbation has grown to the point where it must be reckoned a serious factor in all manner of human affairs, security included. Some of this modern environmental disturbance derived from anxieties about international security, although modern patterns of energy use and population growth were probably more important.

Second, in the past such conflicts were routine if one adopts a generous definition of resources and environment, because there have been numerous wars over land, labor, and energy. But if one adopts more conventional and more restricted definitions, such wars have been rare, and in the modern world confined to struggles to secure oil.

Third, environmental perturbations and resource scarcities will probably figure more prominently in the future than they have in the past, because ecological buffers are becoming thinner with time. Should they lead to wars, they are most likely to concern water and oil.

Finally, in the longer run and the larger sense, the big shifts in energy regime and population growth that are sure to come will revise this picture in fundamental ways, but ones quite impossible to envision. Just what constitutes a resource will always be changing. And just which parts of the environment are valued, which are preserved, which are transformed and on what scales—all of this will be changing too. For all our scientific expertise, modeling skill, and theoretical sophistication, we remain subject to the unforeseen, the unintended consequence, the nonlinear effect. In the security arena, the stakes grew much higher in the modern era, and our knowledge of how both the natural and political worlds work grew too. But we still cannot generate precise and reliable ideas about threats and risks until they are upon us. We must respect the wisdom of King Alfonso.

Notes

1. The best sampler of this literature is the *Environmental Change and Security Project Report*, edited by G. Dabelko and published annually since 1995 by the Woodrow Wilson International Center for Scholars. It contains an invaluable bibliography in each issue.

2. Among the more careful work, which displays fewer of the shortcomings so difficult to avoid in this field, is that of T. Homer-Dixon, e.g., his *Environment, Scarcity, and Violence* (Princeton: Princeton University Press, 1999).

3. My discussion will not extend to intrastate conflicts that involve environmental dimensions, such as the resource wars over diamonds, gold, timber, or oil that bedevil societies with weak states in parts of Africa and southeast Asia. On these, see Michael Klare, *Resource Wars: The New Landscape of Global Conflict* (New York: Henry Holt, 2001).

4. For a thorough treatment see the German government's remote sensing program's Aral Sea Homepage at www.dfd.dlr.de/app/land/aralsee/index.html. See also J. R. McNeill, *Something New under the Sun* (New York: Norton, 2000), 162–66, and the sources cited there.

5. On state ambitions and environmental interventions, see James Scott, *Seeing Like a State* (New Haven: Yale University Press, 1998).

6. See Piero Bevilacqua, "Le rivoluzioni dell'acqua," in *Storia dell'agricoltura italiana in età contemporanea,* ed. Piero Bevilacqua (Venice: Marsilio, 1989), 255–318; J. J. Sadkovich, "The Indispensable Navy," in *Naval Power in the Twentieth Century,* ed. N. A. M. Rodger (Annapolis: Naval Institute Press, 1996), 66–76.

7. It had other preconditions as well, most notably the world's largest industrial sector, which was swiftly converted from civilian to military production.

8. On the American military-industrial buildup, see Richard Overy, *Why the Allies Won* (New York: Norton, 1995); on water management, Donald Worster, *Rivers of Empire* (New York: Pantheon, 1985). American shipbuilders assembled cargo vessels, known as Liberty ships, in an average of eight days.

9. J. W. de Zeeuw, "Peat and the Dutch Golden Age," *A.A.G. Bijdragen* 21 (1978): 3–31.

10. The total population of Britain was about 13 million, so the number of vigorous men was perhaps 3 million.

11. An example on the Gambia River is detailed in Donald Wright, *The World and a Very Small Place in Africa* (Armonk, N.Y.: M. E. Sharpe, 1997).

12. Peter Brimblecombe, *The Big Smoke: A History of Air Pollution in London since Medieval Times* (London: Methuen, 1987), chap. 8.

13. For further elaboration, see McNeill, *Something New under the Sun,* chaps. 2, 8, 10; and Christian Pfister, ed., *Das 1950er Syndrom* (Bern: Verlag Paul Haupt, 1996).

14. Artisans, entertainers, animal keepers, translators, among others. For details, see

Thomas Allsen, *Culture and Conquest in Mongol Eurasia* (Cambridge: Cambridge University Press, 2001).

15. Data from Daniel Yergin, *The Prize* (New York: Simon & Schuster, 1991), 167–89. Clemenceau's words are variously reported and translated.

16. For example, Arthur P. Westing, *Warfare in a Fragile World* (London: Taylor & Francis, 1980); Westing, *Environmental Hazards of War* (Newbury Park, Calif.: Sage Publications, 1990); Daniel Faber, *Environment under Fire* (New York: Monthly Review Press, 1993).

17. On these examples, see Patrick Caffrey, "The Forests of Northeast China, 1600–1953: Environment, Politics, and Society" (Ph.D. diss., Georgetown University, 2002); Karl Appuhn, "Inventing Nature: Forests, Forestry, and State Power in Renaissance Venice," *Journal of Modern History* 72 (2000): 861–89; Jean-Paul Amat, "Le rôle stratégique de la forêt, 1871–1914: Exemples dans les forêts lorraines," *Revue historiques des armées* 1 (1993): 62–69.

18. On the environmental aspects of the Great Leap Forward, see Judith Shapiro, *Mao's War against Nature: Politics and the Environment in Revolutionary China* (New York: Cambridge University Press, 2001), 67–93.

19. For details, see Stephen Schwartz, ed., *Atomic Audit: The Costs and Consequences of U.S. Nuclear Weapons since 1940* (Washington: Brookings Institution, 1998), chap. 6; and McNeill, *Something New under the Sun,* 342—44, and the works cited there. The best English-language source on Soviet and Russian nuclear environmental issues is the Norwegian Bellona Foundation. Visit their website at www.bellona.no.

20. On Romania see Jean-Claude Chesnais, *Le crépuscule de l'Occident: Démographie et politique* (Paris: Robert Laffont, 1995), 171–78. On Chinese population history and policy during the Mao years, see James Lee and Wang Feng, *One Quarter of Humankind: Malthusian Mythology and Chinese Reality* (Cambridge: Harvard University Press, 1999); Judith Shapiro, *Mao's War against Nature,* 21–65.

21. K. N. Deffeyes, *Hubbert's Peak: The Impending World Oil Shortage* (Princeton: Princeton University Press, 2001).

Chapter 9

Demographic Developments
and Security

CHARLES B. KEELY

Overwhelming events make planning difficult. There is also a natural tendency to solve the last problem or fight the last war. The terrorist attacks against the World Trade Center and the Pentagon on September 11, 2001, have generated statements that the world will never be the same, and that there is a virtually inexhaustible supply of suicidal terrorists sympathetic to the ideology underlying these attacks. We should counter tendencies to focus on the immediate and familiar. In politics and war, there are fads and fashions. Assassination and terror historically seem to run in waves. We understand little about what triggers or ends such repetitive and stylized behaviors. In the midst of terror, it seems both cold comfort and hard to believe that such behavior is patterned and that past experience tells us that it comes and goes in waves.

Meanwhile, in the post–cold war environment, reevaluation of the meaning of security goes on. There is decided interest in what may be termed soft security issues such as population, refugees, narcotics, people trafficking and smuggling, international organized crime, environmental degradation, and cyber crime, war, and terrorism. Soft security issues are not perpetrated by or generally reactive to the use of military force, and the use of military force is not the primary response to them. While potentially destabilizing for states in direct or indirect ways, the typical response mechanisms to soft security threats are police powers and other nonmilitary regulatory instruments, and even humanitarian assistance, including activities by nongovernmental organizations.

This chapter analyzes the security issues surrounding demographic factors. It analyzes how population processes may affect security, specific contemporary issues, and patterns of policy responses in the areas of population size and structure, fertility, mortality, and international migration.

Population and State Power

Concern about population and security has a long history. Population size and distribution and the underlying processes of fertility, mortality, and migration periodically emerge as sources of anxiety for the security of states.[1] It was once quite popular to speculate about whether a state could be powerful without having a large population. States with large populations, however, are not uniformly great powers. But countries, perhaps most typically France, have worried about their relative size and the effects of fertility and war losses on their ability to achieve the greatness they felt called to. France during Napoleon's era had the largest population of any European state. But declining fertility and losses in the Franco-Prussian war led to national debates, which have continued sporadically, about France's low fertility.[2]

A variation on the theme of a state's absolute population size is how population is distributed among the countries of the globe. This was a major concern, even if expressed privately, among Western European elites worried by rapid population growth in developing countries after World War II. Their worry was not confined to the pressures of population on the capacity for sustainable economic development, but extended to the inevitable reduction of the proportion of the world's population in developed countries, if current trends persisted.[3] In 1958–59, William H. Draper Jr., an investment banker, general in World War II, and central official in the postwar assistance to Germany, headed a presidential committee to study the United States' Military Assistance Program.[4] Based on econometric work on the relation between population growth and investment, Draper's committee recommended developing family planning programs to deal with rapid population growth. Failure was seen in terms of a loss to the communist threat and a contributor to "international class warfare" and widespread international insecurity.[5] Rapid population growth has generally been estimated by subsequent officials in administrations of both political parties as a bar to economic development, a threat to stability, and a danger to the environment and global resources. In the 1960s and 1970s rapid population growth became a more popular concern, as people in developed nations grew alarmed by what they termed the "population bomb"; these concerns contributed to the formation of the environmental movement.[6]

Most of the rapid population growth, whether measured in terms of absolute increase or rates of growth, was and remains concentrated in the developing countries. Demographic projections based on differentials in the rates of growth by country clearly indicated that the bulk of the world's population would be in the developing world. The relative size of the developed, industrial countries' populations would decrease from about 33 percent in 1950 to 25 percent in 1980. The decline was projected to continue to 21 percent in 2000 and 17 percent by 2025. Between 1950 and 2025, the decline in the relative share of the developed countries' percentage of the earth's population (that is, North America, Europe, the Soviet Union, Oceania, and Japan) was projected to decline by half.

The sorts of projection used to analyze the issue and sensitize decision makers and the public point up some problems with the use of population projections for these purposes. The projections have been generally accurate, with minor overestimations at the global level and increasingly larger errors with smaller units (country level and especially smaller countries) and with increasing time horizons.[7] Nevertheless, in terms of relative size the projections have proved to be relatively accurate and their main points about changing distribution among countries and about the magnitude of the differences expected through the end of the twentieth century were correct.

But the projection exercises provide food for thought in relation to assumptions about state stability. Projections from the cold war era refer to the Soviet Union. Aside from the obvious fact that the USSR no longer exists as a state (or three states, if one counts the Ukrainian SSR and Belorussian SSR, which held separate seats at the United Nations), are all Commonwealth of Independent States (CIS) countries now to be considered developed? In addition, many states have large variation in levels of economic development. Brazil is a good example. The state may not be the best unit of analysis in some respects, but it is the unit for which data are collected and reported, and there is no gainsaying the importance of the state in regard to economic and military decisions. But we must not presume that current states or boundaries will persist indefinitely or that state-level data tell the whole story. Contemporary projections referring, for example, to Indonesia ought to be carefully scrutinized, especially if extended out twenty-five to fifty years.

The concern over rapid population growth and its effects on sustainable development and international stability were used to justify aid for international family planning efforts both by UN agencies and bilaterally by states.[8] A large regime of international organizations, state-aid agencies, and nongovernmental organizations developed to provide technical expertise, supplies, and education, which has led to widespread adoption of family planning methods and subsequent fertility declines in many countries, though not universally so. In a little more than a generation (using 1968—the year of the initiation of the UN Fund for Population Activities—as a marker), the proportion of couples who use modern methods of family planning has mushroomed to almost 60 percent worldwide and about 55 percent in developing countries as of 1998.[9]

While microstates will probably not become great powers, there seems to be a range of population size that allows for being an important power. Population itself seems not to be the defining issue. States like Australia even talk about "punching above its weight," using the boxing metaphor to indicate that a welterweight can at time carry a heavyweight's punch. In addition, alliances and political institutions such as the European Union require a different calculus than the simple toting up of individual country population size. Furthermore, for both states and coalitions, technological and organizational skills can have a multiplicative effect for the overall power of a state. Size is not everything.[10]

More recently, the shifting concentration of the earth's population to the developing countries, as a result of rapid population growth in less developed countries and low fertility and aging populations in industrial societies, has resurfaced in analysis and commentary. Especially if one thinks in terms of Huntingtonian clashes of civilizations or similar macrostrategic designs, such figures may give us pause.[11]

The concern in this instance is not so much about the absolute size of a state's population and its relation to state power, but that the shift in relative population size among states or groups of states presages a shift of state power globally. The concern is developed against a background of European and North American dominance in the modern era, when, in the early stages and into the twentieth century, the share of the world's population living in the industrial powers was much larger and, as noted above, projected to decline even further. To put it perhaps a little too dramatically, does the shift in population ratios to less developed and non-Western states point to a "decline of the West?"

Industrial powers in the West are still large states in population terms. Developments like the European Union, alliances like the North Atlantic Treaty Organization, and control of military technology, advanced organizational techniques, and dominant military forces lead reasonably to the conclusion that any effect of growth in population size and the redistribution of relative population shares will be blunted. This does not mean that there are no vulnerabilities, as terrorist attacks attest, but the shift in population ratios globally does not map any similar shift in state power distribution. Put in terms of specific countries, the growth of Nigeria, Indonesia, or even India (which is projected to replace China as the world's largest country in the next twenty-five years), will probably not affect the balance of military power or global influence of the United States or leading European countries such as France and the United Kingdom. Of course there will be change in power relations. But India's emergence, for example, will probably have more to do with the strength of its economy, its advances in technology, and its possession of nuclear weapons than with the absolute or relative growth of its population base.

Overall growth in population size does not mean that a country will become a great power, nor does a changing distribution of the world's population necessarily imply a shift in the balance of geopolitical power. What is the effect on stability in states experiencing rapid population growth?

Population Growth and State Stability

Population growth is related to instability that can lead to internal and international security threats. The pathways by which population growth influences political violence, instability, and change are not straightforward. There are a number of specific situations, noted by Goldstone, in which population growth, mediated by economic and political factors, seems to breed political violence and social instability.[12]

First, political violence is connected to an expanding agricultural population with constricted access to land controlled by an economic or political elite. This is a specific instance of the general problem of resource scarcity and its impact on political insecurity. In a sense, resource scarcity has an inherent population component. Whether the issue is water supply, air and water quality, food self-sufficiency, or a similar issue of resources, the nub of the problem is supply relative to demand of the relevant population. In effect, the hypothesis is proposed that a lack of a sufficient supply per capita of a necessity for life will lead to political violence. However, environmental change (whether resource depletion, population increases that make greater demands and raise prices or threaten supply, or catastrophic events) may lead to nonviolent conflict. It may also help generate new forms of technology or social organization to secure and distribute resources. The presumption that environmental change is or will be a major source of conflict is deeply questionable.[13]

There are specific kinds of population change associated with political instability. In the case of an expanding agricultural population in an economy where cultivated land is in the hands of elites, there is often increased cultivation of marginal land. Who controls the marginal land and its output can lead to conflict, as can increases in marginal land cultivation not resulting in sufficient food or income for the expanding population. Pressure on peasant access to food and other forms of income can lead to conflicts with landlords. Recent political violence in Chiapas in Mexico exhibits this pattern of peasant-landlord relations, which has been an element in revolutions since the French Revolution of 1789. Land reform is often among the central demands of those espousing social transformation. A trigger for such demands has been the increase of agrarian populations within an economic structure that confines control of land to elites.

At the urban end of the spectrum, an economy unable to generate enough jobs for a growing urban population is a second source of political and social instability. Migration from the countryside to the city, often a response to deteriorating peasant access to land, can trigger or exacerbate the problem of urban unemployment. The lack of sufficient jobs for the growing population creates a breeding ground for destabilizing activities, including violence. Goldstone notes that a recent state failure task force study of sub-Saharan crises found that the risk of crisis doubled with the combination of above-average urbanization and below-average GDP/capita levels.[14]

A third factor contributing to political violence is lack of access to economic or political power among growing urban populations. Of particular note is a "youth bulge," or expansion of the fifteen to twenty-five age cohort relative to the rest of the population. In fact, since World War II, absent a youth bulge, ethnic conflict has been rare.[15]

Higher education seems to increase the problem of the youth bulge. Not only do the young urbanites lack access to employment or political power, they have the time, intellectual resources, and organizational skills to create instability of various sorts and threaten prevailing structures. Examples range from Tudor England and Enlightenment France to Tokugawa Japan and modern Iran.[16]

Finally, migrations into areas with distinct ethnic, religious, or national identities can be a source of instability, violence, and social tension. The results can be the restructuring of societies and redistribution of political power, often after periods of struggle and attempts at accommodation. The movement of Albanians into Kosovo and the former Yugoslav Republic of Macedonia led to war in Kosovo and threatened war in Macedonia and remains a source of tension. Migration will be dealt with in more detail below.

None of these situations is the result of purely demographic factors. Each is a result of a population variable or variables, such as change in size, age, or ethnic composition. Each is affected by population processes of fertility, mortality, or migration. But the political and economic contexts are crucial and can be decisive.[17] Population factors affect stability within specific contexts. In combination with other political, economic, material, and social factors, they can motivate people to work for social, political, or economic change. This desire for change, the means available to bring it about, and the general acceptability of change to the larger society determine whether political instability and political violence result. A simple correlation between population factors and violence or instability is erroneous.

Fertility

The security effects of fertility have most often been associated with rapid population growth. Many assumed that population growth would lead to instability in Third World countries in the post–World War II era, since those countries were thought to be incapable of sustained economic growth under the pressure of increasing population. It was assumed that the costs of education, health, and other infrastructure would inhibit both domestic savings and the capacity to attract direct foreign investment necessary for sustained economic growth. Julian Simon and others questioned these assumptions, and saw population growth as a source of economic vitality by engendering the very talents needed to create healthy, self-sustaining economies.[18] And indeed the experience of some developing countries supported Simon's theory, though that experience was far from universal. Rapid population growth does put tremendous strains on a country's capacity to invest when there is a large number of dependent children, children who will soon reach the age where they will need jobs. Unless there are infusions of government or foreign investment, the pressures on savings capacity can cause a downward economic spiral in such situations.

In addition, the gap between declining mortality rates and high fertility rates in the developing world led to enormous rates of population growth that were economically unsustainable without external investment on a massive scale. The promotion of family planning and contraception became an important feature of bilateral assistance programs and the United Nations Fund for Population Activities (UNFPA).

Some argued that the industrialized nations' concern with population growth was a diversionary tactic, that it was easier (and much cheaper) to support contraception in the Third World than to contribute to economic development. At the UN conference on population in Bucharest in 1974, the Indian delegate spoke for many countries when he proposed that economic development was the best contraceptive.

The potential security effects of fertility go beyond the impact of rapid population growth on a country's economy. Differential fertility within states between racial, ethnic, religious, or class groups is also a basis for concern. Many countries are multinational or have other politically sensitive religious or racial divisions. Some, such as Lebanon, have even organized political institutions to take into account such divisions in the distribution of offices and power. Israel, for one, pays attention to the relative populations of Jews and Arabs within its borders in order to ensure that the country remains both a Jewish and also a democratic state. The key to understanding the security implications of differential fertility within a state is a detailed knowledge of the politics of its racial, ethnic, religious, or class divisions.

Mortality

Mortality rates are another area of concern. Three aspects deserve particular notice. First, reduction of infant mortality rates is often part of family planning programs, because high infant mortality rates encourage parents to have as many children as possible to ensure that at least some survive. Current thinking about fertility programs emphasizes reproductive health broadly. This means not only safe and effective contraceptive use by couples who choose it, but also healthy mothers and children. Advocates of this approach emphasize that the results will not only be more effective in fertility reduction but will effectively address the needs of mothers and children and respect their dignity. From the standpoint of fertility reduction and slowing population growth rates, child survival is a key. If women and couples see high levels of child survival, they will come to trust that their children will survive into adulthood. The benefits of children, both for increasing family income at an early age and for their role as caretakers of elderly parents later on, become less important factors. High child-survival rates reduce the value of large families and encourage smaller family size. Smaller families, with spacing between births, means healthier children and mothers. Lower child mortality, then, is part of a package of changes that support microdecision making in favor of smaller families after general mortality has declined while fertility rates remain high. Lower infant and child mortality, good in themselves, generally accompany fertility reduction.

Second, rising infant mortality rates are a reliable indicator of social collapse. Infant mortality itself is not the causal mechanism but a reliable measure of crumbling social infrastructure of a state that increasingly is unable to operate. There are numerous examples, from the former Zaire to the Soviet Union in the 1980s. Currently North Korea is experiencing increasing infant mortality rates.[19] This is a case of a demographic variable providing important intelligence about impending instability, rather than being a cause of that instability.

Finally, mortality and security are linked in the case of HIV-AIDS. The link is not so much that AIDS will lead to huge population reductions; typically, high mortality rates are quickly made up, in the short term, by a rise in births. Increased mortality generally does not result in long-term reduction of a country's population. For example, the Black Death killed about one-third of Europe's population in the second half of the fourteenth century. By 1500 population had recovered to its size in 1350. And the situation in Europe at that time was one of generally high fertility and mortality regardless of the plague. In a situation of generally low mortality, deaths caused by a pandemic can be replaced by births in a much shorter period. The influenza epidemic of 1918, the high mortality rates caused by the Russian famine of 1932–33, and the accompanying dekulakization of the 1930s resulted in the deaths of almost 15 million. China's famine from 1959 to 1961 killed about 30 million people. None of these events had lasting effects on population growth within these countries.

The effect of AIDS on security comes not from population reduction itself but from its selectivity in killing young adults and, in some countries, a disproportionate number of the educated. If a whole generation is lost, the talented and educated among them are also lost, with repercussions that can last for years.

In short, reducing infant and child mortality is a necessary element of lowering fertility rates. High and increasing infant mortality rates are a reliable indication that a state is in crisis or decline. The impact of AIDS is more in the realm of lost opportunity than a pause in population growth.

Migration, Refugees, and Internally Displaced Persons (IDPs)

Migration is often thought of as the demographic variable most likely to cause security problems.[20] Refugee flows can lead to destabilization in receiving states and the ethnic, religious, or national composition of refugees can add to their destabilizing potential.[21] Even nonrefugee flows can lead to violent conflict, as the effects of Albanian migration over time into Kosovo and Macedonia indicate.

The relatively large number of state breakups and secessions since the late 1980s has been followed by population exchanges and in some cases by resistance to forced population exchange, such as we saw among Russians residing in the Baltic states. Between the end of World War II and the late 1980s secession accounted for the creation of only one new state, Bangladesh. The geopolitical system did not encourage or support secession after the state realignment following the war. How long the international system will tolerate secession at recent levels is unclear. Mild international reaction to the Russian Federation's actions in Chechnya, and the lack of international support for an independent Kurdistan, may indicate a preference for predictability and stability over a state's self-determination. The process of realigning state boundaries that followed the end of the cold war may not yet have played itself out. These border shifts are similar to the boundary changes that took place after both world wars, and after wars in earlier centuries as well. It is worth noting that when states agree or the international community decrees that populations will move to "homelands," these shifts are called population transfers. When a state does the same thing unilaterally, it is called ethnic cleansing.

States also need to pay attention to the consequences of military action for refugees. During the Gulf War of 1991, the Kurds of northern Iraq were kept out of a Turkey reluctant to provide asylum (as required by international law) because Turkey was preoccupied with its own Kurdish population. This development created the need for Operation Provide Comfort and the current political/military arrangements in northern Iraq. Likewise, bombing in Kosovo and the reaction of the Yugoslav government had important implications for the movement of Albanians into both Albania and Macedonia. Macedonian stability, given its already large Albanian population in the west, was a source of particular concern.[22] The lessons of these experiences should be factored into current planning about response to the terrorist attacks of 2001 and the possible effects of military actions. Attention should also be given to the likelihood that more refugees will be created by other antiterrorist campaigns.

Migration and security have salience beyond refugee flows. Internally displaced persons (IDPs) also cause international concern. Because IDPs remain within their own country, they are at least nominally under the jurisdiction of their home government. The question of international action on behalf of IDPs has been raised within the Security Council and by the UN secretary general, Kofi Annan, sovereignty notwithstanding. A set of guiding principles for internal displacement has been developed by a UN special rapporteur, Francis Deng, which has been widely acknowledged to reflect current international law and practice.[23] The growing international attempt to establish clear principles for IDP protection and assistance stems from the concern over the implications of IDPs for international stability and security, as well as human rights concerns. The relationships between IDPs, sovereignty, and international initiatives is an obvious cause of concern. The security implications of IDPs have created pressure for changes in the interpretation of the doctrine of national sovereignty.

Migration and security issues are also connected for states in the area of migration controls that affect both regular migration and asylum seeking. The upsurge in 1984 of people from developing countries seeking political asylum in Europe awakened European governments to security implications of asylum that they had failed to consider. One concern was that asylum seekers and other refugees could use the European countries to which they fled as bases from which to foment plans to overthrow their home governments. The possibility that terrorists could gain entry into a country by seeking political asylum was also a serious concern. The murders at the Munich Olympics and the assassination of Swedish prime minister Olaf Palme were still fresh. Moreover, European governments suspected that the Soviet Union was engaged in a cold war game of overloading Western countries with applicants for asylum, which overburdened the economic systems of these countries and created political tensions.[24] One result has been a change in the perception and treatment of political asylum, which is now often considered less a humanitarian than a security issue.

Since the terrorist attacks on the United States of September 11, 2001, there has been heightened concern about immigration controls generally, and not only in the United States. Greater security is imposed on both international and domestic travelers, especially those traveling by air. Stricter document requirements have been imposed for nationals of some countries. The United States suspended its refugee resettlement program for about two months in October and November 2001. There was even a call for strengthening procedures for entry control and the subsequent monitoring of visitors, both nonimmigrant long-term visitors and immigrants and refugees. There have also been calls for suspending the admission of foreign students until new screening and monitoring systems can be installed.

While new requirements and procedures may have value for other reasons, their capacity to prevent the entry of dedicated terrorists is minimal. New procedures may up the ante a bit for determined terrorists, but most of the participants in the September 11 attacks entered the United States legally and had legal status at the time of the attacks. Reliance on immigration controls to identify and weed out potential terrorists is unlikely to be effective. September 11 was not an immigration but an intelligence failure.

Policy Responses

The dominant response to rapid population growth in the developing world has been the creation of programs to reduce fertility levels. The programs have been described successively as population control, family planning, and, more currently, reproductive health. These labels themselves have a complex political and ideological history.[25]

Family Planning

Originally resisted by many developing countries and spurned by communist countries in their early stages, most countries in the less developed world have come to adopt and even embrace family planning programs. The same India that declared development the best contraceptive in 1974 ousted the government of Indira Gandhi in 1977, in part over the issue of forced sterilization. China, once a staunch opponent of birth control, eventually developed an activist family planning program and a one-child-family norm.

Ironically, it was the United States, once a strong supporter of family planning, a major donor through its foreign aid program, and a prime mover for the creation of UNFPA, that did an about-face on international fertility policy. At the 1984 UN Population Conference in Mexico City, the U.S. government under President Ronald Reagan questioned the need for international population assistance. This stance was bound up with domestic differences over abortion policy and the relation between family planning and abortion assistance. It should be noted, however, that during the Reagan and Bush presidencies and continuing through President Clinton, the population line in the foreign assistance budget did not decrease and in fact was often increased by Congress.

Advocates for women, however, and especially for women's health concerns, were also critical of family planning programs, which they considered instrumentalist, target-oriented, and little concerned with women's rights and women's need for information. These critics developed an approach to women's reproductive health that included access to family planning but also to choice of method and adequate information with which to make informed choices. This approach was adopted by the U.S. government during the Clinton years and championed at the 1994 UN Conference on Population and Development in Cairo.

International reproductive health programs are an institutionalized part of international bilateral and multilateral aid programs and are embedded in many countries' health systems. The dominant response to rapid population growth and the consequent changes in population size and age structure in the developing world have been the result of programs designed to reduce fertility levels and enhance reproductive health, as well as the health of women and children more generally. The result has been a remarkable change, in a little more than a generation, in an intimate aspect of behavior of enormous social importance.

Child Mortality and HIV-AIDS

The policy responses to mortality have focused primarily on infant and child mortality and HIV-AIDS. While family planning and reproductive health have been incorporated into countries' health systems in many ways, additional attention has typically been given to child survival, both as an end in itself and as part of a family planning/reproductive health package. Not all policymakers agree that family planning and reproductive health have received adequate emphasis, but they have at least been components of overall health policy. In addition, the United Nations International Children's Emergency Fund (UNICEF) has carried out child survival programs, as have many NGOs, such as Save the Children. While oral rehydration of children suffering from diarrhea may not seem to be a security concern, its implications make it one. Child survival should contribute to fertility reduction, which lowers population growth rates, which contributes to sustained economic development, which is conducive to political stability and the avoidance of political violence.

Only recently have international AIDS programs begun to focus on the need to address the high levels of HIV infection and full-blown AIDS in the developing world. The battleground is Africa and the issue is the availability of treatments for AIDS, which are expensive. Divisive issues include intellectual property rights and patent protections, the cost of drugs, and the development of medical infrastructures to sustain large programs of complicated drug regimens. Although the ultimate impact of HIV-AIDS in Africa (and elsewhere) is in the balance, a satisfactory outcome is by no means assured. The capacity for some states to survive the dire social and economic costs of the AIDS epidemic is very much in question.

Migration, Refugees, and Internally Displaced Persons

Policy responses to migration have focused until quite recently on refugee movements, though concern has grown about internally displaced persons as well. Individual states have focused on visa and other border controls in particular since September 11, 2001.

The international community, and specifically the Western powers, developed an international refugee regime following World War II. Originally very Eurocentric, the international organizations (especially the UN High Commissioner for Refugees, or UNHCR) and the NGOs in the refugee regime focused primarily on the less developed world. European, North American, and Australian governments ran their own refugee resettlement programs, focused mainly on asylum seekers and refugees resettled from communist countries. The end of the cold war, the growing numbers of people from the global south seeking asylum in Europe and from Cuba, Haiti, and Central America seeking asylum in the United States have led to major challenges around refugee protection and assistance.

The postwar international refugee programs of the industrialized West came under attack from many quarters, as persons with questionable claims of persecution used asylum procedures to gain access to industrial countries. Domestic constituencies questioned their governments' judgment and motives for restricting access as more and more of those seeking asylum came from the noncommunist countries of the southern hemisphere. Other domestic constituencies opposed refugee immigration as a threat to national identity. In Europe the movement toward a European Union complicated the process and raised difficult questions about national identity and the future of nation-states themselves. Deep ideological divisions on these issues persist in the liberal democratic countries of the West.

Industrialized countries have pressured UNHCR and other protection and assistance agencies to reduce the flow of refugees, to contain them in "safe areas" within their own conflicted countries or neighboring countries. Refugees have been pressured to repatriate, sometimes even under conditions of continued conflict in their homelands. Refugee resettlement has caused controversy within countries, within humanitarian organizations, and within international organizations. While few overtly question the basic principle of political asylum for the truly persecuted, many are uneasy about how the process works and about whether the doctrines developed during the cold war are relevant today.

International practice and policies concerning refugees and asylum are in flux. The issues include the safety of aid personnel, the relation between military force and humanitarian organizations, the conditions appropriate for repatriation, the capacity for preventive action, and the commitment of states to providing practical protection, among others. While there seems to be a role for militaries in protection of humanitarian operations and logistical assistance in some situations, the provision of security for refugees and asylum seekers is mainly a civilian matter. Developments in humanitarian assistance, however, will matter for international security.

The fate of internally displaced persons is now on the international agenda. Given their destabilizing potential, efforts to date have consisted mainly of broaching the possibility that sovereignty requirements should not be allowed to close off further discussion. The reports of the special rapporteur, Francis Deng, have focused on codifying existing international law outlining the obligations of states in this area. The number of internally displaced people has been rising and will probably continue to rise. Confining potential refugees to safe areas in their own countries will by definition increase internal displacement. How far states will be willing to go collectively, under UN auspices or otherwise, in interventions of various sorts, including the use of force, remains to be seen.

Finally, in reaction to terrorist attacks, states are paying closer attention to visa and border control issues. The requirements of the global economy for international travel will probably limit the use of immigration control as a frontline defense against terrorism. Rather, increased intelligence and changes in operations will probably be the main defense against terrorist activities, with immigration regulation brought into the picture when useful and appropriate.

Population Aging

A final issue has recently given pause to policy planners and observers. In industrial countries, low fertility and increasing life-span (the result of advances in nutrition, education, and health care) have led to aging of the population. The average lifespan in industrialized countries is increasing, as is the proportion of persons over age sixty-five. This obviously entails social and economic costs, which have recently become the subject of intense debate. In the United States, for example, debates about the sustainability of the Social Security and Medicare systems have become increasingly urgent and at times quite heated in the past twenty years. Similar debates have taken place in Europe, Japan, and other industrial countries.

The population division of the United Nations issued a report in March 2000 entitled "Replacement Migration: Is It a Solution to Declining and Aging Populations?" which analyzed population projections and simulated migration requirements for eight industrial countries and for Europe as a whole, to determine what would be needed to maintain working-age populations at about their current size and the ratio of retired to working-age population.[26] The report was controversial, especially in Europe, as it contained controversial findings related to too-low fertility estimates and assumed that immigration would cease by 2035. The report estimated how much international migration would have to take place to avoid the impacts of low fertility and increases in elderly populations. While the report did not advocated exclusive reliance on migration, and noted other ways to substitute for losses to the labor force, it focused on the level of immigration necessary to sustain the labor forces of industrial countries. There were, of course, differences from country to country, but the report essentially concluded that the number of immigrants that would be needed to maintain the projected size of the retired populations of industrialized countries has never been reached. And if the required migration did take place, by 2050 "the proportion of post-1995 immigrants and their descendants would range between 59 percent and 99 percent."[27] Such immigration levels are beyond political feasibility.

Population aging is a serious problem that will require a variety of social and economic adjustments, some of them painful. A package of items could help meet labor-force requirements for industrial countries. Slight increases in fertility from their current low levels are indeed possible. Later retirement, increased female participation in the labor force, especially in Mediterranean countries, modest levels of immigration, increased reliance on temporary high-skill personnel, and increased labor productivity are all possibilities. Even modest decreases in overall population size do not spell economic or security doom. Pursued as part of a large-scale policy, a package of adjustments could potentially make the problem manageable.

Social dislocation is difficult, even harsh. But it is unlikely that population aging will translate into militarily vulnerable elderly populations unable to defend themselves or to operate viable economies hobbled by the costs of caring for a dependent elderly population. If adequately addressed, the aging of populations is unlikely to become a threat to security or a source of political instability.

Conclusion

Elsewhere in this volume the relationship between security and the environment is addressed. This discussion must include the role of population and its relation to resources. Population size and rates of growth certainly affect the environment and ecological resources. Population size is not the only factor, of course; consumption patterns also are at work. It is all too easy to spin out possible connections between some aspect of demography and a security concern, but perspective is needed to rein in speculation. Awareness of population and its possible role as one of many contributing factors is of utmost use to the analyst. It is neither necessary nor prudent to view population as a major security issue.

The discussion of security and population presented here allows for some tentative conclusions. First, demographic factors are typically not dominant causes of insecurity but rather increase the likelihood of problems or tend to exacerbate problems. Population size, distribution, and structure, and the demographic processes of fertility, mortality, and migration, generally work indirectly through other social and economic factors. They become salient within contexts that give them meaning or through which they affect state capacity to operate or defend itself.

Second, demographic factors are generally not amenable to military solutions. Manipulating population variables and outcomes generally falls within social policy, domestic or foreign. The effects of high fertility, low fertility, and excess mortality are generally addressed most effectively through social policy such as health care, female education, and labor policy. Family planning is a notable example of an aid program that has had considerable quantifiable success and has brought about major social changes in decision making by individuals and couples.

Third, migration, not fertility or mortality, is the factor most likely to exacerbate security concerns. Sometimes migration can have a fairly direct impact on a political situation already defined in ethnic, religious, racial, or class terms. Sometimes sheer numbers of migrants or refugees can overwhelm a country's infrastructure and capacity to respond. In the area of migration controls, particularly those connected to forced mass movements, military force can be useful in prevention and control. In such cases the threat to state security will be more direct and familiar. The value of the military, however, lies not in its capacity to defeat an enemy but in its ability to impose order and control on a situation.

Finally, demography as a security issue clearly points in the direction of an expanded notion of security, one that goes beyond the threat of military force and beyond the use of military assets to protect a country's interests. To incorporate population in a security agenda requires expanding the traditional concerns of security and the usual means analyzed to address threats to security. To incorporate population into security studies requires adjustments in scope and methods for addressing threats to state stability.

Attention to demography, like attention to all soft security issues, tends to be overblown. Security analysts who have recently "discovered" population issues sometimes exhibit the enthusiasm of the newly converted. Longtime students of the subject can be flattered and beguiled by the attention suddenly given to their field of expertise by politicians, the intelligence community, and the military. A little humility is in order all around. All of the "new" security issues have been around and have a history, even a history of discussion within a security framework. They deserve attention. They are not the sum and substance of security in the coming decades.

Notes

1. A number of books in the general area of population and security have appeared, most of them, since the late 1980s, written or edited in the main by Myron Weiner, Michael S. Teitelbaum, and Jay Winter, individually or in some combination. These include Michael S. Teitelbaum and Jay M. Winter, *The Fear of Population Decline* (Orlando: Academic Press, 1985); Michael S. Teitelbaum and Jay M. Winter, *Population and Resources in Western Intellectual Traditions* (Cambridge: Cambridge University Press, 1989); Myron Weiner, *International Migration and Security* (Boulder: Westview, 1993); Myron Weiner, *The Global Migration Crisis: Challenge to the State and to Human Rights* (New York: HarperCollins, 1995); Michael S. Teitelbaum and Myron Weiner, eds., *Threatened Peoples, Threatened Borders: World Migration and U.S. Policy* (New York: Norton, 1995); Michael S. Teitelbaum and Jay M. Winter, *A Question of Numbers: High Migration, Low Fertility, and the Politics of National Identity* (New York: Hill and Wang, 1998); Myron Weiner and Sharon Stanton Russell, *Demography and National Security* (New York: Berghahn, 2001).

2. Teitelbaum and Winter, *The Fear of Population Decline.*

3. Peter J. Donaldson, *Nature against Us: The United States and the World Population Crisis, 1965–1980* (Chapel Hill: University of North Carolina Press, 1990).

4. Ibid., 23–25.

5. Ibid., 23.

6. Paul R. Ehrlich, *The Population Bomb* (New York: Ballantine Books, 1968).

7. John Bongaarts and Rodolfo A. Bulatao, eds., *Beyond Six Billion: Forecasting the World's Population* (Washington, D.C.: National Academy Press, 2000), chap. 2.

8. Donaldson, *Nature against Us.*

9. United Nations, Department of Economic and Social Affairs, population division, *Levels and Trends in Contraceptive Use as Assessed in 1998* (New York: United Nations, 2000).

10. Ronald R. Krebs and Jack S. Levy, "Demographic Change and the Sources of International Conflict," in Weiner and Russell, *Demography and National Security,* 62–105; Teitelbaum and Winter, *The Fear of Population Decline*; Teitelbaum and Winter, *A Question of Numbers.*

11. Samuel Huntington, *The Clash of Civilizations and the Remaking of World Order* (New York: Simon & Schuster, 1996); Robert Kaplan, "The Coming Anarchy," *The Atlantic* 273, no. 2 (1994): 44–76; Paul Demeny, "A Perspective on Long-Term Population Growth," *Population and Development Review* 10, no. 1 (1984): 103–26.

12. Jack A. Goldstone, "Demography, Environment, and Security: An Overview," in Weiner and Russell, *Demography and National Security*, 38–61.

13. Ibid.

14. Ibid., 47.

15. Ibid.

16. Ibid.

17. Krebs and Levy, *Demographic Change*.

18. Julian Simon, *The Ultimate Resource* (Princeton: Princeton University Press, 1996).

19. Goldstone, *Demography, Environment, and Security*, 52.

20. Weiner, *International Migration*; Teitelbaum and Winter, *Question of Numbers*; Kaplan, *Coming Anarchy*; Teitelbaum and Weiner, *Threatened Peoples, Threatened Borders*.

21. Charles B. Keely, "How Nation States Create and Respond to Refugee Flows," *International Migration Review* 30 (winter 1996): 1046–66; Aristide Zolberg, Astri Suhrke, and Sergio Aguayo, *Escape from Violence* (New York: Oxford University Press, 1988).

22. Kelly M. Greenhill, "People Pressure: The Coercive Use of Refugees in the Kosovo Conflict" (paper presented at the American Political Science Association meeting, Washington, D.C., Aug. 2000).

23. United Nations, Office of the Commissioner of Humanitarian Affairs, *Guiding Principles on Internal Displacement* (New York: United Nations, Dec. 2000), 14; Roberta Cohen and Francis M. Deng, *Masses in Flight: The Global Crisis of Internal Displacement* (Washington, D.C.: Brookings Institution Press, 1998); Roberta Cohen and Francis M. Deng, *The Forsaken People: Case Studies of the Internally Displaced* (Washington, D.C.: Brookings Institution Press, 1998); United Nations, Office of the Commissioner on Humanitarian Affairs, *Handbook for Applying the Guiding Principles on Internal Displacement* (New York: United Nations, June 2000), 61.

24. Sharon Stanton Russell, Charles B. Keely, and Brian P. Christian, "Multilateral Diplomacy to Harmonize Asylum Policy in Europe: 1984–1993" (Institute for the Study of International Migration (ISIM) working paper, Edmund A. Walsh School of Foreign Service, Georgetown University, 2002), 68.

25. Donaldson, *Nature against Us*; Jason L. Finkle and Alison C. McIntosh, eds., *The New Politics of Population* (New York: Oxford University Press, 1994); Alison C. McIntosh and Jason L. Finkle, "The Cairo Conference on Population and Development: A New Paradigm?" *Population and Development Review* 21, no. 2 (1995): 223–60; Jason L. Finkle and Alison C. McIntosh, "United Nations Population Conferences Shaping the Policy Agenda for the Twenty-first Century," *Studies in Family Planning* 3 (March 2002): 11–23.

26. United Nations Department of Economic and Social Affairs, Population Division, "Replacement Migration: Is It a Solution to Declining and Aging Populations?" available at www.un.org/esa/population/publications/popdecline/popdecline.htm.

27. Ibid., 94.

Chapter 10

Security and Conflict in the Developing World

Timothy D. Hoyt

Concerns over wars in the developing world have been a constant in international security since the end of World War II. At the end of the cold war, consideration of these conflicts took on new importance. Previously underappreciated dimensions of political and military conflict in the developing world emerged as policy priorities; these included global campaigns to ban land mines, concerns about failed states and internal conflict, and the creation of a new category of "rogue states"—an issue that then became the focus of U.S. defense planning.

The end of the cold war fundamentally changed the international security environment. The specter of nuclear war diminished dramatically with the collapse of the Soviet Union. European states redefined their defense policies and slashed their defense budgets and military preparedness, as the rationale for high levels of peacetime armament disappeared.

The European experience, however, was far from universal. The developing world, scene of some of the most brutal conflicts of the cold war, did not benefit nearly as much from the Soviet collapse. Some states, like Israel, did experience tangible benefits; one of the most important results of the Soviet collapse was the removal of an enormous supplier of subsidized heavy armaments to potential opponents of Israel and the West. Arms once supplied gratis, or under liberal terms of credit, suddenly had to be paid for in hard currency on the international market—a substantial blow to overmilitarized states such as Syria and North Korea.

In general, though, the developing world did not experience the cascade of security benefits that Europe enjoyed. The most important benefits—the end to the threat of inadvertent nuclear escalation, for example—had always lain far beyond the control of the developing states. It could even be argued that the threat of inadvertent escalation had exercised a moderating force on regional conflicts. The superpowers sought to contain regional wars in both duration and scope, for fear that success by one side's client might lead to direct intervention or other forms of escalation.

Conflict in the developing world, in fact, poses an increasing threat to international security, particularly in the aftermath of the September 11 terrorist attacks on the United States. The increasing importance of this conflict, however, was apparent long before that tragedy. Analysts of international security have focused increasingly on the developing world since 1990, identifying difficult issues that were simply overlooked during the cold war and troubling trends in the international system as a whole that will require skillful and courageous management in the future.[1]

To understand the nature of emerging threats in the developing world, this chapter will examine the evolution of U.S. and international concerns during the cold war and post–cold war period. The first section, an examination of priorities during the cold war, will focus on several key questions intended to illuminate the gradual shift in international priorities concerning conflict in the developing world. What types of conflicts were of particular concern? What threats did they pose, and how were those threats defined? What other actors were concerned, and why? How were the wars fought? What types of weaponry were used in these wars, and what were the sources of those arms? How did the United States and the international community respond to these conflicts? The second section will examine conflict in the developing world in the 1990s, applying this same set of questions. This comparative approach demonstrates the shifting priorities of the international system as it viewed regional conflicts in a new international perspective. The third section examines the changing international response to regional crises and internal conflict. The international community increasingly recognizes the difficult problem of conflict resolution, particularly in the case of extended civil wars and insurgencies, and the problem of failed states and the collapse of domestic governance. The fourth section looks at prospects for the future. The growing gap between "haves" and "have-nots," the rise of nontraditional security threats, and the potential impact of the war on terrorism all pose significant challenges for international stability. The final section assesses the policy ramifications of conflict in the developing world, and the potential responses of the United States, the West, and the international community.

Cold War Concerns

For most of the cold war, the United States and the West focused on conflict in regions of strategic interest, particularly on areas where important economic resources were located or where the Soviet Union sought influence.[2] Types of conflict of particular concern were conventional military campaigns aimed at overthrowing U.S. allies or important unaligned states (South Korea in 1950, the Sino-Indian War of 1962, various conflicts in the Middle East), or unconventional wars waged by pro-Soviet forces against pro-Western or unaligned governments (Vietnam, Latin America). Priority was given primarily to regional conflict that might affect the global balance of power, either by swaying important states to the other side (as experienced in the Chinese civil war) or that might be perceived as the beginning of a significant acceleration of communist influence (the "domino effect").

The United States and its allies were concerned with several sets of actors in their response to crises in the developing world. The first concern was the role of the USSR. At various points during the cold war, U.S. leaders prioritized regional conflicts in terms of Soviet involvement—the Middle East, South Asia in 1971, and even sub-Saharan Africa from the mid-1970s were all seen as "vital interests" in the struggle against Soviet influence. Direct Soviet intervention in Afghanistan, following closely on the collapse of the shah in Iran, caused a major reorientation in U.S. foreign policy.

A second concern was Chinese involvement, particularly in Southeast and northern Asia. U.S. intervention in Vietnam was profoundly affected by concerns over Chinese response, and British operations in Malaya focused on Chinese support for communist insurgents there.[3] The Southeast Asian Treaty Organization was formed, at least in part, to include China in the geostrategic policy of containment, and also to respond to Chinese-backed movements in many of the member states.[4]

A third, although lesser, concern was hegemonic actions by regional powers. Concerns over Vietnam (post–1975), India (post–1971), postrevolution Iran, Indonesia (under Sukarno), and Nasser's interference in Algeria and Yemen all prompted various forms of U.S. and/or international intervention. The United States also viewed efforts to unify the political leadership of the Arab world, either under Nasser (the United Arab Republic) or under various Ba'athist pretenders including Saddam Hussein, with alarm. The actions of pro-Western potential hegemons, including Israel and South Africa, also provoked responses in the international community and, at times, the United States.[5]

The conflicts of greatest concern were primarily conventional, mid-intensity wars of relatively short duration—for example, the Middle East conflicts of 1967 and 1973, the South Asian conflicts of 1965 and 1971 (and quasi-nuclear confrontations of 1986–87 and 1990), and the Sino-Indian war of 1962.[6] In each of these conflicts significant superpower interests or allies were, theoretically, at risk. A quick victory by one side could significantly reduce the capabilities of one side's allies—a blow to prestige and potentially to regional and global balances of power.

The employment of modern major weapons systems (particularly tanks, artillery, and jet aircraft; naval forces played a lesser role in these conflicts) facilitated quick advances, attacks on distant targets, and the possibility of rapid, decisive victory. The provision of military training, advisors, and in some cases actual combat troops by the superpowers or their close allies raised the relative combat capabilities of these forces further, again posing the potential for rapid, destabilizing victory, something the initiators of many of these conflicts hoped to achieve even if they lacked the means. Many of the most important conflicts in the developing world began as preemptive or surprise attacks with limited aims focused on seizing disputed or strategically important territory.[7]

The result was "moderation," in many but not all cases, of high-priority conventional conflicts by the superpowers. The United States or Soviet Union would intervene in a region, diplomatically or by projecting military forces, to halt a conflict that was beginning to threaten its interests. The United States sent the aircraft carrier *Enterprise* and its escorts into the Bay of Bengal in 1962 to support the Indians against China, and again in 1971 to coerce the Indians into halting their war on Pakistan.

The Soviet Union used its growing naval presence to intervene in the Middle East in 1973. In addition, arms resupply was used, particularly by the Soviets in the Middle East, both to restore the military strength of its proxies and to reassert Soviet interest in the regional military balance.[8] On occasion overt or implied nuclear threats were used to reinforce the importance of war termination or nonintervention—in Korea in 1953, Hungary in 1956, and the Middle East in 1973.

Extended conventional wars in the developing world occurred primarily when neither superpower felt a need to intervene. As a result, the Iran–Iraq war was allowed to drag on for eight bloody years, and conflicts in the Horn of Africa sputtered sporadically for lack of superpower attention. More problematic were low-intensity conflicts or insurgencies where neither the governing regime nor the insurgents were capable of quick success—El Salvador and Cambodia, for example, in the 1980s. These conflicts could become the scene of extended wars, which had much higher humanitarian costs. States threatened by dissidents or insurgencies, indigenous or externally sponsored, turned to the superpowers for training and assistance in internal security. The result was the creation of repressive regimes like those in Iraq and Syria, the warping of civil-military relations in Latin America, and the extended and brutal internal conflicts in Sudan, Ethiopia, and Angola, among others.

Wars of Concern in the 1990s

The end of the cold war presented an opportunity for substantial change in the international system, a promise that appeared to be partially fulfilled by the international response to Iraq's aggression against Kuwait in the late summer of 1990.[9] Multinational cooperation, however, proved more difficult than many hoped. National interest remained a major element in decisions for intervention, particularly on the part of the United States. Iraq's unwillingness to cooperate with UN-mandated arms inspectors, and the linkages between those inspectors and national intelligence agencies of various countries, raised further complications.[10] The extended commitments and long-term political and economic costs necessary for successful peacekeeping and peacemaking operations deterred intervention as well.[11] Finally, the collapse of the "Second World" (Eastern Europe and the Soviet bloc) brought many of the problems of the developing world much closer to home for European powers, and issues in the Balkans received a higher priority than did equally pressing issues in other regions.[12]

Nevertheless, the wars of concern in the 1990s differed significantly from those of the cold war, simply because the threat of escalation to the superpower level no longer existed. Iraq had signed a treaty of "peace, friendship, and cooperation" with the Soviet Union, but received no support during the 1990–91 crisis. The Indo-Pakistani nuclear crisis of 1990 spurred prompt U.S. diplomatic intervention, but also resulted in the rapid imposition of economic sanctions on Pakistan as a result of its nuclear program, an action that had been deferred by the Reagan administration because of the Soviet presence in Afghanistan. India, in return, received no significant Soviet support in the crisis. In a nonideological global environment, the thresholds and justifications for intervention required thorough reexamination.

During the 1990s the international community directed its attention to intrastate conflict. This focus reflected both the decreased interstate conflict and the abrupt changes, particularly in the former Eastern bloc, in territorial borders and state cohesion. During the cold war, superpower concerns and international norms usually sufficed to maintain the territorial boundaries of even the most fragile states in the developing world, with the rare exception of a significantly effective regional war (Vietnam, Bangladesh). If fractured states in Eastern Europe and the former Soviet Union were worthy of attention, so were failing states elsewhere. The human cost of collapsing states became evident, and both policymakers and academics focused increased attention on the moral and ethical obligations of the developed states to control and resolve these conflicts.

The primary actors of concern, for both the United States and the international community, were no longer traditional "great" powers. Rather, the new conflicts demonstrated the increasing importance of regional rivals as supporters, instigators, and/or sanctuaries for adversaries in these intrastate wars. Although the largest state sponsor of terrorism (the Soviet Union) collapsed, other "rogue states" continued to support unconventional wars and terrorist attacks that threatened both regional stability and global travel and communications.

Threat definition shifted from concerns over the bipolar balance of power to the primacy of regional stability and the denial of revisionist efforts.[13] The impact of state failure, manifested in the form of civilian suffering, refugee flows, and the spillover of political conflict and violence across local borders, became especially evident with the collapse of Yugoslavia, but the situations of Lebanon, Zaire, Afghanistan, and Somalia also drew international attention and, in some cases, intervention. These were long, slow wars of attrition utterly lacking in proportionality, as opposed to the quicker, more sophisticated, but also cleaner regional wars of the cold war period.

The weapons that attracted attention also changed during this period. So-called weapons of mass destruction—nuclear, biological, chemical, and radiological weapons and the missiles that can be used to deliver them—had always been a concern during the cold war. In the post–cold war era, however, they took on new importance.[14] Iraq, in particular, had demonstrably used them on both external and domestic enemies. U.S. conventional military predominance, demonstrated in the Gulf War, spurred potential adversaries to find new capabilities to deter the United States and deny it access to their regions. Finally, the United States and the international community hoped to create a new environment in which the utility of nuclear weapons would be thoroughly discredited, the costs of entry into the arena of weapons of mass destruction made prohibitively high, and the number of states actually possessing the weapons absolutely capped and their arsenals gradually rolled back to lower levels.[15]

The international community also made efforts to stem the arms trade and force arms purchasers and exporters to register their transactions, efforts that were undercut by the economic interests of both firms and nations actively involved in these transactions.[16] More interesting, and distinctly connected to the emerging focus on internal conflict, were efforts to ban or control sales of the least sophisticated forms of weapons—land mines and small arms. The land mine question, in particular, symbolizes the emerging priority of intrastate conflict. In interstate wars, the land mine represents perhaps the ultimate defensive weapon. A passive device that cannot be used to project force, land mines were generally posted within a state's own territory to channel or prevent offensive enemy operations. In internal conflicts, however, land mines become a potentially indiscriminate weapon used to contain insurgencies and their supporting communities, and create dire humanitarian crises in some parts of the world. As a result, the United States finds itself outside the emerging international norm by seeking to preserve the use of land mines in the demilitarized zone between North and South Korea—an action perfectly consistent with a profoundly defensive, nonaggressive, and ethical policy.

Based on the experience of the 1990s, two key trends can be observed in conflict in the developing world. First, large-scale conventional conflict is becoming less likely. One of the advantages of a bipolar world, from the perspective of developing states, was the willingness of superpower patrons to provide copious quantities of sophisticated weaponry on generous terms of credit. These massive and easily replaced arsenals of tanks and aircraft raised the potential for a quick victory, either through destruction of the enemy's similarly armed forces or through the occupation and successful defense of enemy territory on the border for long enough to encourage negotiations. As these arsenals degrade, through lack of maintenance and inadequate funding for replacement equipment, many states no longer see short conventional wars as a viable option. Some states—Syria and North Korea, to name two—find themselves in possession of vast quantities of obsolete equipment, and the unenviable example of Iraq demonstrates the inadequacy of these kinds of forces against the United States and its allies. They remain useful against local adversaries, but used too aggressively they might prompt U.S. intervention.

A second trend is the increased duration and lethality of internal wars. In the past, low-intensity conflict was the term used to describe these kinds of conflicts, where small numbers of guerrillas (or a cabal within political leadership or elites) would attempt, over time, to create the proper conditions for a successful coup d'etat. Internal conflict in the developing world since the 1970s, however, has increasingly violated this concept. The civil wars and insurgencies in Africa, Asia, and Latin America have become extended conflicts lasting years or decades, using limited military means for virtually unlimited political ends (the overthrow, over time, of ruling regimes and ideologies). Whether supported by great powers, in the cold war, or fueled by genuine local ethnic, religious, or political differences, these conflicts have become terribly bloody, and are marked by a fading distinction between soldier and noncombatant. Victory, or at least territorial control, is achieved through terror and mayhem. Civilian casualties have skyrocketed, and the list of weapons used against opponents of existing regimes now includes chemical weapons and environmental terrorism.

The causes of these conflicts, and the driving forces behind those already under way, now lie more in local or regional issues and less in the exploitation of those issues by foreign powers for ideological purposes.[17] Environmental and demographic pressures contribute to conflict in many regions. The Israeli–Palestinian conflict, for example, is exacerbated by tensions over water rights—also a problem between Senegal and Mauritania and between other African states. Turkey and India hold the option of using water supplies for political coercion against powerful neighbors, including Syria, Iraq, and Pakistan. Drought has contributed to conflicts in the Horn of Africa, and deforestation has expanded insurgency in the Philippines.

Environmental crises often result from increased population pressures. Population growth in the poorest areas of the developing world continues at astounding rates, but population pressures are also felt in the Islamic world, particularly in Saudi Arabia. Demographic trends in Iran, Brazil, and other states point to an increasingly younger population that will demand economic opportunity and, quite possibly, create profound political tensions if that opportunity does not emerge.[18]

The precarious political stability and legitimacy of developing states further exacerbates internal tensions. Many of these states suffer from artificial boundaries inherited from European colonial powers, boundaries that divide lands formerly inhabited by ethnically homogenous populations among multiple states.[19] These areas then become potential trouble spots, at a minimum providing promising opportunities for smuggling across borders but often serving in addition as sanctuaries for criminals, political opposition, or even active insurgents. In nonhomogenous but weakly governed states, social and ethnic differences are frequently used artificially to create political support and a domestic enemy. Slobodan Milosevic's use of the Albanian minority in Yugoslavia is only one example of this phenomenon.

International Responses

The very nature of these changing wars and weapons requires fundamentally different forms of intervention. "Solutions" to these conflicts are costly, difficult, and require extended commitments that few states can or will justify in the national interest. As a result, interventions are increasingly multilateral and deeply politicized, as the various coalition partners and institutions argue over the ends, means, and relative importance of each of the dozens of conflicts in the developing world. The end of the superpower competition eliminated the threat of inadvertent escalation or intervention in regional crises. It also increased the potential for the use of regional, multinational, and international forces in peacekeeping or even peacemaking roles.

As mentioned above, economic, demographic, environmental, and regional threats all menace the territorial integrity and legitimacy of states in the developing world. These pressures can create the potential for internal conflict or full-blown civil war, the very kind of conflict that now concerns the international community to a much greater degree. Cynical political leaders can manipulate them for personal and political reasons—to shore up faltering regimes, to secure international financial or military support, or perhaps simply to add to personal or family fortunes. These internal conflicts, however, have substantial potential to overflow national boundaries and become regional problems. This is particularly true in former colonial areas like sub-Saharan Africa, where ethnic groups are divided by artificial boundaries, but also in collapsing states (Congo, Lebanon, Yugoslavia) and regions where international borders are not fully demarcated or remain politically contentious (South and Central Asia).

This linkage between internal conflict and regional instability creates new incentives for international, multinational, or regional forces to intervene in civil conflicts. West Africa, a region of chronic internal strife, has organized ECOWAS, a regional peacekeeping force based around the army of Nigeria, the dominant power. The Association of Southest Asian Nations (ASEAN) is organized at least in part to ensure that internal security threats menace neither neighbors nor regimes.[20] UN interventions have become increasingly important, and the war on terrorism requires even more creative multinational forces in Afghanistan and perhaps elsewhere to help with human security concerns and nation building.

In many of the most important and conflicted regions, however, internal divisions are deliberately manipulated by both internal and external actors for political ends, a technique that Carl von Clausewitz would have immediately understood.[21] The current crisis in Israel and Palestine represents the most dangerous of these circumstances. The Palestinian Authority, and particularly Chairman Arafat, deliberately uses violence to attempt to shift the failing peace process to more favorable terms. Other factions in Palestine, however, use violence to attack both the Israelis *and* the legitimacy of the Palestinian Authority. Outside forces, particularly Syria, Iraq, and Iran, provide support for Palestinian insurgents. Hezbollah seeks to reclaim disputed territory on the border of Israel, Lebanon, and Syria. Israel, too, suffers from internal divisions, based on ethnicity and orthodoxy, which are reflected in support for settlement policies and domestic political trends and party affiliation (these tensions still exist, but they have been minimized because of the severity of the current crisis).

In South Asia, the Kashmir dispute remains the fundamental barrier to regional stability, and Pakistani assistance has expanded the insurgency in both duration and intensity.[22] The induction of nuclear weapons into the arsenals of both sides has not created a situation of stable deterrence; both states now publicly argue that "limited war" is possible under the nuclear shadow, and the attack on the Indian parliament on December 13, 2001, has raised the level of border militarization to unprecedented levels.[23] The existence of the South Asian Association for Regional Cooperation (SAARC) is irrelevant to the security issue, as that organization's mandate focuses on economic and political cooperation. India's relative power within the region is so great that it has been able to coerce or interfere with all of its regional neighbors since 1971, and no purely regional alliance can balance this power disparity. Violence remains endemic both within and across borders, based on ethnicity (Tamils in Sri Lanka, tribal groups in the Indian northeast, and Pashtuns in northwestern Pakistan), religion (Kashmir, the Sikh desire for an independent Khalistan), ideology (Maoist rebels in Nepal) and even caste and economic-driven violence in the Indian state of Bihar and elsewhere.

Use of internal disputes to justify violations of sovereignty is not reserved, of course, to regional rivals. The emerging tension between cold war norms regarding human rights, violence against innocents, and genocide create increasing pressures on Westphalian norms of sovereignty and nonintervention. Similarly, the issue of state failure—the collapse or weakening of central authority—can create security problems from nonstate actors crossing borders to attack neighboring countries.

Foreign military intervention to resolve the problems associated with failed states has been a constant in the international system for twenty years, arguably beginning with Israel's invasion of Lebanon in 1982. The U.S. intervention to help stabilize the situation resulted in disaster in Beirut in 1983. More recently, the intervention in Somalia demonstrated the limits of effective intervention and the unwillingness of the United States to remain militarily engaged in extended peace operations, a decision that contributed to the Rwandan genocide.[24] The domestic political impact of casualties during peace operations profoundly influences Western decisions about intervention, a lesson that has not been lost on actors in the developing world.

Military operations in the Balkans in the 1990s emphasized high-tech military intervention and violation of sovereignty, particularly through the use of precision air strikes.[25] Iraq was crushed by an international intervention that included seven weeks of relentless, effective, and comparatively proportionate air attacks. U.S. and coalition threats to Iraq over violations of UN inspection regimes also took the form of air strikes and the longstanding "no-fly zones" in northern and southern Iraq. The United States launched cruise missile strikes on targets in Sudan and Afghanistan in an effort to retaliate for attacks by Al Qaeda in 1998. All of these operations demonstrated the ability of high-tech forces to intervene cheaply and formidably across the national borders of even the most powerfully armed developing states.[26]

The war on terrorism has not ended this threat to sovereignty in the developing world. The United States successfully engaged in a war in Central Asia using mobile special forces, air power staged from a combination of aircraft carriers and distant allied bases, and highly effective and still inadequately studied covert forces and weaponry controlled by the CIA. Despite the formidable logistical obstacles, the difficult terrain, and the onset of winter, the ruling Taliban regime in Afghanistan was overthrown in a matter of weeks. U.S. forces continue to operate in Afghanistan and Pakistan, as well as in the southern Philippines and other areas. The amorphous nature of the Al Qaeda terrorist network and its roots in literally dozens of states provides the United States with reasons to intervene in countries from Colombia to Indonesia, virtually the entire southern hemisphere. In 2003 the United States, supported by the United Kingdom and a small coalition of mainly Western powers, invaded Iraq, overthrew Saddam Hussein and his regime, and assumed a temporary trusteeship over this large and strategically significant country.[27]

This new era of international intervention creates difficult problems for developing states. In the post–cold war era, many developing states with weak governing institutions and low-quality militaries relied on normative concepts, particularly the Westphalian notion of sovereignty, for protection of otherwise vulnerable borders. In an emerging era of economic globalization and military intervention, sovereignty is increasingly threatened. Regimes must be much more careful in their authoritarian acts, and the economic costs of political isolation have become increasingly oppressive for most smaller states.[28] Relying on international institutions for protection is increasingly problematic, given the grudging UN acceptance of U.S.-led intervention in Kosovo. As a result, sovereignty is becoming a crucial issue in the developing world once again.

Prospects for the Future

The future of security problems in the developing world is cloudy at best. Even the areas that appeared to be thriving—Southeast Asia, for instance—have demonstrated their vulnerability to economic and political disruption. Other regions have been virtually abandoned by the international community, falling behind in basic measures of economic and political development. The gap between "haves" and "have-nots" in the international system is widening rather than shrinking, and divisions within the developing world have prevented and continue to prevent the adoption of collective measures to redress these issues through international forums.

Nontraditional security threats are likely to put increasing pressure on existing regimes, particularly in the absence of a global consensus on the long-term impact of key trends. Environmental issues, for example, force developing states to make difficult trade-offs between long-term global commitments (only partially supported by the industrial states) and short-term economic gain. Deforestation is becoming a major issue in many parts of the developing world, as is soil fertility and salinity. Access to clean water is becoming an increasingly contentious issue in the Middle East and elsewhere.

Population remains a major concern as well. The rapid drop in Western birthrates and the substantial aging of the population in the northern hemisphere in general raise a number of long-term security implications, including immigration, population flows, and resource allocation in the future. Immigration to Europe has already led to a rise in right-wing political parties in many members of the European Union. Younger populations in the developing world with little hope of economic prosperity may become restless, hostile, or aggressive, leading to regional conflict or perhaps increased willingness to join national or transnational groups that oppose globalization or other Western concepts.

Dangerous instability exists in many parts of the world, particularly the poorest areas (like sub-Saharan Africa) and the most politically fragmented states (Indonesia, former Congo, Afghanistan). Even with significant international attention and commitment, these regions pose political and economic challenges that are quite daunting, and represent flashpoints for potential conflict. States without central authority quickly become havens for criminals, scenes of internal conflict between competing elites and ethnic groups, potential bases for transnational terrorist or other organizations, and possibly centers for nationalist movements intent on rearranging regional borders.

As the United States wages its war on terrorism and state supporters of terrorist groups, it may leave a series of similarly shattered or unstable states in its wake. The interim government in Afghanistan requires enormous support in order to establish and maintain central authority—a long-term commitment of military personnel and financial resources that is not popular in the U.S. administration. Even with multinational peacekeeping contingents and international economic support, establishing and maintaining a stable central authority will take many years.

The demise of the regime of Saddam Hussein in Iraq also poses a significant threat to regional stability. The war itself imposed even further damage to Iraq's civilian infrastructure—a network already badly damaged by the Gulf War and a decade of punishing sanctions. The domestic consequences of the 2003 war remain unpredictable. American analysts feared the dissolution of Iraq after the Gulf War and its collapse into a northern Kurdish area, a central region ruled from Baghdad, and a southern Shi'ite mini-state that might then favor Iran. It is equally possible that a successor regime will assert itself in Baghdad, imposed by the invading forces or perhaps drawn from remnants of the military, the Ba'ath Party, or the Iraqi exile community.

In any case, the potential for significant regional instability exists. A collapsed Iraqi state creates opportunities for covert Iranian intervention in the north and south—the regions that control most of Iraq's oil. Iraq has a tradition of gradual centralization from the center around Baghdad, and whether a successor regime rapidly asserts itself or not, problems in outlying areas can be expected. The collapse of central authority poses multiple opportunities for criminal or terrorist groups.

Finally, the role of the United States in the aftermath of the conflict will also shape the nature of the Iraqi regime. U.S. forces may stay in Iraq, hoping to promote a new democratic regime and enforce an international monitoring system. This will act as a magnet for anti-American sentiment and for terrorist networks and operations, and may delegitimize any regime or institutions that actively cooperate with it. Alternatively, the United States could attempt to withdraw rapidly and hope for the best—a likely recipe for instability even if some kind of peacekeeping force is left in place.

An additional issue of importance for the future is the apparent success of very limited military means—whether terrorism, foreign-supported insurgency, or low-intensity conflict—to achieve virtually unlimited political ends through perseverance and ruthlessness. Afghanistan drove out the Soviet Union with copious foreign support. Pakistan effectively placed the Taliban in power with only modest investments, and has tied up Indian forces in Kashmir for a dozen years at relatively little political or economic cost—until September 11, 2001.[29] The second *intifada* in the West Bank and occupied territories has fundamentally changed Israel's perception of its security and has caused enormous loss of life on both sides. While the perpetrators of the *intifada* might view this as a tactical success, their efforts have indisputably undermined the peace process and driven the Israeli public much farther to the political right than it was in 1999.

The apparent success of these movements, carried out at relatively low economic cost (although the human and social costs have been quite high) sets them up as an example for "wars of the weak." Weaker powers seeking a change in the status quo will attempt to exploit ethnic cleavages in neighboring states, using low-intensity wars of attrition to test the patience and commitment of their more powerful adversaries. In some cases, such as Kashmir, this may lead to extended and only partially successful counterinsurgency campaigns with high losses of civilian life. In other situations, like that in the West Bank, it may lead to an overwhelming military response, which in turn risks possible escalation to regional conflict. As Pakistan demonstrated in the Kargil war of 1999, even possession of nuclear weapons by both sides does not protect a state from invasion or covert attack.[30]

The combination of unstable regimes, changing normative conceptions of sovereignty and the limits of international intervention, and the weakness of international institutions raises the potential for significant changes in national borders in the coming century. As countries like Zaire collapse, their neighbors may seek to take advantage of fragmentation, establishing de facto (if not yet de jure) control over large portions of national territory through local proxies. In regions where no significant international interest or regional hegemon is present to reassert order, these changes may eventually either become official, leading to a redrawing of international boundaries, or lead to outright conflict with a successor regime in the collapsed state.

In a similar manner, the combination of failing states, waning notions of sovereignty, and determined external intervention may also lead not to the preservation of existing states but to their dissolution. Efforts to preserve Yugoslavia in the early 1990s failed due to lack of support by many European states, a policy that led not only to state breakup but also to brutal civil war and genocide. In an effort to prevent human rights violations, a multinational military intervention succeeded in accelerating the breakup of Serbia, establishing a near-independent Kosovo (*not* an initial war objective), and fanning the flames of greater Albanian nationalism, causing insecurity in other states in the region. Developing states once relied on the UN to protect their sovereignty from rapacious postcolonial powers. Kosovo apparently demonstrated that the UN could be dragged in to provide legitimacy for a multinational invasion after the fact, and the accidental bombing of the Chinese embassy suggested to many that the United States could now operate militarily without constraints in the emerging international system.

Policy Implications

The United States, as a global leader, must respond to conflict in the developing world. This is particularly true as the war on terrorism progresses. As Sir Basil Liddell-Hart once wrote, the object of war is to achieve a better peace.[31] If the rise of terrorism, to some extent, can be traced to institutional weakness and state collapse in the developing world, one aspect of a better peace will be the establishment of more secure successor states and the denial of sanctuary to terrorist groups. If terrorism is linked to social and cultural resentment, political engagement is a means of lessening that tension.[32]

It may be difficult to justify extended American commitment in the developing world on the basis of narrow national interest, particularly in Africa. However, that continent is the locus of major forces of instability, ranging from state collapse to a dangerous HIV epidemic. It is a region where population growth is rapid, natural resources are quickly being depleted, and demographics point to an enormous young population exposed to Western technologies and culture but without hope of economic prosperity or, increasingly, even a reasonable lifespan. Similar but less catastrophic conditions can be found elsewhere in the developing world, and an increasingly embittered population of young men and women looks to anti-Western ideologies and organizations as a means of fighting against their current condition.

The United States remains constrained, however, by a Congress and public that believe, incorrectly, that a vast portion of America's taxpayer dollars are spent on international aid. The foreign assistance budget is currently less than 10 percent of the defense budget, and much of that total remains earmarked for Israel and Egypt. As the country pursues a war on terror, the requirements for postconflict state building (Afghanistan and Iraq) and the rewarding of key allies (Colombia and Pakistan) may outweigh the use of economic assistance as a long-term tool to prevent future crises.

This is an area where other developed states already play an important role, and they must increase their presence. The European Union and Japan have established a reputation as solid international donors. Due in part to military weakness, in part to constitutional prohibitions on military operations abroad, and in part to public and political preference, the EU and Japan rely on economic aid as an alternative means of international influence. International economic assistance as a tool, however, is likely to be constrained in the West because of slowing economic growth. Under these circumstances, the EU can also play an important role through military support for peacekeeping missions.

International organizations and institutions can, and must, play a greater role. Private investment and assistance now play a far more important role in economic aid than do government-provided funds. It will be necessary to work through other institutions and organizations, including the UN, the World Bank and International Monetary Fund, and humanitarian nongovernmental organizations to resolve long-term problems to which Western governments simply cannot commit unilaterally.

The role of regional and international organizations in peacekeeping and conflict resolution must also expand. If internal conflict and regional rivalry represent crucial security issues in the developing world, the role of regional players—and particularly regional organizations—will only expand. ECOWAS represents an outstanding example of the potential utility of a regional organization.[33] UN peacekeeping forces will continue to be a mainstay, but these operations are contingent not only on adequate funding but also on political consensus. To be truly effective, however, the UN may have to reassess its definition of conflict resolution. Currently the UN is most comfortable with short-term solutions such as temporarily defusing a crisis or preventing an immediate outbreak of hostilities. UN operations may have to take greater risks and be given broader powers, in an effort to *end* conflicts rather than simply contain them and hope to wait them out. In a world of greater instability, increased access to weapons of mass destruction and other powerful weapons makes the ramifications of continuing conflicts far more serious than in the past.

Finally, the long-term implications of the decline of sovereignty require further study. If the Westphalian concept of sovereignty is becoming obsolete in a globalized world—a condition the United States still does not formally accept, given its rejection of many international bodies—what can replace it? What legal or other guarantees can ensure the borders of weaker states? Under what conditions should a state be allowed to fail and its boundaries be redrawn to reflect changed political conditions? Can these issues be resolved peacefully, or is the weakening of Westphalian sovereignty simply an invitation to war?

For the United States and the developed countries, the problems of the developing world, particularly the most impoverished and politically weak states, remain second- or third-order concerns. As the world's greatest power and the organizer of the current international system, the United States bears primary responsibility for maintaining that system, a system that ultimately both reflects and sustains important American values, including free trade, democracy, and human rights. It is ultimately in the enlightened self-interest of the West to pay greater attention to the developing world, to develop a better understanding of the causes of instability, and to craft long-term responses to these problems. This will also require the United States to become more politically, economically, and militarily engaged in the developing world.

Acknowledgments

The author would like to thank his students in the Security Studies Program at Georgetown University for their challenging questions about the issues raised in this chapter. He would also like to thank Audrey Kurth Cronin, Bernard Finel, Jim Ludes, Dinshaw Mistry, and Elizabeth Stanley-Mitchell for their insightful comments, generous assistance, and intellectual camaraderie. The views expressed in this chapter are those of the author and do not reflect the policy or official position of the Department of Defense, the U.S. Navy, or any other government organization.

Notes

1. An extensive study of this subject is Robert E. Harkavy and Stephanie G. Neuman, *Warfare and the Third World* (New York: Palgrave, 2001).

2. John Lewis Gaddis, *Strategies of Containment* (Oxford: Oxford University Press, 1982).

3. An interesting study of both wars is Sir Robert Thompson, *Defeating Communist Insurgency,* vol. 10 of *Studies in International Security* (New York: Praeger, 1966). On Vietnam, see Guenter Lewy, *America in Vietnam* (London: Oxford University Press, 1978); Andrew F. Krepinevich, *The Army and Vietnam* (Baltimore: Johns Hopkins University Press, 1986); Leslie H. Gelb and Richard Betts, *The Irony of Vietnam: The System Worked* (Washington, D.C.: Brookings Institution, 1979); H. R. McMaster, *Dereliction of Duty* (New York: HarperCollins, 1997); David Kasier, *American Tragedy* (Boston: Belknap Press, 2000).

4. An updated study of the cold war is found in John Lewis Gaddis, *We Now Know: Rethinking Cold War History* (Oxford: Oxford University Press, 1997).

5. An interesting approach to these and other states, which were rejected by most international institutions, is Robert Harkavy, "The Pariah State System" *Orbis* 21 (fall 1977): 623–49.

6. On the Arab–Israeli conflict, see Chaim Herzog, *The Arab-Israeli Wars* (New York: Vintage Books, 1984). On South Asia, see T. V. Paul, *Asymmetric Conflicts: War Initiation by Weaker Powers* (Cambridge: Cambridge University Press, 1994), 107–25; Robert Jackson, *South Asia in Crisis* (London: International Institute for Strategic Studies, 1975); Richard Sisson and Leo B. Rose, *War and Secession: Pakistan, India, and the Creation of Bangladesh* (Berkeley: University of California Press, 1991); Devin T. Hagerty, *The Consequences of Nuclear Proliferation* (Cambridge: MIT Press, 1998); Kanti P. Bajpai et al., *Brasstacks and Beyond: Perception and Management of Crisis in South Asia* (Urbana-Champaign, Ill.: ACDIS, June 1995); *Conflict Prevention and Confidence-Building Measures in South Asia: The 1990 Crisis,* occasional paper no. 17, ed. Michael Krepon and Mishi Faruqee (Washington, D.C.: Henry L. Stimson Center, April 1994); and Steven A. Hoffman, *India and the China Crisis* (Berkeley: University of California Press, 1990).

7. The best work on this remains Eliot A. Cohen, "Distant Battles," *International Security* 10 (spring 1986): 143–71. See also Harkavy and Neuman, *Warfare and the Third World.*

8. Robert E. Harkavy, "Arms Resupply during Conflict: A Framework for Analysis," in *The Economics of Military Expenditures,* ed. Christian Schmidt (New York: St. Martin's Press, 1987), 239–79.

9. Lawrence Freedman and Efraim Karsh, *The Gulf Conflict, 1990-1991: Diplomacy and War in the New World Order* (Princeton: Princeton University Press, 1993).

10. Richard Butler, *The Greatest Threat: Iraq, Weapons of Mass Destruction, and the Crisis of Global Security* (New York: PublicAffairs, 2000); Tim Trevan, *Saddam's Secrets: The Hunt for Iraq's Hidden Weapons* (London: HarperCollins, 1999); Scott Ritter, *Endgame: Solving the Iraq Problem—Once and for All* (New York: Simon & Schuster, 1999).

11. Daniel Byman, *Keeping the Peace: Lasting Solutions to Ethnic Conflicts* (Baltimore: Johns Hopkins University Press, 2002).

12. General Wesley K. Clark, *Waging Modern War* (New York: PublicAffairs, 2001).

13. See *A National Security Strategy for a New Century* (White House, Dec. 1999), available at www.fas.org/man/docs/nssrpref-1299.htm.

14. This included a brief flirtation with policies of preemptive military strikes. See Thomas G. Mahnken, "Counterproliferation: A Critical Appraisal" in *Twenty-First Century Weapons Proliferation*, ed. Henry Sokolski and James M. Ludes (London: Frank Cass, 2001), 72–83.

15. Mitchell Reiss, *Bridled Ambition: Why Countries Constrain Their Nuclear Capabilities* (Washington, D.C.: Woodrow Wilson Center, 1995).

16. See, for instance, William D. Hartung, *And Weapons for All* (New York: HarperCollins, 1994); and William D. Hartung, "Curbing the Arms Trade: From Rhetoric to Restraint," *World Policy Journal* 9 (spring 1992): 219–47. An excellent study of the arms trade in this period is *The Arms Trade: Problems and Prospects in the Post–Cold War World,* ed. Robert E. Harkavy and Stephanie G. Neuman (special issue of *The Annals of the American Academy of Political Science* 535, Sept. 1994).

17. For a theoretical examination of the importance of internal and regional issues, see Barry Buzan, *People, States, and Fear,* 2d ed. (Boulder: Lynne Rienner, 1991).

18. Thomas F. Homer-Dixon, "Environmental Scarcities and Violent Conflict: Evidence from Cases," *International Security* 19 (summer 1994): 5–40.

19. Mohammed Ayoob, *The Third World Security Predicament: State Making, Regional Conflict, and the International System* (Boulder: Lynne Rienner, 1995).

20. W. Howard Wriggins et al., *Dynamics of Regional Politics: Four Systems on the Indian Ocean Rim* (New York: Columbia University Press, 1992).

21. Carl von Clausewitz, *On War,* indexed ed., ed. and trans. Michael Howard and Peter Paret (Princeton: Princeton University Press, 1976).

22. Robert G. Wirsing, *India, Pakistan, and the Kashmir Dispute* (1994; New York: St Martin's Press, 1998); Sumit Ganguly, *The Crisis in Kashmir: Portents of War, Hopes of Peace* (Cambridge: Cambridge University Press, 1997).

23. "Fernandes Unveils 'Limited War' Doctrine," *The Hindu,* Jan. 25, 2000; "When Words Hurt: No Limits on a 'Limited War,'" *Asiaweek* 26 (March 31, 2000); "India Builds Up Forces as Bush Urges Calm," *New York Times,* Dec. 30, 2001. This report cites Pakistani intelligence officials as having identified twenty-three Indian divisions on the border, in addition to six hundred aircraft. India moved troops from the border with China (III Corps) as well. As of September 2002, approximately 1 million troops remain positioned on both sides of the border—an unprecedented nine-month mobilization. On at least three occasions, India has reportedly been within hours of initiating a war.

24. Mark Bowden, *Black Hawk Down: A Story of Modern War* (New York: Signet, 1999).

25. Clark, *Waging Modern War.*

26. For a cautionary note, see Daniel Byman and Matthew Waxman, *The Dynamics of Coercion: American Foreign Policy and the Limits of Military Might* (Cambridge: Cambridge University Press, 2002).

27. Although the U.S.-led war was an operational success, the challenges of maintaining stability in postwar Iraq will be complex and long-lasting.

28. Thomas L. Friedman, *The Lexus and the Olive Tree: Understanding Globalization* (New York: Anchor Books, 2000).

29. Ahmed Rashid, *Taliban* (New Haven: Yale University Press, 2000).

30. Pakistan's apparent aims are discussed in the *Kargil Review Committee Report* (New Delhi: SAGE, Dec. 15, 1999); Waheguru Pal Singh Sidhu, "In the Shadow of Kargil, Keeping Peace in Nuclear South Asia" in *Managing Armed Conflicts in the Twenty-first Century,* ed. Adekeye Adebajo and Chandra Lekha Sriram (London: Frank Cass, 2001); and Timothy D. Hoyt, "Pakistani Nuclear Doctrine and the Dangers of Strategic Myopia," *Asian Survey* 41 (Nov.–Dec. 2001): 956–77.

31. B. H. Liddell-Hart, *Strategy,* 2d rev. ed. (New York: Meridian, 1991), 322.

32. This concept is discussed in Samuel P. Huntington, *The Clash of Civilizations and the Remaking of World Order* (New York: Touchstone, 1996), and Benjamin R. Barber, *Jihad vs. McWorld: Terrorism's Challenge to Democracy* (New York: Ballantine, 1995).

33. SAARC, because of its institutional reluctance to engage in security issues, represents the other end of the spectrum.

Part III   Transnational Actors and Security

Chapter 11   # Transnational Mass Media Organizations and Security

Diana Owen

Technological advances, global economic factors, and dynamic social and political conditions have facilitated the development of a worldwide media infrastructure with significant implications for international security. Transnational mass media organizations are a prominent force shaping the relationships between states and societies even as they transcend national boundaries. As international relations scholar Martin Shaw observes, "The expanded role of media should be seen as part of a sea-change in world politics, in which old ways of understanding are brought into question."[1]

The media's potential to influence diplomacy, foreign affairs, and security matters has grown since the end of the cold war. The rationale behind U.S. foreign policymaking became less focused, and American political leaders failed to convey a clear international relations agenda.[2] The complexity and number of situations in which nations could become engaged has increased, and the pressure to become involved has escalated.[3] The end of the cold war also witnessed the transition of media from primarily domestic agencies to components of an interdependent transnational order.[4] Initially, policymakers did not anticipate the consequences of global news coverage of international events, and did not have effective media management strategies in place. As a result of these trends, mass media gained a freer reign to identify international hot spots and determine the standpoint of coverage.

The media's relationship to security is constantly evolving. Government and military leaders face the difficulty of managing media in an intricate and often unpredictable environment. Decision makers must continuously adapt their strategies to meet the demands of a shifting array of media actors armed with advanced technological tools for reaching broader audiences.

This chapter examines trends in the development of the transnational mass media system, focusing on its emergence and evolution to its present status. It focuses specifically on industry operations and reporting trends, media effects on diplomacy and foreign affairs, and media/military relations and coverage of war and peacekeeping missions. Some perspectives on future trends and policy recommendations are offered.

The Arrival of Global News

The advent of CNN's twenty-four-hour satellite television news operation in the 1980s ushered in a new era of global news reporting. CNN defied established operating procedures for news organizations by making live news its trademark.[5] Faced with the need to fill air time, CNN devoted 30 to 40 percent of its domestic news coverage to international affairs. This strategy paid off, as satellite coverage of international news stories, including the Falkland Islands War of 1982, the overthrow of President Ferdinand Marcos in the Philippines in 1986, and the fall of the Berlin Wall in 1989 attracted viewers.[6]

CNN's coverage of the Tiananmen Square Massacre in 1989 was a defining moment in the development of the global news order. Live news reports highlighted student protestors' occupation of Tiananmen Square and their demands for reform, exacerbating the political crisis for the Chinese government. This unprecedented event demonstrated the power of continuous satellite television coverage to immediately influence public opinion and foreign policymaking. Government officials around the world monitored CNN for information about the uprising.[7] The U.S. government condemned the Chinese government's actions and briefly imposed trade sanctions. Lacking the media's beaming of sensational images across the globe, a similar uprising in 1986 prompted no action from Western leaders.[8]

Tiananmen Square set the stage for global news coverage of the Gulf War of 1991, which firmly established the paradigm shift in international affairs reporting. CNN journalists broadcast reports live from Baghdad against a dramatic backdrop of pyrotechnics. The Gulf War established CNN as a communication system linking world leaders, diplomats, and the public.[9] Prior to the Gulf War, CNN's audience rating rarely reached 1 million viewers, most of them in the United States. CNN's war coverage attracted an international audience nearly seven times as large.

Global News Structure and Organization

The global news order has developed haphazardly, resulting in a highly fluid multitiered system. At present, CNN and BBC News remain at the top of the global news hierarchy. These organizations can be characterized by their technological innovations in international news because they serve as delivery systems connecting audio and video sources, newsrooms, and foreign ministries to television sets and online news resources even in remote locations.[10] The middle tier is composed of regional media organizations outside the United States. Organizations such as the European Community's Euronews, which broadcasts in seven languages, and Televisa, which provides Spanish-language services to Latin America, have emerged largely in response to the perceived American bias of international news. In the United States CNN's success has prompted established news organizations to alter their approach to international news and encouraged new entrants into the marketplace. Twenty-four-hour news channels with a more restricted international reach than CNN, such as MSNBC and Fox News Network, also occupy the middle tier. Finally, small satellite news operations have been established in countries and territories throughout the world. These outlets can play significant supporting roles by providing feed to organizations with a global infrastructure, especially when crises arise. In addition, national broadcasting networks such as CBS and

ABC, which primarily serve a domestic U.S. audience, have the capacity to become part of the global mix in times of crisis.

The Major Global Players: CNN and BBC News

Launched on June 1, 1980, CNN became the pioneer in the field of twenty-four-hour news service and remains a major force in international markets. The organization's assets include multiple television networks, radio news channels, a wholesale news service that sells video and radio news to other broadcast entities, and online services in multiple languages. The network engages in vast cross-promotion of the holdings of its parent company, AOL–Time Warner, including film, entertainment television, and Internet products.

CNN International (CNNI), the network's international television news service, is available to more than 151 million households in more than 212 countries and territories worldwide, reaching approximately 800 million people daily who are linked via twenty-three satellites. Since 1997 CNNI has operated five separately scheduled but closely associated regional channels, catering to audiences in Europe/Middle East/Africa, Asia/Pacific, South Asia, Latin America, and the United States.[11]

One of the keys to CNNI's prominence in the transnational media system is its capacity to forge alliances with other news operations to provide feed and commentary from remote or dangerous locales, and to have news delivery systems in place when conflicts arise. In 1982, for example, CNN became the first American network to broadcast from Cuba since 1952.[12] CNN's ability to gain strategic advantage in its coverage by targeting potential hot spots and negotiating agreements with local media is illustrated by its deal with the Al-Jazeera television network, which gave CNN exclusive access to Afghanistan in the weeks immediately following the terrorist attacks against the United States of September 11, 2001. Launched in 1996, the Qatar-based Al-Jazeera is the only pan-Arab twenty-four-hour news station. Al-Jazeera first gained recognition in the global media arena when CNN used its footage of the bombing of Baghdad in December 1998. Rather than establish its own offices in Afghanistan when granted permission by the Taliban in 1999, CNN courted Al-Jazeera, which had studios in Kabul and Kandahar. CNN and Al-Jazeera entered into a long-term agreement prior to the events of September 11. Al-Jazeera became a *CNN World Report* contributor and gained access to CNN's syndicated news feed. CNN negotiated the right to break into Al-Jazeera's newscasts with its own correspondents and stories. The deal specified resource sharing and exclusive rights to broadcast footage.[13] This deal enabled CNN to be the first to break news stories about the situation in Afghanistan at a time when U.S. access was limited, giving CNN an initial advantage over its competitors. CNN's relationship with Al-Jazeera also illustrates the delicate nature of resource-sharing alliances. A controversy arose when Al-Jazeera's policies over the airing of videotapes produced by Osama bin Laden differed from those advocated by the U.S. government, which encouraged media organizations to restrict broadcasting of the tapes. The relationship with CNN ended on January 31, 2002, when CNN aired footage from an interview with bin Laden conducted by Al-Jazeera that the network had chosen not to broadcast. Al-Jazeera claimed that CNN had obtained the tape illegally.[14]

CNN's prominence has been challenged by disputes over the integrity of its reports and the emergence of other all-news networks. CNN suffered a major blow to its credibility in 1998 when it was forced to retract its "Operation Tailwind" story after CNN correspondents alleged that the U.S. military used nerve gas on American defectors during the Vietnam War. This highly publicized mistake precipitated a three-year decline in ratings and prestige. During this same period, the number of actors in the global news arena increased substantially. Venues for information dissemination and commentary have grown exponentially in conjunction with technological advances. New entrants MSNBC and Fox News Network have cut into CNN's domestic market share significantly, sparking a reorganization and format changes at CNN in 2001. Still, CNN is able to maintain a solid audience during times of crisis because it is perceived as more serious and less entertainment-oriented than its U.S. competitors.

CNN is rivaled internationally by the British Broadcasting Corporation (BBC), whose combined media services reach the largest global news audience in the world. CNN's tendency to evaluate the importance of international news stories through an American lens often limits the scope of its coverage and its audience. In the mid-1990s BBC News challenged CNNI's dominance in the world television news market when the BBC's more extensive coverage of events in such places as Rwanda, Kosovo, and East Timor drew the attention of viewers and policymakers.[15] Political observers began to speak of a "BBC effect," as opposed to the more familiar "CNN effect," as human rights offenses were subject to public scrutiny, prompting leaders to react.[16]

BBC World Service, funded by a grant from the British Foreign Office, leads the global radio news market, with a steadily growing audience that reached 153 million in 2001. The radio service, heard in 120 capital cities and hundreds of other locations around the world, is broadcast in forty-three languages. The use of digital XM satellite radio technology has allowed World Service to extend its penetration into global markets by offering high-quality transmissions of its news and commentary programs, especially in the United States. Among global news organizations, BBC World Service plays an activist role in providing services to regions in crisis. After September 11, 2001, World Service initiated a twenty-four-hour rolling news and current affairs Arabic service using medium and shortwave frequencies broadcast in five languages spoken in Afghanistan and the surrounding area. In Afghanistan, where television had been banned by the Taliban and a national newspaper did not exist, BBC World Service was a primary source of information for many people.[17] World Service also operates a nonprofit organization, the BBC World Service Trust, with the goal of "promoting development through the effective use of the media." Among the projects initiated by the trust are special informational broadcasts to aid Afghan refugees, a radio series transmitted in twenty languages to help people understand their rights, and a multimedia training program for journalists in Nigeria.[18]

Global Media and Political Culture

That media organizations' reach transcends traditional political boundaries has significant implications for cultural identity and ultimately for international security. The global power structure is inherently tied to the mass media system. This power structure represents the hierarchy of international relationships. Global news is dominated by Western, some argue predominantly American, media. As global media presence translates into global political power, nations with superior communications technology have a greater hold over the flow of information and the construction of international images.[19] Thus participation in global dialogue is extremely uneven, as the interests and views of many states and actors are excluded.

There is a concern that Western global news can obliterate indigenous cultures by creating a single world market that spreads American consumer values.[20] CNN's guiding content practice of "synergistic ownership" allows the movement of characters and stories across various corporate holdings. These messages and symbols can reinforce the dominant American news and cultural values represented by media/entertainment organizations. In addition, global media undermine the ability of groups in less-powerful nations to represent themselves, as they are introduced to the world through a Western lens. Most often they are portrayed as victims and, less sympathetically, as combatants, which serves to reinforce the existing power structure.[21] Western journalists frequently speak for these groups rather than allow them to speak for themselves.[22] These factors can breed resentment and hostility in the transnational arena.

Some challenge the media imperialism argument, as it underestimates the power of citizens of non-Western states to protect their own cultures and manage their own destinies. News is culturally dependent; to be considered credible, it must conform to audience expectations within a society. World news broadcasts, even in nations that rely heavily on Western media, vary widely, as native journalists reprocess content to fit their own cultural conventions and social needs.[23]

While much of the debate surrounding media globalization dwells on its negative implications, there are occasions when global television contributes to a civil view of the global community. When natural disasters such as earthquakes and floods strike, the global media system can help to orchestrate assistance efforts. Thus global news can foster an international public sphere of cooperation, civility, and humanity.

Industry Operations and Reporting Trends

Technology and market forces have influenced news organizations' global expansion and operational structures. News industry procedures and operations have undergone a significant transformation over the past decade, as advanced telecommunications technologies have made information from around the world available to millions globally in real or near-real time. The competition for audience shares and influence among the growing number of media outlets has intensified, causing media organizations to resort to more dramatic methods for gathering and reporting news. The pressure to get stories into the public domain at an accelerated pace has undercut established norms of reporting and has compromised news values. Journalists have come to play an increasingly active role in the making, as opposed to the reporting, of news. While these patterns of media operations and influence are highly visible in the United States, they also are evident in news reporting around the globe.[24]

Driven by a deep concern with profits, news organizations have scaled down their news gathering and investigative reporting units, especially in foreign lands. To decrease their cost per news minute, CNN has downsized its number of foreign correspondents and replaced them with in-studio commentators. There is heavy reliance on press agencies, such as the Associated Press and Reuters, which translates into a uniformity of information and sources. As the global media market has become more crowded, tenuous alliances have formed between organizations to cut costs. Information increasingly comes from pooled sources, whereby a single journalist or camera will supply text, commentary, and audio/video feed for many outlets. News and bureau sharing arrangements have become commonplace.[25] Professional or specialist defense correspondents have been replaced by reporters with little knowledge or understanding of military or world affairs. Further, the widespread availability of inexpensive video cameras and recording devices makes it possible for virtually anyone anywhere to become a news agent by turning over a tape to a news organization. These arrangements facilitate a "point-to-point" structure of global news, making it is possible to report on events instantaneously from almost anywhere in the world.

The integrity of news can be compromised significantly by these arrangements. With fewer resources committed directly to international affairs coverage, media organizations rely heavily on second-hand information that is then reported by journalists who lack particularized expertise. Further, the possibility for information to be disseminated in ways that compromises national security interests is intensified as news organizations focus on the bottom line and lack the foresight and experience to anticipate the consequences of their actions. The controversial footage of the body of a dead American soldier being dragged through the streets of Mogadishu in October 1993 was taken by a Somali driver "using a Hi-8 video camera left behind by a departing Reuters team which had employed him as a stringer."[26] By some accounts, the U.S. peacemaking operation in Somalia was derailed as a result of CNN's ratings-boosting reports, which repeatedly aired this image. Others claim that the Clinton administration was already making plans to extract troops and that this incident simply accelerated the process.[27] Over the objections of officials from the State and Justice Departments, *CBS Evening News* broadcast on May 15, 2002, portions of a videotape of *Wall Street Journal* reporter Daniel Pearl's murder produced by his abductors in Pakistan. In addition to considering the airing of the tape to be insensitive to Pearl's family, the Bush administration feared that terrorists would be encouraged by the publicity it generated. *CBS News* anchor Dan Rather defended the move by stating that viewers could "see and judge" for themselves "the kind of propaganda terrorists are using in their war against the United States."[28]

When situations warrant on-site coverage, correspondents who frequently have little or no experience in the area to which they have been assigned are sent to cover trouble spots based on their perceived audience appeal. The ratings competition has fostered a star system among journalists, who seek maximum visibility by making themselves part of the stories they are covering. Because few high-profile journalists are knowledgeable about international security affairs, typical story frames focus on the experience of the reporters themselves as events unfold. The potential for reporters to mislead the public when placing themselves at the center of the action is illustrated by an incident involving Geraldo Rivera on assignment in Afghanistan for Fox News Network. Using the title, "war correspondent," Rivera, reporting live, attempted to mimic the U.S. Special Forces while brandishing a gun and rolling on the ground, claiming that he was searching caves for Al Qaeda members while under fire. Fox gave this and other incidents staged by Rivera liberal air time, as the reports increased the network's ratings. The deception ended when it was exposed by a cameraman, yet Rivera continued his reports.

"Parachute journalism," where correspondents are dispatched to the scene of the most recent crisis, makes it difficult to track down appropriate sources to provide nuanced or even accurate information. The "live-coverage" and "breaking-news" formats promoted by CNN have become trademarks of mass media, and have contributed to the decline in information quality. Fact checking and proper sourcing are abandoned as speed is stressed over accuracy. Information increasingly is attributed to anonymous sources.[29]

Errors in reporting rarely are corrected, and misinformation can resurface, especially as the Internet provides a readily accessible archive. A classic example of unverified information recirculating and driving the news involves TWA Flight 800, which crashed soon after takeoff from New York en route to Paris. On August 22, 1996, a civilian in Virginia posted a document on the Internet claiming that Flight 800 had been brought down by a U.S. Navy missile undergoing testing. The document was widely circulated on the web via e-mail, and its contents were reported by news organizations. In November, Pierre Salinger, President Kennedy's former press secretary, held a news conference during which he used the web document to accuse the U.S. military and the FBI of withholding the truth from the public about the navy's involvement in the crash. Salinger's allegations continued to make news for more than a year after the crash despite compelling contrary evidence.[30]

The overriding characteristic of global news is that it is conflict-driven. The popularity of rolling news operations, especially, is cyclical; they thrive during times of crisis and struggle to maintain market share in periods of political quiet. Rolling news organizations' audiences swelled to unprecedented levels for several weeks following the September 11 terrorist attacks, only to level off as the war on terrorism continued.[31] Journalists strive to find story angles that are ever more sensational in an effort to stave off audience attrition. Appeals to fear have long been used by journalists to stimulate audience attention. Each new crisis is presented as riskier, deadlier, and more extreme than similar past situations.[32] Important but less sensational stories are not covered, despite the need to provide a steady stream of content. News organizations rely heavily on repeated messages and talk and speculation that is linked to the drama de jour. News blurs into opinion, analysis, and debate by reporters and commentators, as the entertainment orientation obscures serious and, more important, accurate discussion of critical affairs.

Media Effects on Diplomacy and Foreign Affairs

Media industry operations and reporting norms present challenges for government and military decision makers who must manage information and opinion and at the same time protect national security. Officials must work against an information environment that accommodates misinformation and rumor. They must provide briefings for correspondents who lack the foundational knowledge that is necessary to provide proper context for fast-breaking events. To receive positive coverage, leaders also must create opportunities that showcase the journalists themselves, such as allowing reporters access to military bases and personnel, without compromising the security of their missions. Further, journalists and commentators may publicly second-guess official policies and strategies, and thus undermine public support.

The public's perceptions of and reactions to events are an important component of security affairs, and they are shaped largely by media coverage. Not only do mass media play an agenda-setting role in terms of telling the public what to think about,[33] they also are influential in shaping public perceptions of policies and events, especially in the international arena.[34] Public support becomes critical when policies result in tangible costs, such as loss of life, restrictions on resources, and limitations on personal freedoms.[35]

Although the increase in the amount of global news has resulted in enhanced awareness of world events among the general population, the public is not necessarily well informed.[36] Unbalanced, fragmented, and repetitious news coverage fails to provide meaningful context to facilitate the audience's understanding of events and issues.[37] The format of news products, such as those used by rolling news organizations featuring news fragments presented simultaneously to consumers in boxes and banners, magnifies the superficiality of coverage. People's unfamiliarity with world affairs renders public opinion volatile and enhances the ability for media to influence viewpoints, especially in the short term. Media reports also can generate fear, often unnecessarily, that can adversely affect political and social relations. News stories exacerbated the American public's fears after the September 11 terrorist attacks, as more than 70 percent of audience members found the news frightening to watch.[38] Fear caused many to curtail traveling and spending for months after the attacks, and contributed to adverse economic conditions.

Media Diplomacy

Prior to World War II, diplomatic relations were conducted largely in private. The diffusion of radio and television technologies sparked a transition to an era of media diplomacy characterized by the "use of the media to articulate and promote foreign policy."[39] The information age has changed the criteria by which national superiority is assessed, from military might to the ability to use domestic media to promote a powerful national identity and international image.[40] The capacity to conduct media diplomacy enhances a nation's position in the global power hierarchy.[41]

A nation's media diplomacy is greatly influenced by its governmental system. In absolutist regimes the government tends to own the mass media and use it openly and directly to influence foreign policy. The relationship between the media and the government is often adversarial in libertarian societies, as the press maintains legal independence from government and defines itself as a watchdog. The adversarial relationship between the press and government in democratic regimes creates special challenges for media diplomacy, especially during crises and conflicts.

Conventional wisdom suggests that the adversarial relationship between media and governments in democratic regimes turns collaborative when serious concerns over national security arise. Balancing the public's right to know against the security interests, the press routinely would suppress information. For example, the *New York Times* did not publish information about the U.S. government flying U-2 spy planes over the Soviet Union.[42] The media stood by the American government's claim that Libyan terrorists were behind the bombing of a Berlin disco in 1986 despite information that Syria was probably responsible. The disco bombing served as justification for the U.S. attack on Libya.[43] The cooperative relationship between journalists and government has extended even further, as journalists have gathered covert intelligence for the CIA.[44]

The collaborative relationship between government and journalists over security issues is less likely to pertain in the global media era. This situation is due in part to the decline in the number of career diplomatic correspondents who have established connections with government officials and accumulated enough experience to anticipate the consequences of security breaches. Moreover, the free-for-all global news system rewards journalists who are able to break stories, no matter what the costs. Government leaders have adopted defensive strategies, such as leaking misinformation to divert media attention from actual operations. For example, in 1988 Pentagon officials leaked a story to a television correspondent that an aircraft carrier would be delayed in heading to the Persian Gulf, where Iran and Iraq were at war, when in fact the carrier was dispatched immediately. Spokesman for the Joint Chiefs of Staff Jay Coupe stated, "We actually put out a false message to mislead people. The idea was not to give information about the movement of our carrier. We were trying to confuse people."[45]

The "CNN Effect"

The "CNN effect" is a catch-all phrase describing the global mass media's ability to leverage the conduct of U.S. diplomacy and foreign policy. During times of crisis, news agencies become part of the operating environment within which government and military leaders must act. The media become an international battleground for public opinion. The "CNN effect" implies a loss of policymaking control on the part of decision makers because of the power and immediacy of press reports.[46] Driven by American media values, this situation promotes a foreign policy of media-specific crisis management.

Many government and military leaders perceive that the "CNN effect" is real. Political leaders routinely monitor CNN to keep abreast of daily events. An NBC News special report documenting a day in the West Wing of the White House during the early days of the war on terrorism revealed televisions in nearly every room tuned into CNN. National Security Advisor Condoleeza Rice was shown informing visiting Israeli dignitaries that she was monitoring an outbreak of violence in the region via CNN.[47] In addition, policymakers admit that they take twenty-four-hour news coverage into account when planning their actions and believe that CNN has the ability to influence public and elite perceptions worldwide.[48] For example, White House officials were greatly disturbed by a CNN report that aired worldwide on March 28, 2002, and began with the statement, "The U.S. military is not quite ready for another major war," and continued with, "The U.S. military needs more time to retool its ships, aircraft, and weapons, restock munitions, and to rest its troops." Leaders feared that this report would give the impression that American troops were not prepared to continue the war on terrorism.

There is little consensus about the scope, significance, and implications of the "CNN effect," or even about whether it actually exists. It is clear that there is no simple cause-and-effect relationship at work. Media coverage is but one factor of many that can influence foreign policy. Case studies indicate that the "CNN effect" is conditional and unsystematic; it is evident in some circumstances and not in others. Real-time news coverage may be a factor for the entirety of a security or military operation, or it may be short-lived and narrowly focused. Media scholar Steven Livingston identifies several types of "CNN effects" that depend on particular sets of events and circumstances, including the media's role as agenda setters and catalysts or impediments to foreign policymaking and crisis management.[49]

The media can act as agenda-setting agencies when their coverage establishes foreign policy priorities. Media agenda-setting is most likely to occur when grisly pictures are used to expose humanitarian abuses. Leaders face pressure to intervene when activist groups seize the media moment. Attention can be diverted away from situations that are most severe or where intervention has the potential for greatest success.[50]

The press can be an accelerant to decision making by creating a sense of urgency and prompting officials to act prematurely when dealing with crises in response to public pressure. Veteran BBC journalist Nik Gowing terms this phenomenon "policy panic."[51] In 1962 President Kennedy had six days to deal with the Cuban missile crisis before the press broke the news to the public. Today intelligence officials compete with news organizations to get their message out first, especially as the potential for leaks looms large. There is no longer a predictable "news cycle" that allows leaders time to contemplate events and develop strategies. Journalists often pressure leaders for immediate reactions, and a failure to respond may be reported as government unpreparedness or a policy void.[52]

CNN can serve as a diplomatic party line, immediately conveying messages internationally to those involved in conflicts and crises. The media also provide a mechanism for communication between branches of a nation's government, as occurs when the U.S. president "goes public" to build support for policies he would like Congress to adopt.[53] Thus the media spotlight compromises leaders' ability to reach private agreements.

News organizations may be impediments to policymakers' achieving their desired goals. Negative crisis coverage can hinder the ability of public officials to rally support for their actions. Strategic decision making and military operations become subject to criticism when put on public display, especially when casualties result. Leaders fear a recurrence of "Vietnam syndrome," which occurs when horrific images and media commentary undermine morale and create opposition to military interventions.[54] Some argue that the "CNN effect" may be responsible for a decline in public support in Europe for the military action in Afghanistan associated with the war on terrorism. Support in Britain declined from 72 percent shortly after the campaign started in September 2001 to 62 percent in early November, and similarly dropped from 66 percent to 51 percent in France. According to a European diplomat, "The main reason is the 'CNN effect.' On the European television screens you see the collateral damage, the humanitarian crisis that some people relate to American bombings."[55]

Because warring parties recognize that they will be scrutinized by a global audience, they may tailor their actions to television coverage and run the risk of compromising their missions. The media may pose a threat to operational security by exposing technical details of planned maneuvers. Further, the press may be used to spread propaganda unwittingly.[56]

The presence of a "CNN effect" often is contingent on the strength of government leadership regarding a particular situation. According to former diplomatic correspondent turned media scholar Marvin Kalb, "If the government has a strong vision, then television is not likely to have a major effect. If the government has an ambivalent position with respect to a problem, then pictures can have a big effect."[57]

The belief that Western media, particularly the U.S. press, can be manipulated so as to bring about military deployment, deter military intervention, or prohibit further action constitutes another type of "CNN effect." This scenario can involve public relations firms as part of a media diplomacy strategy. The first major instance of such a strategy occurred in 1990, when the Kuwaiti government, under

Iraqi occupation, paid $10.8 million to the U.S. firm of Hill & Knowlton to wage a propaganda campaign to influence American public opinion. The goal was to equate Saddam Hussein with Adolph Hitler.[58] Fabricated stories, complete with pictures of Iraqi soldiers throwing Kuwaiti babies from their incubators, made their way from CNN to President Bush to the UN Security Council. The Gulf War was authorized shortly thereafter.[59]

As leaders have become more adept at managing the media, the notion of a negative "CNN effect" has lost credence. Government officials can manage CNN as part of a strategy to direct attention toward a particular trouble spot. By being attentive to public opinion, political leaders can use the media to set the agenda and mobilize support for their actions. One of the most effective strategies for establishing public support for humanitarian and military operations is to use the media to vilify an enemy leader and create a common target. Evidence suggests that significant American bombing campaigns are preceded by the vilification of a government or movement leader.[60] Negative media coverage of Saddam Hussein began long before the Gulf War. President George W. Bush used the media to connect the war on terrorism directly to Osama bin Laden after the September 11 attacks. This strategy contributed to President Bush's unprecedented approval ratings during the bombing of Afghanistan, even as news reports of civilian casualties mounted. This strategy is not without its liabilities, as public opinion polls indicate that support for military action associated with the war on terrorism would diminish markedly with the death or capture of bin Laden.

In addition, the existence of a "CNN effect" has been disputed on the basis that the media neither control the foreign policy agenda nor force leaders to make decisions. Further, scholarly investigations increasingly reveal that the "CNN effect" rarely undermines policymakers' objectives. Finally, commentators employed by media organizations during crisis situations tend to be supportive of the government's positions and actions. Many come from the ranks of retired military officers.

The Media and the Military

Tension between the media and the military in democratic nations has existed for centuries and endures today.[61] In the United States journalists feel it is their responsibility to provide information to the public and act as a check on military actions. They protest abridgement of their First Amendment freedoms. Military authorities are concerned that journalists' activities can compromise their operations by providing information to the enemy and placing soldiers in life-threatening situations. They do not want the home front demoralized, or to have their mistakes and failures exposed. In addition, journalists putting themselves at risk pose a problem for military security. Veteran journalist H. D. S. Greenway observes that "as one side fights for information, the other side fights either to deny or control it."[62] Yet it is clear that both sides are mutually dependent, and efforts have been made by both parties to close the gap.

Journalists and military personnel reflect the views and ideologies of their respective cultures.[63] Lt. General Bernard Trainor (ret.), a military officer turned journalist, provides a compelling description of these differences:

> Journalists tend to be creative, while the military is happy with traditional approaches. Reporters are independent, while military are team players. The media are liberal and skeptical, while the military is conservative and accepting. The military is hostile toward the journalist; the journalist is indifferent toward the military. Journalists are not used to the fact that the military do not court journalists for their own purposes, but rather avoid them. Given these feelings, the natural inclination of the military is to suppress the press.[64]

The tensions between the military and the media are illustrated by the actions taken by the Israeli government in April 2002 to limit the press's access to and ability to report on military actions in the West Bank. The Israeli government press office revoked the credentials of two reporters from Abu Dhabi Television, a satellite channel, for their account of the deaths of five Palestinian policemen. The press office stated that the reporters showed "utter disregard" for Israeli military censorship rules, broadcast anti-Israeli propaganda, and were creating "an uproar in the Arab world." The press office also threatened legal action against CNN and NBC for continuing to broadcast from the city of Ramallah after Israel had declared the city off limits to journalists as a closed military zone. Israeli forces also fired on working journalists and expelled a CBS television news crew. These actions provoked an outcry among journalists, as organizations such as the Committee to Protect Journalists and the International Federation of Journalists voiced strong opposition to censorship "that will not bring peace, but will only lead to more ignorance, rumor, and fear."[65]

Global television exacerbates military personnel's anxiety about the media. They express concern that the ubiquitous television presence places constraints on the way military power is deployed. Through television the public has gained a greater awareness and understanding of how troops are deployed and military operations are undertaken, which causes people to be more critical in their evaluations.[66] As General Anthony Zinni (ret.) states, "There is a constant lens on your operation" that can immediately affect troop morale and safety.[67]

War Coverage

The formal and informal procedures governing media coverage of war change with every conflict. They are shaped by the experiences of the prior conflict, the nature of the current intervention, the characteristics of available media technologies, and the reporting conventions that are operative at the time. An examination of media coverage of conflicts involving the United States in the global news era illustrates these points.

The legacy of the Vietnam War, the first of the television era, continues to loom large in defining the parameters of media coverage of deadly conflicts. Journalists were given virtually free rein to cover the war, as there was no official government censorship policy. Coverage initially was positive but became more critical over time as U.S. policy became less defined and casualties mounted. In order to sustain interest in the war, reporters, who had open access to the battlefield, took to broadcasting increasingly gruesome images. The Tet offensive of 1968 is generally considered the turning point in media coverage. Images of a South Vietnamese officer shooting a Viet Cong prisoner in the head at the American compound in Saigon horrified American viewers and fueled the antiwar movement at home. There is a lingering belief among military personnel that the media undermined American efforts in Vietnam by stimulating homeland protests and damaging troop morale.[68] Journalists contend that for fifteen years after Vietnam, the Pentagon would not cooperate with the press on any issue.[69]

The Vietnam experience prompted the American government to place clear restrictions on media coverage of subsequent conflicts. A news blackout was instituted during the 1983 invasion of Grenada. Correspondents were allowed to enter the country only after it had been secured. At least one journalist chartered a boat but could not get close to the action. To contend with media outcry, the government instituted a "pool" format. A select number of journalists were given access to government briefings and then permitted to share their notes with other reporters. Tight control was maintained over information, as only a select group of reporters was given access to soldiers and the battlefront. The format was used again in 1989 during the invasion of Panama, causing outrage among journalists.[70]

The Gulf War presented a logistical challenge to military officials seeking to manage the press, as more than 1600 American reporters and countless journalists from other nations converged on Baghdad. Unprecedented government restrictions were placed on the press during this first war of the global news era. The pool system was implemented and correspondents were forced to rely heavily on press releases and official government sources for information because of limited access to battle fronts. Reporters could not conduct interviews even with doctors and nurses in the rear areas of the war zone without a military escort. Journalists' dispatches and film were subject to censorship by military officials.[71]

At the time journalists were largely content to follow these rules. The war unfolded rapidly, and reporters were unfamiliar with the weapons systems and strategies employed. They relied on the explanations of military experts, as they had no time to track down other sources.[72] Further, the equipment used to transmit the exciting satellite images that characterized global news coverage lacked portability. Correspondents consented to military restrictions as they provided cover for the fact that technological limitations would not permit them to broadcast live from the battlefield.[73] For CNN, the restrictions on information access were tempered by the commercial and popular success of the Gulf War. Watching the war on television became an immediate obsession for many people, as viewers were mesmerized by reports showcasing American military and technological strength in the heat of battle. American viewers welcomed this kind of reassuring coverage, especially as many reserve units were deployed.

Despite the steps taken by American government and military leaders to contain the press, they did not anticipate the need to control the flow of information from the enemy to global media. The Gulf War marked the first time that American media provided a global platform for the enemy to make his case. CNN gave significant air time to Saddam Hussein, which he used as part of his public relations efforts and to send messages to supporters in the Arab world.

After the Gulf War media organizations criticized the sanitized perspective that was provided to the public as well as the fact that information they were disseminating about the accuracy of American weapons proved incorrect. Constitutional lawsuits were filed charging that the Pentagon and the White House had violated the press's First Amendment rights. Journalists vowed that they would never again allow themselves to be subject to these types of restrictions.[74] The public, however, supported the government's decisions to limit press access in the interest of national security.[75]

The rules governing media coverage are once again being revised for the war on terrorism. Journalists' access to information about the antiterrorism campaign has been more restricted than at any time in recent history, especially during the first stage of the operation. President Bush expressed government policy with the following statement: "Let me condition the press this way. Any sources and methods of intelligence will remain guarded in secret. My administration will not talk about how we gather intelligence, if we gather intelligence, and what the intelligence says. That is for the protection of the American people."[76]

Accordingly, military briefings have been cautious. To limit press complaints, the Bush administration employed a Gulf War tactic by giving reporters and the public access to key leaders, including Defense Secretary Donald Rumsfeld and Secretary of State Colin Powell. Reporters are effectively kept away from the story but given access to military and government leaders, which conveys to audiences that journalists are close to the command center.[77] Following a request by U.S. authorities, American networks adopted the policy of not airing tapes from Osama bin Laden live, agreeing instead to review and edit them in consultation with government officials.

Access to soldiers and the battlefield has been controlled strategically, as well. During the early phases of the war on terrorism, in September and October 2001, the press was kept away from Afghanistan. In early November the press was allowed to go along on a limited number of Pentagon-controlled military operations. After the defeat of the Taliban, journalists were given greater freedom, especially as their reports heralded the success of the operation. The decision to allow greater press access to the war zone was not without consequences, as the military was forced to manage news of civilian casualties.

The military's strategic control over access and information results in part from the unique nature of the war on terrorism. The operation is not a traditional fight against another nation and it lacks clear criteria for determining enemies and declaring a winner. The need to guard intelligence is essential, as this conflict involves many special operations that rely on the element of surprise. Leaking information could cost lives. Further, the military does not want to publicize the fact that the search for terrorists will involve operations where the enemy eludes U.S. forces.

The content, tone, and style of global television reporting of the war on terrorism also has shifted with events. Reporters were caught especially off guard by the events in motion on September 11, as they knew little about terrorism or the situation in Afghanistan.[78] Lacking information and expertise, the press was initially careful to cite multiple sources and check facts. As time went on and information was not forthcoming from official sources, media organizations returned to their stock reporting rituals.[79] The amount of commentary and speculation in reports increased, as did anonymous sourcing. Global news disseminated from Western stations was decidedly one-sided, as coverage was almost exclusively pro-United States. Domestic news was overwhelming patriotic.[80]

More than 500 journalists were embedded with troops from all branches of the service during the invasion of Iraq in 2003. A number of these journalists received special Pentagon-sponsored military training prior to their assignments. In explaining its reasons for embedding journalists, the Defense Department emphasized the centrality of media coverage to the success of the operation because of its influence on global public opinion. The introduction to their ground rules for embedded journalists stated, "We need to tell the factual story—good or bad—before others seed the media with disinformation and distortions, as they most certainly will continue to do. Our people in the field need to tell our story—only commanders can ensure the media get to the story alongside the troops."[81] While many journalists welcomed the opportunity to cover the Iraqi situation with the cooperation of the military, others questioned whether the relationship would compromise objective reporting.

Peacekeeping and Humanitarian Missions

Over the past two decades, the focus of military operations increasingly has shifted to peacekeeping, humanitarian activities, and emergency services. Early on, the military and intelligence community did not see a compelling need to manage the press, especially when vital Western interests were not at stake.[82] This view miscalculated the potential of the press to undermine public support when a government chooses to engage in these missions, especially as casualties featured prominently in global news reports have the potential to jeopardize operations.[83]

There is an antagonistic disconnect between the role military leaders and policymakers expect the media to play and the role journalists see for themselves, especially as perceptions change with virtually every situation. Ambiguities exist on both sides of the equation. The mandate and scope of peacekeeping and humanitarian operations are frequently unclear. Governments, NATO, and the UN often seek to appear as if they are taking humanitarian action without committing themselves to engaging in conflict. For example, delayed humanitarian interventions in Rwanda, Kosovo, East Timor, and Burundi can be interpreted as substitutes for concrete political commitment and meaningful military engagement by Western powers.

As the preceding discussion of the "CNN effect" illustrates, the media's function in these types of interventions also is indeterminate and frequently misconstrued. The uncertainty surrounding media influence places political leaders on continuous alert for the day when coverage of a particular situation will resonate with domestic and global publics. More often than not, humanitarian disasters will remain off the radar screen of journalists until armed conflict breaks out. No matter how horrific the broadcast images, media influence generally takes a back seat to policymakers' assessments about compelling strategic national interests.[84] CNN beamed images of atrocities in Bosnia around the globe for years without compelling the Bush administration to become involved. The Clinton administration's intervention in Bosnia in 1995, which led to the Dayton peace agreement, was prompted by the prospect of American forces being sent in to extract UN peacekeeping troops who were suffering casualties under a Serbian advance.[85]

Media organizations' decisions to cover humanitarian crises are driven heavily by commercial incentives and budgetary issues. They are reluctant to invest resources on a humanitarian situation for which the return may be a decrease in audience. International institutions, embassies, and nongovernmental organizations identify trouble spots and work to initiate interventions with far greater frequency than the media. Embassies, in fact, disregard internal strife, political instability, and human suffering at their own peril. Nongovernmental organizations work hard to attract media attention to problem areas but realize that they cannot count on press coverage to bolster fundraising and volunteer efforts or cause governments to act. While there was more media coverage of Rwanda before and during the 1994 genocide than of Somalia at any time before 1992, media attention failed to stimulate intervention by major powers. However, ninety relief organizations, working in conjunction with bureaucracies established in the country, dispatched assistance.[86]

Because of the unique nature of peacekeeping operations, the media generally have greater power and freedom in their reporting than in battlefield situations. There are many more sources of information in a humanitarian situation than in a war. In some instances, the media aid the military by providing intelligence and sorting through the abundance of sources.[87]

Prospects for the Future

As British media scholar Stephen Badsey has observed, "A recurring part of the story of the new relationship between media and international security has been the manner in which technological developments have upset old and established certainties and relationships."[88] Few predicted that television would alter the course of the Vietnam War by transmitting vivid and brutal images to Americans at home that print, radio, and even film could not convey. It is difficult to imagine what twenty years of technological innovation will do to change the relationship between media and security affairs.

Examining current trends, however, can provide some idea of what the future holds. New communications technologies create the potential for a new type of transnational media, or "hypermedia," effect on transnational information management. Myriad communications technologies, from wireless telephones and fax machines to the Internet, facilitate the distribution of information to increasingly fragmented audiences. The amount of information available to the public and elites has proliferated and will only multiply.

Actors in the transnational security arena are already contending with the glut of information. It has become increasingly difficult to separate factual information from rumor, propaganda, fiction, or material taken out of context. This information involves not only traditional text, audio, and video but newer hybrid formats facilitated by computer technology. The situation is complicated further because all forms of information are available for widespread transmission instantaneously. There is great potential for power to become vested in those individuals, agencies, or institutions that manage information by sorting through, repackaging, and disseminating it to target populations.

In addition, traditional barriers to the flow of information, such as state boundaries, will be obliterated further by new technologies. New political arrangements and alliances will be organized around media. There are already indications of the emergence of a global state predicated on global media dominance. According to Martin Shaw, one possible configuration of this global state is "the Western state together with its legitimation framework, the UN system, through which other states—and to a lesser extent world society—are drawn into political relationships with it."[89] Additional alliances would be formed based on economic, political, and military allegiances orchestrated through the media system. Finally, entrepreneurs who introduce and manage new communications technologies in the global arena also stand to become powerful actors in the political community, as they align themselves with governmental and nongovernmental actors. These arrangements are likely to be highly unstable and even combustible in times of global crisis.

Predictions about the future based on current power relationships should be made with the caveat that trends are shifting in the global media arena. There is evidence that Western/American dominance of the global news market has diminished slightly, and this tendency is likely to continue as more nations gain technological advantage. When the Gulf War experience demonstrated the viability of satellite technology as a cost-effective news-delivery system, nations around the world established their own network services. Local services now provide American networks with much of their foreign news, whereas the opposite was true less than a decade ago.[90] As the barriers to entry are lifted and new, less costly, more portable communications technologies are diffused in remote and developing nations, their influence on the transnational scene is likely to grow.

Policy Recommendations

Policy recommendations with the greatest potential for implementation and effectiveness focus on diplomatic and military actors. It is difficult to establish policies governing the operation of global media, particularly in peacetime. The global media system itself is largely unregulated. In democratic nations, industry pressures and social norms work against regulation, including cooperation with leaders in wartime. Individual media organizations are primarily self-regulated and fight hard against efforts to control their operations.

Members of the military and diplomatic communities can take measures to enhance their strategic position in the global media environment. The first step is to stay on the cutting edge of communication technologies and use them to develop innovative media diplomacy strategies and to anticipate how to manage media relations in wartime. Government technology should be upgraded to corporate standards.[91] In addition, leaders should hone their media management skills beyond the current level of competence. Media relations training that takes into account the new realities of the global media system and anticipates the effects of emerging communications technologies is imperative. Political actors should develop a detailed understanding of the norms and operating procedures that drive the media. The commercial imperatives that are central to media organizations are directly at odds with the public service incentives of military and government personnel. Strategies should take these fundamental differences in orientation into account and capitalize on them. One way is to produce media products for global consumption that have high levels of commercial audience appeal.[92] Finally, global media resources should be employed to enhance public outreach that is unfiltered by mass media. Internet technologies are well suited to this goal.

Concerns about the ability of mass media to adversely affect democratic objectives in international affairs are longstanding, despite the difficulties surrounding policy development and implementation. Much of the debate surrounds the issue of media ethics and content. The call for "international media monitoring" has gained some support, particularly in academic circles. Taking the lead from Karl Deutsch's suggestion of forty years ago, advocates of "media monitoring" believe that content analysis of global news products should be conducted to determine the amount of coverage given to particular events, the accuracy of reports, and the tone of stories, especially if they convey hostility. The goal, essentially, is to ward off a potential "CNN effect" that would lead to violence or loss of life. This concept has been proposed in the form of an international media alert system, which would monitor the media climate for early signs that coverage was motivating crimes against humanity.[93] The possibility for proposals like this to be implemented formally is minimal, especially as they border on censorship and are likely to be ineffective in accomplishing their goals.

Conclusion

The past twenty years have witnessed major transformations of the mass media's relationship to national and international security. Many of the consequences of the emergent transnational mass media order have been unanticipated, if not unintended. The advent of satellite television news in particular has had vast implications for the conduct of foreign affairs, diplomacy, peacekeeping missions, and war. New technologies and reporting norms have together created a news environment that emphasizes immediacy at the expense of accuracy. At times the pressure to provide a constant stream of breaking news stories can compromise national security. Journalism that features "star" reporters who lack expertise in international and military affairs creates difficulties for officials attempting to convey information about complex situations and operations. The media's influence on the public has moved beyond agenda setting to opinion formation, as the number of mass media outlets has vastly increased and coverage of security-related news has expanded. The importance of media diplomacy for a nation's position in the global power hierarchy has swelled. At the same time, the challenge of conducting diplomatic relations by democratic governments has become more difficult. Evidence of "CNN and BBC effects," while not unimpeachable, is compelling enough to persuade government and military leaders to continually monitor real-time news and to contemplate its effects when developing public relations and diplomatic strategies.

The longstanding tension between the media and the military persists in the current age, especially as the focus of operations has shifted to peacekeeping and humanitarian missions. Each intervention requires that government strategies for press management be adapted or rewritten to contend with technological advances in reporting and information dissemination, increasingly intrusive journalistic practices, and infotainment-style coverage. The eradication of the line between hard news and commentary has significant implications for reporting about military operations. As coverage of the "war on terrorism" illustrates, news organizations have come to rely heavily on "expert commentators" who speculate about military operations or second-guess leaders, especially when government sources seek to restrict information in the interest of national security. News consumers find it difficult to distinguish between fact and speculation, which can impede government leaders' ability to maintain support for their actions.

The media/security nexus has been characterized by volatility and uncertainty, and there is little evidence to suggest that the situation will stabilize in the foreseeable future. Mass media technologies and practices are an integral component of the shift toward new types of political arrangements that defy traditional physical state boundaries and alliances. As media power and political power become increasingly synonymous, it will be imperative for political and military leaders to track developments in the transnational media arena.

Acknowledgment

The author would like to thank Jeffrey S. Owen, Christine Chianese, and Hugh Curnutt for their assistance.

Notes

1. Martin Shaw, "Global Voices: Civil Society and Media in Global Crisis," in *Human Rights in Global Politics,* ed. Timothy Dunne and Nicholas Wheeler (Cambridge: Cambridge University Press, 1999), 214.

2. James Schlesinger, "Quest for a Post–Cold War Foreign Policy," *Foreign Affairs* (winter 1992); James F. Hoge Jr., "Media Pervasiveness," *Foreign Affairs* (summer 1994); Richard N. Haass, "Paradigm Lost," *Foreign Affairs* (winter 1995).

3. Richard Dunaway, "National Security Decision-Making and the Global Telecommunications Revolution," *United States National Security* (Sept. 2001).

4. Robert O. Keohane and Joseph S. Nye, *Power and Interdependence: World Politics in Transition* (Boston: Little, Brown, 1977); James N. Rosenau, *Along the Domestic-Foreign Frontier* (Cambridge: Cambridge University Press, 1990).

5. The decision to center CNN's reporting around live news was primarily financial. The network had paid for the satellite time, and it was economically advantageous to rely more on live feed than on high-priced on-air correspondents. See Hank Wittemore, *CNN: The Inside Story* (Boston: Little, Brown, 1990).

6. CNN devotes approximately 60 to 70 percent of its coverage to international events in its foreign markets, with 30 to 40 percent focusing on U.S.-based news. See Lewis A. Friedland, *Covering the World: International Television News Services* (New York: Twentieth Century Fund Press, 1992).

7. Joan Shorenstein Barone Center, *Turmoil in Tiananmen: A Study of U.S. Press Coverage of the Beijing Spring of 1989* (Cambridge: Harvard University, John F. Kennedy School of Government, 1992).

8. Center for Defense Information, "The 'CNN Effect': TV and Foreign Policy," *America's Defense Monitor*, program transcript 834, May 7, 1995.

9. Friedland, *Covering the World,* 42.

10. William A. Hatchen and Harva Hatchen, *The World News Prism: Changing Media of International Communications* (Ames: Iowa State University Press, 1999).

11. CNN News Group Businesses, "CNN International," available at www.aoltimewarner.com (2002).

12. Wendy J. Williams, "The CNN Effect: The First 24-Hour News Channel Has Reshaped the TV Landscape," *Boston Herald,* May 28, 2000, 6.

13. Abdallah S. Schleifer, "The Sweet and Sour Success of Al-Jazeera," *Transnational Broadcasting Studies* (fall/winter), available at www.tbsjournal.com/Jazeera_sas.html (2001).

14. CNN, "Al-Jazeera Statement and CNN Response on bin Laden Interview," Jan. 31, 2002, available at www.cnn.com/2002/US/01/31/gen.aljazeera.statement.

15. Stephen Badsey, "Air Power and Joint Forces: Manipulating the Media" (paper presented at the 2000 Air Power Conference, Aerospace Centre, London, 2000).

16. When a story warranting international headlines involves the United States, CNNI's

ratings increase markedly. The U.S.-focused events in the wake of the September 11 terrorist attacks boosted CNNI's ratings in the short term.

17. Surveys conducted by BBC World Service prior to Sept. 11, 2001, indicated that 72 percent of Pashto-language speakers and 62 percent of Persian speakers in Afghanistan listened to BBC broadcasts daily. The Urdu speakers in the region were switching to the new rolling news format in significant numbers (see BBC World Service, "Extra BBC World Service Transmissions: Listen to News Reports Arabic, Hindi, Urdu and Pashto on Digital Satellite in the UK," 2002, available at www.bbc.co.uk/worldservice/us/011005_sky_transmissions.shtml).

18. BBC offers a subscription service, BBC Monitoring, which serves government departments, journalists, academics, and businesses. BBC Monitoring provides customized synopses of news and information culled from more than 2,000 radio, television, print, Internet, and news agency sources, as well as translation services for one hundred languages. As the BBC sorts through the glut of information and provides translation services for government and business officials, it has the potential to act as an informational gatekeeper (see BBC World Service, "BBC World Service Trust: Using Communications for Development," 2002, www.bbc.co.uk/worldservice/us/trust/index.shtml).

19. Bosah Ebo, "War as Popular Culture: The Gulf Conflict and the Technology of Illusionary Entertainment," *Journal of American Culture* 18, no. 3, 1995.

20. Benjamin Barber, *Jihad Versus McWorld* (New York: Time Books, 1995); Larry Strelitz, "Where the Global Meets the Local: Media Studies and the Myth of Cultural Homogenization," *Transnational Broadcasting Studies* (spring 2001), available at www.tbsjournal.com/Archives/Spring01/strelitz.html.

21. Alice Hall, "The World in the Screen: The Impact of Character Representativeness, Social Variability, and Presentation on Audiences' Conceptualization of Cross-cultural Media Meanings," *Transnational Broadcasting Studies* (spring 2001), available at www.tbsjournal.com/Archives/Spring01/Hall.html.

22. Herbert Schiller, *Communication and Cultural Domination* (White Plains: M. E. Sharpe, 1976); Shaw, "Global Voices," 214–32.

23. Rebecca Carrier, "Global News and Domestic Needs: Reflections and Adaptations of World Information to Fit National Policies and Audience Needs," in *News Media and Foreign Relations: A Multifaceted Perspective,* ed. Abbas Malek (Norwood, N.J.: Ablex Publishing, 1997), 177–94.

24. Satellite television news stations outside the United States have used CNN as a model and have combined live coverage using correspondents and news reports with in-studio talk shows. The result has been coverage that is entertainment-oriented, emotional, and ideological (remarks made by Rami G. Khouri at panel discussion, "Covering the War on Terrorism," Georgetown University, Jan. 24, 2002).

25. Scotti Williston, "Global News and the Vanishing Foreign Correspondent," *Transnational Broadcasting Studies* (spring 2001), available at www.tbsjournal.com/Spring01/Williston.html.

26. Badsey, "Air Power and Joint Forces."

27. Steven Livingston and Todd Eachus, "Humanitarian Crises and U.S. Foreign Policy: Somalia and the CNN Effect Reconsidered," *Political Communication* 12 (1995); Warren P. Strobel, "The CNN Effect," *International Communication Online*, vol. JOUR/IR, 246, 1998, available at www.lehigh.edu/~j10d/J246-98/strobel.html.

28. Howard Kurtz, "CBS Defends Decision to Air Part of Pearl Tape," *Washington Post,* May 16, 2002, C1.

29. Bill Kovach and Tom Rosenstiel, *Warp Speed: America in the Age of Mixed Media* (New York: Century Foundation Press, 1999).

30. CNN, "Federal Agencies Deny TWA Flight 800 Shot Down by Missile," Nov. 8, 1996, available at www.cnn.com/US/9611/08/twa.salinger; Jocelyn Noveck, "Pierre Salinger Claims Navy Missile Shot Down TWA Flight 800," AP story, Nov. 8, 1996; CNN, "Salinger 'Totally Sure' TWA 800 Missile Theory Is True," March 13, 1997, www.cnn.com/US/9703/13/twa.

31. Jon Friedman, "Fox Defeated CNN in Homes for Week," www.CBS.MarketWatch.com, Nov. 14, 2001.

32. Susan D. Moeller, *Compassion Fatigue: How the Media Sells Disease, Famine, War, and Death* (New York: Routledge, 1999).

33. Bernard C. Cohen, *The Press and Foreign Policy,* repr. ed. (Berkeley: Institute for Governmental Studies Press, 1993).

34. Amy Fried, *Muffled Voices: Oliver North and the Politics of Public Opinion* (New York: Columbia University Press, 1997); Maxwell McCombs, Donald L. Shaw, and David Weaver, eds., *Communication and Democracy: Exploring the Intellectual Frontiers of Agenda Setting Theory* (Mahwah, N.J.: Lawrence Erlbaum Publishers, 1997).

35. Carroll J. Glynn et al., *Public Opinion* (Boulder: Westview Press, 1999).

36. Stephen P. Aubin, *Distorting Defense: Network News and National Security* (Westport, Conn.: Praeger, 1998).

37. W. Lance Bennett, *News: The Politics of Illusion,* 4th ed. (New York: Longman, 2001).

38. Pew Research Center for the People and the Press, "Attacks at Home Draw More Interest Than War Abroad," (Washington, D.C.: Pew Research Center, Oct. 22, 2001).

39. Bosah Ebo, "Media Diplomacy and Foreign Policy: Toward a Theoretical Framework," in Malek, *News Media and Foreign Relations,* 43.

40. Simon Serfati, ed., *The Media and Foreign Policy* (New York: St. Martin's Press, 1990); Majid Tehranian, *Technologies of Power: Information Machines and Democratic Prospects.* (Norwood, N.J.: Ablex Publishing, 1990).

41. In an effort to create a positive international image that is perceived as legitimate, nations have retained the services of public relations firms, many of them based in the United States; see Ebo, "War as Popular Culture."

42. Montague Kern, Patricia W. Leving, and Ralph B. Leving, *The Kennedy Crisis: The Press, the Presidency, and Foreign Policy.* (Chapel Hill, N.C.: University of North Carolina Press, 1984).

43. Ebo, "War as Popular Culture."

44. William Preston Jr., Edward S. Herman, and Herbert I. Schiller, *Hope and Folly: The United States and UNESCO, 1945–1985* (Minneapolis: University of Minnesota Press, 1989).

45. Howard Kurz, "Journalists Worry about Limits on Information, Access," *Washington Post,* Sept. 24, 2001, A5.

46. Warren P. Strobel, *Late-Breaking Foreign Policy: The News Media's Influence on Peace Operations* (Washington, D.C.: U.S. Institute of Peace, 1997).

47. The one-hour NBC News special report, anchored by Tom Brokaw, aired on Jan. 23, 2001.

48. Strobel, *Late-Breaking Foreign Policy.*

49. Steven Livingston, *Clarifying the CNN Effect: An Examination of Media Effects According to Type of Military Intervention* (research paper R-18, Joan Shorenstein Center for Press-Politics, Harvard University, 1997).

50. Michael Mandelbaum, "Foreign Policy as Social Work," *Foreign Affairs* (Jan. 1996); Steven Livingston, "Beyond the 'CNN Effect': The Media-Foreign Policy Dynamic," in *Politics and the Media: The New Media and Their Influences,* ed. Pippa Norris (Boulder: Lynne Rienner Publishers, 1997), 291–318.

51. Nik Gowing, "Real-time Television Coverage of Armed Conflicts and Diplomatic Crises: Does It Pressure or Distort Foreign Policy Decision Making?" (working paper 94-1, Joan Shorenstein Center for Press-Politics, Harvard University, 1994); Jennifer Byrne, "Interview with Nik Gowing," Australian Broadcasting Corporation News, Aug. 14, 1999.

52. U.S. Institute of Peace, "The Mass Media's Impact on International Affairs," *Peace Watch* (June 1997).

53. Timothy E. Cook, *Governing with the News: The News Media as a Political Institution* (Chicago: University of Chicago Press, 1998); Samuel Kernell, *Going Public: News Strategies of Presidential Leadership* (Washington, D.C.: Congressional Quarterly Press, 1997).

54. Livingston, "Beyond the CNN Effect."

55. William Douglas, "Bush: Time to Deliver Pledges," *Newsday,* Nov. 10, 2001.

56. Livingston, *Clarifying the CNN Effect.*

57. Center for Defense Information, "The 'CNN Effect.'"

58. Saddam Hussein launched his own public relations media campaign to counter these images. He appeared on television with the families of Western hostages and patted the children on the head in an attempt to look compassionate. The move only worsened his image in the West, as he was viewed as manipulating children (Ebo, "War as Popular Culture").

59. W. Lance Bennett and David L. Paletz, eds., *Taken by Storm* (Chicago: University of Chicago Press, 1994); Badsey, "Air Power and Joint Forces."

60. Badsey, "Air Power and Joint Forces."

61. Loren B. Thompson, *Defense Beat* (New York: Lexington Books, 1991); Christopher Young, "The Role of Media in International Conflict" (working paper 38, Canadian Institute for Peace and Security, 1991).

62. H. D. S. Greenway, "This Warring Century," *Columbia Journalism Review* (Sept.–Oct. 1999): 50.

63. Marvin Kalb, remarks made at the panel discussion "Covering the War on Terrorism," Georgetown University, Jan. 24, 2002.

64. Lt. Gen. Bernard Trainor, "The Military and the Media: A Troubled Embrace," in *The Media and the Gulf War: The Press and Democracy in Wartime,* ed. Hedrick Smith (Washington, D.C.: Seven Locks Press, 1992), 72.

65. Steve Weizman, "Israel Warns Journalists of Action," *Washington Post*, April 3, 2002.

66. Dunaway, "National Security Decision-Making."

67. U.S. Institute of Peace, "The Mass Media's Impact on International Affairs."

68. William M. Hammond, *The Military and the Media, 1962–1968: The U.S. Army in Vietnam* (Washington, D.C.: Center of Military History, United States Army, 1988).

69. Kalb, remarks.

70. Noam Chomsky, *What Uncle Sam Really Wants* (Tucson: Odonian Press, 1993).

71. Freedom Forum, *The Media at War: The Press and the Persian Gulf Conflict* (New York:

Gannett Foundation, Columbia University, 1991); Douglas Kellner, *The Persian Gulf TV War* (Boulder: Westview Press, 1992); Robert F. Denton, ed., *Media and the Persian Gulf War* (New York: Praeger, 1993); Bennett and Paletz, *Taken by Storm.*

72. Smith, *The Media and the Gulf War.*

73. Barry Dunsmore, "Live from the Battlefield," in Norris, *Politics and the Press,* 237–74.

74. Smith, *The Media and the Gulf War.*

75. The public sided strongly with the Bush administration's media policy during the Gulf War. A 1991 Times-Mirror Center poll indicated that 80 percent of Americans agreed with the Pentagon's restrictions and 60 percent felt they should have been tighter (Kurtz, "CBS Defends Decision").

76. Ibid.

77. Kalb, remarks.

78. Matthew Rose, "How the Media Got It All Wrong in Afghanistan," *Wall Street Journal*, Oct. 27, 2001.

79. Project for Excellence in Journalism, "Before and After: How the War on Terrorism Has Changed the News Agenda, Network Television, June to October 2001" (research report, Center for Excellence in Journalism, Washington, D.C., 2001).

80. Project for Excellence in Journalism, "Return to Normalcy? How the Media Have Covered the War on Terrorism" (research report, Center for Excellence in Journalism, Washington, D.C., 2002).

81. Joe Strupp, "Why Is Pentagon Inviting Press to Accompany Tropps?" *Editor & Publisher,* Feb. 10, 2003.

82. Strobel, *Late-Breaking Foreign Policy.*

83. Dennis C. Jett, *Why Peacekeeping Fails* (Boston: St. Martin's Press, 2000). Tolerance of casualties may be culturally dependent, as European citizens appear to be more accepting of military casualties than do Americans. There is some limited evidence that public intolerance of casualties in the United States may be exaggerated by politicians' fear of alienating constituents. See James Burk, "Public Support for Peacekeeping in Lebanon and Somalia" (paper presented at the Inter-University Seminar on Armed Forces and Society, Baltimore, Oct. 22, 1995). However, public opinion polls conducted since the Gulf War repeatedly reveal that Americans' support of military operations diminishes as the body count increases.

84. Government and media values are often at odds over the definition of "national interest." Governments increasingly construe national interest in terms of noninterventionist policies. In 1994 President Clinton issued Presidential Decision Directive number 25 on multilateral peace operations (PDD25), which severely limits the deployment of ground troops for peacekeeping missions. In 1996 U.S. National Security Advisor Anthony Lake presented a seven-point checklist of national interests, specifying that force would be used only in situations of extreme urgency. Journalists, on the other hand, feel that it is their responsibility to bring atrocities to light, and to prompt action to alleviate them (Gowing, "Real-Time Television Coverage").

85. Richard Holbrooke, *To End a War* (New York: Random House, 1998).

86. Andrew S. Natsios, *U.S. Foreign Policy and the Four Horsemen of the Apocalypse* (Washington, D.C.: Center for Strategic and International Studies, 1997).

87. Strobel, "The CNN Effect."

88. Badsey, *The Media and International Security,* xxvii.

89. Shaw, "Global Voices," 216.

90. Williston, "Global News."

91. Center for Strategic and International Studies, "Reinventing Diplomacy in the Information Age" (Washington, D.C.: CSIS, 2001), available at www.csis.org/pubs/diaexecsum.html.

92. An example of this strategy is the primetime U.S. television program "American Fighter Pilots," which follows the real-life story of air force pilots training to fly the F-15. The program employs high-tech audio-visual representations to drive home its positive message about the military.

93. Kaarle Nordestreng and Michael Griffin, eds., *International Media Monitoring* (Cresskill, N.Y.: Hapton Press, 1999).

Chapter 12   # Transnational Crime, Corruption, and Security

Roy Godson

One of the most dangerous threats to the quality of life in the contemporary world is at once old and new. It is the collaboration of political establishments with the criminal underworld—the political criminal nexus (PCN). These partnerships increasingly undermine the rule of law, human rights, and economic development in many parts of the world. States in transition are especially at risk. The insidious effects of PCNs, and even their very existence, are often obscured, not only deliberately by the players themselves but also by the tendency of security specialists to underestimate groups that operate outside the formal political structures and channels.

In some areas the PCN problem is chronic—for example, in Mexico, Nigeria, Turkey, and Taiwan. In such cases only the forms and players change. In other countries and regions—Colombia, Afghanistan, Sierra Leone, the Balkans, and the Caucuses—the problem is more acute, violent, and kaleidoscopic, and it often dominates political, economic, and social life.

As local problems become global and global problems have local effects, the complex and murky relations between criminals and political elites explain much, not only about local politics but about regional and global trends in world politics as well. These increasingly complicated dynamics have created different kinds of security challenges, the contours of which are only gradually coming into focus.

The first part of this chapter highlights the significance of the PCN problem and explains why it has become so important. The second part analyzes the causes of and the driving forces behind the PCN problem. Some will doubt that valid causal generalizations are possible about clandestine relationships. Indeed, such generalizations—and well-grounded theory and data—are not easy to come by. However, there have been a number of well-documented studies of these issues, which enable us to identify patterns, develop generalizations and hypotheses, and draw implications for policy.

Significantly, actors from the global level—the UN, the G-8, and the World Bank—to the regional—the EU and OAS—to national and subnational elites have begun to grapple with the PCN problem. They are prescribing solutions, passing international conventions, and authorizing expenditures for the use of force and other techniques of statecraft to manage the malady. Having reached conclusions about the cause of the problem, they are developing and implementing policy aimed at its management.

The final section of the chapter develops policy lessons and recommendations, identifying problems that have been underestimated or overestimated by others for ideological and bureaucratic reasons. It also suggests directions for future research that would strengthen analysis and ultimately help to prevent and ameliorate this global security challenge.

The Nature of the Political-Criminal Nexus

Definitions and Actors

Definitions are necessary to avoid the confusion that accompanies the many different types of political and criminal actors. Nonetheless, some definitions now in use are extremely broad. For example, some define regimes or governments as "criminal" because they systematically violate international conventions, such as the UN's 1948 Universal Declaration of Human Rights. While not disputing the criminal nature of some of these regimes, this definition is too broad for analytical purposes. It would include most if not all authoritarian regimes, from the Nazis and communist regimes of twentieth-century Europe to Panama under Noriega, and would erase the distinctional problems created by the collaboration of two sets of actors, politicians and the professional criminals.

Other definitions focus on individual political leaders and define their governments as criminal because the leaders themselves, or the political systems they manage, regularly violate the criminal statutes of their own societies. This category would include what have come to be known as "kleptocracies," systems headed by very corrupt leaders who use their political authority to enrich themselves, their families, and their political allies. Mobutu (The Congo), Abacha (Nigeria), and Estrada (Philippines) would appear to fall into this category.

The focus here is on the collaboration between two sets of groups and institutions, the political establishment and the criminal underworld. The involvement is sustained, although it may take different forms. Sometimes it is easy to distinguish between the two sets of players, as in the case of the American Cosa Nostra and the U.S. political establishment. When a political establishment knowingly and regularly does business with gang leaders, or when professional criminals are actually elected to power, as has happened in Sicily and Taiwan, the distinction is less straightforward. The lines between the two sets of players become less distinctive; and sometimes the political and the criminal merge.

The Criminals (Underworld)

The criminals, whose activities are substantially shielded from public view in the underworld, have a number of characteristics.[1] They are usually, but not always, professionals, and they make their livelihood primarily from crime. Some engage in legal as well as illegal professional activities. Their principal motive is profit, but they have secondary motives as well. The most important criminals are part of an organization, that is, they have ongoing relationships with other criminals.

The organization can be a hierarchical, vertical structure, such as the U.S. or Sicilian Cosa Nostra, or a more horizontal, egalitarian network, such as those found in organized crime in and around China and the Chinese communities scattered throughout the world. Geographic location can be local, regional, or transstate. The criminals purposefully violate national and often international conventions (for example, most importantly, the anti-drug-trafficking regime).

The Political Establishment (Upper World)

The political establishment, by contrast, must conduct at least some of its business in public. It is important to note the major distinction between the legal governmental establishment and the nonlegal, terrorist/separatist, revolutionary groups, such as Al Qaeda, Colombia's FARC, the Irish IRA, and Kosovo's KLA. The focus here is on the legal, governmental, and political establishment. Within this establishment there are diverse players and levels.

The first are officeholders in the executive, legislative, and judicial branches of government. They include those in security bureaucracies, the military, paramilitary, intelligence and security services, diverse police and law enforcement, prosecutors and judges. Usually these are both national and local, but they interact with transstate criminals who operate both inside and outside their territory. At the top are the president, prime minister, and various other ministers. These usually operate at the national level, but sometimes they also interact with transstate criminals.[2]

A second group are front men who work for or support official officeholders. They include political party officials, public relations firms, businesses, legal advisers, accountants, and NGOs supportive of parties. They usually are based nationally, but they often operate across state borders.[3] The third group is the legal opposition that rotates in and out of official positions; they and their front men and organizations are usually nationally based but often have transstate links to both legal and criminal actors.[4]

A PCN consists of relationships of varying degrees of cooperation among these political and criminal participants at the local, national, and transstate levels. These patterns fluctuate between various combinations of collaboration and conflict.[5] An initially stable pattern may become unbalanced over time, until a new, more stable equilibrium is reached. It sometimes evolves into open war between the partners, and the PCN is seriously weakened if not destroyed. For example, after decades of collaboration, both the criminals and the politicians were seriously damaged in Sicily in the 1980s and 1990s.[6] In most cases where a crime group has endured and prospered, however, whether in a democracy or an authoritarian regime, the criminals have reached some type of accommodation with political authorities at the local, national, or interstate level.

Criminal organizations that exist over a period of time benefit from collaboration, at least in their home state or region. Typically, where one sees a long history of organized crime, there is a PCN—for example, in southern Italy and on the U.S.–Mexican border.[7]

It should be noted, however, that not all political actors engaged in criminal or corrupt activities require a PCN. Political actors can behave in a criminal fashion—for example, they can become corrupt—without collaborating with the underworld, yet often they believe that such alliances are advantageous.

Why PCNs Are Transnational Security Threats

Why are PCNs transnational security threats and not simply local law enforcement or policy problems? Security threats interfere dramatically with the functioning of society. Conditions that threaten the political, economic, and social infrastructure of a country cannot be considered ordinary crime problems. Normally the infrastructure or framework provides the means for the reconciliation of differences within the system. For example, street crime and public health problems are not generally a security problem in the United States. The infrastructure can handle such problems, and they generally do not threaten the functioning of the legal or health system. By contrast, contemporary organized crime in Mexico and the spread of AIDS in much of southern Africa threaten the legal, economic, and social infrastructure of those societies. Even the perception that they threaten the infrastructure creates a security problem by diminishing confidence in central authority, or by creating alternative structures of power.

Especially in the world's many weak states and small states, the PCN is a major threat to governability and the rule of law. The PCN may not become the government. There may be major foreign policy or economic decisions that the top political leaders make without the consultation or major participation of criminal groups. But the PCN in these societies plays a role in determining major aspects of the infrastructure. For example, in elections or the appointments of key executives or judicial figures, or in key public investment decisions, tax policy, or trade policy, coalitions on diverse issues will be formed between political and criminal leaders. This will result in political appointments in the security area, prosecution policies, border controls, and so on. In the courts it will extend to who is prosecuted, who is convicted, what prison conditions or sanctions prevail. The PCN involves much more than a few corrupt officials. It can and sometimes does substantially control the politics of a country and how it normally works. It affects the functioning of much of the system and threatens the security of the rule of law. The balance within the PCN may at times go back and forth, however. Sometimes the politicians will dominate, sometimes the criminals. The specifics of how the PCN dominates a state vary. Regardless of who is dominant, the politicians or the criminals, the coalition of forces that is created influences many aspects of government, and the reconciliation of differences inside the country.

A key factor in the ability of the PCN to maintain power is its use of violence and intimidation. In addition to the use of violence by criminals, the PCN can mobilize the forces of the state when necessary to attain its goals. Once the public comes to fear those who should be their protectors—the police, intelligence, and security forces—and loses confidence in the electoral and judicial systems, they will seek alternatives, creating different patrons and loyalties, and further weaken the national infrastructure.

Particularly in a globalizing world, these are all areas of concern, because the PCN can operate on a local, national, regional, or transstate level. Its activities in one country or region undermine democratic governability, the rule of law, economic development, human rights, and the environment in that region. But a local or regional PCN also can, and often does, take advantage of zones of impunity or sanctuary in other regions to operate more effectively in its home state as well as in other regions. For example, a PCN in one state will use safe havens in others for production of illegal products, such as drugs and counterfeit goods; it uses transit zones in other regions for illegal activities, such as smuggling and access to markets; and it uses services in still other regions for money laundering, safe meetings, and false documents, particularly passports, including diplomatic passports. That the central governments of such states often have difficulty maintaining control over all their territory makes the possibility of an effective governmental response less likely.

This influence now often reaches beyond domestic activities. The PCN in one country or region is in a position to influence regional and global security concerns. It can affect state-to-state relationships, making normal relations all but impossible. For example, political decisions in the Balkans, on the U.S.–Mexican border, in Central and Southwest Asia, and in the Golden Triangle and Central Africa are affected by the PCN in other countries. Smuggling routes for drugs, arms, resources, and people from Southwest Asia are controlled by PCNs in the former CIS, the Balkans, and southern Italy. The reverse is also true. The Colombia PCN has played a major role in the evolution of politics and security in Mexico and the Caribbean. Decisions by the Colombian cartels to use the Mexican and Caribbean smuggling routes to the United States have resulted in massive national PCNs in these regions. Prior to these developments, they were local organizations, affecting local crime and corruption. This transformation changed the nature of politics and security in Central and South America, Mexico, the Caribbean, and the U.S. border area during the 1990s.

Of 192 states in the world today, approximately thirty-five have characteristics that maintain strong governance and rule of law and weak PCNs. Approximately 120 others can be classified as medium to weak to failed states (zones with very weak to nonexistent infrastructures).[8] They have medium to strong PCNs. In these states PCNs threaten the security of their own people as well as the security of people in other regions.

For example, the United States is affected by the activities of the PCNs of Eurasia, Mexico, and the Caribbean. Their involvement in drugs, illegal migration, violation of intellectual property rights, and the dissemination of weapons of mass destruction has a direct impact within the United States even though the United States itself appears to be relatively free of a domestic regional or national PCN.

To take another example, the People's Republic of China faces current and future threats both from inside the country and from PCNs abroad. Organized crime appears to be growing in China, and the PCN is also expanding. In some regions there is considerable Chinese public acknowledgment of these developments.[9] In others the sources are murkier. But it appears that inside mainland China the PCN gives power to particular coalitions that can use money and violence to maneuver against other groups and undermine decisions that affect the infrastructure of society.

The activities of the PCNs on the borders of China can also affect the infrastructure inside the country. For example, drug trafficking from Southeast Asia appears to be contributing to the spread of AIDS inside China as well as to increased levels of drug addiction. These internal effects may be strengthening political-criminal coalitions inside major areas of China. More powerful PCNs in China facilitate PCNs in other parts of the world through their involvement in intellectual property violations, piracy in the South China Sea, and the manufacture of precursor chemicals, all problematic developments. China has vast borders that are difficult to control, and its economy is now developing at a rapid rate, offering attractive opportunities for exploitation, both legitimate and illegitimate.

The activities of PCNs become particularly important in certain circumstances. For example, in regions that possess weapons of mass destruction, PCNs can facilitate the export of these weapons or their components and also facilitate the import of components into their own or other states. This could be a threat in Russia and perhaps China.[10]

Regions and sectors that are important to the global economy, such as the economic and financial sectors, are vulnerable to PCNs. China, South Asia, and Mexico, for example, are involved in massive counterfeiting of goods and violations of intellectual property rights damaging to the economies of the United States and other countries. PCNs may also help criminals gain control of key sectors of the economic security infrastructure, such as telecommunications or financial services. PCNs affect regional cooperation, color relations with other states, and contribute to local instability in geostrategic regions of concern.

International Responses

Many governments and international institutions now maintain that organized crime, interstate crime, and corruption are security threats. There also has been increasing recognition of the linkage between the upper and underworlds, although few have explicitly recognized the PCN as a security threat.

The United States first spelled out the security threat from organized crime in a comprehensive manner in 1995 and has been incorporating it into policy and planning ever since. The Clinton administration's Presidential Decision Directive (PDD) 42 states unequivocally that organized crime is a threat to national security. The same year, President Clinton's address to the UN's fiftieth anniversary assembly drew attention to organized crime as a global threat. Three years later "The U.S. International Crime-Control Strategy," the first attempt to devise a national strategy, was published. It recognizes the threat of international crime to the integrity of government. By 2000 there was specific recognition of the dangers of PCNs. A

U.S. interagency working group published the first "International Crime Threat Assessment," recognizing the PCN as a security threat.[11]

At its 1998 Summit in Birmingham, England, the G-8 began to focus on organized crime as a security threat and established a senior experts group, known as the Lyon group. Not all members of the G-8 specifically endorsed the perception of the PCN as a security problem, but some, especially Germany, regard the PCN as a significant security threat.

The United Nations, and especially its Office of Drug Control and Crime Prevention in Vienna, has been increasingly concerned in recent years with interstate crime, particularly drugs, trafficking in people, and corruption. Budgets for countering high-level crime and corruption have been increased, but as yet there has been little explicit recognition by the UN of the PCN as a significant threat.[12]

Causes and Conditions

Motives

Criminals are insecure. Their lives and well-being are at risk. There is no individual or group to protect them and their families from their own governments, foreign political actors, or rivals inside or outside their own circles. Criminals need protection, impunity, security, and assistance in facilitating their activities. Collaboration with the upper world can bring protection against law enforcement and also some protection from rival criminals, both inside and outside their own organizations. As further protection, through their PCN connections they can obtain information from the police, intelligence, and the military to help neutralize their opponents.[13]

The criminals also want economic information from government sources that can be exploited for profit. For example, advance information on government economic policy and regulatory activity enables them to take advantage of privatization plans, bids for public contracts, sales of licenses, and other opportunities. For states in transition, such as the countries of the former Soviet Union, this has been a particular problem.[14]

Successful criminal elites often want to be accepted by the upper world and seek social mobility for themselves and their families. They often want to mix with celebrities, be seen in fashionable places, and have their families blessed by senior religious authorities. They want respect from the best and most powerful in their societies. Often they surround themselves with symbols of wealth and power, large houses, even private zoos.[15]

The political elites who collaborate with the powerful underworld are driven by a variety of motives. A principal motive, obviously, is money for personal or political purposes—to finance lavish lifestyles, win elections, and maintain their leadership roles. Criminal connections can also facilitate services for corrupt business or money laundering for the politicians.[16]

Fear of physical threats to family and position have influenced some. When offered the choice of "silver or lead," most will choose silver. If a politician has collaborated with criminals early in his career and later become successful, he will not be allowed to walk away from the relationship, or may continue it out of physical or psychological pressure.[17] Criminals are often in a position to perform other services and favors, such as providing intelligence on rivals at home and abroad, disrupting or even eliminating political rivals (e.g., Taiwan in the 1970s), or securing votes in particular regions (e.g., Sicily and Taiwan in the 1980s).[18]

There are also areas in which strong cultural and familial connections or long traditions of association and collaboration bring politicians and criminals together. This is the case in southern Italy and on the island of Sicily.[19]

Structural Conditions

It is possible to identify political, social, and economic factors that facilitate the formation and evolution of PCNs.

Political Factors. Where the state is too unitary or noncompetitive, and/or where it and its bureaucracies are too strong relative to civil society, PCNs tend to develop. Examples of the former were Mexico's one-party system, Russia's one-party legacy, and Colombia's clientele-based system, in which state assets and services are viewed as bounty. The lack of checks and balances, in the form of either civil society or opposition political parties, helps explain this tendency. Even in the United States, there are particular regions where this condition appears to be present—New York City, for example. In spite of a generally vibrant civil society, contractors for decades worked with the U.S. Cosa Nostra and local officials in order to meet construction schedules and avoid becoming bogged down in red tape or labor strife. The PCN was used to bypass bureaucratic inefficiencies. In this case as elsewhere, checks and balances, the development of civil society, and particularly, various types of watchdog groups help to weaken the PCN.[20]

Regimes and bureaucracies that are weak relative to society or other political actors tend to develop PCNs. In these circumstances, inefficient premodern institutions, patronage systems, and governmental inability to compel citizens or officials to obey the laws appears to explain the tendency. Examples include Colombia's inability in the 1980s to stamp out prolonged violence associated with drug trafficking and to resolve conflicts in the private sector. Similarly, the Nigerian government's inability to police itself and Mexico's antiquated law enforcement agencies, as it began to engage in a democratic transition in the 1980s and 1990s, also illustrate this condition.

Where these conditions are present efforts should be made to strengthen the state's weak institutions. For example, foreign aid programs to professionalize law enforcement agencies and strengthen conflict-resolution mechanisms could ameliorate this condition. U.S. law enforcement assistance to Italy in the 1980s and 1990s appears to have played a role in dramatically weakening the PCN in Sicily. Aid to Colombia in the 1980s contributed to the near-total destruction of the Medellin and Cali PCNs.[21]

Contemporary political systems in transition appear to be particularly susceptible to the development of PCNs. Russia, Ukraine, Mexico, Georgia, Taiwan, and maybe China illustrate this propensity. (Portugal and perhaps Spain, possibly because their transitions were completed during the cold war, appear to be exceptions to this general pattern.) This seems to be true for most if not all former communist and totalitarian states and authoritarian regimes in the post–cold war era. Economic and political transitions create uncertainty about what norms of behavior are acceptable and provide an extremely favorable environment for former and current state officials to work with criminal opportunists. Moreover, the transition of institutions such as law enforcement appears to be characterized by a period where control is secured neither by the old (authoritarian or premodern) institutions, nor by the new (more modern and democratic) successor institutions. This condition may be amenable over time to change by policy actions, for example, the transfer of institutional expertise and experience from other states. The policy implication is that in aiding transition states, one should be mindful of this problem and focus on developing efficient institutions, perhaps even before the framework of the old ones is discarded. This finding bears directly on current policymaking toward Cuba and China, to name only two.

A criminal organization's capacity to mediate between the state and individuals tends to draw loyalty away from the state and toward the criminal organization, thereby increasing both the strength of the criminal organization and the occasions for political-criminal collaboration. This occurred in Sicily, where for many decades the Mafia mediated between state and local communities.[22] The degree to which state institutions can prevent penetration and exploitation by cohesive subnational groups is another factor. For example, Nigeria's PCN has been entrenched by ethnic groups and probably also secret societies that penetrated and occupied state institutions.[23]

Cultural Factors. Cultural factors also play a role in facilitating PCNs. Certain subcultural traits or characteristics have been identified as significant variables. Patron-client systems, for example, in Mexico and southern Italy, tend to make politics personal. Individuals, both criminal and noncriminal, accept that economic and personal conflicts can be solved by leaders with personal clout and the ability to threaten or provide physical security.

A prevalence of secret societies, as in the case of China and ethnic Chinese societies in many parts of the Pacific Rim, is another contributing factor.[24] Secret societies in Nigeria also appear to have been significant in the rise of the PCN. The Italian Mafia-Freemasonry connection in the 1970s and 1980s helped create conditions of covertness that facilitated the development of PCNs.[25]

A widespread public perception that corruption is "normal," as has been the case in much of twentieth-century Nigeria, Mexico, and Hong Kong, has contributed to the rise of PCNs. When confidence in the accountability, trustworthiness, and efficiency of government is undermined, when the line between criminality and politics blurs, when respect for wealth, regardless of its source, is encouraged, there is fertile ground for the rise of PCNs.[26]

In some societies the public perception of criminals as cultural heroes or "men of honor" bestows an aura of legitimacy on illegal activities.[27] When, for example, "Mafia" leaders are respected or Mexican drug barons are idolized by young people for their power and money—such as we see in the popular music along the U.S.-Mexican border—or when they are applauded by the church for their charitable work, the stigma attached to criminal conduct and violence is diminished.[28]

These factors contribute to the social context that facilitates or retards political-criminal relationships. Changes in culture can facilitate a breakup of a PCN, as evidenced by the apparently effective efforts in Sicily and Hong Kong. In Sicily, over the past twenty years, policymakers and law enforcement officials developed allies from many parts of society—the Church, the arts, entertainment, and education—in order to undermine cultural acceptance of patron-client relationships and the Mafia and weaken the PCN.[29] Similarly, in Hong Kong since the mid-1970s, law enforcement has been combined with extensive education and prevention campaigns. A central component of this effort is a strong community-outreach program, including publicity campaigns (radio, television, and posters), business ethics programs, and moral education for primary and secondary school students. This approach in Sicily and Hong Kong appears to have been successful in weakening the traditional culture of corruption prevalent in these societies and strengthening a culture of lawfulness.[30]

Economic Factors. Not surprisingly, markets and economics bear on the strength or weakness of PCNs. For example, the vast quantity of drug money that needed to be laundered in Colombia made the establishment of national-level PCNs a major goal of the criminals. Another factor is the level of efficiency and service provided to legitimate economic actors by criminal organizations and their political collaborators. For example, when domestic currency is devalued and unstable, entrepreneurs' access to foreign currencies may come only through criminal organizations. Similarly, criminal bankers often provide speed, simplicity, and confidentiality that surpass the services offered by legitimate banks, even for legitimate activities, let alone for tax evasion and money laundering. Specific national economic policies also can contribute to a climate conducive to criminal and political-criminal activities. For example, Colombia's tax-amnesty schemes tended to encourage links between illicit money and the formal economy.[31] Economic factors at the local level also play a role. Local criminal groups in Mexico and Sicily had the capacity to direct local government contracts and exercise control over local job opportunities.[32]

The supply-and-demand dynamics of illegal goods and services strengthen PCNs. The demand for illegal goods and services and the effort to supply that demand can contribute in a significant way to the creation of organized crime and hence PCNs. But this general concern is often so broad and amorphous as to be unhelpful when formulating concrete diagnoses and policy prescriptions. The policy implications of economic factors will vary according to the specific economic factor in question. However, attentiveness to the kinds of economic situations that promote PCNs can help analysts detect and minimize them.

Although difficult to use from a rigorous scientific perspective, it is important to recognize the role of contingent, accidental, or coincidental factors in the development of PCNs. Among the contingent factors that have been identified so far are specific individuals and specific political circumstances. PCNs often develop opportunistically, as when a specific person occupying a particular government or criminal position at a particular time may have a singular impact. Individuals who were critical to PCNs were Pablo Escobar and the Rodriguez-Orejuela brothers of the Colombian Medellin and Cali cartels, respectively, and Amado Carillo Fuentes in Mexico. In the 1970s and 1980s these leaders brought the Colombian and Mexican drug-producing and smuggling organizations into global prominence, in the process developing entrenched PCNs in Colombia, Mexico, and elsewhere.[33]

In certain cases one can identify particular political circumstances that have led to the emergence of a PCN. For example, in Italy in 1948 the Christian Democratic Party's need for political support in Sicily in order to compete with the Communists allied the Christian Democrats with the reviving Mafia.[34] This electoral reliance on the Mafia was a particular contingent condition. When this condition changed, as it did in the late 1980s with the end of the cold war, the relationship became less important. This change in conditions helped lead to the weakening (but not the elimination) of the Sicilian Mafia.[35] There are clear policy implications for contingent factors. For example, where individuals appear to be the keys to a PCN, these people can be identified and targeted for law enforcement or other disruptive actions. In the 1980s U.S. law enforcement came to the aid of specific parts of the Colombian and Mexican governments by helping to target the key figures of their drug cartels. This contributed to the incarceration, death, or removal of key members of the cartels' leadership, the splintering of the criminal organizations, and the weakening of the PCNs.[36]

Different types of criminal activity and diverse concentrations of criminal actors lead to different types of PCNs. Local smugglers and criminal organizations need to develop relationships with local law enforcement authorities, but they may have few relationships with state or national officials. In this case the PCN would be narrow, focused, and likely to have only limited impact on the larger society. By contrast, a criminal organization with a broader and deeper local or regional base, such as the Sicilian Mafia, with diverse profit-making activities, may seek numerous and varied relationships with political actors of all types at all levels. A PCN of this type would have more serious implications for the host society. Understanding these differences can inform policy by allowing the more dangerous types of PCN to be prioritized and targeted. As resources are limited, devising criteria for differentiating among PCNs is significant.

PCN relationships, like others, are dynamic. Early on in a given relationship one partner (either the political actor or the criminal) will be dominant. Over time, as conditions change, this dynamic may be reversed. In Sicily from the 1950s to the

1970s, the criminals were the dominant partners. When they felt their power waning in the 1980s, they went to war, that is, they used terrorism against the political class and the state, including some of their former partners. For this and other reasons, the PCN was weakened and nearly destroyed, as other political forces and civil society mobilized against the Mafia and their former political allies.

In Mexico PCNs for decades tended to be dominated by political actors, but this changed as political and economic transitions began taking place in the 1980s.[37] During the 1980s an increased concern for democracy and law enforcement consistent with human rights left government weaker and law enforcement less effective. Increasing resources from the cocaine trade and other activities enabled criminals to become more assertive and violent. At present the two sides appear to be fairly equal in strength, as is demonstrated by the large-scale violence among political and criminal actors in that country.

In the twentieth century PCNs tended to arise, evolve, and sometimes disappear. In the United States the creation of oversight bodies for state contracting, programs to increase competency of government officials and administrators, the use of special prosecutors and task forces, and witness protection programs substantially diminished PCNs in various regions, particularly in the case of the American Cosa Nostra and its political connections.[38]

As this diagnosis has shown, PCNs have a variety of causes, both motivational and structural, and these appear in many complex combinations. Monocausal explanations are incomplete and insufficient. Money is not always the sine qua non; other interests and insecurities may also play a role. Remedies aimed solely at one type of motivation or one type of structural factor are less likely to be successful than more comprehensive ones. Some elements can be generalized, but not all. States in transition, for example, in their fluid and complex conditions, need to be addressed differently from those with well-established institutions.

Many diagnoses tend toward political explanations and the financial motivations of criminals. Their policy implications emphasize professionalization of law enforcement, for example. Because they also tend to subscribe to the theory that money is the principal motivation of criminals, policy is focused on the effort to cut off the money and seize the assets. Those who employ economic explanations also seek to use market forces to affect outcomes by controlling the supply of drugs. However, the economic and law enforcement or regulatory approach appears to be inadequate because it fails to address the many other contributory factors.

Policy Lessons

In recent years governments and global and regional bodies have focused primarily on ameliorating the causes and conditions that facilitate organized and transstate crime. Increasingly, some have addressed corruption and protecting the integrity of the political establishment. The PCN itself, however, has rarely been the focus, and when it has governmental policy has addressed the political and institutional factors that facilitate organized crime, rather than the motivations of the establishment. Usually the focus on criminals has been on improving the effectiveness of law enforcement and regulatory systems in weak or transitional states, as well as on regional and global law enforcement cooperation. Hence the focus has been on interdicting local and transstate criminals, with less attention sometimes focused on criminal efforts to corrupt government officials, particularly at the lower levels.

There have also been efforts to affect the supply of some illegal goods and services. Most efforts have been devoted to influencing the producers of opium and coca by providing opportunities to raise alternative crops.[39] There have also been other financial incentives and sanctions for establishment figures involved in laundering drug money, both of the criminals and of the political establishment generally.[40]

So far, however, there have been only a few efforts to address the global challenge of the PCN. The problem has been viewed by governments and nongovernmental specialists primarily from a criminal law enforcement perspective, with supplementary assistance requested from diplomats and intelligence practitioners and specialists in alternative development.

There also has been little effort to develop strategic approaches to managing the problem. Such an approach would involve detailed assessments of the problem, prioritization of objectives, the sustained mobilization and calibration of resources and the means to achieve priority objectives, and evaluations of performance.

Assessments are needed to identify the specific threats and their causes and to exploit opportunities to prevent or break the linkages between the upper and underworlds. What factors or conditions that spawn PCNs are amenable to change, and over what period of time? What practices have been effective in preventing or breaking such linkages, and are they replicable?

Second, what are the key priorities? Presumably some PCNs are more important than others. Several G-8 nations have become particularly concerned with "Russian organized crime" and its political linkages in Russia. What should the other priorities be? Should the PCN in China also be of regional and global concern? What efforts are being made to establish a global coalition to identify and build consensus on the priorities?

Third, there is a need for a realistic appraisal of the long-term means and resources that will be needed to address, manage, and minimize the priority PCNs. The relatively meager resources and means that have been mobilized to fight and prevent even transstate organized crime in the past decade have been insufficient. No doubt the problem would have been worse had governments not taken the steps they have. But even the United States, the United Kingdom, and the Federal Republic of Germany, among the most mobilized and capable of governments, have not been able to reverse the general growth of transnational organized crime and PCNs, although there have been some successes.[41]

It appears that more than governments will be needed to manage the problem of the PCNs. There is almost certainly a necessary and important role for civil society and private sectors in the mix, particularly in the management of cultural factors.

In recent years there has been growing recognition in some governments and international institutions that cultural and educational resources are necessary to complement law enforcement and intelligence in managing and preventing major crime and corruption.

The term "culture of lawfulness" describes a dominant or mainstream culture and ethos sympathetic to the rule of law. In such a culture the average person believes that legal norms are a fundamental part of justice and that the culture's legal and judicial system enhances the quality of life of individuals and society as a whole. To achieve a culture of lawfulness, various social institutions must be mobilized. In places as diverse as Western Sicily and Hong Kong, formal school-based education for all youngsters, centers of moral authority such as religious institutions and NGOs, and the mass media have all played a part in contributing to a culture of lawfulness.[42]   These cultural methods of combating PCNs are very inexpensive in comparison to the material costs of paramilitary activities, intelligence, and law enforcement. For a medium-sized state, it is estimated that as little as $1 million per year, for five to ten years, would be needed to design and implement a basic program for the creation of a culture supportive of the rule of law.

Some of those resources also could be devoted to intensifying the sense of insecurity among criminals and in deterring some from entering a life of crime in the first place. Depicting the criminal lifestyle as one of permanent anxiety, albeit under a thin veneer of glamour, is one part of such a strategy. In addition, security can be offered to those willing to give up criminal lifestyles through witness protection programs for key figures who need it. Exposure and publicity in the media are powerful tools that can shatter the links between criminals and their political allies. But there has been almost no planning or implementation, on the regional or global level, to synchronize what have been called "two wheels of the cart"—law enforcement and culture—and until this changes we can expect to see little progress from exclusively political and economic "solutions."

Finally, there will be a need for a periodic review and evaluation of performance outputs. It is relatively easy to measure inputs, such as how much money is spent. It is much more difficult, intellectually and politically, to measure outputs. But such measurements are needed to guide strategic planning to manage this very complex and murky problem of the collaboration between the political establishment and the underworlds. Evaluation, recalibration, and reevaluation are usually the weak point in strategy, however. While the U.S. "International Crime-Control Strategy" was an important first step, almost no evaluation was built into the process to determine whether the means were achieving the intended goals. Nor were the goals prioritized, and there is confusion between ends and means. (Only the U.S. Office of Drug Control Policy has proposed to engage in systematic evaluations of U.S. efforts.)[43]

Developing and refining the strategies are the work of both governments and nongovernmental specialists, both within and across state boundaries. One impediment in this case, however, is that many governmental leaders are uncomfortable with investigating their senior foreign political, intelligence, and law enforcement counterparts. This makes it very difficult to conduct official business, especially countering crime and corruption with officials or bureaucracies known to be corrupt. Moreover, some bureaucracies also are not comfortable with the dangerous work of probing the links between criminals with the political establishments of the world.[44]

While some of this work can be undertaken by academics and other nongovernmental specialists, the global security requirement of the early twenty-first century requires a partnership between governmental and nongovernmental sectors. Democratic governments have the primary resources and capabilities to assess the clandestine linkages of the PCN, while nongovernmental specialists have the independent analytical capabilities to help governments in such assessments and to study effective practices and evaluate performance.

Although there has been some teaching, research, and training on the security threat of nonstate actors in the United States, UK, and some other countries (for example, about terrorism and ethnic conflict), systematic work on these problems is only just beginning.

Conclusion

Collaboration between governments and gangsters, in ways that significantly affect security, is much more than the stuff of fiction. While it is not new, the magnitude of the problem today is unprecedented. Some regions are affected more than others, but in an era of increasing globalization the problem reaches into most corners of the world. The causes, however, do not lend themselves to straightforward solutions. These causes can be viewed from the perspectives of economic, political, and cultural structures that give rise to the incentives for the collaboration of political and criminal elites. Or they can be ascertained from examining the motivations of the respective elites, given the condition of contemporary world politics and the specific conditions in their environment.

Many governmental players—at both the national and the international levels—and some civil society or "third-sector" actors have begun to recognize the severity of the problem. On the whole, however, their prescriptions are not based on multicausality or on a strategic approach to the problem. Usually the search for solutions has focused on criminals rather than on the dynamic relationships between the political and criminal players. Moreover, the explanation for PCNs most often given is that in the current era of multiple transitions to democracy, the problem is primarily one of weak governments and the absence of strong legal institutions. While these appear to be major contributing factors, they are not the sole determinants.

Finally, few governmental players in the United States and elsewhere appear to have taken a strategic approach to the global challenge of the PCN. Very little exists in the way of detailed assessments and studies. There has been little prioritization of objectives, too few calculations of the required resources for the mobilization and calibration of means both in government and the private sector that are needed over the short as well as the medium term. Nor has there been a systematic attempt to evaluate and recalibrate performance.

The outlook for the near to medium term is not particularly encouraging. Since the 1980s there have been some successes—for example, in Sicily and the United States. The PCNs involving the Sicilian and the U.S. Cosa Nostra and the political establishments in their respective regions have declined dramatically. In other regions the problem probably would have been worse if governments and third-sector organizations had not made some efforts to prevent or to break up PCNs. On balance, however, it is difficult to find reasons for optimism.

Governments and civil society were moving in the right direction prior to September 11, 2001. Since then, attention has shifted away from transnational crime and its connections to political establishments and has focused instead on terrorism and its connections to strong and weak states. It is possible that the shift in priorities will have a positive effect in helping to combat and prevent PCNs. Terrorist-political linkages, particularly in regions that have weak governments, are now viewed as important. Moreover, there is overlap between terrorists and other criminals. Both need money, arms, money laundering, false documents, secret methods of communication, and safe havens, and both stand to gain from political connections. As governments and civil societies in various regions mobilize and collaborate to prevent and manage terrorist groups and their political linkages, they may find it useful to develop a strategic approach, which also will be helpful in preventing and curtailing PCNs.

Notes

1. There have been many attempts to define organized crime and transstate organized crime; definitions vary among countries, organizations, and agencies. For my purposes, *crime* refers to illegal activities conducted either by organized groups/networks or individuals acting independently. *Organized crime* refers to individuals and groups with ongoing working relationships who make their living primarily through activities that one or more states deem illegal and criminal. Organized crime can take a variety of institutional or organizational forms. This includes tight vertical hierarchies with lifelong commitments, as well as looser, more ephemeral, nonhierarchical relationships. *Transstate crime* refers to organized criminal activities and enterprises that operate across national boundaries. *Disorganized crime*, by contrast, is crime committed by individuals or small groups acting in isolation.

The UN Convention against Transnational Organized Crime defines "organized criminal group" as "a structured group of three or more persons, existing for a period of time and acting in concert with the aim of committing one or more serious crimes or offences established in accordance with this Convention, in order to obtain, directly or indirectly, a financial or other material benefit" (G.A. res. 55/25, annex I, 55 UN GAOR Supp. (no. 49) at 44, UN Doc. A/45/49 (vol. 1), 2001). The United States is one of 124 countries to sign this UN convention at the Palermo conference of Dec. 12–15, 2000. See also Howard Abadinsky,

Organized Crime, 6th ed., (Stamford, Conn.: Thomson Learning, 2000). On the problem of defining organized crime, see Michael D. Maltz, "Defining Organized Crime," in *Handbook of Organized Crime in the United States,* ed. Robert J. Kelly et al. (Westport, Conn.: Greenwood Publishing Group, 1994), 21–37; Mark Findlay, *The Globalization of Crime: Understanding Transitional Relationships in Context* (Cambridge: Cambridge University Press, 1999). Klaus von Lampe has compiled a useful compendium of definitions by organized crime specialists from various countries. It can be accessed at his website, http://people.freenet.de/kvlampe/OCDEF1.htm. Criminologists in mainland China have also sought to differentiate between various types or levels of organized crime according to their levels of sophistication and organizational needs, namely, ordinary and relatively disorganized groups and gangs, "underground groups of a criminal nature," and the highest level, almost certainly involving significant political collaboration, "underground criminal organizations." See especially the work of Professor He Bingsong of the China University of Law and Political Science.

2. On the Salinas-Citibank connection, see U.S. General Accounting Office, "Private Banking: Raul Salinas, Citibank, and Alleged Money Laundering," report to the Permanent Subcommittee on Investigations, Committee on Governmental Affairs, U.S. Senate, Oct. 1998, GAO/OSI-99-1. See also John Bailey and Roy Godson, eds., *Organized Crime and Democratic Governability: Mexico and the US-Mexican Borderlands* (Pittsburgh: University of Pittsburgh Press, 2001); Eduardo Varela-Cid, *Hidden Fortunes: Drug Money, Cartels, and the Elite Banks,* trans. Michael C. Berman (New York: Hudson Street Press, 1999).

3. See also June T. Dreyer, "The Emerging Political-Criminal Nexus in the People's Republic of China" (draft paper prepared for joint meeting of the U.S. and Chinese Working Groups on Political-Criminal Collaboration in the PRC, National Strategy Information Center, Dec. 2001).

4. See, for example, KoLin Chin, "Black Gold Politics: Organized Crime, Business, and Politics in Taiwan" (draft paper prepared for joint meeting of the U.S. and Chinese Working Groups on Political-Criminal Collaboration in the PRC, National Strategy Information Center, Dec. 2001); Paul Klebnikov, *Godfather of the Kremlin: Boris Berezovsky and the Looting of Russia* (New York: Harcourt, 2000).

5. For a description of a typology of PCNs within one country, see Bailey and Godson, *Organized Crime and Democratic Governability,* esp. the introduction.

6. For the recollections of key leaders in the anti-Mafia movement, see Leoluca Orlando, *Fighting the Mafia and Renewing Sicilian Culture* (San Francisco: Encounter Books, 2001). Among the best analyses in English and Italian is Letizia Paoli, "The Pledge to Secrecy: Culture, Structure and Action of Mafia Associations," (Ph.D. diss., European University Institute, Florence, 1997).

7. Stanley A. Pimentel, "The Nexus of Organized Crime and Politics in Mexico"; Luis Astorga, "Organized Crime and the Organization of Crime"; Louis R. Sadler, "The Historical Dynamics of Smuggling in the U.S.-Mexican Border Region, 1550–1998," all in Bailey and Godson, *Organized Crime and Democratic Governability.*

8. This calculation is based on several data sources, originally brought to my attention by Matthew M. Taylor, a Ph.D. candidate at Georgetown University. The major data sources are listed below. The combination of these sources suggests that most of the states in the world can be categorized as having medium to weak to failing governmental systems. It can be deduced further that in many if not all of these states, the PCN tends to be medium to strong. As far as is known, there is no published survey of the strength and weakness of the

PCN in states characterized as having weak or strong governments. See UN membership list, accessed at www.un.org/Overview/unmember.html; www.worldaudit.org/polrights.html; Daniel Kaufman, Aart Kraay, and Pablo Zoido-Lobaton, "Governance Matters," accessed in May 1999 at www.imf.org/external/pubs/ft/fandd/2000/06/kauf.html; Freedom House, "Annual Survey of Freedom Country Scores 1972–73 to 1999–2000," accessed at http://216.119.117.183/.

9. June T. Dreyer, "The Emerging Political-Criminal Nexus."

10. Former Senate Majority Leader Howard Baker and former counsel to the president Lloyd Cutler chaired a U.S. Department of Energy bipartisan task force in 2000–2001 that concluded, "The most urgent unmet national security threat to the United States today is the danger that weapons of mass destruction or weapons-usable material in Russia could be stolen and sold to terrorists or hostile nation states and used against American troops abroad or citizens at home" (Howard Baker and Lloyd Cutler, "A Report Card on the Department of Energy's Nonproliferation Programs with Russia," Jan. 10, 2001. The report can be accessed at www.hr.doe.gov/seab/).

11. White House, *International Crime Threat Assessment,* esp. 10–13, accessed at http://clinton4.nara.gov/WH/EOP/NSC/html/documents/pub45270/pub45270index.html.   See also Anthony Lake, *Six Nightmares: Real Threats in a Dangerous World and How America Can Meet Them* (Boston: Little, Brown, 2000.)

12. UN Convention against Transnational Organized Crime. For estimates of the prevalence and costs of transnational crime according to the UN's eighteen categories of transnational crime, see Gerhard O. W. Mueller's "Transnational Crime: Definitions and Concepts" in *Combating Transnational Crime: Concepts, Activities and Responses,* ed. Phil Williams and Dimitri Vlassis (Portland: Frank Cass, 2001).

13. See, for example, Pimentel, "The Nexus of Organized Crime and Politics in Mexico."

14. Louise I. Shelley, "Russia and Ukraine: Transition or Tragedy," *Trends in Organized Crime* 4 (spring 1999); U.S. Government Interagency Working Group, "International Crime Threat Assessment"; Richard Palmer, with Vladimir Brovkin, *The New Russian Oligarchy: The Nomenklatura, the KGB, and the Mafiya* (unpublished manuscript).

15. Robert J. Nieves, *Colombian Cocaine Cartels: Lessons from the Front* (Washington, D.C.: National Strategy Information Center, 1997).

16. See Pimentel, "The Nexus of Organized Crime and Politics in Mexico."

17. Nieves, *Colombian Cocaine Cartels;* Roberto E. Blum, "Corruption and Complicity: Mortar of Mexico's Political System?" *Trends in Organized Crime* 3 (fall 1997).

18. David E. Kaplan, *Fires of the Dragon: Politics, Murder, and the Kuomintang* (New York: Atheneum, 1992); Orlando, *Fighting the Mafia.*

19. Enzo Lodato, "The Palermo Renaissance," *Trends in Organized Crime* 5 (spring 2000).

20. Robert J. Kelly, "An American Way of Crime and Corruption," *Trends in Organized Crime* 5 (winter 2000).

21. Nieves, *Colombian Cocaine Cartels.*

22. Paoli, "The Pledge to Secrecy."

23. Obe N. I. Ebbi, "Slicing Nigeria's 'National Cake,'" *Trends in Organized Crime* 4 (spring 1999).

24. W. P. Morgan, *Triad Societies in Hong Kong* (Hong Kong: Government Press, 1960); W. P. Morgan, *Triad Societies* (general briefing paper, Royal Hong Kong Police, 1996); Jean Chesneaux, ed., *Popular Movements and Secret Societies in China 1840–1950* (Stanford: Stanford

University Press, 1972); Frederic Wakeman Jr., *Policing Shanghai, 1927–1937* (Berkeley: University of California Press, 1995).

25. Paoli, "The Pledge to Secrecy." See also Pino Arlacchi, *Addio Cosa Nostra: La vita di Tommaso Buscetta* (Milan: Rizzoli, 1994); Ebbe, "Slicing Nigeria's 'National Cake'"; Bailey and Godson, *Organized Crime and Democratic Governability.*

26. T. Wing Lo, "Pioneer of Moral Education: Independent Commission against Corruption (ICAC)," *Trends in Organized Crime* 4 (winter 1998).

27. Paoli, "The Pledge to Secrecy."

28. Terrence E. Poppa, *Drug Lord: The Life and Death of a Mexican Kingpin, A True Story,* 2d ed. (Seattle: Demand Publications, 1998).

29. Orlando, *Fighting the Mafia.*

30. Lo, "Pioneer of Moral Education"; Alan Lai, "A Quiet Revolution: The Hong Kong Experience," *Trends in Organized Crime* (spring 2000); Richard C. LaMagna, *Changing a Culture of Corruption: How Hong Kong's Independent Commission against Corruption Succeeded in Furthering a Culture of Lawfulness* (Washington, D.C.: National Strategy Information Center, 1999).

31. Rensselaer W. Lee III and Francisco E. Thuomi, "Did the Traffickers Subvert Democracy in Colombia?" *Trends in Organized Crime* 5 (winter 1999).

32. Orlando, *Fighting the Mafia.*

33. See Pimentel, "The Nexus of Organized Crime."

34. Salvatore Lupo, "The Allies and the Mafia," *Journal of Modern Italian Studies* 2 (spring 1997).

35. Jane C. Schneider and Peter T. Schneider, *Reversible Destiny: Mafia, Antimafia, and the Struggle for Palermo* (Berkeley: University of California Press, 2003).

36. Nieves, *Colombian Cocaine Cartels.*

37. Bailey and Godson, *Organized Crime and Democratic Governability.*

38. James B. Jacobs, *Gotham Unbound* (New York: New York University Press, 1999); James B. Jacobs, Christopher Panarella, and Jay Worthington, *Busting the Mob: The United States vs. Cosa Nostra* (New York: New York University Press, 1996).

39. *UN Action Plan on International Cooperation on the Eradication of Illicit Drugs and on Alternative Development,* 1998, accessed at the website of the UN Office for Drug Control and Crime Prevention, at www.undcp.org/resolution_1998-09-08_3.html#E.

40. See, for example, UN, *Declaration against Corruption and Bribery in International Commercial Transactions,* Dec. 1996; Organization For Economic Cooperation and Development (OECD), *Convention on Combating Bribery of Foreign Officials in International Business Transactions,* Dec. 1997; *Guiding Principles for Fighting Corruption and Safeguarding Integrity among Justice and Security Officials,* A Global Forum on Fighting Corruption: Safeguarding Integrity among Justice and Security Officials, Washington, D.C., Feb. 24–26, 1999, accessed at www.state.gov/g/inl/rls/rpt/fgcrpt/2001/3161.htm.

41. For one critique of "The U.S. International Crime-Control Strategy" and the responses of some U.S. officials, see the U.S. General Accounting Office Report, "International Crime Control: Sustained Executive Level Coordination of Federal Response Needed," GAO-01-629, Aug. 2001, Washington, D.C.

42. See, for example, the autobiography of Leoluca Orlando, *Fighting the Mafia.* See also the special issue of *Trends in Organized Crime* 5 (spring 2000), which is devoted to building a culture of lawfulness.

43. White House Office of National Drug Control Policy, *Performance Measures of Effectiveness, Report for 2001*, Washington, D.C., 2001. For a discussion of measuring outputs, see David H. Bayley, *Police for the Future* (New York: Oxford University Press, 1994).

44. There is also the matter of conflicting governmental priorities. It may be judged to be more important to secure the support of a foreign government or element of a foreign government to achieve overarching foreign policy objectives than to deal with the PCN relationships in that country. Many believe that this explains the U.S. government's apparent failure to confront, for example, the Italian and Mexican governments about their PCNs during much of the cold war.

Chapter 13   Transnational Terrorism
and Security

Audrey Kurth Cronin

As the world's predominant military and economic power, the United States is in a position to pursue its interests around the globe with unprecedented strength and reach. Even in the wake of the attacks of September 11, 2001, and especially after the U.S. military action in Afghanistan and Iraq, the threat of transnational terrorism, mostly consisting of underfunded and ad hoc cells motivated by radical fringe ideas, seems almost frivolous in comparison. American strategic culture has a long tradition of downplaying such atypical concerns in comparison to more conventional state-based centers of military and political power. This has been an effective approach, on the whole, as was clearly and dramatically demonstrated in Afghanistan and Iraq, the U.S. military knows how to destroy governments and their armed forces, and the American leadership and public have a natural bias toward using power in the manner that has yielded the greatest success.

The United States has been much less impressive, however, in its consistent use of other, more subtle tools of international statecraft, and in an important and ironic twist, it is these tools that now become central to the security of the United States and its allies. In an era of globalized terrorism, the old, familiar threats have not gone away, but they have been joined by new competing concerns that are only superficially understood. An examination of the recent evolution of international terrorism and an understanding of the prospects for future developments will lead to the conclusion that old attitudes are not just anachronistic; they are dangerous.

My main argument is that power—more precisely, the reaction to preponderant power—is the most general explanation for international terrorism since the creation of the Westphalian state system. However, the nature of the power catalyzing most terrorist activity has changed over time. Thus it is possible to examine terrorism within major powers from the time of the French Revolution to the downfall of tsarist Russia from the perspective of terrorism aimed at democratization or, at least, political change from within these powers. A second, overlapping era would be the revulsion to imposed colonial power, which culminated in the numerous conflicts surrounding the protracted period of decolonization, especially in Africa, the Middle East, and Asia. A third epoch can be lumped under the heading of antihegemonic terrorism in opposition to the international system led by the United States. This third epoch, however, entered a new dimension when the cold war ended and U.S.-led globalization became the most dominant actor in the international system. I contend that terrorism is the biggest threat to the future of globalization.

There is nothing inevitable or linear about globalization, and the fact that most of the world's people and nations still live outside that system (although in many developing world countries the elites enjoy its fruits) is likely to be the major cause of transnational terrorism that could directly affect U.S. interests and global security in the years ahead. Prescriptions for coping with or deflecting these threats will require both strategic and tactical policies that provide sticks for dealing with terrorists themselves and with short-term threats, but also with long-term incentives to help countries step out of poverty and squalor—factors that help breed terrorists and especially their supporters—through good governance, economic growth, and education, health, and other social benefits. These solutions, of course, are impossible to implement fully in the short term, and even fully implemented would not ensure that other abuses of power would avoid eventually promoting further terrorist activity. Nonetheless, a failure to address these underlying causes and support mechanisms for terrorism would be less effective than a comprehensive approach to addressing this major threat to globalization in general and U.S. interests in particular.

This chapter will first provide an overview of key trends and developments in international terrorism, placing the events of September 11 in the context of modern terrorism. It will examine the causes and types of terrorist activity, and significant innovations in transnational terrorist tactics and behavior. Included here will be a discussion of the benefits and pitfalls of relying on analyses of past trends as indicators of future terrorist activity. Second, it will analyze the implications of these developments for the stability and security of the international community generally, and the United States, its allies, and other developed countries more specifically. This section will touch briefly on counterterrorist methods that hold greater or less potential for successful suppression of terrorist activity, understanding that interactions between terrorism and counterterrorism reflect some of the same offense/defense dynamics that characterize other domestic or international conflict relationships.[1] Third, the chapter will outline the prospects of these developments for the foreseeable future, including projections of challenges to the stability of the international community. Finally, it will conclude with a range of policy recommendations suggested by the foregoing analysis.

Terrorism and the Struggle for Power

No treatment of "terrorism" can escape the inevitable discussion of the definition of the term, an exercise fraught with frustration. Terrorism is notoriously difficult to define, in part because the term has evolved through several meanings since its first use during the French Revolution, and in part because the term is associated with an activity that is designed to be subjective. Generally speaking, the targets of a terrorist episode are not the individual victims who are killed or maimed in an attack, but governments, publics, or constituents among whom the terrorists hope to engender a reaction—of fear, repulsion, intimidation, overreaction, or radicalization, for example. Eminent specialists in the field have devoted dozens of pages to the effort to develop an unassailable definition of terrorism, only to conclude that the effort is fruitless: terrorism is *intended* to be a matter of perception and is thus seen differently by different observers.[2]

While individuals can disagree over whether particular actions constitute terrorism, there are nevertheless certain fundamental aspects of the concept that can be identified. First, terrorism always has a political nature. Terrorism involves the commission of outrageous acts in order to precipitate political change. At its root terrorism is about justice, or at least someone's perception of justice.

Second, although many other uses of violence are inherently political, including and especially conventional war between states, terrorism is distinguished by its non-state character, even when terrorists receive military, political, economic, and other means of support directly or indirectly from states. States obviously use force for political ends: when state force is used internationally it is considered an act of war; when it is used domestically, it is called various things, including law enforcement, state terror, oppression, or civil war. While states can terrorize, they cannot by definition be terrorists.

Third, terrorism deliberately and specifically targets the innocent, and that also distinguishes it from state uses of force that inadvertently kill innocent bystanders. In any given example, the latter may or may not be seen as justified; but again, this use of force is different from terrorism. Hence, the fact that precision-guided missions sometimes go astray and kill innocent civilians is a tragic use of force, but not terrorism. On the other hand, sometimes the "innocent" victims of terrorism can be military or military-related targets, and thus one would include the bombing of the Khobar Towers military housing facility in Saudi Arabia and the suicide boat attack on the USS *Cole* while docked in Yemen, because in neither case was the military target involved in a state of war in international legal terms.

Finally, state use of force is subject to international norms and conventions that may be invoked or at least consulted; terrorists do not abide by international laws or norms and, in order to maximize the psychological effect of an attack, their activities have a deliberately unpredictable quality.[3]

For the purposes of this discussion, therefore, terrorism is defined as "the threat or use of seemingly random violence against innocents for political ends by non-state actors."[4] All of these common elements are manifested in recent examples of terrorism, from the kidnapping of tourists by the Abu Sayyef group in the Philippines to the various incidents committed by Al Qaeda, including the 1998 attacks on U.S. embassies in Kenya and Tanzania, and the September 11, 2001, attacks on the World Trade Center and the Pentagon.

The Historical Origins of Terrorism

Terrorism is as old as human history, probably dating back to the first organized human interactions. One of the first reliably documented instances of terrorism came in the first century CE. The Zealots-Sicarii, Jewish terrorists who operated for about twenty-five years, among other things murdered their victims by the use of the dagger (*sica*) in broad daylight in the heart of Jerusalem, eventually creating such anxiety in the population at large that they generated a mass insurrection.[5] Other early terrorists emerged in the intervening centuries, notably the Hindu Thugs and the Muslim Assassins; but modern terrorism is generally considered to have originated with the French Revolution.[6]

The term was not used until 1795, when it was coined to refer to a policy systemically used to protect the fledgling French republican government against counterrevolutionaries. Although that positive connotation of the word has certainly changed, Robespierre's practice of using revolutionary tribunals as means of publicizing a prisoner's fate for broader effect within the population (quite apart from questions of legal guilt or innocence) can be seen as a nascent example of the much more highly developed blatant manipulation of media attention by terrorist groups in the mid- to late twentieth century.[7] Since then the concept has evolved through several phases and associated meanings.

The Driving Forces Behind Terrorism

The historian David Rapoport has described contemporary terrorism, such as that perpetuated by Al Qaeda, as part of a religiously inspired "fourth wave" following three earlier phases in which terrorism emanated from the breakup of empires, decolonization, and anti-Americanism.[8] The argument here is that modern terrorism can best be seen as a power struggle: central power versus local power, big power versus small power, modern power versus traditional power. And while contemporary terrorism emanating from largely Muslim countries has more than a patina of religious inspiration, it is more useful to see it as part of a larger phenomenon—antiglobalization and the struggle between the have and have-not nations. Thus the distinguishing feature of modern terrorism is the connection between sweeping political or ideological concepts and increasing levels of terrorist activity internationally. Terrorists' broad political aims have been against empires, colonial powers, and the American-led international economic system marked by globalization. This is not so much to disagree with Rapoport as to refine his typology in the hope of making it easier to draw policy recommendations. If it is correct that Al Qaeda, while a band driven by religious extremism, is in fact able to do so much harm because of the secondary support and sanctuary it receives from vast areas left out of globalization, then it follows that the prescription for dealing with Osama bin Laden and his followers is not just eradicating a relatively small number of terrorists, but also addressing the environment that enables them to acquire so much power.

In the nineteenth century, the unleashing of powerful concepts such as universal suffrage and popular empowerment raised the hopes of radical intellectuals throughout Europe and the Western world, eventually resulting in the first kind of modern international terrorism—democratic uprisings against monarchies and empires. Originating in Russia, it was stimulated not by state repression but by the efforts of the tsars to placate demands for economic and political reforms, and the inevitable disappointment of popular expectations that were raised as a result. This type of modern terrorism was thus initially characterized by the activities of the Russian anarchists and later the development of a series of movements throughout the United States and Europe, especially in the territories of the former Ottoman Empire. The dissolution of empires and the search for a new distribution of political power has been a powerful catalyst for terrorism in the past century, which Rapoport sees as culminating in the assassination of Archduke Franz Ferdinand, an event that catalyzed the major powers into violent action not because of the significance of the distinguished gentleman himself but because of the suspicion of rival state involvement in the sponsorship of the killing. World War I, the convulsive systemic cataclysm that resulted, ended the first era of modern terrorism, according to Rapoport.[9] But it would be a mistake to assume that this kind of terrorism has ceased. It has continued, perhaps most notably in the 1990s in the Balkans after the breakup of the former state of Yugoslavia. But it also continues in diverse locations around the globe such as Kashmir, Chechnya, Aceh, and Shinxiang, to mention but a few of the trouble spots within vast former empires. Likewise, the dashed expectations that inspired the Russian anarchists are akin to the dashed expectations fueling much of the hatred that directly and indirectly supports Al Qaeda and other terrorist networks in the twenty-first century.

A second, related kind of modern terrorism developed beginning after World War I and continues to the present day. These struggles for separate power are another facet of terrorism against larger political powers and are specifically aimed at the positive objective of winning political independence (as opposed to the broader goal above of striking at the sinews of an empire). The era of rapid decolonization spawned national movements in territories as diverse as Algeria, South Africa, Israel, and Vietnam.[10] This was an age of ambivalence toward the phenomenon in the international community, with haggling over the definition of terrorism reaching a fever pitch in the United Nations. The question of political motivation became important in determining international attitudes toward terrorist attacks, as the post–World War II backlash against the colonial powers and the attractiveness of national independence movements led to the creation of a plethora of new states often born in violence. Arguments over the justice of international causes and the designation of terrorist struggles as "wars of national liberation" predominated, with consequentialist philosophies excusing the killing of innocent people if the cause in the long run was just. The U.S. intervention in Vietnam, and especially the subsequent American defeat by the nationalist, left-wing Viet Cong, excited the imagination of revolutionaries throughout the world and helped lead to a resurgence in leftist terrorist violence, especially in Western Europe. The Soviet Union underwrote the nationalist and leftist terrorist agendas of many of these groups, nudging the United States into a caricature as the new colonial power—an easy task following Vietnam—and furthering an ideological agenda oriented toward achieving a postcapitalist, international communist utopia.[11] Even though the cold war ended more than a decade ago, however, the search for national self-determination has continued, not only in the areas mentioned above with respect to the dissolution of large empires, but also in specific recent hot spots such as Sri Lanka, East Timor, the Basque region, and Sudan, to mention but a few.

Revolutionary terrorism achieved a truly international dimension during the 1970s and 1980s, evolving in part as a result of the technological advances and in part as a result of a dramatic explosion of international media influence. Individual, scattered national causes began to develop into international revolutionary organizations with links and activities increasingly across borders and among differing causes. This development was helped along greatly by the covert sponsorship of states such as Iran, Libya, and North Korea, and, of course, the Soviet Union, which found the underwriting of terrorist organizations an attractive way to accomplish clandestine goals while avoiding clear responsibility and potential retaliation from the United States. Sometimes the lowest common denominator among the groups was the force against which they were reacting—for example, imperialism—rather than the specific goals that were sought, but the important innovation was the increasing commonality of international connections among the groups. Especially after the 1972 Munich Olympics massacre, for example, the Palestinian Liberation Organization (PLO) captured the imaginations of many young radicals and served as a spiritual role model. In Lebanon it also provided practical training in the preferred techniques of mid-twentieth-century terrorism, such as airline hijacking, hostage taking, and, of course, bombing.

Since the events of September 11, 2001, the world is witnessing the maturation of a new sort of terrorist activity, spawned by the Iranian revolution of 1979 as well as the Soviet defeat in Afghanistan shortly thereafter. The powerful attraction of religious and spiritual movements has replaced the nationalist or leftist political revolutionary ethos and become the central characteristic of a growing international trend. It is perhaps ironic that the forces of history seem to be driving international terrorism back to an earlier era, with echoes of the behavior of earlier "sacred" terrorists like the Zealots-Sicarii clearly apparent in the terrorist activities of organizations like Al Qaeda and its erstwhile hosts, the Taliban. The implications of this trend for the United States and the international community will be explored in greater depth in the next section. But it would be a mistake to see this religious terrorism as new, rather than as a continuation of an ongoing modern power struggle between those with power and those without it. Above all, the main target of these terrorists remains American power and the American-led global system.

There is nothing truly new about religious terrorism, but in a post-Enlightenment materialist era, the motivating factors seem alien to most in the secular West, and the potential technological manifestations of radical religious zeal more ominous. Like earlier movements, however, this latest wave of terrorism has roots that are much deeper than are immediately apparent, and it is not likely to be short-lived: thus it behooves leaders in the developed world and their publics to understand its characteristics so as to counter its effects. What is different is the recognition of the solutions, which must deal both with the specific religious fanatics who are the terrorists and the far more politically motivated states, entities, and people who would support them because they feel powerless and left behind in a world of globalization. Thus, if there is a trend in terrorism, it is that we now are living with a two-level challenge: the hyperreligious motivation for small groups of terrorists, and the much broader enabling environment of bad governance, nonexistent social services, and unmet expectations that characterizes much of the developing world. Leaving aside for the moment the enabling environment, it is worth focusing on the chief motivations of the terrorists themselves, and therefore contrasting secular and spiritual motivations of terrorism.

Types of Terrorism

There are four main types of terrorist organizations currently operating through-out the world, categorized mainly by their source of motivation: left-wing terror-ists, right-wing terrorists, ethno-nationalist/separatist terrorists, and religious or "sacred" terrorists. All four types have enjoyed eras of relative prominence in the modern era, with left-wing terrorism intertwined with the communist movement,[12] right-wing terrorism drawing its inspiration from Fascism,[13] and the bulk of ethno-nationalist/separatist terrorism accompanying the wave of decolonization in the immediate post–World War II years.[14] These categories are not perfect, as many groups have a mix of motivating ideologies. Many ethno-nationalist groups, for example, have religious characteristics or agendas[15]—but usually a dominant ideology or motivation can be gleaned.

The reasons why these categories are useful is not simply that classifying the groups gives scholars a more orderly way to study them, but also because different motivations tend to lead to different styles and modes of behavior. Understanding the "type" of terrorist group involved can provide insight into the likeliest manifes-tations of their violence and the most typical patterns of their development. While generalizations are always dangerous, left-wing terrorist organizations, driven by liberal or idealist political concepts, tend to prefer revolutionary, antiauthoritar-ian, antimaterialistic agendas (here it is useful to distinguish between the ideal-ism of individual terrorists and the frequently contradictory motivations of their sponsors). In line with these preferences, they often employ brutal criminal-type behavior such as kidnappings, murders, bombings, and arson; but they have a difficult time defining clear long-term visions. Most of the left-wing organiza-tions in twentieth-century Western Europe, for example, were brutal but relatively ephemeral. Of course, right-wing terrorists can be ruthless, but in their most recent manifestations they tend to be less cohesive and more impetuous in their violence than are leftist terrorist groups. This makes them potentially explosive but difficult to track.[16] Ethno-nationalist and separatist terrorists are the most understandable in conventional terms, usually having a clear political or territorial aim that is ra-tional and negotiable, if not always justifiable in any given case. At the same time, it can be difficult to distinguish between goals based on ethnic identity and those rooted in the control of a piece of land. With their focus on gains to be made in the traditional state-oriented international system, they often transition in and out of more conventional paramilitary structures, depending on how the cause is going, and they typically have sources of support among the local populace of the same ethnicity with whom the separatist political goals (or appeals to blood links) may resonate. That broader popular support is usually the key to the greater average longevity of ethno-nationalist/separatist groups in the modern era.

All four types of terrorists are capable of egregious acts of barbarism. That said, religious terrorism may be especially dangerous to international security in the foreseeable future for at least five reasons. First, religious terrorists often consider themselves to be engaged in a Manichean struggle of good against evil, implying an open-ended set of targets in the human world: anyone who is not a member of the religion or religious sect may be "evil" and thus fair game. While indiscriminate attacks, in and of themselves, are not unique to religious terrorists, the exclusivity of the faith may lead religious terrorists to dehumanize victims even more than most terrorist groups do, since nonmembers are "infidels," be they children, noncombatants, or innocent bystanders—as perhaps, for instance, Al Qaeda operatives may have viewed Muslims killed in the World Trade Center.

Second, religious terrorists engage in violent behavior directly or indirectly in order to please the perceived commands of a deity. This has a number of worrisome implications: the whims of the deity may be more or less obvious to those who are not a part of the religion, so the actions of violent religious organizations can be especially unpredictable; and religious terrorists are not as constrained in their behavior by concerns about the reactions of their human constituents. (Their audience lies elsewhere.)

Third, religious terrorists, by definition, consider themselves to be unconstrained by secular values or laws. Indeed, the very target of the attacks may be the law-based secular society that is embodied in most modern states. The driving motivation, therefore, is to overturn the current post-Westphalian state system—a much more fundamental threat than, say, ethno-nationalist terrorism purporting to carve out a *new* secular state or autonomous territory.

Fourth, religious terrorists often display a complete alienation from the existing social system. They are not just trying to correct the system, making it more just, more perfect, more egalitarian, and so on, but are trying to replace it completely, ushering in a new age through the violent catharsis that they hope to perpetuate. In some groups, apocalyptic images of destruction are seen as a necessity—even a purifying regimen—and this makes them uniquely dangerous, as was painfully learned on September 11, 2001.[17]

Finally, in addition to the seemingly infinite and unpredictable objectives of religious terrorists, religious terrorism is also especially worrisome because of its dispersed popular support in civil society. On the one hand, groups such as Al Qaeda are able to find support from Muslim nongovernmental foundations throughout the world, making it truly a global transnational network. On the other hand, in the process of trying to weed out the relatively few number of people providing serious support from the majority of most of these groups, there is the real risk of igniting the very holy war that the terrorists may be seeking in the first place.

Militating against the vexing aspects of religious terrorism, however, are several countervailing factors. First, in general, mainstream religious groups, including Islamic groups, seek peace, not war. For instance, the number of peaceful Muslims—or Jews or Christians—overwhelms the number of putative followers of Islam who would condone the atrocities committed when suicide hijackers slammed jumbo jets into the World Trade Center and the Pentagon.

Second, the end of the cold war and the advance of globalization have increased the common interests among former cold war adversaries in limiting the access of lethal means to potential religious fanatics who might actually be willing to use weapons of mass destruction. If there is a silver lining in the dark cloud of September 11, then perhaps it is the clarifying focus that the tragedy wrought: namely, that the United States, Europe, and even Russia and China, share a strong common interest in international stability and against international terrorism (though this is distinct from efforts to curb weapons proliferation by pariah state actors).

Third, the sanctuaries for massive terrorist training camps, such as those that were allowed to exist in Afghanistan under the Taliban, are now widely viewed as a global security problem that we cannot afford to ignore. The American people understand the direct link between failed states and national interests in a way they did not appreciate before September 11. Before the tragic strikes on American soil, few Americans felt that Afghanistan mattered; after September 11, few Americans doubted it.

Finally, while the motives of religious terrorists may be apocalyptic, the resources and means that they need to conduct sophisticated and lethal operations can be interdicted through a range of nonmilitary means such as cracking down on money laundering. In fact, an effective suppression of terrorism requires a combination of short-term measures, including military force tailored for special missions, and long-term steps, mostly political, economic, and legal in nature.

In sum, there are both enduring and new aspects to contemporary terrorism. The enduring features center on the common political struggle that characterizes major acts of international terrorism in the past century or more. The newest and perhaps most alarming aspect is the increasing religious nature of modern terrorist groups.

Implications for Stability and Security

Statistics show that even before the dreadful attacks by Al Qaeda, religiously motivated terrorist organizations were becoming increasingly common. The acceleration of this trend has been quite dramatic: according to the RAND-St. Andrews University chronology of international terrorist incidents, in 1968 none of the identified international terrorist organizations could be classified as "religious"; in 1980, in the aftermath of the Iranian revolution, there were two (out of sixty-four), and that number had expanded to twenty-five (out of fifty-eight) by 1995.[18] Thus, even before the tragedies of September 11, the role of religiously motivated international terrorism had become increasingly prevalent. As mentioned above, religious terrorism is the predominant threat of the current era, and it is also the type of terrorism that has the longest pedigree internationally.

In addition to the evolving motivation and character of terrorist attacks, there has been a notable shift in the geography of terrorism, a trend that is likely to continue well into the current century. While the Middle East continues to be the locus of most terrorist activity, Central and South Asia, the Balkans, and Transcaucasia have been growing in significance over the past decade. The tightening of links among terrorist organizations around the globe, a phenomenon established in the past two decades, characterizes the current era, with the use of technologies such as the Internet, mobile phones, and instant messaging increasing the global reach of many groups, for recruitment purposes as well as coordination of operations. Consider the lethal impact of synchronized attacks—whether on the U.S. embassies in 1998 or on New York and Washington in 2001—which would not have been possible without the revolution in information technology. Globalization has enabled terrorist organizations to reach across international borders in the same way (and often through the same channels) that commerce and business interests do. The dropping of barriers through the North American Free Trade Agreement and the European Union, for instance, has enabled the smooth flow of many things, good and bad, between countries; in a sense, terrorism is becoming like any other international enterprise, a very ominous development. But the up side of the globalization of terrorism is that the international response to terrorist networks has also begun to be increasingly global, with international cooperation on law enforcement, intelligence, and especially financial controls being areas of notable recent innovation.[19]

As I have argued, however, looking at terrorism as something separate from globalization is dangerous. The more basic reality is that globalization and terrorism are the two largest forces marking international security in the twenty-first century, and the main question is whether terrorism will be allowed to disrupt the promise of improved livelihoods for millions and millions more of the people on earth. Globalization is not an inevitable, linear development, but rather a trend that can be disrupted and set back through such unconventional means as international terrorism. Conversely, international terrorism is the danger it is only because of the power that it derives from globalization, whether access to weapons of mass destruction, global media outreach, or a diverse network of financial and information resources.

Other important trends become more apparent after studying the available data regarding international terrorist incidents from the mid-twentieth century to the present. The good news is that there were fewer attacks in the period immediately before September 11, 2001: internationally, in the 1990s, the number averaged below 400 per year, whereas in the 1980s the number of incidents per year was well above 500 (see Figure 13.1).[20] It is worth noting, in this regard, that some eminent observers of international terrorism argued that the threat of terrorism was *declining* before September 11. To quote from an article by a former State Department counterterrorism specialist, prominently published in July 2001 by the *New York Times*:

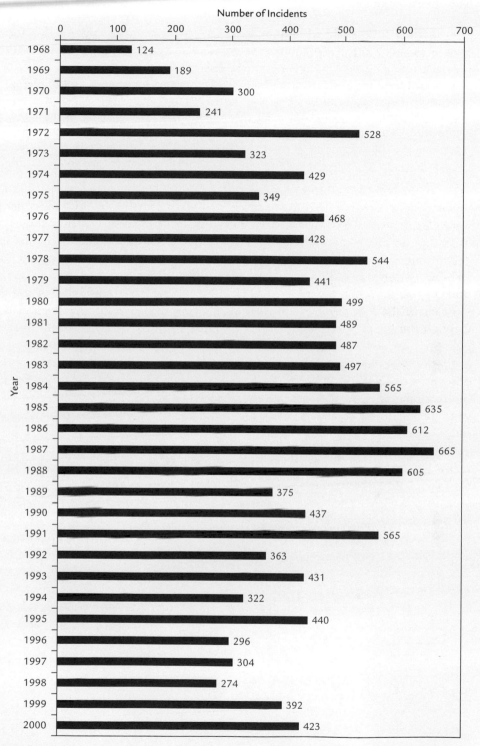

Figure 13.1   International Terrorist Incidents, 1968–2000

Source: U.S. Department of State

Although high-profile incidents have fostered the perception that terrorism is becoming more lethal, the numbers say otherwise, and early signs suggest that the decade beginning in 2000 will continue the downward trend. . . . [T]here are bureaucracies in the military and in intelligence agencies that are desperate to find an enemy to justify budget growth. . . . In the 1980's when international terrorism was at its zenith, NATO and the United States European Command pooh-poohed the notion of preparing to fight terrorists. . . . While terrorism is not vanquished, in a world where thousands of nuclear warheads are still aimed across the continents, terrorism is not the biggest security challenge confronting the United States, and it should not be portrayed that way.[21]

The conclusions reached in the article are based largely on extrapolations of State Department data for the year 2000—a healthy reminder of the danger of attaching too much significance to the predictive value of short-term changes in statistical data. Of course, the attacks on New York and Washington occurred just over two months later.

Nonetheless, there are certain obvious conclusions to reach from an examination of the number, type, and pattern of international terrorist incidents in the past several decades. First, even before September 11, 2001, the absolute number of casualties of terrorism had been increasing (see Figure 13.2). This jump in deaths and injuries can be partly explained by a few high-profile incidents, especially the

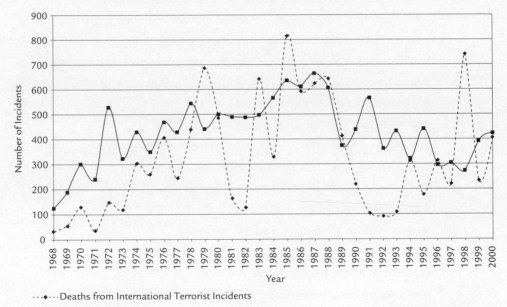

- - -◆- - - Deaths from International Terrorist Incidents

——■—— Total International Terrorist Incidents

Source: U.S. Department of State

Figure 13.2   Number of International Terrorist Incidents and
Deaths Caused by International Terrorist Incidents

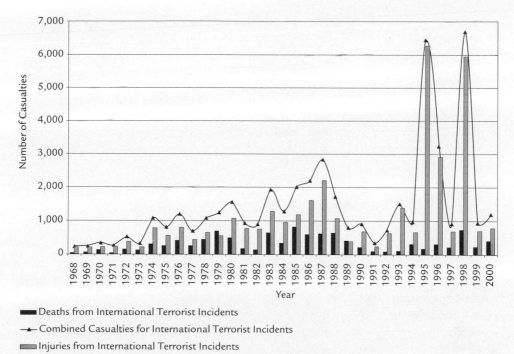

Deaths from International Terrorist Incidents

Combined Casualties for International Terrorist Incidents

Injuries from International Terrorist Incidents

Source: U. S. Department of State

Figure 13.3   Casualties from International Terrorist Incidents

Riyadh bombing and the Oklahoma City bombing in 1995, the Khobar Towers attack in 1996, and the bombing of the U.S. embassies in Nairobi and Dar-es-Salaam
in 1998. In the latter embassy attacks alone, for example, 224 people were killed
(including twelve Americans) and 4,574 were injured (including fifteen Americans).[22] But it is significant that more people were being hurt by terrorism as the
decade proceeded. Second, and related to this, the number of people who died and
were wounded per incident was increasing (see Figure 13.3). Thus, even though
the number of incidents declined in the 1990s, the number of people killed or
wounded in each incident was increasing.

Another important trend is related to attacks that involve United States targets,
either U.S. citizens or U.S. interests. The number of international terrorist incidents
involving the United States generally increased in the 1990s, from a low of sixty-six
in 1994 to a high of two hundred in the year 2000 (see Figure 13.4). Interestingly, the
highest number of attacks ever recorded involving the United States, 312, occurred
in 1991, when the United States was engaged in Operation Desert Storm; of those,
275 international terrorist incidents occurred during the war itself.[23] This is a long-
established problem: U.S. nationals consistently have been the most targeted since
1968.[24] But the percentage of international attacks against U.S. targets or U.S. citizens
increased over the course of the 1990s, from about 20 percent in 1993–95 to almost

292   Audrey Kurth Cronin

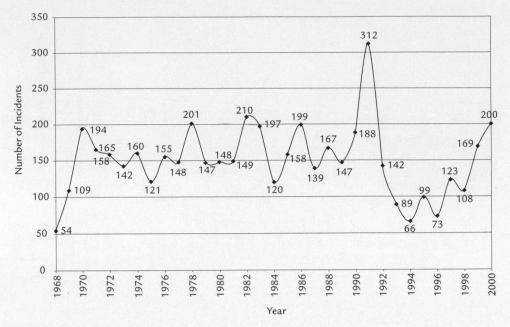

Source: U.S. Department of State

Figure 13.4   International Terrorist Attacks Involving the United States

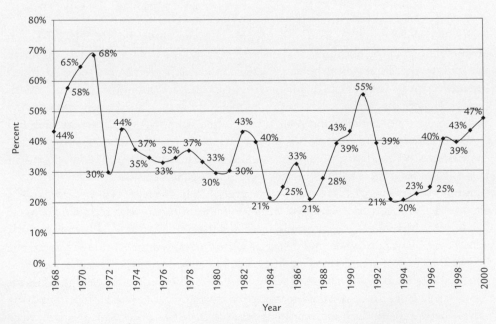

Source: U.S. Department of State

Figure 13.5   International Terrorist Incidents Involving the U.S. as a Percentage of Total Incidents

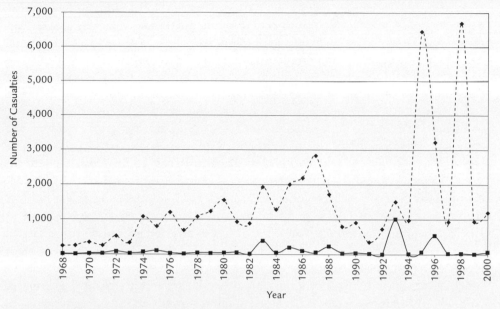

--◆-- Casualties from International Terrorist Incidents

—■—U.S. Casualties from International Terrorist Incidents

Source: U.S. Department of State

Figure 13.6   Comparison of Total versus U.S. Casualties as
a Result of International Terrorist Attacks

50 percent in 2000 (see Figure 13.5). Looking at the data in another way, when we examine the absolute number of casualties strictly from terrorist attacks involving the United States, the increase at the turn of the century is dramatic (see Figures 13.6 and 13.7). This is perhaps a natural side effect of the increased role and profile of the United States in the world; but the degree of increase is nonetheless troublesome.

One must note the dangers of studying trends too closely and drawing conclusions too confidently on the basis of what has happened in the past: terrorists want to shock observers, and shock usually requires a radical departure from the norm. While it is obviously useful to understand historical patterns, it is also dangerous to become too dependent on the belief that the prelude is a completely reliable indicator of what will follow. As Richard Betts points out in his examination of why the September 11 tragedies were not prevented, major intelligence failures often reveal a bright analyst who was so knowledgeable of past trends that he or she was unable to anticipate an exception to the previous experience.[25] Knowledgeable observers can see broad outlines and discern changes in tactics, motivations, and means; but studying the patterns and trends in international terrorism is useful only if done with a hearty dose of humility about the number of times the best counterterrorism experts have been surprised. If terrorism were predictable, it would not be so terrifying.

For example, before September 11, 2001, experts in the field of counterterrorism generally pointed to the sharply declining number of attacks against airliners between the 1970s and the 1990s as an example of success (see Figure 13.9).[26] The number of both skyjackings and bombings had dropped precipitously, a result that was generally credited to better (though not perfect) airline screening of passengers and carry-on baggage. The number of people killed per incident had admittedly increased (see Figure 13.10). But the overall picture was considered favorable and was credited to better deterrence of attacks. As is now known, however, such assumptions and complacency probably led, directly or indirectly, to the success of the Al Qaeda-sponsored attacks, where the use of civilian airplane "missiles" to drive directly into the World Trade Center and the Pentagon was an innovation that took knowledgeable counterterrorism specialists completely by surprise. Most depressing is the fact that the terrorists, who passed without incident through the normal airline screening devices on that fateful morning, would not have been arrested for cause in any case: the box-cutter knives that they wielded were less than four inches long and thus perfectly legal. Modern terrorists are innovators—sometimes with types of technology, more often with target selection, location, timing, and/or style of attack; and when faced with relatively static laws, countermeasures, and assumptions, including conclusions based on "trends," they have a built-in advantage. This is not to argue that we should avoid studying trends—it is the best means of gaining general insight into modern terrorist behavior over time; it is only to caution that examining the recent history

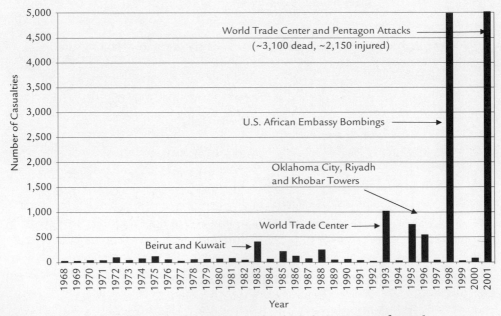

Source: U.S. Department of State; CNN [at www.cnn.com] and Stratfor [at www.stratfor.com]

Figure 13.7   Casualties from International Terrorist Attacks Involving the U.S.

of terrorist behavior must be done with an open mind and an appreciation of the potentially deadly importance of exceptions to the rule.

The increasing lethality of terrorist attacks was already receiving an inordinate amount of attention in the late 1990s, with many experts on terrorism arguing at that time that the trend toward more casualties per incident implied a number of things. First, it meant that, as had been feared, religious "apocalyptic" terrorism was more dangerous than the other types that had predominated earlier in the twentieth century. The world was facing the resurgence of a far more malignant type of terrorism, whose lethality was borne out in the increased death toll from incidents that increasingly involved a religious motivation. Second, with a premium now apparently placed upon causing more casualties in each incident, it was feared that the incentives for terrorist organizations to use so-called "weapons of mass destruction" would be greatly increased. The breakup of the Soviet Union and the fear of the resulting increased availability of Soviet nuclear, biological, and chemical weapons led to an argument that terrorist groups, seeking more dramatic and deadly results, would be increasingly inclined to use chemical, biological, and nuclear technologies.[27] The 1995 sarin gas attack by the Japanese cult Aum Shinrikyo in the Tokyo subway seemed to confirm that fear.

Increasing globalization is also at the heart of the danger of potential use of chemical, biological, nuclear, and radiological weapons. Of course, access to the

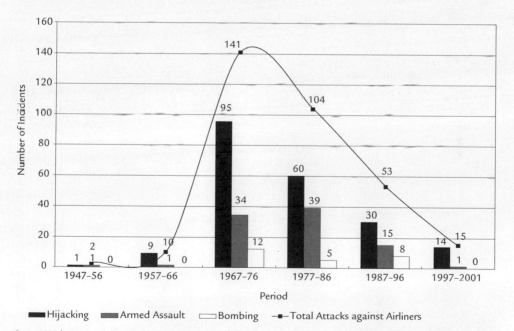

Source: Web version of "Criminal Acts against Civil Aviation," FAA Office of Civil Aviation Security, available at http://cas.faa.gov/crimacts/, and Ariel Merari, "Attacks on Civil Aviation: Trends and Lessons," in *Aviation Terrorism and Security*, ed. Paul Wilkinson and Brian M. Jenkins [Portland, Ore.: Frank Cass, 1999]

Figure 13.8   History of Terrorist Attacks against Airliners

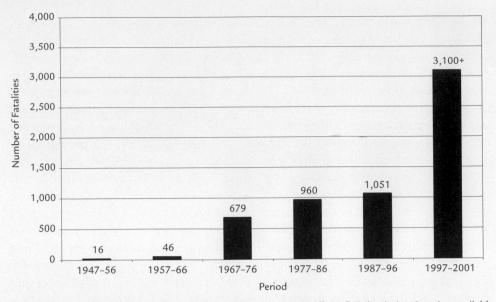

Source: Web version of "Criminal Acts against Civil Aviation," FAA Office of Civil Aviation Security, available at http://cas.faa.gov/crimacts/, and Ariel Merari, "Attacks on Civil Aviation: Trends and Lessons," in *Aviation Terrorism and Security*, ed. Paul Wilkinson and Brian M. Jenkins [Portland, Ore.: Frank Cass, 1999]

Figure 13.9   Fatalities from Terrorist Attacks on Airliners

knowledge needed to build these weapons has become increasingly ubiquitous as a result of the much-ballyhooed information revolution. This subject has been thoroughly (perhaps too thoroughly) covered in the terrorism field elsewhere: the technologies are increasingly available.[28] But more to the point, the political incentives to attack powerful targets like the United States with powerful weapons have increased, with the threat to indigenous customs, religions, languages, economies—and the accompanying distortions in local communities as a result of exposure to the global marketplace of goods and ideas—increasingly blamed upon American-sponsored modernization. At the heart of the threat to the United States and the international community, therefore, is not the advancement of technologies for carrying out terrorist deeds, but the political frustrations and international movements increasingly inclined to react to U.S.-led globalization.

Prospects for the Future

The fundamental new causes of international terrorism can be placed under the heading of antiglobalization. But it must be made clear that this is not to equate antiglobalization protests on the margins of major international forums, such as the 2001 G-8 meeting in Genoa, with the kinds of deadly terrorism on which this article focuses. Nor is it to suggest that poverty and the widening gap between the North and the South can be directly correlated to the rising lethality of terrorism.

After all, if poverty and not politics were the root cause of terrorism, than surely Africa—which has the highest number by far of least-developed countries—would be the primary locus of terrorism rather than the Middle East, South and Central Asia, and the Balkans. Oversimplified generalizations about poverty and terrorism, or any other single-factor explanations of terrorism, are highly problematic.

Instead, the argument is simply that the terrorism that threatens international stability, and particularly U.S. global leadership, is centered on political causes that are enduring: the weak against the strong, the disenfranchised against the establishment, and the revolutionary against the status quo. The fact that expectations around the world have been raised by the information revolution is not necessarily helpful, in the same way that rising expectations led anarchists to take up violence against the tsar in Russia a century ago. Indeed, the fact that so many people in so many nations have been left behind—and were visibly left behind during the dramatic growth of wealthy nations in the 1990s—led to new sanctuaries for terrorists, produced more sympathy for terrorists who were willing to take on the United States, and promoted radical religious movements to recruit, propagandize, and support terrorism throughout many parts of the mostly Muslim world. So, while the Al Qaeda network can be called a religious terrorist organization, and while surely its Taliban puppet regime was filled with religious zealots, and while its suicide recruits may have been convinced that they were waging a just holy war, to dismiss the broad enabling environment would be to focus more on the symptoms than on the causes of contemporary terrorism.

Terrorism is a by-product of broader historical shifts in the international distribution of power in all of its forms—political, economic, military, ideological, and cultural. These are the same forms of power characterizing the forces of Western-led globalization. At times of dramatic international change, human beings (especially those not benefiting from the change, or not benefiting as much or as rapidly from the change) grasp for alternative means to control and understand their environments. If current trends continue, widening global disparities, coupled with burgeoning information and connectivity, are likely to accelerate well into the twenty-first century, unless the terrorist backlash, increasingly taking its inspiration from radical misoneistic religious or pseudoreligious concepts, successfully counters these trends.

From a Manichean perspective, the ad hoc and purportedly benign intentions of the secular West (and its allied governments throughout the world) do not seem benign at all; an adherence to radical religious philosophies and practices can seem a rational response to a perceived assault, especially when no feasible or attractive alternative for progress is offered by a home government. This is not to suggest that those who engage in terrorist behavior can be excused because of environmental factors or conditions. The point is that the tiny proportion of the population that ends up in terrorist cells cannot exist without the availability of broader sources of active or passive sympathy, resources, and support, and that those avenues of sustenance are where the proverbial center of gravity for an effective response to the terrorist threat must reside. The response to transnational terrorism must deal with the question of whether the broader enabling environment will increase or decrease over time, not just in Central Asia or the Middle East but throughout the globe, and the answer will be strongly influenced by the policy choices that are made in the near future.

Policy Lessons

The United States and other international actors need to develop a two-track strategy for preventing and countering terrorism: a set of short-term actions that address immediate threats and challenges, and a set of longer-term actions that will shape the environments that enable terrorist networks to develop. The latter must focus on those whom globalization has left behind. Paradoxically, this will entail employing and exploiting the tools of globalization itself.

In the short term, the United States needs to continue to focus on capable military forces that can sustain punishing air strikes with even a greater capacity for special operations on the ground. This will require not only stealthy, long-range power projection capabilities but also agile, sophisticated, and lethal ground forces, backed up by greater intelligence, including human intelligence supported by people with language skills and cultural training. The use of military force continues to be important as one means of responding to terrorist violence against the West, and there is no question that it effectively preempts and disrupts some international terrorist activity.

Homeland defense is of course another priority, especially for the United States. Terrorism will continue to reach American shores and the U.S. government needs to have better tools to prevent or minimize future attacks. The tradeoffs between comprehensive attempts to prevent terrorism and civil liberties will be especially difficult to balance, and decision makers will struggle to make prudent choices. Unfortunately, however, homeland defense is a mission inevitably destined to be characterized by its failures, because the attacks that are prevented by the measures undertaken on American soil are unlikely to be known publicly, while gaps in the protective measures taken will be inevitably exploited and painfully exposed. It is simply not possible to defend against all means and manners of attack. This is not to argue that efforts to tighten border controls, improve interagency coordination, and increase domestic security are unimportant; rather, it is to acknowledge that, due to the very avenues of globalization that have served Western interests in other ways, American soil is no longer impervious to international terrorism. Better advance planning for the management of the consequences of terrorist attacks will therefore be critically important. The history of modern terrorism contains many episodes of copycat attacks, inspired by the dramatic successes of well-publicized incidents, and the attacks on the World Trade Center and the Pentagon are unlikely to be an exception.

When all is said and done, however, the more effective policy instruments in the long run will be nonmilitary. The United States needs to expand and deepen its nonmilitary instruments of power: intelligence, public diplomacy, cooperation

with allies, international legal instruments, and economic assistance and sanctions. This is hardly an earth-shattering suggestion. In his original description of
containment, George Kennan made the same fundamental argument, albeit in a
radically different context. When faced with a long-term threat, American power
is most strongly bolstered by political, economic, and military elements, in that
order. The point is not that the United States and its allies need to be involved
in a kind of global welfare reform, but that the roots of terrorism are complex,
important, prevalent, increasingly worrisome, and demanding of as much subtlety
in response as they display in their genesis. The United States must therefore be
truly strategic in its response: an effective grand strategy against terrorism involves
planning a campaign with *all* of the most effective means available, not just the
most measurable, obvious, or gratifying, and includes plans for shaping what the
nature of the global environment will be after the military campaign has ended.
The evolution of terrorism in the past has been clearly tied to broad-based political
forces and resulting power shifts throughout the globe. Contemporary terrorism
is no exception.

In particular, the United States, working with other major donor nations in the
international community, needs to provide an effective incentive structure to reward
"good performers"—countries with good governance, inclusive education programs,
and adequate social programs—and be prepared not to ignore but to work around
"bad performers" and intervene in so-called failed states. The United States and its
allies must also develop and project a vision of sustainable development—of economic growth, of meeting basic social needs such as education and health, and of
good governance—for the developing world. This is especially important with respect
to Muslim countries, which are most likely to be angry with the United States over
Washington's longstanding support for Israel at the expense of Palestinians, over
U.S. policies toward Iraq, and over the abundance of American power, including the
U.S. military presence in the Middle East. This is not to accept the revisionist propaganda of Osama bin Laden; rather, it is simply to note that the response to terrorism
must take into account these important political perceptions.

In the final analysis, terrorism is the leading threat to the continued success of
globalization, of bringing more people and nations into a prosperous global trading order. If globalization is to continue—and its continuance is not foreordained—
then the tools of globalization, including international norms, the rule of law, and
international economic power, will have to be fully exercised against the terrorist
backlash. In this struggle, the United States will not and cannot act alone.

Notes

The views expressed in this chapter are those of the author. They do not represent
the official position of the Congressional Research Service or any other part of the
U.S. government.

1. Modern terrorists often learn from mistakes and innovate on everything from type, target, timing, or location of attack, so static conclusions about effective counterterrorist methods are inherently perishable and subject to review.

2. On the difficulty of defining terrorism, see, for example, Omar Malik, "Enough of the Definition of Terrorism!" (Royal Institute of International Affairs paper [London: RIIA, 2001]); and Alex P. Schmid, *Political Terrorism: A Research Guide* (New Brunswick, N.J.: Transaction Books, 1984), which spends more than a hundred pages grappling with the question of a definition, only to conclude that there is no one universally acceptable definition.

3. The diabolical nature of terrorism has given resonance to Robert Kaplan's view that the world is a "grim landscape" littered with "evildoers" and requiring Western leaders to adapt a "pagan ethos." But such conclusions deserve far more scrutiny than space allows here. See *Washington Post*, Outlook section, Feb. 17, 2002.

4. R. G. Frey and Christopher W. Morris, "Violence, Terrorism and Justice," in *Violence, Terrorism and Justice*, ed. R. G. Frey and Christopher W. Morris (Cambridge: Cambridge University Press, 1991), 3.

5. Walter Laqueur, *Terrorism* (London: Weidenfeld and Nicolson, 1977), 7–8; and David C. Rapoport, "Fear and Trembling: Terrorism in Three Religious Traditions," *American Political Science Review* 78 (1984): 658–77.

6. David C. Rapoport, "The Fourth Wave: September 11 in the History of Terrorism," *Current History* (Dec. 2001): 419–24; and David C. Rapoport, "Terrorism," in *Encyclopedia of Violence, Peace, and Conflict* (New York: Academic Press, 1999).

7. Ironically, Robespierre's tactics during the Reign of Terror would not be included in my definition of terrorism for this chapter, because it was state terror.

8. Rapoport, "The Fourth Wave."

9. Ibid., 419–20.

10. Ibid., 420.

11. Rapoport actually divided these into two "waves"—separating the sweep of postwar decolonization from the reaction to the U.S. intervention in Vietnam; but since the sources of the Vietnam War were also a manifestation of postcolonial nationalism, I believe they are better treated as one era in modern terrorism.

12. Groups such as the Second of June Movement, the Baader-Meinhof Group, the Red Brigades, the Weathermen, and the Symbionese Liberation Army belong in this category.

13. Among right-wing groups would be some members of the American militia movements, such as the Christian Patriots, other neo-Nazi organizations (in the United States and Europe), and the Ku Klux Klan. Right-wing groups tend to be less well organized and more impulsive in their violence than left-wing terrorist groups. There is also, of course, usually a racist element to their agendas.

14. The list here would be extremely long, including groups as different as the Tamil Tigers of Sri Lanka, the Basque separatist party, the PLO, and the Irish Republican Army (and its various splinter groups).

15. Bruce Hoffman notes that secular terrorist groups that have a strong religious element include the Provisional IRA, the Armenians, and perhaps the PLO; however, the political/separatist aspect is the predominant characteristic of these groups. Hoffman, "Terrorist Targeting: Tactics, Trends, and Potentialities," in *Technology and Terrorism*, ed. Paul Wilkinson (London: Frank Cass, 1993), 26, n. 25.

16. It is interesting to note that, according to Chris Harmon, in Germany, 1991 was the

first year that the number of indigenous rightist radicals exceeded that of the leftists. Christopher C. Harmon, *Terrorism Today* (London: Frank Cass, 2000), 3.

17. On the characteristics of modern religious terrorist groups, see Bruce Hoffman, *Inside Terrorism* (New York: Columbia University Press, 1998), chap. 4, esp. 94–95; and Hoffman, "Terrorism Trends and Prospects," in *Countering the New Terrorism*, ed. Ian O. Lesser et al. (Santa Monica: RAND, 1999), esp. 19–20. On the peculiar twists of one apocalyptic vision, see Robert Jay Lifton, *Destroying the World to Save It: Aum Shinrikyo, Apocalyptic Violence, and the New Global Terrorism* (New York: Metropolitan Books, 1999).

18. Hoffman, *Inside Terrorism*, 90–91; and Nadine Gurr and Benjamin Cole, *The New Face of Terrorism: Threats from Weapons of Mass Destruction* (London: I. B. Tauris, 2000), 28–29.

19. On these issues, see Audrey Kurth Cronin and Jim Ludes, eds., *Attacking Terrorism: Elements of a Grand Strategy* (Washington, D.C.: Georgetown University Press, forthcoming).

20. Statistics compiled from data given in U.S. Department of State, *Patterns of Global Terrorism*, published annually by the Office of the Coordinator for Counterterrorism, U.S. Department of State.

21. Larry C. Johnson, "The Declining Terrorist Threat," *New York Times*, July 10, 2001, A19. See also Ehud Sprinzak, "The Great Superterrorism Scare," *Foreign Policy* (fall 1998); and Ehud Sprinzak, "Revisiting the Superterrorism Scare," *Foreign Policy* (Sept.–Oct. 2001).

22. All data come from U.S. Department of State, *Patterns of Global Terrorism*.

23. Harmon, *Terrorism Today*, 52.

24. Hoffman, "Terrorist Targeting," 24.

25. Richard K. Betts, "Fixing Intelligence," *Foreign Affairs* (Jan.–Feb. 2002): 49.

26. Paul Wilkinson and Brian Jenkins, eds., *Aviation Terrorism and Security* (New York: Frank Cass, 1998), a special issue of the journal *Political Violence and Terrorism* 10, no. 3 (1998). See especially the article by Ariel Merari, "Attacks on Civil Aviation: Trends and Lessons," which includes very helpful data, some of which is reproduced here in Figure 13.9.

27. See, for example, Steven Simon and Daniel Benjamin, "America and the New Terrorism," *Survival* 42 (spring 2000): 59–75, as well as the responses in the subsequent issue, "America and the New Terrorism: An Exchange," *Survival* 42 (summer 2000): 156–72; Hoffman, "Terrorism Trends and Prospects," 7–38.

28. There are many recent sources on chemical, biological, nuclear, and radiological weapons. A selection of the best of them includes Jonathan B. Tucker, ed., *Toxic Terror: Assessing Terrorist Use of Chemical and Biological Weapons* (Cambridge: MIT Press, 2000); Joshua Lederberg, *Biological Weapons: Limiting the Threat* (Cambridge: MIT Press, 1999); Richard A. Falkenrath, Robert D. Newman, and Bradley A. Thayer, *America's Achilles' Heel* (Cambridge: MIT Press, 1998); Nadine Gurr and Benjamin Cole, *The New Face of Terrorism: Threats from Weapons of Mass Destruction* (New York: I. B. Taurus Publishers, 2000); Jessica Stern, *The Ultimate Terrorists* (Cambridge: Harvard University Press, 1999); and Brad Roberts, ed., *Terrorism with Chemical and Biological Weapons: Calibrating Risks and Responses* (Alexandria, Va.: Chemical and Biological Arms Control Institute, 1997).

Conclusion

Conclusion   # Security Problems and Security Policy in a Grave New World

MICHAEL E. BROWN

We have tried to accomplish three main things in this book: to advance understanding of contemporary national and international security problems, to assess the prospects for security problems over the next decade or two, and to derive policy lessons that will help to promote national and international security in the future. In this concluding chapter, I will outline a framework for thinking about current and emerging national and international security problems, make some projections about future developments, and suggest some policy recommendations.[1]

I argue that, contrary to those who see only stasis or novelty in security affairs, there is both continuity and change in the security arena. Indeed, we can distinguish between continuing, changing, and emerging security problems. I also suggest that we broaden the security agenda to include the full range of factors that can affect the prospects for security. At the same time, we must do this without creating a vast, amorphous morass of undifferentiated policy problems. I argue that it is useful to distinguish the military and nonmilitary challenges that create security problems, on the one hand, and interstate, intrastate, and transnational arenas, on the other.

The forecast for the next decade or two is gloomy at best. There are only a few areas where policy problems are easing. Some issue areas will see a continuation of the current dangerous state of affairs, while others will probably witness gradual deterioration or even a more dramatic turn for the worse. Cataclysmic developments—such as terrorist use of weapons of mass destruction—cannot be ruled out. It might be hard to imagine and distressing to contemplate, but security problems will probably become more widespread, more intense, more complex, speedier, and deadlier in the future.

Unfortunately, national, regional, and international policy responses are inadequate in many of the issue areas examined in this volume. Many security problems are receiving insufficient attention from policymakers. In most areas, policymakers are not thinking far enough ahead; instead of anticipating problems and devising strategies to deal with them, they are reacting to events with uncoordinated, ad hoc responses. In addition, policymakers often favor simple, single-factor options and hope for quick fixes, when they should be developing multifaceted approaches that will be pursued diligently over the long haul. In the fluid, dynamic security environment of the twenty-first century, policymakers will not be able to recycle old policy approaches. They will have to be creative and adapt to changing circumstances. They will, in short, have to become more adept at strategic thinking.

305

Continuity and Change in Security Affairs

Experts in the field of international relations disagree categorically about the impact of the end of the cold war and the advent of globalization on national and international security affairs. Some contend that the fundamental features of the international security landscape have not changed at all, while others insist that everything has changed.

At one end of the spectrum, realists argue that the main features of the international system have not changed, even though the cold war has ended and globalization has become a growing force in international relations. The international system, they contend, is still anarchic in that states and other actors still have to provide for their own security; there is no international authority capable of providing security for one and all. States, they maintain, are still the dominant actors in the international system, and states are still determined to preserve their survival. The result, these analysts say, is that security competitions and confrontations will still be common features of international relations in the twenty-first century.

For example, Kenneth Waltz argues that the world "has not been transformed" by the end of the cold war. Rather, "the structure of the system has simply been remade by the disappearance of the Soviet Union." A true transformation in international relations, he says, "awaits the day when the international system is no longer populated by states that have to help themselves." In the meantime, he maintains, "the essential continuity of international politics" remains.[2] Similarly, John Mearsheimer argues that "international anarchy—the driving force behind great-power behavior—did not change with the end of the Cold War, and there are few signs that such change is likely any time soon. States remain the principal actors in world politics."[3] The future will therefore look much like the past: "The state system is alive and well, and although regrettable, military competition between sovereign states will remain the distinguishing feature of international politics for the foreseeable future."[4]

At the other end of the spectrum are those who argue that the nature of the international system is indeed changing. They contend that powerful, technology-driven developments—the information revolution, the proliferation of global telecommunications systems, and growing economic interdependence—are changing the nature and distribution of power in the international system. States, they say, have lost their information monopolies and control over their economies. They contend that states are therefore becoming less important while non-state actors are gaining ground. They predict that increasingly empowered individuals, non-governmental organizations (NGOs), and multinational corporations will form a new international civil society that will soon supercede the state system.

For example, Jessica Mathews argues, "The end of the Cold War has brought no mere adjustment among states but a novel redistribution of power among states, markets, and civil society. National governments are not simply losing autonomy in a globalizing economy. They are sharing powers—including political, social, and security roles at the core of sovereignty" with nonstate actors. A "power shift" from states to nonstate actors is taking place: "Increasingly, NGOs are able to push around even the largest governments." In the future, she says, "the relative power of states will continue to decline." The main features of the state-centered system that has dominated the world for centuries "are all dissolving." "If current trends continue," she concludes, "the international system 50 years hence will be profoundly different."[5]

Thomas Friedman has a similar but more nuanced view of globalization. He argues that "if you want to understand the post–Cold War world you have to start by understanding that a new international system has succeeded it—globalization." He maintains that globalization is "not just some passing trend. Today it is the overarching international system shaping the domestic politics and foreign relations of virtually every country." Friedman argues that globalization is creating a complex balance of power among states, between states and markets, and between states and individuals, but he does not foresee the demise of states. States in general and the United States in particular "are still hugely important today," but so are markets, individuals, and other nonstate actors.[6]

I believe that there is both continuity and change in national and international security affairs. The fundamentals of the international system have not yet changed: the international system is still anarchic; states are still the dominant actors in international relations; states still seek security; and interstate security competitions and confrontations will continue to be important features of the security landscape. At the same time, globalization is increasingly impinging on state power, nonstate actors are becoming increasingly influential, and the security agenda contains an increasingly complex set of issues. Many of the issues on the security agenda today do not fall under the rubric of interstate problems. Some of these problems are entirely new and potentially momentous.

If there is both continuity and change in national and international security, it is not enough to say that the truth is somewhere "in the middle" and leave it at that. We need to differentiate as sharply as we can between different kinds of security problems. We can start by looking at the security agenda in temporal terms and distinguishing between three sets of security problems: continuing problems, changing problems, and emerging problems.

Something Old

Continuing problems are the hardy perennials of national and international security: competitions and conflicts between states. The names of the players and the arenas of competition change over time, but the interstate character of this important set of problems remains the same. These problems have been central features of international relations for centuries, and they will continue to be important in the twenty-first century. The 2003 war in Iraq demonstrated in a vivid way that interstate security problems are still very much on the international security agenda.

Specific problems include the possibility of armed clashes between states, the proliferation of weapons of mass destruction in dangerous states and unstable regions, and the rise and fall of great powers. Current concerns include the possibility of recurring war between India and Pakistan as well as armed conflict on the Korean peninsula, perhaps involving other powers. The acquisition of nuclear, biological, or chemical weapons by potentially aggressive states is a major worry. The open acquisition of nuclear weapons by India and Pakistan in 1998 has complicated the stability equation in South Asia; the potential consequences of war between these two regional powers are now many times more devastating than they were in the past.

Although the United States currently stands alone as the world's only super-power, great-power competition will also be an important feature of international relations in the twenty-first century. A key issue will be the evolution of relations between the United States and China, as the latter's economic power and regional aspirations grow.[7] Interstate security problems—these and others yet unknown—will continue to be critical security problems.

Something New

Changing problems have long-standing roots in national and international security affairs, but they have changed qualitatively due to the end of the cold war and the advent of globalization. This large set of problems includes a wide range of inter-state, intrastate, and transnational problems.

Changing interstate security problems include the evolving nature of the nu-clear balance between the United States and Russia; the former has reenergized its effort to deploy national missile defenses, and the latter has experienced nuclear command-and-control problems due to the deterioration of the Russian nuclear establishment. More generally, Russia is in the midst of a profound political and economic transformation that has weakened the ability of its military establish-ment to maintain custody of its nuclear, biological, and chemical weapons stock-piles. It is now a potential source of nuclear, biological, and chemical capabilities for would-be proliferators, including both state and nonstate actors.[8] The interna-tional trade in conventional weapons and technologies has also been transformed by the end of the cold war. The driving forces behind conventional arms transfers are no longer political but economic. This makes conventional proliferation sub-stantially harder to control.[9] Although it is not yet clear whether technological ad-vances in sensors, information processing, precision guidance, and other advanced conventional weapon systems will constitute a true "revolution" in military affairs, it is clear that the United States has developed conventional power-projection capabilities that are vastly superior to those of any other country, including its al-lies. This is affecting the prospects for great-power military intervention as well as relations between the United States and its partners.[10] Finally, important changes are taking place in nonmilitary arenas, with defense industries becoming more in-tegrated, the global energy market becoming more interconnected, and advances in information technology all having implications for interstate relations in the twenty-first century.[11] New links and new vulnerabilities are being created at the same time.

Intrastate security problems are not new, but they too are changing. It is often said that security problems in the developing world were neglected during the cold war, but the historical record suggests otherwise. The United States and the Soviet Union were deeply concerned about and involved in security problems in what was then called the Third World, but their actions were often destabilizing. The superpowers viewed the Third World through cold war lenses and sought political advantages wherever they could. Their support for different actors intensified, militarized, and prolonged many armed conflicts in the developing world. At the same time, their interest in keeping local and regional conflicts from escalating into superpower confrontations helped to control escalation in some cases. Now that the cold war has ended, the dynamics of conflict in the developing world have changed dramatically. Conflicts that were driven to a large degree by superpower patronage—in Cambodia, El Salvador, Mozambique, Namibia, and Nicaragua, for example—have moved toward settlement. Other conflicts are no longer constrained by external moderating forces and have escalated. Today, intrastate security problems are driven by a wide range of nonmilitary issues, including environmental and demographic pressures, resource competitions, fierce power struggles, and crises over the political stability and legitimacy of states.[12] Weak, failing, and failed states are increasingly serious concerns. Intrastate violence is facilitated by the changing nature of the conventional arms market: state and corporate suppliers are eager to sell weapons, and the black market in light weapons and small arms has grown substantially.[13] The result is a high level of violent conflict, with around twenty-five major armed conflicts taking place in the developing world at any one time.[14]

A final subset of changing security problems is transnational in character. This includes relatively localized regional problems as well as transnational problems that transcend any one area. Some of the latter are global in nature.

Many intrastate conflicts have regional dimensions.[15] When intrastate conflicts become violent, refugees often flee across international borders in large numbers. Refugees are not just humanitarian problems; they are also security problems. Fighters often mingle with refugee populations, using refugee camps to rest, recuperate, reorganize, rearm, and relaunch their military campaigns. Large refugee populations can strain economic resources, aggravate ethnic tensions, and generate political instability in host countries. Global refugee populations surged from an average of 11.6 million in the 1980s to an average of 14.7 million in the 1990s; they declined to just over 12 million in the early 2000s.[16]

Intrastate conflicts can also affect neighboring states at a military level. The territory of neighboring states can be used to ship arms and supplies to insurgent groups, which can lead to interdiction campaigns. Outlying regions of neighboring states can also be used as bases from which terrorist assaults or more conventional attacks can be launched. This can lead to hot-pursuit operations across borders and reprisals. Although they pretend otherwise, neighboring states are not always the innocent victims of turmoil in their regions. To the contrary, they often meddle in these conflicts for self-serving reasons. In short, many intrastate conflicts have regional dimensions that do not fit neatly into either the "interstate" or "intra-state" categories. These are complex, hybrid, regional conflicts that can best be thought of as transnational in character.

The expanding capabilities of transnational media organizations, transnational criminal organizations, and transnational terrorist organizations are also growing security concerns.[17] Although media organizations have long played important roles in national and international security affairs, the advent of around-the-clock television news in the early 1980s was a watershed development.[18] The impact of the "CNN effect" on policymaking is often overstated, but the growing influence of these organizations is nonetheless real. Transnational criminal organizations pose increasingly grave threats to stability in a growing number of countries. It is estimated that 120 of the more than 190 states in the international system are now challenged by medium-to-strong criminal networks.[19] These networks undermine the rule of law, human rights, economic development, and governance in general. They are not just crime problems; they are security problems. Many of these networks operate throughout and across regions; some have global operations.

The threats posed by transnational terrorist organizations—Al Qaeda, in particular—have become horrifyingly clear, but the worst may be yet to come.[20] Although Al Qaeda's base of operations in Afghanistan has been decimated, its capacities for action have not been eliminated. One possibility might be a physical attack on a target in the West combined with a cyber attack that would disrupt response capacities.[21] Another might be an attack involving nuclear, biological, chemical, or radiological weapons. This is another longstanding security problem that is changing in potentially devastating ways.

Something Out of the Blue

A third and final category of security problems consists of developments that are genuinely new. Since their trajectories and implications are not yet perfectly clear, it might be useful to call these issues *emerging problems*. The driving force in this area is technology. Information technology is already changing the world in a multitude of ways, and the implications of genetic engineering are just starting to be appreciated. Some of these developments will have incremental effects on national and international security, while others could bring about truly revolutionary transformations. (These issues will be discussed in greater detail later in this chapter.)

The New Security Landscape

The debate over the composition of the contemporary security agenda is mainly a debate over parameters and priorities: What exactly is a "security" issue? And what are the most important security problems?[22]

Realists tend to answer these questions in narrow terms. Security problems are issues involving states, and they involve the threat, use, or potential use of military force. For realists, the most important issues on the security agenda today are the same issues that have been on the agenda for centuries: the search by states for security; competitions among states for security; and the interstate competitions, confrontations, arms races, and wars that result from these quests.[23] Sophisticated realists understand that there are other conflict problems in the world—at the intrastate level, for example—but they believe that the security landscape is dominated by interstate problems that have prominent military dimensions.

Others have a more expansive conception of the security agenda.[24] Many argue that intrastate and transnational security problems should be added to the agenda. For example, Michael Klare argues that "many of the most severe and persistent threats to global peace and security are arising not from conflicts between major political entities but from increased disorder within states, societies, and civilizations along ethnic, racial, religious, linguistic, caste, or class lines."[25] Edward Kolodziej similarly contends that it is misguided to confine the security agenda to "state-centric analysis."[26] Many scholars and analysts have suggested that the security agenda needs to be expanded to consider a wider range of nonmilitary influences on conflict problems. Richard Ullman warns that "defining national security merely (or even primarily) in military terms conveys a profoundly false image of reality." This is dangerous, he says, because "it causes states to concentrate on military threats and to ignore other and perhaps more harmful dangers."[27] Jessica Mathews maintains that global developments call for a broader conception of national security that includes resource, environmental, and demographic issues.[28] Advocates of "human security" argue that the focus of concern should be redirected from states to groups and individuals, and that a very wide range of issues should be added to the security agenda: economic security, food security, health security, environmental security, and political security.[29] Michael Klare goes so far as to argue that, given the prevalence of intrastate, nonmilitary security problems, "it is questionable whether there is a role for military power at all."[30]

I believe that each school of thought is half correct. Realists are correct to point to the fundamentally anarchic nature of the international system and the continued importance of states and interstate problems within it, but they focus too narrowly on traditional, interstate, military security issues. Realism's critics are correct when they argue that intrastate, transnational, and nonmilitary factors must be placed on the security agenda, but some broaden the concept of "security" to the point where it has no meaning.

Advocates of "human security," for example, define security as "safety from such chronic threats as hunger, disease, and repression." For them, security "means protections from sudden and hurtful disruptions in patterns of daily life—whether in homes, in jobs, or in communities."[31] If one employs this broad definition, then "security problems" and "public-policy problems" become indistinguishable. Barry Buzan, Ole Wæver, and Jaap de Wilde argue that a public-policy issue becomes "securitized" when it requires "emergency measures" and "actions outside the normal bounds of political procedure."[32] If one follows this line of thinking, then "security problems" and "public-policy emergencies" become indistinguishable. This is unsatisfactory. As Lawrence Freedman convincingly argues, "once anything that generates anxieties or threatens the quality of life in some respect becomes labeled a 'security problem,' the field risks losing all focus."[33]

The challenge, therefore, is to broaden the agenda to include the full range of factors and actors that can affect the prospects for security, while defining meaningful parameters for this set of problems and, correspondingly, the field of security studies.

I believe that the central issue on the security agenda, and the heart of the field of security studies, is the problem of violent conflict. We should therefore endeavor to understand the full range of military and nonmilitary factors that can contribute to the *causes* of violent conflicts, including the most organized, most intense forms of violence—war and genocide.[34] Nonmilitary factors that can contribute to the outbreak of violent conflicts include historical, political, economic, social, cultural, religious, demographic, environmental, and technological issues and developments. The security agenda should also include all of the issues associated with the *conduct* of violent conflicts, including the dynamics of escalation and de-escalation, as well as the threat and use of military force and other deadly policy instruments.[35] Another set of critical issues involves the challenges of conflict *control,* including efforts aimed at conflict prevention, conflict management, and conflict resolution.

The scope of this agenda is broad; some structure is therefore needed. I argue that it is useful to distinguish the military and nonmilitary challenges that create

Table 14.1   The New Security Landscape: A Framework with Some Illustrations[a]

	Interstate Problems	Intrastate Problems	Transnational Problems
Military Challenges	Interstate Wars	Military Coups	Cross-Border Insurgencies
	Great-Power Competitions	Ethnic Conflicts	Transnational Terrorism
	Weapon Proliferation to Unstable States or Regions	Civil Wars	Weapon Proliferation via or to Nonstate Actors
Nonmilitary Challenges	Trade Disputes	Population Growth	Transnational Media
	Resource Conflicts	Economic Migrations	Transnational Crime
	Energy Competitions	Resource Competitions	Technology Proliferation

[a] Many scholars have called for adding nonmilitary factors to the security agenda. See Richard H. Ullman, "Redefining Security," *International Security* 8 (summer 1983): 129–53; Jessica T. Mathews, "Redefining Security," *Foreign Affairs* 68 (spring 1989): 162–77. Others have called for adding intrastate and transnational problems to the equation. See Edward A. Kolodziej, "Renaissance in Security Studies? Caveat Lector!" *International Studies Quarterly* 36 (Dec. 1992): 421–38; Michael T. Klare, "Redefining Security: The New Global Schisms," in *Globalization and the Challenges of a New Century,* ed. Patrick O'Meara, Howard D. Mehlinger, and Matthew Krain (Bloomington: Indiana University Press, 2000), 131–39. An excellent overview of both sets of issues can be found in Richard H. Schultz Jr., Roy Godson, and George H. Quester, eds., *Security Studies for the 21st Century* (Washington, D.C.: Brassey's, 1997). A similar but less elaborate matrix is developed in Roland Paris, "Human Security: Paradigm Shift or Hot Air?" *International Security* 26 (fall 2001): 87–102.

security problems, on the one hand, and interstate, intrastate, and transnational arenas, on the other. These distinctions can be depicted in the form of a matrix (see Table 14.1).

Interstate security problems include traditional military competitions, arms races, and armed conflicts, as well as weapon proliferation to aggressive regimes or unstable regions. As discussed above, these problems will continue to be on the security agenda in the future. Many interstate problems will be driven by nonmilitary disputes; those that have the potential to become violent conflicts qualify as security problems. Some of the possibilities include resource competitions over water, oil, and gas;[36] interstate disputes over cross-border economic migration or refugee populations;[37] and changes in defense industries that have the potential to affect national military capabilities.[38]

Intrastate security problems are often driven by underlying nonmilitary developments that generate social, economic, and political instability, thereby making violent conflict more likely. Particularly important in this regard are demographic developments (population growth and population movements) and environmental developments (resource degradation and depletion) that can combine to produce intrastate resource competitions. The resolution of these competitions frequently depends on the political and administrative capacities of the states in question. Unfortunately, resource competitions in the developing world are common in places where institutional capacities are weak. Violence is often the result.[39]

Many intrastate conflicts are simply the products of elite competitions for power, whether between civilian factions, factions of the military leadership, or civilian and military leaders. Many of these disputes have ethnic dimensions, but it would be a mistake to categorize all of these problems as "ethnic conflicts." Leaders who are motivated primarily by personal gain often claim to be the champions of their ethnic constituents and they often polarize ethnic relations over the course of their political campaigns, but it is important to distinguish between the parochial motivations that galvanize these conflicts and the ethnic consequences that follow. Many intrastate conflicts are driven primarily by parochial political and criminal agendas.[40]

Finally, transnational security problems can also have either nonmilitary or military dimensions. Transnational media organizations are nonmilitary in character, but they can have effects on the course and conduct of military operations. The expanded role of the media in the 2003 war in Iraq is a dramatic example of this phenomenon. Transnational criminal organizations are motivated primarily by profit and power, but their operations can undermine state authority and their black market operations often involve the sale and transfer of weapons. Proliferation issues range from the comparatively benign to the truly terrifying. The proliferation of information technologies, for example, might not have immediate, direct effects on political conflicts, but they could have powerful longer-term implications for stability and security. The proliferation of weapons of mass destruction in particular is of course a more immediate and deadly security threat.

Specific policy priorities will of course vary from country to country and region to region, and they will also evolve over time. At this juncture, some parts of the world—Latin America and Southeast Asia, for example—mainly have to contend with intrastate and transnational security problems. Others, such as northeast Asia, find interstate security issues higher on the agenda. Some regions have to contend with almost every kind of security problem imaginable; others with relatively few.

This simple framework is most certainly not the final word on a complex and changing set of issues. Indeed, many security problems overlap two or more of the categories discussed above. That said, it provides a useful starting point for distinguishing between the many security problems that are on the security agenda today.

Prospects for the Future

One of this book's most striking conclusions is that the prospects for national and international security over the next decade or two are grim. In issue area after issue area, one finds only a few glimmers of optimism. Some forecasts call for a continuation of the current perilous state of affairs. Others predict that things will get worse, but in an incremental, evolutionary fashion. Still others see radical and possibly cataclysmic turns for the worse.

Military Challenges

The least pessimistic forecasts are in traditional security areas, mainly involving the military position of the United States, nuclear balances, and interstate weapon proliferation. But even here, the picture is far from encouraging.

The United States will continue to be the dominant military power in the world for at least the next decade or two. Indeed, its current military advantages, both quantitative and qualitative, will probably grow due to its high levels of defense spending. Current U.S. defense spending makes up more than 38 percent of worldwide defense expenditures, and U.S. spending is projected to increase dramatically over the course of the decade, from $397 billion in FY 2003 to $470 billion in FY 2007. The United States spends more on military research and development (almost $54 billion in FY 2003) than any other country spends on total defense, so its technological and qualitative advantages will probably continue to grow as well. The gap between the United States and its potential military adversaries becomes even more impressive when one takes U.S. allies into account: the United States, its NATO allies, Australia, Israel, Japan, New Zealand, and South Korea account for more than 67 percent of worldwide defense expenditures; other allied and friendly states add to this total.[41]

Although the United States will retain its current military superiority for some time to come, this does not mean that others will be powerless. Any U.S. military action will involve the projection of military power over long distances; this will complicate the task for U.S. military planners and diminish military effectiveness. Timothy Hoyt believes that some adversaries will be capable of mounting significant resistance to U.S. military actions, possibly by employing unconventional tactics, engaging in asymmetric warfare, and perhaps resorting to terrorism. The 2003 war in Iraq showed signs of this. Hoyt expects that, contrary to the images of highly effective "surgical" air strikes generated by recent U.S. military operations, combat in the future will be "much murkier, less decisive, and less controlled."[42] In any event, even if U.S. military superiority is seen as benign and stabilizing in many quarters, it will be viewed differently in places such as Baghdad and Beijing. The impact of U.S. military power on national and international security will be seen by many, though not by all, as positive.

The prospects for the control of nuclear, biological, and chemical weapons are mixed at best. The good news is that the United States and Russia are continuing to make deep cuts in their nuclear arsenals, and U.S. efforts to push ahead with national missile defense has not derailed the U.S.–Russian nuclear relationship. In addition, India and Pakistan's 1998 nuclear tests have not yet triggered an intense nuclear arms race between these bitter rivals, as one might have expected. Even so, it is hard to be optimistic about the nuclear balance in South Asia, given that India and Pakistan have a volatile relationship marked by intense political disputes, periodic open warfare, and, now, rudimentary nuclear arsenals.

The bad news is that many problems remain, some appear to be intractable, and others are getting worse. The United States is exploring the possibility of using nuclear weapons in new ways, perhaps in preemptive attacks, perhaps to retaliate against the use of biological or chemical weapons on U.S. military forces or the U.S. homeland. Russian nuclear forces remain on a launch-on-warning posture, which is dangerous even under the best of circumstances. Unfortunately, as Bernard Finel, Brian Finlay, and Janne Nolan observe, Russian command, control, and early warning capabilities are deteriorating badly. The possibility of a nuclear catastrophe involving Russian nuclear forces cannot be ruled out. China's nuclear modernization program could embolden Beijing and make a U.S.–China confrontation over Taiwan more likely.

The proliferation picture is ominous with respect to nuclear, biological, and chemical weapons. The main challenge in the nuclear arena is preventing the proliferation of Russian nuclear weapons, fissile materials, component parts, and expertise to other state or non-state actors. Unfortunately, the U.S.–Russia programs to deal with these issues have been underappreciated and underfunded. As a result, these programs have addressed "only a small percentage of the weapons and materials still held—and often inadequately secured—by Moscow." Controlling the proliferation of biological and chemical weapons will be inherently difficult because of the dual-use problem: many biological and chemical facilities can be used to produce either civilian products or weapons. This makes arms control in this area exceedingly difficult. Globalization compounds the problem: trade in general is growing, border controls are weaker, and weapon proliferation is consequently facilitated. Significant progress in this area is unlikely; significant deterioration is more likely.

Unfortunately, international efforts to address these proliferation problems have been stymied by a policy split between the United States and most of the rest of the world. The administration of U.S. President George W. Bush favors unilateral approaches to these problems, with preventive and preemptive military attacks being among the options on the table. Almost every other leading power favors multilateral arms control initiatives. Coordinated international efforts to address proliferation problems are therefore stalled at a critical juncture in world affairs. This deadlock is unlikely to be broken by the current cast of characters.[43]

The forecast is also dismal in the area of conventional weapons proliferation. The international market in conventional weapons and technologies is now driven by economics. Large inventories of weapons, excess production capacities, and reduced levels of defense spending combine to give many countries and corporations irresistible economic incentives to export arms. According to Jo Husbands, supplier restraint is unlikely in the foreseeable future unless there is a shock to the system. In addition, the black market in conventional weapons is growing. Unfortunately, the powerful forces that are driving the conventional arms trade are not being met by vigorous policy responses in the West. To the contrary, Western countries are among the most energetic participants in this market. Arms control successes, Husbands says, have been "small and infrequent." She concludes that the policy challenges are enormous and that available policy tools are woefully inadequate.[44] In short, the best that can be hoped for is a continuation of the current, discouraging state of affairs.

Nonmilitary Challenges: Economic, Demographic, and Environmental

The dominant trend in the international economic arena is integration. This will have important effects on defense economics, the international energy market, and the prospects for security in both areas.

Defense and defense-related industries constitute an important economic sector in transition. The important military advantages currently enjoyed by the United States and its allies depend to a large degree on advanced technologies in the areas of microelectronics, data processing, telecommunications, cryptography, sensors, precision guidance, propulsion, and materials. Theodore Moran notes that in recent decades an increasing portion of these technologies has been coming from "innovations developed by commercial companies for the commercial market." The future of these firms is therefore an increasingly important national and international security question.

Many countries face formidable challenges. Europe and Japan are hampered by rigidities in labor and capital markets that impede innovation. Given the enormous size of U.S. research, development, and procurement budgets and existing U.S. technological leads, European and Japanese firms might be relegated to "a second-class and possibly subordinate status" for years and perhaps decades to come. Russia must institute regulatory and tax reform and rein in the oligarchs who currently dominate key sectors of the economy. This is easier said than done. It will be difficult for Russia to generate internationally competitive high-technology firms in the near term. China also needs to bring companies up to international standards, but the prospects are brighter here.

To make this great leap forward, it will seek to forge alliances with Western firms to improve program management and system integration capabilities.

Looking ahead, Moran foresees greater international integration in these key industries. Non-American high-technology firms will seek to have a presence in the United States because this will give them important competitive advantages. This means that the U.S. military will continue to have access to a wide range of new, high-performance capabilities. At the same time, because of "a macroeconomic tidal wave" caused by low U.S. savings rates and high U.S. balance-of-payments deficits, foreign ownership of U.S. corporate assets is likely to increase from 13 percent in 2000 to 24 percent in 2015; it could reach 50 percent in some high-technology sectors. This will reduce the ability of the United States to confine high-technology capabilities within its borders. More important, this growing economic interpenetration will constrain American economic and political autonomy, thereby diminishing the magnitude of U.S. unipolarity.[45]

The global energy market became increasingly integrated in the final decades of the twentieth century. This trend has continued since the end of the cold war and is likely to continue in the future. Martha Harris predicts that the future is not rosy. Global energy consumption is expected to increase by two-thirds over the next twenty years, which means that interruptions in energy supplies could be highly disruptive. Unfortunately, key components of the energy infrastructure—pipelines, terminals, power plants, and transmission grids, for example—are increasingly vulnerable. Policymakers consequently face significant security challenges ahead.

Harris argues that the increasingly integrated character of the global energy market and rising energy demand call for a fundamental departure from the parochial, national approach that dominated energy policy in the last century. A broader conception of energy security and a multilateral approach to these problems are needed in the new one. The reality, she says, is that "no country can achieve energy security independently today." The United States must take the lead in adopting a global perspective and a multilateral approach to energy security problems, and not for purely altruistic reasons. According to Harris, "the United States will not be secure if competition for control of energy resources around the world leads to conflict, market disruptions, and environmental disasters."[46]

Demographic and environmental factors will continue to generate intrastate and interstate security problems in the future. The world's population is expected to grow by approximately 50 percent—from around 6 billion to a projected 9 billion—by 2050. It is expected that at least 95 percent of the increase will be in the developing world—the part of the world least capable of sustaining additional population pressures. In addition, more and more of the world's population will live in cities. The portion of the world's population living in cities of more than 100,000 people is projected to grow from around 50 percent today to more than 60 percent in 2030.[47] Population movements—migration, urbanization, and populations displaced by violent conflicts—will continue to be sources of tension in many countries and regions.

Demographic and environmental factors often interact to generate instability and security problems. Significantly, important ecological buffers such as forests, fisheries, and fresh water are shrinking and will continue to shrink in the years ahead. This will generate more economic and environmental migration, which in turn will lead to economic, social, and political tensions, and perhaps violence. Water and oil will continue to be sources of contention and perhaps contributing factors in interstate conflicts. John McNeill observes that "environmental perturbation has grown to the point where it must be reckoned a serious factor in all manner of human affairs, security included." He believes that linkages between environmental and security issues will exist with greater force in the future.[48] It is highly probable that demographic developments, environmental factors, and resource scarcities will become increasingly important security issues in years ahead.

Although security problems in the developing world pose increasing threats to international security, international responses to these problems continue to be inadequate. According to Timothy Hoyt, some regions have been "virtually abandoned by the international community." He concludes that it is "in the enlightened self-interest of the West to pay greater attention to the developing world, to develop a better understanding of the causes of instability, and to craft long-term responses to these problems."[49] This, he believes, will require a level of leadership and engagement that the United States has not yet demonstrated.

Nonmilitary Challenges: Technological

Information technology and genetic engineering are two areas where forecasts range from generally pessimistic to potentially catastrophic. Dorothy Denning argues that the likely effects of advances in information technology on security are not encouraging. The number and severity of cyber attacks has increased dramatically in recent years, and this trend is likely to continue. Information technology is becoming faster, more powerful, more mobile, and more ubiquitous around the world. As a result, she says, "There are more perpetrators, more targets, and more opportunities to exploit, disrupt, and sabotage systems." In addition, computer networks are becoming increasingly integrated with critical infrastructures such as telecommunications, transportation, banking, electrical grids, oil and gas distribution systems, water supply systems, government services, and emergency services. Cyber attacks on these infrastructures have already become common, and deadly attacks on increasingly vulnerable systems could be launched in the future. Terrorists could combine a physical attack with a cyber attack on government response and emergency services systems, for example. "The bottom line," Denning says, "is that we will never have secure systems." In the future, "We can expect to see more attacks, and more mass attacks."[50]

Looking at two clusters of emerging technologies—digital networking and genetic engineering—Loren Thompson predicts that both "are sure to have tremendous effects on security and stability," with the former being the most important in the near term and the latter having potentially epochal effects in the long run. Together, they "will transform human relations within a few generations."

Thompson notes that digital networking is already transforming commerce, culture, and politics, but not always in benign ways. Information and communications technology is diffusing unevenly, both within and between nations, thereby reinforcing existing economic stratification. The proliferation of information and communications technology is also having disruptive effects on traditional societies, changing group loyalties and identities. It is having political effects, moreover, because it is strengthening the capacities of groups that seek to challenge established political authorities. These trends are likely to continue, and they are likely to generate a tremendous amount of instability.

According to Thompson, genetic engineering might have truly cataclysmic implications. In the near term, genetic engineering could be used to fashion extremely potent biological weapons, or weapons targeted at specific groups of people. Alternatively, genetic engineering might enable people to live decades longer; this, in turn, would have momentous demographic effects. In the long term, genetic engineering "may change the course of evolution, in the process redefining human nature."

Thompson maintains that these new technologies need to be understood, monitored, and in some cases regulated and suppressed. However, for better or worse, many of these technological advances will be socially irresistible and nearly impossible to control for technical reasons. Even if they could be regulated, economic interests would oppose the creation of control mechanisms. He concludes, "Major consequences for world order appear to be inevitable."[51]

One final point about technology and security in the twenty-first century should be kept in mind. As Timothy Hoyt points out, the nature of international competition is becoming increasingly knowledge-intensive. Many technologies could have potentially momentous consequences for the international balance of power and international stability. The United States and the West will not necessarily dominate in all of these areas, and controlling the diffusion of technology will be difficult. In the future, Hoyt concludes, "Education will become a major security asset."[52]

Transnational Challenges

As we have seen, transnational media organizations, transnational criminal organizations, and transnational terrorist organizations are not new actors in international affairs, but their influence has increased because of the developments comprised by globalization. Advancing information and communications technologies, increasing international trade, eroding border controls, and declining state capacities in many parts of the world have created environments that allow transnational organizations to operate more freely. The scope of transnational organizations has increased accordingly. Unless a catastrophic shock to the international system brings about a breakdown of the system, these trends will continue in the years ahead.

The arrival of around-the-clock television news operations in the early 1980s made transnational media organizations qualitatively more important than they had been in the past. Their influence has continued to grow since the end of the cold war. Although transnational media organizations will continue to be important actors in national and security affairs in the twenty-first century, several problems are unfolding. First, as more media organizations have launched new commercial operations, the competition for profits and ratings has intensified. Diana Owen argues that these economic pressures have already had pernicious effects on the quality of news coverage: news-gathering operations are being scaled back to cut costs; journalists with genuine expertise are being replaced by celebrity personalities; and, increasingly, speed is being stressed over accuracy.

Another problem is that the most powerful transnational media companies in operation today—CNN and BBC—are Western-based organizations. Since the ability to control information and shape images is an important source of power, the ability to shape the global conversation on many issues is uneven, and largely in Western hands. This is generating considerable resentment elsewhere. In the future, Western dominance of the transnational media scene will erode. Satellite technology is relatively inexpensive, and non-Western organizations are launching media operations of their own. This will lead to alternative sources of information and commentary for many, but new problems as well. The West's ability to control the flow of information around the world, which was always far from absolute, will continue to decline.

Finally, the emergence of extraordinarily powerful transnational media organizations is having effects on the international state system itself. Owen predicts that in the future, "traditional barriers to the flow of information, such as state boundaries, will be obliterated."[53] What this will mean for the nature of international politics remains to be seen.

The trend lines for transnational criminal organizations are even more worrying. Roy Godson contends that national and transnational criminal networks are already undermining political and economic stability in many countries and regions. He warns that "in an era of increasing globalization the problem reaches into most corners of the world." These problems will probably intensify and become more widespread in the future.

To date, policy responses have been inadequate. This crisis is starting to be recognized as an important policy problem, but it is still not universally recognized as a security problem. Many international actors fail to appreciate that these networks are complex security problems driven by combinations of political, economic, and cultural problems that vary from place to place and over time. Many focus instead on the criminal components of the networks, which leads them to treat it as a straightforward law enforcement issue. Unfortunately, narrow policy diagnoses lead to narrow and deficient policy remedies. To be effective, policy responses must be multifaceted, adaptable to circumstances, and flexible over time. According to Godson, the outlook is not encouraging. Given the growing magnitude of the problem and the lag in effective policy responses, "it is difficult to find reasons for optimism."[54]

Transnational terrorist organizations will continue to pose grave threats to national and international security in the future. Audrey Kurth Cronin argues that if the current wave of terrorism is indeed an intensely violent backlash against

U.S.-led globalization, then it is "not likely to be short-lived."[55] She observes that many people in many states are being left behind by globalization, and that this is happening in highly visible ways. Expectations around the world are being raised by the information revolution at a time when global disparities are growing.[56] The possibility that terrorist organizations might acquire nuclear, biological, or chemical weapons is a growing concern. Terrorist organizations that are not constrained by state sponsorship—such as Al Qaeda—might be inclined to use these weapons, and they might be impossible to deter.[57]

Cronin argues that the United States and other Western powers need to develop a two-track strategy for preventing and countering terrorism: "a set of short-term actions that addresses immediate threats and challenges, and a set of longer-term actions that will shape the environments that enable terrorist networks to develop. The latter must focus on those whom globalization has left behind."[58] This will entail devising a comprehensive strategy for sustainable development in the developing world, a vision that includes economic growth, good governance, education, and the provision of basic needs such as health care. The most effective policy instruments in this long-term campaign, she concludes, will be nonmilitary instruments.

Policy Lessons

One of the main reasons why security prospects are grim is the inadequacy of current and likely policy responses. In a dynamic and increasingly complex security setting, old policy formulas will quickly become outmoded. Unfortunately, the costs of policy failures will be high because security problems will continue to be deadly. It is imperative, therefore, that policymakers in both the developed and the developing worlds prepare themselves for the policy challenges of the future. In addition to the policy recommendations developed elsewhere in this book for specific policy problems, three general sets of policy lessons emerge: timing lessons, conceptual lessons, and international lessons.

Timing Lessons

A good place to start is with timing: When should policymakers begin to tackle security problems? And what planning horizons should they adopt?

First, it is naive and dangerous for policymakers to neglect current and emerging security problems, hoping that they will take care of themselves or go away on their own. Policy problems are rarely self-correcting. To the contrary, if left to themselves, policy problems usually get worse as time goes by. Wishful thinking is not a policy; it is the self-deluding refuge of the short-sighted and the faint of heart. Unfortunately, policy problems are often ignored until they become crises; then and only then do they find their way onto the agendas of busy policymakers. The result is that policy problems are neglected when they are relatively easy to solve, and they are addressed only after they become formidable. In effect, policymakers wait until problems become unsolvable before they try to solve them. This may overstate the decision-making dynamic, but not by much. The policy lesson is to engage security problems as soon as possible, even if these problems have not yet become deadly conflicts. Security problems become much more formidable once the violence threshold is crossed.

Second, in a dynamic and increasingly fast-paced world, policymakers no longer have the luxury of waiting for events to unfold before devising policy actions. In the twenty-first century, policymakers must become accustomed to thinking five, ten, and twenty years into the future. This will be inherently difficult for most policymakers; their planning horizons are tied to the daily press of events, legislative calendars, and electoral cycles. Many policymakers do not expect to be in office ten or twenty years down the road; it is difficult for them to expend time, energy, and political capital in the short term when the policy benefits, if any, will be reaped by someone else in the long term. The costs of policy engagement are immediate and often quantifiable; the benefits of far-sighted actions are reaped only in a distant future, and they are often unquantifiable. These incentives and calculations are inherent in the policymaking process, and they will continue to discourage policymakers from strategic thinking. Wise policymakers will work to overcome these structural pressures. Those who simply react to events will be overtaken by events.

Third, policymakers generally hope that security problems can be solved quickly and permanently; they hope for quick, permanent fixes to the issues before them. Unfortunately, most security problems are not amenable to quick fixes and many cannot be solved at all; they can only be managed. Security threats and violent conflicts will be deadly facts of life throughout the twenty-first century. There is no light at the end of this tunnel. The policy lesson is that policymakers must prepare themselves psychologically and politically for the long haul. This means thinking about problems in long-term time frames, as discussed above, and it means making long-term and even open-ended policy commitments.

It is generally difficult for policymakers to make long-term and open-ended programmatic commitments. In the United States, for example, presidents are challenged to outline their "exit strategies" whenever they deploy U.S. military forces abroad. Even so, post–cold war history suggests that long-term, open-ended commitments can be made at least some of the time. NATO brought three new members into the alliance in March 1999, and in November 2002 it extended membership invitations to seven additional countries. These were open-ended security commitments to the alliance's new members; they did not come with expiration dates attached. In short, making long-term and open-ended policy commitments is difficult but not impossible. This is a security challenge that policymakers will have to strive to meet.

Conceptual Lessons

This study also suggests three general guidelines about the way security problems should be conceived and how security policies should be framed.

First, many policymakers still define security problems in narrow terms, giving undue weight to interstate conflicts and the military dimensions of security problems. As discussed earlier in this chapter, policymakers should develop broader security agendas that give appropriate weight to the full range of interstate, intrastate, transnational, military, and nonmilitary challenges that are unfolding today. The policy lesson is to think inclusively about the security agenda.

Second, if security problems are complex, multidimensional, and interconnected, it follows that security policies should be multifaceted. Unfortunately, policymakers often favor simple, single-factor policy approaches; they hope that a single "silver bullet" will solve complex problems. This is another example of wishful thinking. The main policy lesson here is that complex, multidimensional security problems require multifaceted policy responses, often involving a combination of diplomatic, political, economic, and military elements. This is often challenging conceptually and politically, but it is nonetheless necessary.

A third and related lesson is that many contemporary security problems are not amenable to simple military solutions. Indeed, military responses often turn out to be inappropriate, ineffective, and even counterproductive. The use of military forces can appear to be a panacea, but this is all too often an illusion. Problems with nonmilitary roots will almost always require a range of nonmilitary policy responses, even if military actions are part of the equation as well.

International Lessons

Finally, this study suggests several general policy lessons about the international dimensions of contemporary security problems and the international dimensions of suitable policy responses.

First, many security problems in the twenty-first century will cross national borders and cut across regions. Some will be truly global in scope. It will be beyond the capability of any one actor, even a superpower like the United States, to tackle these problems on its own. National leaders who try to tackle these problems unilaterally will fail; national interests will correspondingly suffer. Therefore, one of the most basic principles of security policy will be multilateralism: national, international, and transnational security problems will require multilateral policy responses. Multilateralism will not be an option; it will be a necessity.[59]

Second, multilateral initiatives will require leadership. Although the United States will not be able to lead on every issue at every juncture, it will continue to be the world's one and only superpower for the foreseeable future. American leadership in identifying problems, devising strategies, forging coalitions, providing resources, and taking actions will therefore be key. If American political leaders play a more energetic and effective global leadership role, many national, regional, and international security challenges will become more manageable. If American leaders are unwilling, disinclined, or unable to play this role, a wide array of security problems will become increasingly formidable.

A short-term challenge for the United States will be undoing the diplomatic damage caused by the Bush administration's handling of the Iraq crisis and by the

U.S.-led war in Iraq in 2003. Although U.S. actions in Iraq had the active support of some governments and the tacit support of others, large numbers of people around the world were shocked and appalled by what they saw as unconstrained American unilateralism. Addressing these concerns and overcoming these impressions will require sustained American diplomacy.

More generally, American officials need to develop a better appreciation of what effective international leadership entails. Since the end of the cold war, and cutting across both Democratic and Republican administrations, the prevailing American approach to international problems has been to set a U.S. course and assume that others will ultimately follow—willingly or grudgingly. Complaints about American presumptuousness and arrogance have consequently become increasingly common. American officials would be wise to appreciate that true leadership is based on true consultation. It is not enough for Washington to inform others of what it intends to do. The United States needs to consult with allies, friends, and others about goals, strategies, and actions. And, above all, Washington needs to make a genuine effort to take the views of others into account. The United States clearly has the capacity to undertake unilateral actions in the international arena, but it will be able to lead only if it listens.

This leads to a third and final set of lessons. Those who seek to forge or sustain multilateral initiatives should keep several operational guidelines in mind.[60] For starters, multilateralism cannot be turned on and off and on again. Building multilateral patterns of cooperation takes steady, sustained engagement. The United States, which often suffers from international attention deficit disorder, will have to pay continuous attention to the maintenance of multiple international coalitions. A related guideline is that multilateralism is not an à-la-carte proposition. The United States cannot champion multilateralism on issues that it cares about, and slight it the rest of the time. The United States must be prepared to engage on issues across the board. In addition, multilateralism is a two-way street. The United States must be willing to give as much as it gets. Indeed, one would hope that the world's wealthiest and most powerful country would be inclined to give *more* than it gets.

Finally, for multilateralism to endure, it needs a strong institutional foundation—the United Nations. It is certainly true that the UN has many structural and political flaws, and that it frequently exasperates even its staunchest supporters. It is also true that the UN has a unique and important role to play in promoting international peace and security. In the twenty-first century, international actors will have to take coordinated steps to address common threats, and the UN provides an indispensable mechanism for facilitating multilateral actions. The United States and the other leading powers in the international system would be wise to put the diplomatic trauma of the Iraq crisis behind them and work to make the United Nations into a more effective instrument for the promotion of international peace and security. Building a strong, effective, and respected United Nations is in the enlightened self-interest of the world's leading powers—the United States in particular.

Most of these policy lessons are simple and commonsensical: act early, think ahead, plan for the long haul, avoid simple conceptual schemes and simple policy responses, recognize the limitations of military actions and the need for multilateral initiatives. They would be banal but for the fact that policymakers around the world routinely fail to meet even these minimal standards. The first step, therefore, is to master these policy fundamentals.

Notes

1. This chapter draws on the analyses and assessments found elsewhere in this volume, but it is not a consensus report. These conclusions are my own. Other contributors to this volume may not agree with my judgments, forecasts, and policy recommendations; they should not be held accountable for the arguments developed herein.

2. Kenneth N. Waltz, "Structural Realism after the Cold War," *International Security* 25 (summer 2000): 5–41, at 39.

3. John J. Mearsheimer, *The Tragedy of Great Power Politics* (New York: Norton, 2001), 361.

4. John J. Mearsheimer, "Disorder Restored," in *Rethinking America's Security: Beyond Cold War to New World Order,* ed. Graham Allison and Gregory F. Treverton (New York: Norton, 1992), 213–37, at 214.

5. Jessica T. Mathews, "Power Shift," *Foreign Affairs* 76 (Jan.–Feb. 1997): 50–66.

6. Thomas L. Friedman, *The Lexus and the Olive Tree: Understanding Globalization* (New York: Farrar, Straus and Giroux, 1999), xviii, 7, 11–13.

7. For a provocative analysis of U.S.–China relations in the twenty-first century, see Mearsheimer, *Tragedy of Great Power Politics*, chap. 10. For a range of views on this issue, see Michael E. Brown et al. eds., *The Rise of China* (Cambridge: MIT Press, 2000).

8. See Bernard I. Finel, Brian D. Finlay, and Janne E. Nolan, "The Perils of Nuclear, Biological, and Chemical Weapons," in this volume.

9. See Jo L. Husbands, "The Proliferation of Conventional Weapons and Technologies," in this volume.

10. See Timothy D. Hoyt, "Technology and Security," in this volume.

11. See Theodore H. Moran, "Defense Economics and Security"; Martha Harris, "Energy and Security"; and Dorothy E. Denning, "Information Technology and Security," all in this volume.

12. See Timothy D. Hoyt, "Security and Conflict in the Developing World"; Charles B. Keely, "Demographic Developments and Security"; and J. R. McNeill "Environmental Factors and Security," all in this volume.

13. Husbands, "Proliferation of Conventional Weapons and Technologies."

14. See Mikael Eriksson, Margareta Sollenberg, and Peter Wallensteen, "Patterns of Major Armed Conflicts, 1990–2001," in Stockholm International Peace Research Institute (SIPRI), *SIPRI Yearbook 2002: Armaments, Disarmament, and International Security* (Oxford: Oxford University Press, 2002), 63–76. A "major armed conflict" is one in which at least 1,000 people have been killed.

15. For more on this issue, see Michael E. Brown, "The Causes and Regional Dimensions of Internal Conflict," in *The International Dimensions of Internal Conflict,* ed. Michael E. Brown (Cambridge: MIT Press, 1996), 590–99.

16. See UN High Commissioner for Refugees (UNHCR), *Refugees by Numbers,* 2002 ed., available at www.unhcr.ch.

17. One could also include insurgency groups—such as the Liberation Tigers of Tamil Eelam in Sri Lanka—that have mobilized ethnic diasporas and used the Internet to generate international financial and political support for their causes. The scope of their international operations has expanded considerably since the 1990s.

18. See Diana Owen, "Transnational Mass Media Organizations and Security," in this volume.

19. See Roy Godson, "Transnational Crime, Corruption, and Security," in this volume.

20. See Audrey Kurth Cronin, "Transnational Terrorism and Security," in this volume. See also Finel, Finlay, and Nolan, "Perils of Nuclear, Biological, and Chemical Weapons."

21. See Denning, "Information Technology and Security."

22. For excellent overviews of the evolution of the security agenda and the security studies field, see Joseph S. Nye Jr. and Sean M. Lynn-Jones, "International Security Studies: A Report of a Conference on the State of the Field," *International Security* 12 (spring 1988): 5–27; Steven E. Miller, "*International Security* at Twenty-Five: From One World to Another," *International Security* 26 (summer 2001): 5–39.

23. See Waltz, "Structural Realism after the Cold War"; Mearsheimer, *Tragedy of Great Power Politics*; Mearsheimer, "Disorder Restored." See also Stephen P. Walt, "The Renaissance of Security Studies," *International Studies Quarterly* 35 (June 1991): 211–39.

24. For an excellent overview of these broader issues, see Richard H. Schultz Jr., Roy Godson, and George H. Quester, eds., *Security Studies for the 21ˢᵗ Century* (Washington, D.C.: Brassey's, 1997).

25. Michael T. Klare, "Redefining Security: The New Global Schisms," in *Globalization and the Challenges of a New Century,* ed. Patrick O'Meara, Howard D. Mehlinger, and Matthew Krain (Bloomington: Indiana University Press, 2000), 131–39, at 133.

26. See Edward A. Kolodziej, "Renaissance in Security Studies? Caveat Lector!" *International Studies Quarterly* 36 (Dec. 1992): 421–38, at 422.

27. See Richard H. Ullman, "Redefining Security," *International Security* 8 (summer 1983): 129–53, at 129.

28. See Jessica T. Mathews, "Redefining Security," *Foreign Affairs* 68 (spring 1989): 162–77.

29. For an overview of the "human security" agenda, see UN Development Program, "New Dimensions of Human Security," in *Human Development Report, 1994* (New York: United Nations, 1994), 22–40. For a thoughtful and balanced assessment of the "human security" school, see Roland Paris, "Human Security: Paradigm Shift or Hot Air?" *International Security* 26 (fall 2001): 87–102.

30. Klare, "Redefining Security," 139.

31. UN Development Program, "New Dimensions of Human Security," 23.

32. Barry Buzan, Ole Wæver, and Jaap de Wilde, *Security: A New Framework for Analysis* (Boulder: Lynne Rienner, 1998), 23–24.

33. Lawrence Freedman, "International Security: Changing Targets?" *Foreign Policy* 110 (spring 1998): 48–63, at 53.

34. War and genocide merit special attention because of their horrific consequences, but less intense, less organized conflicts are also important security problems. It is therefore useful to define the parameters of the security agenda (and the security studies field) in terms of the more general but still distinctive problem of violent conflict.

35. This includes the issues associated with strategic studies, which Richard Betts defines as "how political ends and means interact under social, economic, and other constraints," and military science, "how technology, organization, and tactics combine to win battles." See Richard K. Betts, "Should Strategic Studies Survive?" *World Politics* 50 (Oct. 1997): 7–33, at 9. See also Freedman, "International Security."

36. See Harris, "Energy and Security"; McNeill, "Environmental Factors and Security."

37. See Keely, "Demographic Developments and Security."

38. See Moran, "Defense Economics and Security."

39. See Keely, "Demographic Developments and Security"; McNeill, "Environmental Factors and Security."

40. See Brown, "Causes and Regional Dimensions of Internal Conflict," 572–90. See also V. P. Gagnon Jr., "Ethnic Nationalism and International Conflict: The Case of Serbia," *International Security* 19 (winter 1994–95): 130–66; John Mueller, "The Banality of 'Ethnic War,'" *International Security* 25 (summer 2000): 42–70.

41. Vagaries about the value of the Russian ruble make some of these comparisons difficult, but the overall picture is clear. See IISS, *Military Balance, 2002–2003,* 241–42, 332–37.

42. See Hoyt, "Technology and Security."

43. See Finel, Finlay, and Nolan, "Perils of Nuclear, Biological, and Chemical Weapons."

44. See Husbands, "Proliferation of Conventional Weapons and Technologies."

45. Moran, "Defense Economics and Security."

46. See Harris, "Energy and Security."

47. See United Nations Population Fund, *The State of World Population,* available at www.unfpa.org. See also Keely, "Demographic Developments and Security."

48. See McNeill, "Environmental Factors and Security."

49. Hoyt, "Security and Conflict in the Developing World."

50. See Denning, "Information Technology and Security."

51. See Loren B. Thompson, "Emerging Technologies and Security," in this volume.

52. See Hoyt, "Technology and Security."

53. See Owen, "Transnational Mass Media Organizations and Security."

54. Godson, "Transnational Crime, Corruption, and Security."

55. Cronin, "Transnational Terrorism and Security."

56. This assessment is shared by several other contributors to this volume. See Hoyt, "Technology and Security" and "Security and Conflict in the Developing World"; Thompson, "Emerging Technologies and Security"; Finel, Finlay, and Nolan, "Perils of Nuclear, Biological, and Chemical Weapons."

57. See Finel, Finlay, and Nolan, "Perils of Nuclear, Biological, and Chemical Weapons."

58. Cronin, "Transnational Terrorism and Security."

59. See Chantal de Jonge Oudraat and P. J. Simmons, "From Accord to Action," in *Managing Global Issues: Lessons Learned,* ed. Chantal de Jonge Oudraat and P.J. Simmons (Washington, D.C.: Carnegie Endowment for International Peace, 2001), 690–727, at 722–23.

60. These guidelines come from Chantal de Jonge Oudraat.

Contributors

Michael E. Brown is dean of the Elliott School of International Affairs and professor of international affairs and political science at The George Washington University, and coeditor of the journal *International Security*. Professor Brown is the author of *Flying Blind: The Politics of the U.S. Strategic Bomber Program,* which won the Edgar Furniss National Security Book Award. He is the editor of *Ethnic Conflict and International Security* and *The International Dimensions of Internal Conflict.* He is coeditor of *The Costs of Conflict; Government Policies and Ethnic Relations in Asia and the Pacific; Fighting Words: Language Policy and Ethnic Conflict in Asia,* and ten *International Security* readers. He is writing a book on the causes of ethnic conflict and civil war. He received his Ph.D. from Cornell University.

Audrey Kurth Cronin is a specialist in terrorism at the Congressional Research Service, Library of Congress, where she advises members of Congress on international terrorism. She also teaches a longstanding graduate course on political violence and terrorism in the Security Studies Program, Edmund A. Walsh School of Foreign Service, Georgetown University. She is the author of *Great Power Politics and the Struggle over Austria,* coeditor of *Attacking Terrorism: Elements of a Grand Strategy,* and is currently writing a book on American strategy and terrorism in the twenty-first century. Her articles have been published in *International Security, Survival,* and many other journals. She was a Marshall Scholar at St. Antony's College, Oxford, and a postdoctoral fellow at Harvard University. She received her D.Phil. from Oxford University.

Dorothy E. Denning is a professor in the Department of Defense Analysis at the Naval Postgraduate School. Her work encompasses the areas of cyber crime and cyber terrorism, information warfare and security, and cryptography. She has published 120 articles and four books, her most recent being *Information Warfare and Security.* She is an ACM Fellow and recipient of several awards, including the Augusta Ada Lovelace Award and the National Computer Systems Security Award. She has previously worked at Georgetown University, Digital Equipment Corporation, SRI International, and Purdue University. She received her Ph.D. in computer science from Purdue University.

Bernard I. Finel is executive director of the Center for Peace and Security Studies and the Security Studies Program at the Edmund A. Walsh School of Foreign

Service, Georgetown University. He has written on international relations theory, transparency, and the revolution in military affairs. He is coeditor of *Power and Conflict in the Age of Transparency,* and his articles have appeared in *International Studies Quarterly* and *Security Studies.* He served on the governing council of the international security studies section of the International Studies Association from 1999 to 2002. He received his Ph.D. from Georgetown University.

Brian D. Finlay is director of the Nuclear Threat Reduction Campaign. He was previously a program officer at the Century Foundation, a senior researcher in the Foreign Policy Studies Program at the Brookings Institution, and a project manager for the Laboratory Center for Disease Control in Ottawa, Canada. He also served as a consultant to the Canadian Department of Foreign Affairs and International Trade, working on the Ottawa Treaty on Land Mines and the comprehensive test ban treaty. He is the author of numerous articles on nuclear and biological weapons and coeditor of *Opportunity Costs: The Politics of U.S. Non-Proliferation Policy from the Post–Cold War to Post–September 11th.* He holds a master's degree from the Norman Paterson School of International Affairs at Carleton University, and a graduate diploma from the Johns Hopkins School of Advanced International Studies.

Roy Godson is a professor in the Department of Government at Georgetown University. His research examines the security implications of globalization and the growth of substate and transnational groups, such as organized criminal organizations and ethnic groups, in regional and global affairs. He has written or edited twenty books, including *Security Studies for the Twenty-first Century* (coeditor); *Organized Crime and Democratic Governability: Mexico and the U.S.–Mexican Borderlands;* and *Dirty Tricks or Trump Cards: U.S. Covert Action and Counterintelligence.* He received his Ph.D. from Columbia University.

Martha Harris is a senior fellow at the Atlantic Council of the United States in Washington, D.C. She was an Abe Fellow and visiting researcher at the Institute for Energy Economics (Tokyo) doing research on energy security. She has also been senior vice president at the Asia Foundation, deputy assistant secretary of state for export controls, director of the Office of Japan Affairs at the National Research Council, project director and senior analyst at the Office of Technology Assessment, and an adjunct professor in the Security Studies Program at the Edmund A. Walsh School of Foreign Service, Georgetown University. She has published on a wide range of energy, economics, technology, and Asian issues. She received her Ph.D. from the University of Wisconsin–Madison.

Timothy D. Hoyt is an associate professor in the Department of Strategy and Policy at the U.S. Naval War College. He was previously a visiting assistant professor in the Security Studies Program at the Edmund A. Walsh School of Foreign Service, Georgetown University, and professor of strategy and policy for the U.S. Naval

War College's program in Washington, D.C. He has worked for the U.S. Army, the U.S. Department of State, and as a researcher on defense issues for the Library of Congress. He has written on a variety of subjects, including the diffusion of military technologies and practices, the proliferation of conventional and unconventional weapons, and the evolution of security problems in the developing world. He received his Ph.D. from Johns Hopkins University.

Jo L. Husbands is director of the Committee on International Security and Arms Control of the National Academy of Sciences (NAS). She is also an adjunct professor in the Security Studies Program at the Edmund A. Walsh School of Foreign Service, Georgetown University. She has served as director of the development, security, and cooperation division in the NAS Office of International Affairs. Previously she was director of the Academy's Project on Democratization and a senior research associate for its committee on international conflict and cooperation. She has published widely on the topics of arms control, arms transfers, weapons proliferation, and international negotiations. She is a member of the Advisory Board of Women In International Security and sits on the editorial boards of several journals. She received her Ph.D. from the University of Minnesota.

Charles B. Keely is the Donald G. Herzberg Professor of International Migration at Georgetown University. His research focuses on international migration and refugee issues. He has written or edited nine books and more than fifty research articles on migration. Professor Keely has been a senior associate in the Center for Policy Studies of the Population Council of New York, a member of the Committee on Population of the National Academy of Sciences (NAS), and a member of the Joint Committee on Contraceptive Development of the National Academy of Sciences and the National Institute of Medicine. He also has served on NAS working groups on the decennial census, the development of the U.S. statistical system on immigration, and the demography of forced migrants. He received his Ph.D. from Fordham University.

J. R. McNeill is a professor in the Department of History and the Edmund A. Walsh School of Foreign Service, Georgetown University. He has taught at Goucher College, Duke University, and Athens College. He has also been a researcher and consultant in Latin American ecological history, Ecosystems Center, Marine Biological Laboratory, Woods Hole. His publications include *Something New under the Sun: An Environmental History of the Twentieth-Century World; The Mountains of the Mediterranean World: An Environmental History; The Atlantic Empires of France and Spain: Louisbourg and Havana, 1700–1763; The Human Web: A Bird's-eye View of World History* (coauthor); *Atlantic American Societies from Columbus to Abolition* (coeditor); and numerous articles in professional journals. He is currently researching and writing a history of yellow fever. He received his Ph.D. from Duke University.

Theodore H. Moran is the Marcus Wallenberg Professor of International Financial Diplomacy and the founding director of the Landegger Program in International Business Diplomacy at the Edmund A. Walsh School of Foreign Service, Georgetown University. He is widely known for his work on international economics and national security, political risk analysis, corporate strategy, and multinational corporations. His publications include nine books and some sixty scholarly articles. In 1993–94 he was appointed senior advisor for economic policy on the policy planning staff of the Department of State. He has been a consultant to corporations, governments, and multilateral agencies on investment strategy, international negotiations, and political risk assessment. He received his Ph.D. from Harvard University.

Janne E. Nolan is an adjunct professor in the Security Studies Program at the Edmund A. Walsh School of Foreign Service, Georgetown University. She was previously director of international programs at the Eisenhower Institute, director of international programs at the Century Foundation, senior fellow at the Brookings Institution, a staff member on the Senate Armed Services Committee, and an official at the U.S. Arms Control Agency. She has been a member of the Defense Policy Board and the congressionally appointed National Defense Panel. She also served as chair of the presidential advisory board on technology proliferation. She is the author or editor of five books: *Military Industry in Taiwan and South Korea; Guardians of the Arsenal: The Politics of Nuclear Strategy; Trappings of Power: Ballistic Missiles in the Third World; Global Engagement: Security and Cooperation in the Twenty-First Century;* and *An Elusive Consensus: Nuclear Weapons and American Security after the Cold War.* She received her Ph.D. from the Fletcher School of Law and Diplomacy at Tufts University.

Diana Owen is associate professor of political science at Georgetown University. Her publications include *New Media and American Politics* (with Richard Davis), *Media Messages in American Presidential Elections,* and numerous articles in scholarly journals and popular publications. She is completing two major book projects, *Mass Communications and the Making of Citizens* and *American Government and Politics: Realities and the Media* (with David Paletz and Timothy Cook). Her areas of expertise include political behavior and institutions, mass communications, and statistical methodology. She is a fellow of the Center for New Designs in Teaching and Scholarship and cofounder of Georgetown's graduate program in Communication, Culture, and Technology. She received her Ph.D. from University of Wisconsin–Madison.

Loren B. Thompson is the chief operating officer and director of the National Security Program at the Lexington Institute. He is also an adjunct professor in the Security Studies Program at the Edmund A. Walsh School of Foreign Service,

Georgetown University. He is former associate director of Georgetown's Security Studies Program and a former senior fellow at the Alexis de Tocqueville Institution. He frequently advises the Department of Defense and major corporations on strategic communications, management initiatives, and defense-related policy issues. Much of this work is conducted through Source Associates, a professional services firm of which he is chief executive officer. His publications include *Low Intensity Conflict* and *Defense Beat: The Dilemmas of Military Coverage*. He received his Ph.D. from Georgetown University.

Index